Paul's Epistle to the Romans

A Commentary on
Paul's Epistle to the Romans

Dr. Ian A. Fair

HCU Media LLC
Accra, Ghana ◆ Frisco, TX

A Commentary on Paul's Epistle to the Romans

HCU Media LLC

PUBLISHED AND COPYRIGHT © 2023
BY DR. IAN FAIR

ISBN-13: 978-1-939468-27-7 (Paperback Edition)

Printed in the USA

Scripture quotations, unless otherwise noted, are from The Holy Bible, Revised Standard Version, copyright 1971, Zondervan Bible Publishers.

Cover Design by Dale Henry - www.dalehenrydesign.com

First Edition April 2023
10 9 8 7 6 5 4 3 2 1

CONTENTS

Preface

This book is an introductory commentary on Paul's Epistle to the Romans.

Although we will draw on several major commentaries and study materials relevant to such a study of Romans—mention of these can be found in the Bibliography to this study—this book is ***primarily an introductory study of Paul's Epistle to the Romans***, examining Paul's major themes of *atonement, salvation, righteousness,* and the *righteousness of God.*

In each chapter we will demonstrate that:

Paul underscores that God is a righteous God who shows no partiality to gender or ethnic makeup. A guiding principle throughout Romans is that *God is a righteous God* who treats all people equally, Rom 1:16, 17; 3:22.

The overwhelming theme of Paul's theology is that God created all things well but man chose by exercising his God-given free choice to leave God's design for a right relationship with him. Sin is at its root a human decision to turn away from God and his way and pursue a different lifestyle.

As Paul traces the trajectory of man's fall he highlights God's call of Abraham and covenant promise to redeem and bless all men through faith in a redeemer savior, Jesus, the Christ-Messiah.

In a remarkable chapter, Rom 1:18-32 Paul traces the outline of man's fall which resulted in a worldwide habit of decay and human depravity.

But underlying this dramatic outline of human decline Paul lays a foundation of God's unfailing love for his creation, his steadfast grace, and his eternal plan of redemption fortified by his unfailing faithfulness to his promises and profound righteousness.

This point reaches a "climax of hope" when Paul states, *21 **But** now the righteousness of God has been manifested apart from law, although the law and the prophets bear witness to it, 22 the righteousness of God through faith in Jesus Christ for all who believe. For there*

i

is no distinction; [23] *since all have sinned and fall short of the glory of God,* [24] *they are justified by his grace as a gift, through the redemption which is in Christ Jesus,* [25] *whom God put forward as an expiation by his blood, to be received by faith. This was to show God's righteousness, because in his divine forbearance he had passed over former sins;* [26] *it was to prove at the present time that he himself is righteous and that he justifies him who has faith in Jesus.*[1]

Paul argues that the entire world (every person) is *under the power of sin*, Rom 3:9. He contends that all people have sinned by falling short of the glory of God and consequently need God's grace and forgiveness, Rom 3:23, 24.

Righteousness is a gift from God, it cannot be earned by works, and is available only by God's grace through faith in Jesus Christ, Rom 3:20-24.

In the cross of Jesus, Christians die to the demands of the *Torah* Law and sin, and are made alive again in Christ through being united with Christ in baptism, Rom 6:1-11.

In human effort, only frustration results, Rom 7:24, but in Christ there is forgiveness and no condemnation, Rom 8:1.

God, the Holy Spirit, and Jesus Christ are working on behalf of Christians so that no power can separate them from the love of God in Christ, Rom 8:26-39.

Contrary to the views of many Jews, God has not rejected Israel, but Israel has rejected God by not accepting the Messiah and refusing to live by faith in Jesus, Rom 9-11.

Paul outlines an appropriate Christian response to God's redeeming grace—surrendering one's life to God in everyday worship and not being conformed to the world, Rom 12:1ff.

As a practical example of Jewish-Gentile community harmony, not being conceited and haughty is a key to Christians demonstrating love and concern for one another

---

[1] Rom 3:21–26.

culminating in not judging one another. Christians should welcome (accept) one another just as Christ has welcomed and accepted them, Rom 14:1-15:13.

Bibliography

Since this is not intended to be a major commentary on Romans, we include a brief bibliography of the scholarly work that will be referenced in the study.

Achtemeier, Paul, *Romans*, Interpretation, 1985.

Aland, Barbara, *et al.*, *The Greek New Testament*, Deutsche Bibelsellschaft, Fourth Edition, 2001.

Aland, Kurt, et al., *Novum Testamentum Graece*, Duetsche Bibelstiftung, Stuttgart, 1979.

Beasley-Murray, G. R., *Baptism in the New Testament*, Wm. B. Eerdmans-Lightning, 1973.

Bruce, F. F., *Romans*, Tyndale, 1985.

Cottrell, Jack, *Baptism a Biblical Study*, College Press, 1990.

Cottrell, Jack, *Romans*, College Press, 2 vols., 1996.

Cranfield, C. E. B., *Romans*, T. & T. Clark, 1975.

Donfried, Karl P., *The Romans Debate*, Hendrickson, 1977, 1991.

Dunn, James D. G., *Romans*, Word Biblical Commentary, 2 vols., 1988.

Ewell, Walter, ed., *Baker Encyclopedia of the Bible*, 1988.

Fair, Ian A., *Biblical Personal Righteousness*, HCU Media, 2021.

Fergusson, Everett, *Baptism in the Early Church: History, Theology, and Liturgy in the First Five Centuries,* Wm. B. Eerdmans, 2009.

Fitzmyer, Joseph A., *Romans*, Anchor Bible Commentary, 1993.

Freedman, David Noel, *ed., The Anchor Yale Bible Dictionary*, 1922.

Hagner, Donald, *Matthew 14-28*, Word Books, 1995.

Kittel, Gerhard, *Theological Dictionary of the New Testament*, Wm. B. Eerdmans, 1964.

Louw, J. P., & Nida, E. A., *Greek-English Lexicon of the New Testament: Based on Semantic Domains,* United Bible Societies, electronic edition of the 2nd edition, vol. 1, p. 610, 1996.

Metzger, Bruce, *Textual Commentary on the Greek New Testament*, United Bible Society, 1971-2004.

Morris, Leon, *The Epistle to the Romans*, IVP, 1998.

Mounce, R. H., *Romans*, p. 234. Broadman & Holman Publishers, 1995.

Swanson, James A., *Dictionary of Biblical Languages with Semantic Domains: Greek (New Testament)*, Logos Research Systems, 1997.

Zodhiates, Spiros, *A Complete Word Study Dictionary: New Testament,* 1993.

The Revised Standard Version, Grand Rapids, Michigan, 1946-1952, 1971.

Novum Testamentum Graece, Barbara and Kurt Aland, Johannes Karavidopoulos, Carlo M. Martini, Bruce M. Metzger, Deutsche Bibelgesellschaft, 27th edition, 1993.

Chapter 1 - The Author, Authenticity, Date, and Theology of Romans

Context and Message

The basic reason for this first chapter is to introduce you to Paul's reason for writing his great Epistle to the Christians in Rome. It explains that the Epistle was intended to be an apostolic ambassadorial missionary and epideictically[1] oriented Epistle stressing Paul's missionary interest of carrying the gospel of Christ to the West of Italy into Western Europe, even Spain (Rom 15:28).

A fundamental point to understanding this epistle and its message is that Paul was explaining that God is a righteous God who declares all men not guilty in Christ Jesus, and forgives all men by the same means; through the faithfulness of Jesus and Christian faith in God's atoning work in the death of Jesus and his resurrection.

We will learn that there are several types (genres) of New Testament epistles. Remember, Paul was a missionary. Furthermore, Paul had not established the church in Rome. It had possibly been in existence for approximately 30 years when Paul decided to visit Rome and write this letter, circa 56-58 CE. Rome was an important city and a good base for mission work. Paul wanted the Christians in Rome to support him in his mission journey to the West, even to Spain (Rom 15:28).

Although Paul was concerned for all people, his primary mission from God was to go to the Gentiles and preach the Gospel to them. This did not exclude the Christians and Jews in Rome, but they were not the primary purpose of his going to Rome, note Rom 1:8-15, paying attention to vs 13-15:

---

[1] *Epideictic* is a word that discusses *shared values and concerns*. Paul understood that the Christians in Rome would probably share his missionary zeal, and desire to reach the lost with the Gospel of Christ with a fundamental doctrinal issue of salvation by faith in Jesus Christ and not Law Keeping.

"I want you to know, brethren, that I have often intended to come to you (but thus far have been prevented), in order that I may reap some harvest among you as well as among the rest of the Gentiles. ^{14} I am under obligation both to Greeks and to barbarians, both to the wise and to the foolish: ^{15} so I am eager to preach the gospel to you also who are in Rome."

The Roman Christians were not collected in large churches, mostly meeting in house churches, Rom 16. They were mixed groups, some Jewish, some Gentile. Several possibly questioned Paul's fundamental doctrine of justification by faith in Jesus and not by works of the Jewish Mosaic Law.

Paul needed to correct any misinformation they might have regarding his gospel message.

A Key Text - Rom 1:16, 17 *"For I am not ashamed of the gospel: it is the power of God for salvation to everyone who has faith, to the Jew first and also to the Greek. ^{17} For in it the righteousness of God is revealed through faith for faith; as it is written, "He who through faith is righteous shall live."*

If you have not already done so, you need to memorize this text! Why? Because it is the foundation of Paul's theology and the Christian faith.

Remember that a key thought to Paul's theology and the reason for this epistle was that God is a righteous God who desires that all men be saved, both Jew and Gentile. This was a pivotal reason for this epistle and Paul's visit to Rome.

Paul will make the point in this Epistle that all men have sinned and need forgiveness, not only the Jews but all men can be saved by an obedient faith in Jesus, the Christ-Messiah!

The authenticity of Pauline authorship

Few scholars today question the Pauline authorship and authenticity of Romans. Some question the ending of Romans, Rom 15:22-16:27, claiming that these verses were not written by Paul but added by one of his disciples, but few follow this view. Several scholars will note that we have no manuscripts with a different conclusion from the one in our current Epistle.

The occasion for writing this epistle

Paul clearly stated that he had completed his ministry in Palestine, Asia, and Eastern Europe and *was looking for new mission fields.*

Rom 1:8-15.

> *⁸ First, I thank my God through Jesus Christ for all of you, because your faith is proclaimed in all the world. ⁹ For God is my witness, whom I serve with my spirit in the gospel of his Son, that without ceasing I mention you always in my prayers, ¹⁰ asking that somehow by God's will I may now at last succeed in coming to you. ¹¹ For I long to see you, that I may impart to you some spiritual gift to strengthen you, ¹² that is, that we may be mutually encouraged by each other's faith, both yours and mine. ¹³ I want you to know, brethren, that I have often intended to come to you (but thus far have been prevented), in order that I may reap some harvest among you as well as among the rest of the Gentiles. ¹⁴ I am under obligation both to Greeks and to barbarians, both to the wise and to the foolish: ¹⁵ so I am eager to preach the gospel to you also who are in Rome.*

Rom 15:17-20, 22-29.

> *¹⁷ In Christ Jesus, then, I have reason to boast of my work for God. ¹⁸ For I will not venture to speak of anything except what Christ has accomplished through me to win obedience from the Gentiles, by word and deed, ¹⁹ by the power of*

signs and wonders, by the power of the Spirit of *God, so that from Jerusalem and as far around as* *Illyricum I have fully proclaimed the good news of* *Christ.* [20] *Thus I make it my ambition to proclaim the good news, not where Christ has already been named, so that I do not build on someone else's foundation,* [21] *but as it is written,*

"Those who have never been told of him shall see,

and those who have never heard of him shall understand."

Paul's Plan to Visit Rome

[22] *This is the reason that I have so often been hindered from coming to you.* [23] *But now, with no further place for me in these regions, I desire, as I have for many years, to come to you* [24] *when I go to Spain. For I do hope to see you on my journey and to be sent on by you once I have enjoyed your company for a little while.* [25] *At present, however, I am going to Jerusalem in a ministry to the saints;* [26] *for Macedonia and Achaia have been pleased to share their resources with the poor among the saints at Jerusalem.* [27] *They were pleased to do this, and indeed they owe it to them; for if the Gentiles have come to share in their spiritual blessings, they ought also to be of service to them in material things.* [28] *So, when I have completed this, and have delivered to them what has been collected, I will set out by way of you to Spain;* [29] *and I know that when I come to you, I will come in the fullness of the blessing of Christ.*

We note that Paul was seeking aid from the Roman house churches for his planned travels to Spain and was therefore outlining his apostolic and missionary credentials and his Gospel message. Many in Rome did not know Paul personally since he had not yet visited Rome.

Jewish teachers, as in Galatia, possibly Judaizing Christians, had criticized Paul's gospel message charging that he wished only to destroy the Old Testament and the Law of Moses. In this Epistle, Paul wished to correct these false charges. So, in this epistle to the Christians in Rome he outlined his primary gospel message of justification through faith in Jesus Christ for all. Consequently, he carefully laid out the gospel message as the good news he had always preached and planned to preach in Rome and Spain.

The kind of epistle we have in Romans

We know from personal experience that there are various kinds of letters one can write. We might write a business letter, a personal letter, a defensive letter, a love letter. Each of these letters takes on a distinctive character, form, or structure.

In our New Testament we find several different genres of epistles/letters. Different church situations, or religious needs, would have required various kinds of epistles, some pastoral, some defensive, some argumentative.

For example, we have the following epistles in the New Testament:

Apologetic Epistles – *Galatians*, written by Paul in defense of the gospel of Christ he preached to both the Jew and Gentile!

Pastoral Epistles – Corinthians, and Thessalonians, reflecting on local church concerns.

Homilies – *Hebrews*, an extended sermon.

Apocalyptic Epistles – Jesus' *seven letters* in *Revelation* each a discussion of crises that would soon take place in the life of the church.

Personal Epistles – *Philemon, 1 and 2 Timothy, and Titus*.

Formal Ambassadorial Epistles – *Romans*, which is missionary ambassadorial in nature in a formal official apostolic manner which sets out Paul's primary beliefs and credentials.

Epideictic Epistles - Romans. In epideictic style Paul sets out common views that he shares with the other apostles and hopefully with the recipients and others.

The recipients of the epistle

The church in Rome was not a Pauline church plant and could have existed as early as the many Jewish Roman conversions on the Day of Pentecost reflected in Acts 2. Note especially Acts 2:11 where Luke adds that there were in Jerusalem at the feast *"visitors from Rome, both Jews and proselytes"* on the Day of Pentecost.

There does not appear to be a central church in Rome as in Corinth and Thessalonica – the salutation in Romans does not mention a church, Rom 1:1-7. The recipients are addressed simply as *all of God's people in Rome* who obviously were members of the several house churches mentioned by Paul at the conclusion of his epistle, Rom 16.

Paul's opening salutation is unique among his epistles, Rom 1:1-7, and is comprised in Greek of one long sentence:

> *[1] Paul, a servant of Jesus Christ, called to be an apostle, set apart for the gospel of God [2] which he promised beforehand through his prophets in the holy scriptures, [3] the gospel concerning his Son, who was descended from David according to the flesh [4] and designated Son of God in power according to the Spirit of holiness by his resurrection from the dead, Jesus Christ our Lord, [5] through whom we have received grace and apostleship to bring about the obedience of faith for the sake of his name among all the nations, [6] including yourselves who are called to belong to Jesus Christ; [7] To all God's beloved in Rome, who are called to be saints: Grace to you and peace from God our Father and the Lord Jesus Christ.*

The word *saints* used by Paul, a favored term, derives from the Greek word *hágios* which is often translated in other contexts as *holy, set apart, consecrated, referring to the nature and character of God,* or His people.

In regard to God, it stresses God's being totally different from all creation; he is *totally other in nature.* However, it has several nuances depending on context. God is a *holy God*! He is different from all other gods! Note Israel's great confession, the *Shema,* Deut 6:1ff:

> [4] *"Hear, O Israel: The LORD our God is one LORD;* [5] *and you shall love the LORD your God with all your heart, and with all your soul, and with all your might.* [6] *And these words which I command you this day shall be upon your heart;* [7] *and you shall teach them diligently to your children, and shall talk of them when you sit in your house, and when you walk by the way, and when you lie down, and when you rise.* [8] *And you shall bind them as a sign upon your hand, and they shall be as frontlets between your eyes.* [9] *And you shall write them on the doorposts of your house and on your gates".*

Spiros Zodhiates below provides an excellent definition and application of *hágios as saint,* referring to one *who has been cleansed by God, forgiven, and set apart for God's service in His kingdom.*

> "ἅγιος *hágios*; fem. *hagía,* neut. *hágion,* adj. from *hágos,* any matter of religious awe, expiation, sacrifice. Holy, set apart, sanctified, consecrated, saint. It has a common root, *hág-,* with *hagnós* (53), chaste, pure. Its fundamental idea is separation, consecration, devotion to the service of Deity, sharing in God's purity and abstaining from earth's defilement.
>
> (I) Pure, clean, ceremonially, or morally clean, including the idea of deserved respect, reverence.
>
> (A) It particularly means perfect, without blemish (Rom. 12:1).

13

(B) Metaphorically it means morally pure, upright, blameless in heart and life, virtuous, holy. **(1)** Generally (Mark 6:20; Rom. 7:12; 1 Cor. 7:34; Eph. 1:4; 5:27; 1 Pet. 1:16; Sept.: Lev. 11:44). **(2)** Spoken of those who are purified and sanctified by the influences of the Spirit. This is assumed of all who profess the Christian name, hence *hágios*, saint, *hágioi*, saints, Christians (Acts 9:13, 14, 32, 41; 26:10; Rom. 1:7; 8:27; 1 Thess. 3:13). Spoken of those who are to be in any way included in the Christian community (1 Cor. 7:14). Holy kiss means the sacred Christian kiss, the pledge of Christian affection (Rom. 16:16; 1 Cor. 16:20; 2 Cor. 13:12).

(II) *Consecrated, devoted, sacred, holy, meaning set apart from a common to a sacred use; spoken of places, temples, cities, the priesthood, men* (Matt. 4:5; 7:6; 24:15; 27:53; Acts 6:13; 7:33; Rom. 11:16, of firstfruit); of a male opening the womb (Luke 2:23); of apostles (Eph. 3:5); of prophets (Luke 1:70; Acts 3:21; 2 Pet. 1:21); of angels (Matt. 25:31)."[2]

As we have already noted, there were several house churches already existing in Rome, cf. Rom 16:1-23. They are comprised of homogenized groups of Jewish and Gentile converts to Christ, those who had been *saved* by God, *cleansed* by God, and *dedicated* to His service.

The house churches and Christian groups in Rome were obviously ethnically mixed groups, being comprised of Jewish and Gentile converts. This homogenization of Jews and Gentiles would prove to be a challenge to Christians for centuries. Even today we seek solutions to how churches of differing racial and ethnic makeup learn

---

[2] Zodhiates, *The Complete Word Study Dictionary: New Testament,* 2000.

that in Christ there are religiously no "Jewish and Gentile" Christians. They might retain their ethnicity but need to learn to surrender that to being spiritually and effectively one in Christ. We learn from Paul that Christians in Ephesus were also still struggling to learn this principle, Eph 4:1-16.

As in most situations in the first century world there would have been some ethnic-political tension between the Jews and Gentiles. Jewish expulsions from Rome under Nero, and their periodic return, must have created some interesting and challenging situations for the Gentiles who had remained in Rome! Who were the original groups, and who were the more recent arrivals? Were they originally the Jewish converts mentioned in Acts 2, who had returned home to Rome? Were some of them transfers from other Gentile regions, like Corinth, or recent Gentile converts in Rome? Settling into a unified congregation with Gentiles, with a sense of Christian unity, would have been a challenge to all Jews!

Some Jewish Christians with roots in Judaism would have been upset over Paul's supposed rejection of the Law (*Torah*) which was a popular criticism by Jews of Paul's teaching. Some Gentile converts to Judaism and then later to Christianity could also have been distressed by this, having previously been proselytes to Judaism and then converted to Christianity!

Lampe, in the *Anchor Bible Dictionary* gives some indication of the issues that may have been of concern to Paul in his proposed ministry in Rome. Lampe sets his discussion in the context of Aquila's experience as a Jewish Christian living in Rome:

> A Jew from Pontus (Acts 18:2), Aquila was among the first Christians in Rome who still belonged to the synagogues of the city. Together with his wife, Priscilla, and others, he propagated Christianity in at least one of the Roman synagogues. This Christian proclamation led to tumultuous controversies among the Roman Jews,

so that the administration of the emperor Claudius expelled the main quarrelers, including Aquila and Prisca, from the city in 49 C.E. (Acts 18:2, Suet. *Claud.* 25.4 ...) Aquila was already a Christian before Paul settled in Corinth: Paul lived in Aquila's dwelling in Corinth (Acts 18:3), but his first christening (sic, *baptism*) in the city was Stephanas, not Aquila. In addition, Paul baptized no one else in Corinth except Crispus, Gaius, and Stephanas' household (1 Cor 1:14–16; 16:15). If Aquila had been christened (*baptized*) by somebody other than Paul in Corinth, e.g., by Silas or Timotheus, Luke would have liked to report such success (cf. e.g., Acts 18:8). (5) It is not likely that the unbaptized Jew Aquila housed the Christian missionary Paul in Corinth and even gave him a job to support him (Acts 18:2–3), especially if the Jew Aquila had acted on the Jewish side of the controversies in Rome, fighting Christian preaching about Christ. Finally.[3]

Dunn reflects on the social and ethnic makeup of the house churches listed by Paul in Rom 16:

The greetings which follow the commendation of Phoebe obviously serve a number of functions: in particular, they give Phoebe herself a list of people to call on when she first arrives, to whom she could look for hospitality and subsequent support; and they ensure that the letter she presumably took with her would be well received, since Paul already knew so many of the Roman congregations, including a number of leading figures.

The list itself has several interesting features. (1) Paul obviously has strong personal links with a number of those named. Prisca and Aquila are preeminent in this regard: they had worked with

---

[3] Lampe, P., "Aquila (Person)," *The Anchor Yale Bible Dictionary*, 1992, vol. 1, p. 319.

him, they had risked their lives for him, and they often provided him a home (vv 3–4). Another of Paul's coworkers in early missionary work was Urbanus (v 9). In other cases Paul makes a point of calling the one greeted "my beloved"—Epaenetus, the first of his converts in Asia, Ampliatus and Stachys (vv 5, 8, 9). Andronicus and Junia were outstanding among the apostles, having become Christians before Paul (v 7). And particularly touching is the note in v 13—Rufus's mother "and mine"—Paul no doubt recalling occasions of warm and comforting hospitality from Rufus's mother in previous travels. Even though Paul obviously attempts to add a special note to those he knew best in the list, these particular greetings stand out.

(2) The social composition of those listed is also noteworthy. There is an absence of specifically Roman names (though note Julia), and Paul indicates that three of those listed are Jews (Andronicus, Junia, and Herodion—vv 7, 11), though it is likely that Aquila and Prisca, Mary, Rufus and his mother (vv 3, 6, 13) were also Jews. Even so, the list is predominantly gentile, and may well reflect the relative balance between Jews and Gentiles in the Roman congregations. Equally notable is the fact that most of the names were common among slaves, freedmen, and freedwomen—Junia, Ampliatus, Urbanus, Stachys, Persia, Rufus, Asyncritus, Phlegon, Hermes, Patrobas, Hermas, Philologus and Julia, Nereus and *Olympas, as well, of course, as the households of Aristobulus and* Narcissus. This gives a fairly clear picture of the extent to which the first Christian groups in Rome drew their strength from the lower strata of Roman society. At the same time Prisca and Aquila would be not without contacts and influence. The hard workers Mary, Tryphaena and Tryphosa, and Persia (vv 6, 12) may have had some

17

means of their own. And several of those listed must have traveled a fair amount—all those indeed listed under (1), since they had all obviously been personally in contact with Paul earlier in his mission work and were now in Rome.[4]

Rom 14:1ff indicates that there must have been some tensions between the various groups or house churches related to food!

> [1] *As for the man who is weak in faith, welcome him, but not for disputes over opinions.* [2] *One believes he may eat anything, while the weak man eats only vegetables.* [3] *Let not him who eats despise him who abstains, and let not him who abstains pass judgment on him who eats; for God has welcomed him.* [4] *Who are you to pass judgment on the servant of another? It is before his own master that he stands or falls. And he will be upheld, for the Master is able to make him stand.*
>
> [5] *One man esteems one day as better than another, while another man esteems all days alike. Let everyone be fully convinced in his own mind.* [6] *He who observes the day, observes it in honor of the Lord. He also who eats, eats in honor of the Lord, since he gives thanks to God; while he who abstains, abstains in honor of the Lord and gives thanks to God.* [7] *None of us lives to himself, and none of us dies to himself.* [8] *If we live, we live to the Lord, and if we die, we die to the Lord; so then, whether we live or whether we die, we are the Lord's.* [9] *For to this end Christ died and lived again, that he might be Lord both of the dead and of the living.*
>
> [10] *Why do you pass judgment on your brother? Or you, why do you despise your brother?*

---

[4] Dunn, *Romans 9–16*, pp. 899–900.

Paul's theological message

The basic theological message of Romans is clearly stated at Rom 1:16, 17, but this will involve some deep theological discussion!

> *¹⁶ For I am not ashamed of the gospel: <u>it is the power of God for salvation to everyone who has faith, to the Jew first and also to the Greek</u>. ¹⁷ For in it <u>the righteousness of God</u> is revealed through faith for faith; as it is written, "He who through faith is righteous shall live."*

The *power* of the gospel always centers on *the death and resurrection of Jesus*! Note Paul's earlier comment on this at 1 Cor 1:17ff:

> *¹⁷ For Christ did not send me to baptize but to preach the gospel, and not with eloquent wisdom, <u>lest the cross of Christ be emptied of its power</u>.*
>
> *¹⁸ For <u>the word of the cross</u> is folly to those who are perishing, <u>but to us who are being saved it is the power of God</u>. ¹⁹ For it is written, "I will destroy the wisdom of the wise, and the cleverness of the clever I will thwart.*

Considerable debate has circled around the full meaning of Rom 1:16, 17, with good reason! We will engage this debate more fully in the following lessons, but the basic message in this text is clearly that *God is a righteous God* who *declares everyone righteous (forgiven, not guilty) by the same means, through faith in Jesus Christ, his death and resurrection, regardless of gender or ethnic background.*

This was precisely the same gospel Paul had preached in his Epistle to the Galatians, cf. Gal 3:25-29:

> *²⁵ But now that faith has come, we are no longer under a custodian; ²⁶ for in Christ Jesus you are all sons of God, through faith. ²⁷ For as many of you as were baptized into Christ have put on Christ. ²⁸ <u>There is neither Jew nor Greek</u>, there is <u>neither slave nor free</u>, there is <u>neither male nor female; for you are all one in Christ Jesus</u>. ²⁹ And if you are*

Christ's, then you are Abraham's offspring, heirs according to promise.

Paul's point was that God declares everyone righteous *on the same grounds, by the same means, by His faithfulness to His covenant promise to Abraham to bless all nations*, and His faithfulness to the fulfillment of that promise to save all people in Jesus the Messiah.

This message is true for both Jews and Gentiles. God *shows no partiality* (Rom 1:17; 3:21, 22). *All people*, without partiality, are declared righteous by God, who is a righteous God, through faith in Jesus the Messiah!

The center of Paul's argument is that *God is a righteous God* which he demonstrates by *treating everyone the same based on the same system of faith in Jesus*! Paul argues that both Jews and Gentiles are declared righteous on the same grounds, and by the same method – *righteousness, that is, being declared not guilty, comes by grace through faith in Jesus Christ, for everyone, with no distinction or partiality*!

If God treated the Jews (who were sinners) and the Gentiles (who were also sinners) differently, justifying the Jews by the Law of Moses and the Gentiles by faith in Jesus, he would *not be a righteous God*, showing partiality to one group over the other.

Because of God's gracious righteousness and his forgiving grace, Paul naturally stressed that there is an appropriate worshipful response expected from Christians, living faithfully to God's covenant, and presenting one's life as a living sacrifice to God, not being conformed to the cultural or religious patterns or standards of their world (Rom 12:1-2).

Chapter 2 – Paul - God's Missionary of the Good News

Context and Message

As mentioned in chapter 1, Romans is an epistle significantly concerned with God's righteousness and faithfulness. This is the basis for Paul's understanding of his God-ordained all-inclusive mission to both Jew and Gentile.

Right up front in his epistolary greeting to the Romans Paul stresses that he was <u>called and set apart by God for just such a mission</u>. Rom 1:1-7: " Paul, a servant of Jesus Christ, <u>called to be an apostle, set apart for the gospel of God</u> [2] which <u>he promised beforehand through his prophets in the holy scriptures</u>, [3] <u>the gospel concerning his Son</u>, who was descended from David according to the flesh [4] and designated Son of God in power according to the Spirit of holiness by his resurrection from the dead, Jesus Christ our Lord, [5] through whom <u>we have received grace and apostleship to bring about the obedience of faith for the sake of his name among all the nations</u>, [6] including yourselves who are called to belong to Jesus Christ; [7] To all God's beloved in Rome, who are called to be saints. "

God's righteousness and faithfulness are a firm foundation for grasping his great love for his creation, Jews and Gentiles, in His inclusive covenant with Abraham, Gen 12, 15, 17, et al.

It is important that we have a good biblical understanding of righteousness.

Righteousness and justification are built of the same Greek root words, δικαιοσύνη dikaiosúnē; δίκη díkē, δικαιόω dikaióō, which relate to justice and being declared not guilty, a just or right person, or righteous.

The Greek terms are primarily legal court terms implying that one has been declared not guilty, or forgiven. When God declares one forgiven that person is not guilty by forgiveness, not by keeping laws!

Paul and the Jews would understand righteousness as being in a right relationship with God. As we will note later in Rom 3:20 righteousness does not come through our ability to keep the Law of Moses, or any law. Rom 3:20: "For no human being will be justified in his sight by works of the law, since through the law comes knowledge of sin."

The Roman epistle includes a gospel message, an euangelion good news element, regarding the arrival of a divine king, the Messiah, who would be their savior, Jesus Christ. He is the one who through his faithful death on the cross restores God's eternal purpose and covenant promise to Abraham.

His faithful fulfillment of God's eternal plan involved dying on a cross to redeem man from his sinful condition according to God's predetermined eternal purpose.

Jesus, by dying on the cross, made it possible for all people, Jew and Gentile to be adopted into God's family by faith. This had been a major point of Paul's epistle to the Ephesians in Eph 2:3-6, "Blessed be the God and Father of our Lord Jesus Christ, who has blessed us in Christ with every spiritual blessing in the heavenly places, [4] even as he chose us in him before the foundation of the world, that we should be holy and blameless before him. [5] He destined us in love to be his sons through Jesus Christ, according to the purpose of his will, [6] to the praise of his glorious grace which he freely bestowed on us in the Beloved."

Romans is a gospel message that builds on the power of God expressed in the cross of Jesus which draws us through our faith or trusting in the faithful death of Jesus to the atoning activity of God.

This gospel message originates in the faithfulness of God, and in turn calls all people to have faith and trust in God and his covenant faithfulness for all nations,

22

Jews, Gentiles. This would notably include in this context, the Romans living in Rome, and those living to the West of Rome, possibly even Spain, to whom Paul wanted to visit and preach.

Paul was primarily a missionary! That is what the word apostle means, ἀπόστολος apóstolos, "one sent out on a mission as an ambassador."

As a missionary Paul hoped that the Christians in Rome would join him in his mission by supporting him in some way on his journey! To be sped on my journey, προπέμπω, propémpō, in vs 24 below in Greek implies help, hopefully including some financial assistance! Rom 15:22-29: "This is the reason why I have so often been hindered from coming to you. [23] But now, since I no longer have any room for work in these regions, and since I have longed for many years to come to you, [24] I hope to see you in passing as I go to Spain, and to be sped on my journey there by you, once I have enjoyed your company for a little. [25] At present, however, I am going to Jerusalem with aid for the saints. [26] For Macedonia and Achaia have been pleased to make some contribution for the poor among the saints at Jerusalem; [27] they were pleased to do it, and indeed they are in debt to them, for if the Gentiles have come to share in their spiritual blessings, they ought also to be of service to them in material blessings. [28] When therefore I have completed this, and have delivered to them what has been raised, I shall go on by way of you to Spain; [29] and I know that when I come to you I shall come in the fulness of the blessing of Christ."

The gospel message proclaimed by Paul and the apostles called for an obedient faith which implies that men need to respond in an appropriate manner, by faith in God and Jesus in order to benefit by the atoning power of the gospel.

Rom 1:16, 17. "For I am not ashamed of the gospel: it is the power of God for salvation to everyone who has faith, to the Jew first and also to the Greek. [17] For in it the righteousness of God is revealed through faith for faith; as it is written, "He who through faith is righteous shall live."

This gospel is not something new and against God's previous covenant with Abraham and his giving of the Law of Moses or the Torah, but is a fulfilment of that Abrahamic covenant and the Law of Moses, including the Torah which was God's instruction to the Jews for maintaining a covenant relationship with Him.

Paul expresses his love and concern for the Roman Christians by stating up front that he is eager and under obligation to preach this gospel to the Romans, both Jew and Gentile.

Why did Paul write this epistle to the Romans?

Scholars continue to debate the question as to Paul's reason for writing the epistle. They produce several possible differing answers! Perhaps there is no one single reason for Romans, and Paul may have had several reasons related to the primary theology of the epistle!

This topic is discussed at length by scholars in Karl Donfried, *The Romans Debate*, and is one of the chief scholarly debates relating to Romans. For a serious scholar of Romans, Donfried is a must read! It is not a required read for many class teachers, but it is a helpful resource for advanced scholars of Romans.

For several reasons I am of the opinion that Paul explains his reason in the epistle as a letter written by *a mature missionary* to the churches in Rome because *he has mission intentions* and wants the Christians in Rome *to send him on to Spain*, Rom 15:17-29, *as a missionary*. He plans also to preach and teach while in Rome and strengthen their spiritual life and commitment and then be sped on his way by the Roman Christians.

An interesting sidebar to Paul's desire to travel on to Spain is that it took several years and other preaching stops, including an imprisonment in Rome, before Paul possibly made it to the West, or Spain.[5]

We will work with the conclusion adopted in this commentary and study that Romans is primarily a mission epistle!

In Romans, Paul explains the theological message he preaches, laying out his apostolic *"ambassadorial"* credentials in an *epideictic* manner (*epideictic, shared values*) to establish the fact that he is worthy of their support, and that his teaching should not be seen as radical although it was uncomfortable for most Jews.

However, knowing the difficulty Christian Jews were having accepting Gentile Christians who were not circumcised, Paul sets his doctrine in the context of the discussion of the Law (*Torah*), arguing that all Christians, both Jew and Gentile, are justified by God *on the same basis of faith in Jesus Christ* and *not by law keeping*, even the Law of Moses, and that God, being a righteous God, does this without partiality or favoring one group above the other. *All people, according to Paul's understanding of the gospel, are saved and justified by the same principle of faith.*

Although Paul carries on a detailed discussion of justification by grace through faith and not by *Torah* keeping (*Torah* is the Hebrew word that lies behind our English word for law and carries the sense of God's *instruction*). Although he debates the issue, he is not "arguing" against supposed *opponents* as in Galatians. There do not seem to be real opponents against whom he is debating, as in Galatians. The style of argument against *hypothetical opponents* is technically called a *diatribe* and Romans is replete with diatribe rhetorical keys. What "opponents" might seem to exist are merely *hypothetical for the sake of the argument Paul is making.* Nevertheless,

---

[5] Clement, Bishop of Rome, ca 90 CE; a fragment of the Muratorian canon, ca 170 CE; and John Chrysostom, Archbishop of Constantinople, ca 350 CE, bear some testimony to such a mission journey.

he does address probable tensions within the Roman Christian community, Rom 14, 15.

The theme and theology of Romans

Paul introduces the *good news* of *God's righteousness and faithfulness* in his remarkable statement of Rom 1:1-17. Paul's message is *good news for all humanity*. There are no ethnic distinctions or partiality in God's scheme of redemption, Rom 1:5, 13b-17. His good news *euangelion* is for all men!

Note that the word *gospel, euangelion*, in some form occurs *five times* in these opening verses, Rom 1:1-16, and *acts as an introduction to the theology of the entire letter.*

Since Paul uses the "good news" word so often it should affect how we view the book as a whole.

Rom 1:16, 17. The meaning of the word *euangelion*, gospel, especially for Roman recipients

Romans in general would have understood the implication of the Greek word "εὐαγγέλιον, *euaggélion"* for *the announcement of the arrival of a new king*, or *a new Caesar*! An inscription discovered in Prienne in northern Turkey dated c.a. 9 B.C. gives us an insight into *the power and meaning of the word gospel* in ancient times. Here's what the inscription says:

> "Whereas *the Providence which has ordered the whole of our life*, showing concern and zeal, has ordained *the most perfect consummation for human life by giving to it Augustus*, by filling him with virtue for doing the work of a benefactor among men, and *by sending in him, as it were, a savior for us* and those who come after us, to make war to cease, *to create order everywhere…and whereas the birthday of the God was the beginning for the world of the <u>glad tidings that have come to men through him</u>…. Paulus Fabius Maximus*, the

proconsul of the province…has devised a way of honoring Augustus."[6]

In the *gospel* or *glad tidings* honoring the emperor Augustus we have what was considered by learned Romans as a *"divine announcement"* of a king who had come with authority to rule Rome. The emperor is praised for restoring *peace* and bringing *salvation* to his kingdom.

The implications of this view can be seen in the fact that *the gospel of God* also *announces a new king* in the person of Jesus who brings *blessings*, *peace*, and *salvation* for his followers.

Thus, it would be clearly understood by Roman Christians, who were citizens of the Roman Empire and familiar with decrees announcing new emperors, that the gospel was a royal *announcement* or *proclamation*, rather than just an invitation to share the joy inherent in the good news.

The above inscription wasn't merely saying that Augustus is lord *if only the people would let him into their hearts*! It claims that the power that governs the universe had established Augustus as lord of the world and *he was its instrument to bring peace and security to that world.*

Now Paul was announcing *a new Caesar who would rule the world*, Jesus the Messiah, in whom the Roman Christians were to believe and entrust their future.

These are some of the ideas that must have been conjured up in Roman minds when Paul spoke of a *gospel of which he was not ashamed*, for it carried the power of God for salvation, Rom 1:16, 17!

Individualism is such a part of our modern culture in which *personal religious decision* is stressed that we forget the full royal divine implications behind the *gospel*, *euangelion*. The gospel includes a strident announcement regarding a powerful king, divinely enthroned, who "demands" our allegiance and who comes to rule in our lives!

---

[6] *New International Dictionary of New Testament Theology and Exegesis*, Moisés Silva, Zondervan, 2014, vol 2, p. 108.

When Paul preached Jesus as Messiah (king) he wasn't simply inviting people to a faith in a new religion, *he was proclaiming a change in the entire creation order because a new king had risen*, and God was acting through him without partiality! Nothing is to be seen any longer in the same way as it had before! *A new king and a new order had arrived*!

Oscar Cullmann, a prominent 20th century Christian theologian, grasped the significance of the Christ event in his major theological study, *Christ and Time*, stating that *Christ was the center of human history*. By this he intended that Christ was that tangent point around which all history rotated.[7]

So, Paul warns the Romans as he approaches the gates of Rome, which many considered to be the world's center of "divine" imperial power, that he is coming with a *gospel* message that spoke of *God's power* to change everything, and in doing so to save anyone and everyone who believes in God's and the world's king, Jesus Christ! Paul was claiming that in Jesus Christ all history and power on earth had changed!

In contrast to the continued cruelty of Nero against both the Jews and the Christians, Paul preached the *good news of a divine Messiah king* who would bring peace and salvation who had now broken into the history of the world in Jesus Christ. There is ample evidence in history of Nero's atrocities against the Jews and Christians.[8] Although many politically inclined Romans defended Nero, the Jews and Christians to whom Paul was writing knew from personal experience of Nero's atrocities!

In contrast to Nero's legacy, Paul preached a *strange gospel* of a king who was willing to die for his people in order to bring peace and salvation.

---

[7] Oscar Cullmann and Floyd V. Filson, *Christ and Time, The Primitive Christian Conception of Time and History*, SCM Press, 1950.
[8] Cf. the articles in the *Anchor Yale Bible Dictionary* on both Nero and Tacitus. Tacitus in his *Histories* and *Annaels* recorded Nero's atrocities.

This was essentially the *good news, euangelion,* that Paul planned to lay before the Romans, a gospel of a real divine king and a truly righteous God who treated all men equally.

That the new king *would die for his people* might be a shock to both Romans and Jews, but Paul mitigated this in his statement at Rom 1:1-5 regarding the divine power behind Jesus' resurrection from the dead.

Paul presents his epistle as *good news* because *it is the "gospel of God"*

The expression "gospel *of* God" may mean it is a gospel that comes *from* God, or a gospel that *God himself makes known.* It may also mean it is a gospel "*about*" God. There is no need to choose between these alternatives since Paul might have had all of these in mind. All three are certainly true and it is important in the book of Romans to see the full truth and authoritative power of the gospel.

The gospel isn't about less important things like the weather, or the economy of the Graeco-Roman world, or how to have a good relationship with our neighbors. *The gospel is about God himself and how he relates to his sinful creation and acts in their regard.* The gospel is in fact *missional;* it is intended to be preached to all creatures, Mark 16:15, Acts 2:8!

But this gospel also comes from or originates in God himself and the covenant he made with Abraham to bless all nations, Gen 12, 15, 17.

This gospel is not some good advice or a philosophy that Paul or others had dreamed up—*this gospel belonged to God and had come directly from God himself.* In fact, we will learn from Paul at Rom 1:2 that this gospel had been proclaimed before his time in the Jewish Scriptures, the *Torah.*

This means that the Romans should pay careful attention to this gospel message and its *missional* nature! It was foundational to God's original plan to redeem his fallen creation. Cf. Eph 1:3ff:

*³ Blessed be the God and Father of our Lord
Jesus Christ, who has blessed us in Christ with
every spiritual blessing in the heavenly places,
⁴ even as he chose us in him before the foundation
of the world, that we should be holy and blameless
before him. ⁵ He destined us in love to be his sons
through Jesus Christ, according to the purpose of
his will, ⁶ to the praise of his glorious grace which
he freely bestowed on us in the Beloved. ⁷ In him we
have redemption through his blood, the forgiveness
of our trespasses, according to the riches of his
grace ⁸ which he lavished upon us. ⁹ For he has
made known to us in all wisdom and insight the
mystery of his will, according to his purpose which
he set forth in Christ ¹⁰ as a plan for the fulness of
time, to unite all things in him, things in heaven
and things on earth.*

Paul proclaims the euangelion, the gospel or good news, because it is a gospel concerning God's Son, Jesus the Messiah, the Christ, God's Messianic King

First, to begin our study of this strikingly profound
pericope we should understand that the word *Christ, in
Christ Jesus,* written in Greek as *Χριστοῦ Ἰησοῦ,* was not
Jesus' *name*, but referred to the *role* he played in God's
eternal purpose as God's *chosen* and *anointed* king![9]

Second, the word order *in Paul's Greek* is not *Jesus
Christ*, but *Christ Jesus, Χριστοῦ Ἰησοῦ,* emphasizing
first his title as *king*. The text actually reads *"Paul a
bond servant of king Jesus"*! Romans would immediately
get the sense of this for in Paul's time one out of every
three people in Rome was a slave![10]

Third, the impact of referring to Jesus as *King Jesus*
would not have been missed by the Roman Christians,
as this was in striking contrast to the Roman reference
to their dominant leaders as Julius *Caesar* or *Caesar*

---

[9] *Jesus* referred to his name, *Christ* his title or divine role.
[10] Cf. www.britishmuseum.org.

Nero. A new system of "kingship" was being announced, not *Caesar* Jesus, but *King Jesus*!

Fourth, this reference to Jesus as *messiah* would resonate with the Jews who would have been familiar to the Jewish expectation of a new king in the lineage of King David.

Fifth, Χριστός, *Christós*, is the Greek equivalent of the Hebrew word *Messiah*, which primarily was a *descriptive title* such as *a divinely chosen and anointed one*, hence, the *divinely chosen* and *anointed one, Jesus!*

Sixth, the concept of *anointing* kings and priests drew on the rich heritage of Israel's priests and kings being *chosen and anointed by God* to the position of priest or king.

Seventh, Jewish literature, notably during the prophetic era of Israel following the Babylonian exile and captivity of Israel, pointed to a future chosen one who would be the *anointed* "messiah king" of God's kingdom who would lead them to redemption. Micah 5:2 is a good example of these prophetic promises which Matthew referred to as a fulfillment of prophecy at Matt 2:1:

> *But you, O Bethlehem Ephrathah,*
> *who are little to be among the clans of Judah,*
> *from you shall come forth for me*
> *one who is to be ruler in Israel,*
> *whose origin is from of old,*
> *from ancient days.*

The New Testament Scriptures claim that Jesus fulfilled the messianic promises to Israel, cf Matt 1:22f, *passim*, and the covenant promises to Abraham, Gal 3:26-29. Prophets like Daniel, Dan 7, *passim*, spoke of a *coming seed who would reign over God's chosen people and kingdom, and establish an eternal kingdom,* cf. John 12:34, Heb 12:18ff, 2 Pet 1:11.

Thus, references to Jesus in the context of the term *euangelion, good news,* of his being of the *seed of David, all resonate with God's promises to Israel.* These fulfilled promises were Paul's foundation and platform for claiming that *Jesus was the fulfillment of God's promises regarding a messiah and a new messianic and eternal kingdom on earth.*

In this opening paragraph to the Roman saints, Rom 1:1-6, Paul stated that God had *clearly made his divine purposes known through Scripture. He had in Scripture prophesied that a new Messiah would come!*

Thus, in Jesus *the messianic Christ, a new era had arrived.* This was *euangelion, good news.*

A new way was present that had never been an option! Rome was full of past Caesars who appeared for a brief while, then were gone. But in Jesus, God's *Messiah*, the *Christ*, a new king, not a temporary Caesar had arrived. *Jesus would reign over God's kingdom for evermore* Dan 7:13, 14.[11]

Notice Paul's opening thoughts in this long theologically packed and loaded statement. In the Greek Rom 1:1-6 is one long sentence!

Jesus was:

> set apart for the gospel of God[2] which <u>he promised beforehand through his prophets in the holy scriptures</u>, [3] the gospel concerning his Son<u>, who was descended from David according to the flesh</u> [4] and <u>designated Son of God in power according to the Spirit of holiness by his resurrection from the dead</u>, Jesus <u>Christ our Lord</u>, [5] through whom we have received grace and apostleship to bring about the obedience of faith for the sake of his name <u>among all the nations</u>, [6] including yourselves who are called to belong to Jesus Christ...

When he referred to Jesus as the Son of God, Paul stated that Jesus had come to the world as a son of David's

---

[11] It is noteworthy that Rome referred to its leaders as *Caesars, καῖσᾰρ, kaîsar,* or Emperors αυτοκράτορας, *autokratas,* but the New Testament writers refer to Jesus as the *king (basileus)* of God's *kingdom (basileia)!*

royal lineage. That would resonate with the Jews! But that Paul adds that Jesus was also powerfully marked out as *God's unique Son* by his resurrection from among the dead, Rom 1:3. The power of Jesus' resurrection as a divine event would resonate with the Romans who had been taught that the Caesars were either powerful gods or sanctioned by powerful gods. Romans were a people impressed by power not by words.

The phrase "*according to the spirit of holiness*" seems to suggest that there was more to Jesus than his *fleshly*, human, nature. Viewed from his *human* side he is David's son but viewed from his incarnational *spiritual* side he is *God's Son*!

There are those who think we should understand that Christ was David's son according to the flesh, but that he was revealed to be God's Son by the Holy Spirit, "the spirit of holiness." This is true but not what Paul stated. Although we recognize that the Holy Spirit was involved in Jesus' resurrection, Rom 8:16 clearly indicates this, Rom 1:4 explains that it was **by his powerful resurrection** from the dead that he was announced as God's Son. Note Rom 1:4, Jesus was *designated Son of God in power according to the Spirit of holiness by his resurrection from the dead.*

Such power would certainly make an impression on Romans who respected the power of their "divine Caesars."

Rom 1:16. The Gospel is *God's power to save*

We're tempted to think of God's *power* as merely *divine muscle* but it's a mistake to think of it as such in this context. Even when speaking about human power we know the difference between the power to move a huge stone and the power to *move* a person. A person *saved* in Paul's sense means God brought that person back into relationship with himself *by his power and so saved him/her from sin and awful loss.* This kind of saving power isn't done with *divine muscle* but is the result of *divine action in history fulfilled in the death of Jesus on the cross.*

1 Cor 1:18. "*For Christ did not send me to baptize but to preach the gospel, and not with eloquent wisdom, <u>lest the cross of Christ be emptied of its power</u>. ¹⁸ For <u>the word</u> (message, IAF) <u>of the cross</u> is folly to those who are perishing, but to us who are being saved <u>it is the power of God</u>.*"

Since God saves us out of his love and the death of his son, Jesus Christ, it is clear that he doesn't bully us into life by his power, and doesn't save us by force. To be saved by God's "power" means God set himself the task of saving his creation *by a power that lay behind human ability. That power is seen in the cross, or the death of Jesus and his resurrection.*

The *gospel*, or *good news*, is the message that a faithful God by his love and power seen in the crucified Jesus saved us. *God entered the confines of the human heart through offering his Son on a cross to bring about what no other power could achieve.*

The heart of the gospel Paul preached is that *a righteous and faithful God* has made it possible for sinners to be *forgiven for sin* through *faith in Jesus*. This forgiveness is by *the power of God* through *faith in Jesus' death and resurrection. It is not by the sinner's own power or effort but by free gift of God's grace. The sinner is declared *not guilty by God, a forgiven and righteous* person, and brought into a *right relationship with God*

Through God's *faithfulness* and *righteousness,* and faith in his covenant purpose in Jesus, God *forgives* people and *restores* them as his children into a *right relationship* with Himself. They are *declared forgiven, not guilty, and righteous. Now that is good news!*

The gospel is God's power to save *all those who have faith* in His atoning work in Jesus, including both Jew and Gentile!

Rom 1:17 speaks of a righteousness *through faith for faith*! Righteousness originates in *God's faithfulness* which leads to *our faith in God.*

God's righteousness flows **out of** his own righteousness and faithfulness **toward** our faith and our subsequent righteousness.

We are declared righteous by a righteous and faithful God for a righteousness based on our faith, not works!

This means that *our faith in God and Jesus* stem from *our acceptance of God's faith and faithful atoning sacrifice of Jesus Christ.*

For the Roman believers Paul stressed the *universal nature of God's plan.*

In the context of being a Roman, the gospel message is that since *God is a righteous God,* he provides *the same atoning message for all people based on faith,* and not based on *any special ethnic or national religious law* such as the Law of Moses.

God's righteousness is seen in *his faithfulness* to save Jew and Gentile alike, through *their faith in Jesus,* Rom 1:16, 17.

> *[16] For I am not ashamed of the gospel: it is the power of God for salvation to **everyone** who **has faith**, to the Jew first and also to the Greek. [17] For in it the righteousness of God is revealed **through faith for faith**; as it is written, "He who through faith is righteous shall live."*

For the Jewish believers Paul stressed the eternal plan of redemption apparent in the calling of Israel through Abraham to be God's people.

One way of understanding God's righteousness could simply be in acknowledging the fact that he is God, Holy, Sovereign, and Creator. But that is not the point Paul was making to the Romans! Paul's Jewish faith, and the faith of all Jews, would have understood the sovereignty of God, but Paul is also writing to Romans who were Gentiles.

So first, Paul emphasizes that God keeps his promises and commitments; when he created humanity, he made a commitment to humanity simply by creating them good with everything they needed for life.

Second, God made a covenant with Adam and Eve, Noah and his family, and then Abraham that he would bless him and their "seed." In Jesus he did this very thing. Gal 3:6-9; Rom 4:16, 17.

Third, God is a righteous God because he does not show any favoritism or partiality. He did not favor the Jews over the Gentiles but included all men in his covenant with Abraham. He justifies both Jew and Gentile on the same grounds, faith in Jesus and his promises to all people. This is a major theme of the Roman epistle!

Fourth, despite our rebellion against God he didn't utterly destroy mankind—he was faithful to his word to make reconciliation possible and that's part of what we mean when we say God is "righteous."

Fifth, the gospel message that proclaims God's faithfulness to all people draws all people to God in response to his faithfulness so that people can put their trust (faith) in him. So the gospel is *"from faith" ek pisteōs, out of faith, **that is God's faithfulness**,* "unto faith" *eis pistin, toward faith, that is for the creation of faith in those who hear of God's faithfulness,* Rom 1:17.

The relationship between God's righteousness and those who are declared righteous by faith must be *a dynamic symbiotic faith* if salvation is to be experienced. *It isn't just God keeping faith with man, it is also man trusting himself to the God who is faithful.* Neither is it simply man's faith, it is a faith *symbiotically cooperative* with God's faith!

God's covenant with Abraham was on the basis of faith, a faith principle, Abraham trusting that God is faithful and that Abraham and his descendants, both Jew and Gentile, would benefit from God's faithfulness!

36

This gospel message is therefore primarily about God's righteousness and faithfulness, but it also stresses that all who will trust, that is have faith in God's faithfulness, will be saved!

The *double meaning* of the righteousness of God *and* the righteousness of man

In our leading text for this lesson, Rom 1:16, 17, Paul introduced his message speaking of the *"righteousness of God."* This could mean *the righteousness that comes from God*, the righteousness *that God gives or declares*, or it could be understood, as is best understood in the context of Romans, as *the righteousness that belongs to God's character out of which he acts and grants righteousness.* We will demonstrate in the study that follows that the fact that God declares everyone righteous by the same method clearly reveals and stresses *that God is a righteous God* who *saves, justifies*, and *forgives all men in exactly the same manner*, through faith in Jesus Christ.

The term euangelion is an inclusio!

As it appears in the Greek text in the opening and closing verses of Rom 1:1-16 *euangelion* forms an *inclusio*[12] *highlighting the leading theme developed in this periscope*! An *inclusio* focuses attention on a major theme.

The theme is that God is not a God of favoritism but *a righteous God who loves his whole creation*, Jew and Gentile equally; and loves them all *without partiality*! *This is good news*!

---

[12] In biblical studies, *inclusio* is a literary device based on a circular principle, also known as *bracketing* or *in parenthesis, held between two gates*, which consists of creating a frame by placing similar material at the beginning and end of a section. The material in the inclusio could consist of a word, a phrase or a sentence. Inclusio is found in both the Old and New Testament literature. The purpose of an inclusio may be structural - to alert the reader to a particularly important theme - or it may serve to show how the material within the inclusio relates to the overall theme of the literature.

However somber some of the parts of Romans may be on occasion, we need to remember that *Paul sees himself as a preacher and teacher of "the good news of God,"* and it's this good news he preaches that he wants to bring to the Romans, and then take on to Spain.

The good news that Paul preaches begins with the fact that *God is a righteous God* and then moves into a discussion of his declaring his saints righteous by faith in Jesus. The *righteousness of God* is boldly stated at Rom 1:17. The construction of this phrase can refer to *the righteousness that God possesses*, which I believe is what is intended in this place, or to *the righteousness which God imparts to others by grace through faith*, which certainly is taught in Romans. The fact that God treats all men equally on the grounds of faith, both Jews and Gentiles alike, demonstrates God's righteousness.

However, scholars today with solid reason adopt the view which I am proposing as a major feature of the good news of Paul's gospel! *God is a righteous God!*

Rom 1:1-17. The heart of this pericope is that Paul was God's *missionary* to both the Jew and the Gentile!

[1] Paul, a servant of Jesus Christ, <u>called to be an apostle, set apart for the gospel of God</u> [2] which <u>he promised beforehand through his prophets in the holy scriptures</u>, [3] the gospel concerning his Son, who was descended from David according to the flesh [4] and designated Son of God in power according to the Spirit of holiness by his resurrection from the dead, Jesus Christ our Lord, [5] through whom we have received grace and apostleship to bring about the obedience of faith for the sake of his name among all the nations, [6] including yourselves who are called to belong to Jesus Christ; [7] To all God's beloved in Rome, who are called to be saints:

Grace to you and peace from God our Father and the Lord Jesus Christ.

⁸ First, I thank my God through Jesus Christ for all of you, because your faith is proclaimed in all the world. ⁹ For God is my witness, whom I serve with my spirit in the gospel of his Son, that without ceasing I mention you always in my prayers, ¹⁰ <u>asking that somehow by God's will I may now at last succeed in coming to you</u>. ¹¹ For I long to see you, that I may impart to you some spiritual gift to strengthen you, ¹² that is, that we may be mutually encouraged by each other's faith, both yours and mine. ¹³ I want you to know, brethren, that I have often intended to come to you (but thus far have been prevented), in order that I may reap some harvest among you as well as among the rest of the Gentiles. ¹⁴ I am under obligation both to Greeks and to barbarians, both to the wise and to the foolish: ¹⁵ so I am eager to preach the gospel to you also who are in Rome.

¹⁶ For I am not ashamed of the gospel: it is the power of God for salvation to everyone who has faith, to the Jew first and also to the Greek. ¹⁷ For in it the righteousness of God is revealed through faith for faith; as it is written, "He who through faith is righteous shall live."

Paul, the Apostle of God

Although we know Paul as an *apostle*, and he is often introduced as an *apostle* in our English translations of the Bible,[13] *he was primarily a missionary who wrote great theological church related epistles*! The word *apostle* in Greek, ἀπόστολος, *apóstolos*, primarily *refers to <u>one sent out on a mission</u> as an ambassador or a <u>missionary</u>!*[14]

Rom 1:1, 2. The *missional* nature of Paul's calling

¹Paul, a servant of Jesus Christ, <u>called to be an apostle</u>, <u>set apart for the gospel of God</u>² which he

---

[13] Gal 1:1; Eph 1:1; Col 1:1; 1 and 2 Tim 1:1.
[14] Zodhiates and Kittel, ἀπόστολος, *apóstolos*.

*promised beforehand through his prophets in the holy
scriptures.*

Paul claims that the purpose of his *apostolic calling*
was to be *a commissioned missionary* to *preach the gospel
good news, the euangelion,* which came *from God, or* was
about God to all people including the Gentiles.

The Greek expression *of God* is θεοῦ, *theou,* a genitive
noun which could be *a possessive genitive* denoting *good
news belonging* to God, or a descriptive genitive, *good
news about God.*

Context normally adds definition to these genitive
nouns, but in the case here in Romans, it can have a *double
meaning!* The gospel Paul preaches is certainly *good news
about God; he is a righteous God* who treats all people
equally, but Paul's gospel is also a gospel *belonging to
God,* not Paul, not Moses, or anyone else.

Luke explains that God himself told Ananias that God
purposely chose Paul *to preach the gospel to the Gentiles,*
but not overlooking the Jews.

Acts 9:13-19:

*[13] But Ananias answered, "Lord, I have heard from
many about this man, how much evil he has done to thy
saints at Jerusalem; [14] and here he has authority from
the chief priests to bind all who call upon thy name."
[15] But the Lord said to him, "Go, for he is a chosen
instrument of mine to carry my name before the
Gentiles and kings and the sons of Israel; [16] for I will
show him how much he must suffer for the sake of my
name." [17] So Ananias departed and entered the house.
And laying his hands on him he said, "Brother Saul,
the Lord Jesus who appeared to you on the road by
which you came, has sent me that you may regain your
sight and be filled with the Holy Spirit." [18] And
immediately something like scales fell from his eyes
and he regained his sight. Then he rose and was
baptized, [19] and took food and was strengthened.*

Rom 1:2. For the Jewish believers Paul explains that the good news of God's righteousness in Jesus Christ was nothing new. It had been promised in the Old Testament Scriptures.

> *Paul… an apostle set apart for the gospel of God* <u>*² which he promised beforehand through his prophets in the holy scriptures*</u>

The gospel preached by Paul, then, was not something new! It had been promised by the prophets of old! Paul will repeatedly make the point in Romans that the Old Testament scriptures (including the covenant *Torah* itself) pointed to the gospel he was preaching about Jesus Christ, God's Son, cf Rom 3:21 with Acts 26:22-23.

The term *Torah* is a Jewish Hebrew word which stood first for the first five books of the Old Testament, the "Pentateuch or five books of Moses," but in time became understood as *God's sacred instruction in a greater and larger sense* to include *all of their sacred writings.*

Our problem is that the Greek word chosen to translate *Torah* is **νόμος**, *nómos*[15] which has a *wide range of meanings*. On occasion it can mean *law* in the strict sense of law. On other occasions it can mean a *principle*. Likewise, it can mean *that by which one is instructed.* We think in terms of legal law, but the Jew thought of the Law of Moses in terms of *divine instruction*. See how Paul refers to the Psalms as *law Torah* in Rom 3:11-18, 19!

So, in some sense Paul's gospel message might be surprising or new to some, but the truth is *Israel had long been given fair warning of how the good news would be worked out in Jesus the Messiah,*

Jesus stressed that the Jews should have believed in him since they had in Moses' writings all they needed for

---

[15] Zodhiates, νόμος *nómos*; to divide among, parcel out, allot. Etymologically something parceled out, allotted, what one has in use and possession; hence, usage, custom …. In the NT, law … rule, norm and / or standard of judging or acting (Rom. 3:27; 7:23, 25; 8:2, 7; 9:31). In the sense of a rule of life, discipline.

faith in a Messiah! Cf. Luke 24:25-27, 44-47. Cf. also John 5:24, 25:

> Do not think that I shall accuse you to the Father; it is Moses who accuses you, on whom you set your hope. *46 If you believed Moses, you would believe me, for he wrote of me. *47 But if you do not believe his writings, how will you believe my words?*

Unfortunately, many in Israel, eager to establish their own national identity with God missed what the Old Testament or *Torah* taught about God and his plan for the whole human race, cf. Rom 9:30-10:4 in light of Rom 1:16.

> *30 What shall we say, then? That Gentiles who did not pursue righteousness have attained it, that is, righteousness through faith; *31 but that Israel who pursued the righteousness which is based on law did not succeed in fulfilling that law. *32 Why? Because they did not pursue it through faith, but as if it were based on works.* They have stumbled over the stumbling stone, *33 as it is written,* (Isa 28:16).

> *"Behold, I am laying in Zion a stone that will make men stumble, a rock that will make them fall; and he who believes in him will not be put to shame."*

> *1 Brethren, my heart's desire and prayer to God for them is that they may be saved. *2 I bear them witness that they have a zeal for God, but it is not enlightened. *3 For, being ignorant of the righteousness that comes from God, and seeking to establish their own, they did not submit to God's righteousness. *4 For Christ is the end of the law, that everyone who has faith may be justified.*

When God called the Jews and made covenants with Abraham and Moses the Jews thought God had excluded the Gentiles, not realizing that the Gentiles had been part of God's plan from the very beginning and that the Gentiles had been included in God's covenant promise to Abraham, Gen 12, 15, 17.

Rom 1:1-6. Paul's mission was to *bring about an obedient faith among all nations.*

> *¹Paul...set apart for the gospel...³the gospel concerning his Son, who was descended from David according to the flesh ⁴ and designated Son of God in power according to the Spirit of holiness by his resurrection from the dead, Jesus Christ our Lord, ⁵ through whom we have received grace and <u>apostleship to bring about the obedience of faith for the sake of his name among all the nations</u>, ⁶ including yourselves who are called to belong to Jesus Christ.*

Paul had a clear understanding of his divinely appointed purpose and made this point clear to the Roman Christians. In his Galatian epistle[16] he stressed that he had been *set apart* for this purpose even *before he was born*! God intended him *to be a missionary to the world*!

Referring to his *apostleship mission* Paul added that his ministry was given by God's grace *"to bring about the obedience of faith for the sake of his name <u>among all the nations</u>, ⁶ including yourselves who are called to belong to Jesus Christ."*

Rom 1:3, 4. The *human* and *spiritual* lineage of Jesus as Son of God

> *Paul...set apart for the gospel...the gospel concerning <u>his Son, who was descended from David according to the flesh ⁴ and designated Son of God in power according to the Spirit of holiness by his resurrection from the dead</u>, Jesus Christ our Lord...*

The physical *incarnation* of Jesus, the *eternal word*, John 1:1, and second person of the *divine godhead* has throughout the ages of Christianity been a theological challenge. It certainly was for the Jews of Jesus' day, but for the Gentile, the incarnation of their gods was a commonplace possibility.

---

[16] Gal 1:15.

However, for the Jew calling Jesus a Son because he descended from David may not have been too shocking since this was already firmly established in Jewish and Christian thinking, cf. Matt 1:1. Furthermore, God had in David's day promised that he would anoint a descendent of David as son and King. Cf. Psalm 132:11; 2:2, and Heb 1:5-8 where the preacher speaks of the supremacy of Jesus:

> [5] *For to what angel did God ever say,*
> *"Thou art my Son,*
> *today I have begotten thee"?*
> *Or again,*
> *"I will be to him a father,*
> *and he shall be to me a son"?*
> [6] *And again, when he brings the first-born into the world, he says,*
> *"Let all God's angels worship him."*
> [7] *Of the angels he says,*
> *"Who makes his angels winds,*
> *and his servants flames of fire."*
> [8] *But of the Son he says, "Thy throne, O God, is for ever and ever,*
> *the righteous scepter is the scepter of thy kingdom.*

However, Jesus being *designated Son of God in power* because of his *resurrection from the dead* may have raised some questions for both the Jew and the Gentile, but this would have been impressive to the Romans who were enthralled by the divine power believed to be present with their kings or Caesars.

The dual nature of Jesus, he was both fully human and fully divine, Col 1:19, 2:9, although difficult to grasp from the human perspective, was essential for God's plan of redemption. It was necessary for a human being who lived without sin to die in place of sinful humans in a substitutionary death and sacrifice for sin.[17]

---

[17] This is not the place to explore the substitutionary nature of God's plan of redemption. The student should refer to the Theological Dictionaries referenced in the Bibliography of this study for a deeper discussion of redemption metaphors.

The resurrection of Jesus was powerful good news.

To refocus attention at this point, we will examine the *death and resurrection of Jesus as gospel good news*, as *euangelion*!

Greeks, steeped in Platonic views, saw the physical body as corrupt, doomed for eternity to be disgraced and discarded in the netherworld. Consequently, they *scorned any doctrine of a resurrection*. In the Greek mind resurrection was *shocking news*—why raise a corrupt body to life again only to suffer and die again!

In contrast to such a Greek Platonic view of death and the corruption of a physical body Paul explained that the resurrection of Jesus was *good news* for *it provided all believers an incorruptible immortal body to take over from the corruption of the physical. The powerful resurrection of Jesus, building on the atoning death of Jesus on the cross, certainly was good news to be celebrated!*

Paul had already had much to say to the Greek Corinthian Christians about the Christian view of a resurrection.

1 Cor 15:51-57. Paul spoke of a *transformed* body in the resurrection of Christ to dispel the Greek Corinthian Christians concern regarding their view of a corrupt nature of the physical body:

> *[51] Lo! I tell you a mystery. We shall not all sleep, but we shall all be changed, [52] in a moment, in the twinkling of an eye, at the last trumpet. For the trumpet will sound, and <u>the dead will be raised imperishable, and we shall be changed. [53] For this perishable nature must put on the imperishable</u>, and this mortal nature must put on immortality. [54] When the perishable puts on the imperishable, and the mortal puts on immortality, then shall come to pass the saying that is written:*
> *"Death is swallowed up in victory."*
> *[55] "O death, where is thy victory?*
> *O death where is thy sting?" [56] The sting of death is sin, and the power of sin is the law. [57] But*

thanks be to God, who gives us the victory through our Lord Jesus Christ.

1 Cor 15:1-19. Note Paul's extensive argument regarding the importance of the good news, *euangelion,* of the resurrection of Jesus for the Christians' resurrection:

*[1] Now I would remind you, brethren, in what <u>terms I preached to you the</u> **gospel**, which you received, in which you stand, [2] by which you are saved, if you hold it fast—unless you believed in vain.*

[3] For I delivered to you as of <u>first importance what I also received</u>, that Christ died for our sins in accordance with the scriptures, [4] that he was buried, that <u>he was raised on the third day in accordance with the scriptures</u>, [5] and that he appeared to Cephas, then to the twelve. [6] Then he appeared to more than five hundred brethren at one time, most of whom are still alive, though some have fallen asleep. [7] Then he appeared to James, then to all the apostles. [8] Last of all, as to one untimely born, he appeared also to me. [9] For I am the least of the apostles, unfit to be called an apostle, because I persecuted the church of God. [10] But by the grace of God I am what I am, and his grace toward me was not in vain. On the contrary, I worked harder than any of them, though it was not I, but the grace of God which is with me. [11] Whether then it was I or they, so we preach and so you believed.

[12] <u>Now if</u> (since[18]) <u>Christ is preached as raised from the dead, how can some of you say that there is no resurrection of the dead?</u> [13] But if there is no resurrection of the dead, then Christ has not been raised; [14] <u>if Christ has not been raised, then our preaching is in vain and your faith is in vain</u>. [15] We are even found to be misrepresenting God, because we testified of God that he raised Christ, whom he

---

[18] *Ei* with the *indicative* verb implying *since!*

did not raise if it is true that the dead are not raised.
[16] For if the dead are not raised, then Christ has not
been raised. [17] If Christ has not been raised, your
faith is futile, and you are still in your sins. [18] Then
those also who have fallen asleep in Christ have
perished. [19] If for this life only we have hoped in
Christ, we are of all men most to be pitied.

In the case of Paul's message to the Romans *the good*
news, the *euangelion*, was that *it was the result of God's*
power working through   his Holy Spirit *that Jesus had*
been raised from the dead resulting in his being designated
Son of God, Rom 1:1-4:

> *[1] Paul, a servant of Jesus Christ, called to be an*
> *apostle, set apart for the gospel of God [2] which he*
> *promised beforehand through his prophets in the holy*
> *scriptures, [3] the gospel concerning his Son, who was*
> *descended from David according to the flesh [4] and*
> *designated Son of God in power according to the Spirit*
> *of holiness by his resurrection from the dead, Jesus*
> *Christ our Lord...*

Rom 1:16, 17. The *good news, euangelion*, implies a
missional instruction and imperative.

> *For I am not ashamed of the gospel: it is the power of*
> *God for salvation to **everyone** who has faith, to the Jew*
> *first and also to the Greek. [17] For in it the*
> *righteousness of God is revealed through faith for*
> *faith; as it is written, "He who through faith is*
> *righteous shall live."*

Paul introduces the theme of his epistle to the Romans
with one of the most amazing theological statements
regarding his challenging ministry. It involves *a righteous*
God, the *power of man's salvation, the working of God,*
and a worldwide missional dimension.

For both the Jew and the Roman Gentile Paul's
mission was amazing, shocking, challenging, and
encouraging!

First, this God whom Paul preached was for all men,
not only the Jews!

Second, Paul was *not ashamed to preach the good news* of God's plan of redemption *for all nations*, and *the righteousness nature of this God in doing so!* Surely this would be shocking to Jewish people!

Third, God's *righteousness* is seen clearly in his missional purpose of redemption *for all people*, Jews and Gentiles.

On the surface there does not seem to be anything to be ashamed of in preaching a good news gospel relating to a righteous God, but there are deep and challenging themes in this message.

To the Jew it would be challenging and disturbing, for Paul intended to include the Gentiles in this gospel. Had the Gentiles not turned away from God in their heathen practices, Rom 1:18-32, and furthermore, in the Jews' minds, the Gentiles were not included in the *Torah* Law of Moses promise of redemption!

For the Jew, it would seem that Paul was turning their religion upside down, challenging the *Torah* Law, and seemingly arguing that God had rejected Israel for Gentiles, Rom 9-11.

Nevertheless, as Paul will so definitively demonstrate, much of the Jews' concern was misplaced and misinformed.

Paul's message would indeed be good news for both the Jews and the Gentiles!

This good news, an *euangelion*, relating to God's redemptive and atoning intentions *hinged around the power of Jesus' death on the cross* and not in man's futile attempts to keep any religious laws such as the *Torah* Law of Moses flawlessly.

Thus, Paul's divinely appointed commission was the initiative behind Paul's writing to Romans. His purpose was to explain to the Roman Christians, both Jews and Gentiles, that the real power of atonement and redemption, the foundation of righteousness and a right relationship with God, is the *death and resurrection of Jesus* and not the *Torah* Law. Paul had earlier in his epistle to the

Corinthian Christians spoken of the power of the gospel, proclaiming that "*the word of the cross is folly to those who are perishing, but to us who are being saved it is the power of God.*"[19]

The gospel message proclaimed by Paul and the other apostles called for *an obedient faith* which implied that man needs to respond in an appropriate manner to the death of Jesus by faith or trusting in God in order to benefit by the atoning power of the gospel message of the cross.

Furthermore, the gospel was *good news* because it did not depend on human works of merit but depended solely on God's saving grace and power.

Rom 1:9-15. Paul explains his missionary intentions.

> *For God is my witness, whom I serve with my spirit in the gospel of his Son, that without ceasing I mention you always in my prayers, [10] asking that somehow by God's will I may now at last succeed in coming to you. [11] For I long to see you, that I may impart to you some spiritual gift to strengthen you, [12] that is, that we may be mutually encouraged by each other's faith, both yours and mine. [13] I want you to know, brethren, that I have often intended to come to you (but thus far have been prevented), in order that I may reap some harvest among you as well as among the rest of the Gentiles. [14] I am under obligation both to Greeks and to barbarians, both to the wise and to the foolish: [15] so I am eager to preach the gospel to you also who are in Rome.*

We learn from the study of this text that Paul as a missionary obviously hoped that the Christians in Rome would join him in his global mission by supporting him in some financial way on an impending mission journey to Spain! At Rom 15:24 Paul used a well-known Greek expression to indicate his hopes that the Roman Christians would join him on his mission to Spain, Προπέμπω, *propémpō,* means *to be sped on my journey.* In Greek this

---

[19] 1 Cor 1:18.

implies *for you Roman Christians to help on my journey, hopefully including some financial assistance!*[20]

Rom 15:22-29.

> *This is the reason why I have so often been hindered from coming to you.* [23] *But now, since I no longer have any room for work in these regions, and since I have longed for many years to come to you,* [24] *I hope to see you in passing as I go to Spain, and to* **be sped on my journey** *there by you, once I have enjoyed your company for a little.* [25] *At present, however, I am going to Jerusalem with aid for the saints.* [26] *For Macedonia and Achaia have been pleased to make some contribution for the poor among the saints at Jerusalem;* [27] *they were pleased to do it, and indeed they are in debt to them, for if the Gentiles have come to share in their spiritual blessings, they ought also to be of service to them in material blessings.* [28] *When therefore I have completed this, and have delivered to them what has been raised, I shall go on by way of you to Spain;* [29] *and I know that when I come to you I shall come in the fulness of the blessing of Christ.*

Understanding of the word *gospel* as *good news*

The word *gospel* derives from the Greek εὐαγγέλιον, *euaggélion,* which is pronounced *euangelion* and simply means "*good news*"! At its root, it can be any kind of good news—political, religious, social, family—depending on context.

The term *euangelion* was widely used in ancient Greek times both *politically* and *religiously*. It was used to announce the *good news* of the *birth of a king*, or the good

---

[20] Zodhiates, προπέμπω *propémpō*; ... to send, to send on before, send forward or forth. In the NT, to send forward on one's journey, bring someone on his way, especially to accompany for some distance in token of respect and honor. (Acts 20:38; 21:5). Hence, generally to help one forward on a journey (Acts 15:3; Rom. 15:24; 1 Cor. 16:6, 11; 2 Cor. 1:16; Titus 3:13; 3 John 1:6).

news that *a new king had come to reign.* It was used to proclaim *the victory and return of a conquering king.*

In similar fashion the word gospel is used in our four canonical New Testament Gospels[21] regarding Jesus, *announcing the beginning of Jesus' kingly messianic ministry,* and *preaching the good news of the arrival of the promised messianic kingdom of God.*

Our four Gospels announce that the kingdom of God was about to be inaugurated. This was seen as good news to faithful Jews, but not good news to Herod and the ruling powers of the Jewish Temple! Mark and Matthew speak of Jesus' preaching of the kingdom as *gospel*, good news, and Jesus' ministry as *gospel*:

Mark 1:14, 15. *Now after John was arrested, Jesus came into Galilee, <u>preaching the gospel of God</u>, [15] and saying, "The time is fulfilled, and <u>the kingdom of God is at hand</u>; repent, and <u>believe in the gospel</u>."*

Matt 4:23. *And he went about all Galilee, teaching in their synagogues and <u>preaching the gospel of the kingdom</u> and healing every disease and every infirmity among the people.*

In different contexts the term *gospel* was used to describe other items of religious good news. In the case of Paul's Corinthian epistles, the gospel referred to by Paul was the *death, burial, and resurrection* of Jesus by which all men, Jews and Greeks could be saved from the powers of sin and death.

This was decidedly *euangelion*, good *news*! Although the death of Jesus, the promised Jewish Messiah, was seen as unwelcome news by many Jews, in the context of what God had been doing since His call of Abraham, Jesus' death and resurrection was in fact a major step in God's plan of redemption and maturing covenant to bless all nations.

The once "for all time" *hapax* death of Jesus achieved what the temporary Mosaic Sinaitic covenant, with its

---

[21] The Gospels of Matthew, Mark, Luke, and John.

recurring *annual sacrifice* for sin, could not accomplish! That is, *create a permanent sacrificial atonement for all people*, both Jew and Gentile that would be offered only once, *hapax*, and not be repeated annually.

In the larger picture of what God had been doing since his call of Abraham and in the annual Mosaic Law sacrifices, this certainly was *good news*. The news of a *permanent, once for all, atoning sacrifice would be good news to thinking Jews!*

Rom 3:21-31. *That God is a righteousness God* **was an important ingredient in the** *good news* **Paul would preach to the Romans.**

The righteousness Paul preached was not based on *Torah* Law keeping! This was shocking to the Jews who treasured their *Torah*. It would be encouraging to the religious Gentile who wanted to have a relationship with God that was not hindered by the Jewish insistence on Jewish *Torah* Law restrictions. Paul will develop this further throughout his epistle to the Romans, but especially at **Rom 3:21-31.**

> *[21] But now <u>the righteousness of God has been manifested apart from law</u>, although the law and the prophets bear witness to it, [22] <u>the righteousness of God through faith in Jesus Christ for all who believe. For there is no distinction;</u> [23] since all have sinned and fall short of the glory of God, [24] <u>they are justified by his grace as a gift, through the redemption which is in Christ Jesus,</u> [25] whom God put forward as an expiation by his blood, <u>to be received by faith.</u> This was to show God's righteousness, because in his divine forbearance he had passed over former sins; [26] it was to prove at the present time that he himself is righteous and that he justifies him who has faith in Jesus.*
>
> *[27] <u>Then what becomes of our boasting? It is excluded.</u> On what principle? On the principle of works? No, but <u>on the principle of faith.</u> [28] For <u>we hold that a man is justified by faith apart from works</u>*

of law. ²⁹ Or is God the God of Jews only? Is he not the God of Gentiles also? Yes, of Gentiles also, ³⁰ since God is one; and he will justify the circumcised on the ground of their faith and the uncircumcised through their faith. ³¹ Do we then overthrow the law by this faith? By no means! On the contrary, we uphold the law.

God is a righteous God because he *redeems, forgives,* and *justifies* **all people,** both Jew and Greek, *by the same method,* that is, *by grace through faith in Jesus Christ, showing no ethnic partiality.* Furthermore, it is good news because no *one is justified by works of the Torah Law of Moses* or *law keeping of any kind.*

Paul will argue later at Rom 3:20, 7:7-11, *passim,* that works of Law can only kill those who fail to keep the whole Law. The good news is that all men are saved from eternal death and ruin, justified by God's grace, and this only through a trusting faith in what God has done in Jesus Christ, that is, his atoning death on the cross and subsequent resurrection.

Righteousness does not come through anyone's ability to keep the Law or earn salvation by good works. This is indeed good news for those who recognize their weakness and sinful nature.

Paul was well aware that the good news of the gospel he preached regarding the death and resurrection of Jesus *posed problems to the Jews who treasured their Law, and to Gentiles who praised human wisdom rather than the wisdom of God.*

1 Cor 1:17ff:

¹⁷ For Christ did not send me to baptize but to preach the gospel, and not with eloquent wisdom, lest the cross of Christ be emptied of its power. ¹⁸ For the word of the cross is folly to those who are perishing, but to us who are being saved it is the power of God. ¹⁹ For it is written, "I will destroy the wisdom of the wise, and the cleverness of the clever I will thwart."

²⁰ Where is the wise man? Where is the scribe? Where is the debater of this age? Has not God made foolish the wisdom of the world? ²¹ For since, in the wisdom of God, the world did not know God through wisdom, it pleased God through the folly of what we preach to save those who believe. ²² For Jews demand signs and Greeks seek wisdom, ²³ but we preach Christ crucified, a stumbling block to Jews and folly to Gentiles, ²⁴ but to those who are called, both Jews and Greeks, Christ the power of God and the wisdom of God. ²⁵ For the foolishness of God is wiser than men, and the weakness of God is stronger than men.

Chapter 3 - Sinful Human Nature: Rom 1:18–3:20

Context Message

In this chapter we explore one of the leading thoughts in Paul's
Gospel message, the *euangelion*, the *good news* regarding sin; God has provided an *atoning action in Jesus' death for sin. Paul explains mans' depravity, and lost condition. He states with clarity that man cannot be saved by any human works, not even by keeping such religious laws as the Law of Moses.* Paul explains that man's only hope is *trusting in the faithful righteousness of God* seen also in *the faithfulness of Jesus* who gave himself as a sacrifice on the cross at Calvary for atonement and salvation. Paul develops the hope for redemption, salvation, and justification through faith in Jesus Christ and his death and resurrection.

To understand man's relationship with God we have to understand the nature and condition of sin and human depravity. To begin with, it was possible that most Jews in Paul's day thought that it was the Gentiles who were the sinners and in a lost and alienated relationship with God. The Jews thought they were safe in that they had the Law of Moses, the Prophets, the Priests, and the sacrifices. As long as they kept the Law of Moses they were safe!

Sometimes Christians fall into the same trap or dilemma in that
Christians often feel that since they have been baptized, go to church and celebrate the Lord's Supper every Sunday and do charitable deeds, they are safe! Like the Jews of Paul's day, Christians too often rely on their human religious activity for salvation and justification.

In this chapter Paul gets to the heart of the problem of sin; *all men, Jews, Gentiles, and Christians live under the power of sin—they* are sinners, and because of sin become *alienated from God by their sin*. Paul argues in Romans that no one is ever saved by Law keeping or doing honorable deeds, even religious deeds.

All people, starting with Adam, are equally corrupted *by their own sin*. In fact, to be honest with themselves, all mankind should realize that they are sinners and alienated from God by their sin! Paul argues at Rom 3:9, that *the entire world is under the power of sin* and *needs God's loving mercy, atoning grace, and forgiveness*, in order to be *born again*[1] into a saving relationship with God which Paul describes as righteousness.

Paul describes in the most vivid terms the real corrupt condition of all humanity because of their sinful behavior. Paul argues that because of this corrupt nature the wrath of God is *already being poured* out on the sinful world, Rom 1:18, *"For the wrath of God is revealed from heaven against all ungodliness and wickedness of men who by their wickedness suppress the truth."* The expression *is revealed* in Greek is αποκαλύπτεται, *apokaluptetai*, a present passive verb implying something that is *already being revealed*!

On the surface, it looks like Paul is discussing the sinful nature of the Gentiles, but Paul quickly clarifies this by arguing in Rom 2:1-20 that *this is a general principle, true of all men, Jews and Gentiles included*. Paul becomes more specific in Rom 2:19, 20 stressing *"Now we know that whatever the law says it speaks to those who are under the law, so that every mouth may be stopped, and the whole world may be held accountable to God. [20] For no human being will be justified in his sight by works of the law, since through the law comes*

---

[1] *Born again*, although not a favored Pauline term, refers even by Paul to being born anew from above, which was Jesus' term for forgiveness, salvation, and justification. Cf John 3:3-5. Paul later in Rom 6:1 ff discusses his view of being born again. Christians are buried and raised with Christ in baptism to begin to walk in newness of life!

knowledge of sin." Clearly, and emphatically Paul argues that this includes the Jew, for they fall equally into this sinful and corrupt category. Paul stresses that *all men, both Jews and Greeks, are under the power of sin*!

In fact, in a clinching argument, and one that will dominate Paul's theology of atonement, Paul will emphasize that "*no human being will be justified in God's sight by works of law*," or any kind of law keeping, since "*through law comes only the knowledge of sin.*" By this he means, the *Law clarifies the nature of sin. Its purpose is to identify sin and not forgive or annul sin*![2] In fact the Law, or any legal system, will not save anyone, *it only condemns and kills the sinner*! Cf. Rom 3:19; 4:15; 5:20; and 7:12.

In the discussion of Rom 7:12 Paul states that the law is holy, just and good because it clarifies the real nature of sin! Slowly throughout his epistle Paul will develop this point. The law only identifies the nature of sin and indicts the sinner; it does not save! Human failure to keep law, any law, *results in death, total destruction and alienation from God*! Human attempts to keep the Law will not save the Jew for they constantly break that law!

As he has already stated clearly in Rom 1:16, 17, the *good news*, the *gospel*, the *euangelion*, is that it is only through faith in God's righteous nature and his powerful work in the death of Jesus that all men, Jew and Gentile, can be put right with God through faith in Jesus Christ!

God is a faithful and righteous God who keeps his promises and is faithful to his covenant with Abraham to bless all men, including the Gentiles, by the same method, through faith in Jesus Christ!

---

[2] The *annulment* of or *forgiveness* of sin, either under the Old Mosaic Covenant, or under the New Covenant of Christ, *is through faith in God's atoning sacrifice for sin, Jesus Christ!*

The focal point of the discussion

To begin this discussion, we need to turn to Rom 3:9ff, a central thought to the business of sin and the human experience.

> [9] *What then? Are we Jews any better off? No, not at all; for I have already charged that all men, both Jews and Greeks, are under the power of sin,* [10] *as it is written:*
>
> *"None is righteous, no, not one;*
> [11] *no one understands, no one seeks for God.*
> [12] *All have turned aside, together they have gone wrong;*
> *no one does good, not even one."*

This text lies at the very heart of an inherited sin discussion held in some form by many, the Roman Catholic and Greek Orthodox churches, and most Reformed traditions. As we will discuss below in an addendum the doctrine of inherited sin is unfortunately a poor interpretation of both David's and Paul's argument in the above text with its citation of Psalm 14:1-3.

It does however stress the clear reality of *the universal nature of sin and the human predicament.* Whether it touches on the transmission of sin, or the inheritance of sin, is questionable!

Note especially at this point Ezek 18:19, 20:

> [19] *"Yet you say, 'Why should not the son suffer for the iniquity of the father?' When the son has done what is lawful and right, and has been careful to observe all my statutes, he shall surely live.* [20] *The soul that sins shall die. The son shall not suffer for the iniquity of the father, nor the father suffer for the iniquity of the son; the righteousness of the righteous shall be upon himself, and the wickedness of the wicked shall be upon himself."*

Rom 1:18-32. The human predicament

Some texts are so densely packed that they need careful unwrapping in order to see their role in the *gospel* Paul is presenting. The text before us, Rom 1:18-32, is one such text! It speaks mostly on the surface of man's depraved and sinful condition, but we should see beyond this to the role that this section of Romans plays in Paul's argument.

To be precise, Paul was making the point that all men are under the power of sin, both Jew and Gentile, and consequently need the powerful salvation and redemption that flows out of God's loving grace, faithfulness, and righteous nature. To develop this point, he begins his *gospel of good news* in an intriguing manner by demonstrating that all men have repeatedly *fallen away from God,* have *become corrupt by following the sinful world* and *face stern judgment.*

Rom 1:18-32 is long, but worthy of your closer attention. We include a few comments from this amazing text to make the point that all people have sinned:

> *For the wrath of God is revealed from heaven against all ungodliness and wickedness of men who by their wickedness suppress the truth.* [19] *For what can be known about God is plain to them, because God has shown it to them.* [20] *Ever since the creation of the world his invisible nature, namely, his eternal power and deity, has been clearly perceived in the things that have been made. So they are without excuse;* [21] *for although they knew God they did not honor him as God or give thanks to him, but they became futile in their thinking and their senseless minds were darkened.* [22] *Claiming to be wise, they became fools,* [23] *and exchanged the glory of the immortal God for images resembling mortal man or birds or animals or reptiles.*
>
> [24] *Therefore God gave them up in the lusts of their hearts to impurity, to the dishonoring of their bodies among themselves,* [25] *because they exchanged the truth about God for a lie and worshiped and served the creature rather than the Creator, who is blessed forever! Amen.*

²⁶ For this reason God gave them up to dishonorable passions. Their women exchanged natural relations for unnatural, ²⁷ and the men likewise gave up natural relations with women and were consumed with passion for one another, men committing shameless acts with men and receiving in their own persons the due penalty for their error. ²⁸ And since they did not see fit to acknowledge God, God gave them up to a base mind and to improper conduct. ²⁹ They were filled with all manner of wickedness, evil, covetousness, malice. Full of envy, murder, strife, deceit, malignity, they are gossips, ³⁰ slanderers, haters of God, insolent, haughty, boastful, inventors of evil, disobedient to parents, ³¹ foolish, faithless, heartless, ruthless. ³² Though they know God's decree that those who do such things deserve to die, they not only do them but approve those who practice them.

We will not understand how great the good news of the gospel is until we note how far people have fallen and how serious the human predicament is as a result of our sinful nature or human inclination to sin!

Without an awareness of how far mankind has fallen one may not understand why the message about God's atoning faithfulness is such good news.

It was Paul's intention to clearly demonstrate this human predicament and its consequences to both the Jews and Gentiles who were inclined to make excuses and fail to see their own predicament!

To make a point, salvation and forgiveness are meaningless unless we understand the real nature of the human tragedy under sin! Part of the answer to this dilemma is implied in Rom 1:18–3:20 where *Paul clearly and dramatically charts the extent of the sinful course of human history.* We will shortly examine this further at Rom 2 :1-11.

In light of humanity's treacherous betrayal of God and their crass abuse of the dominion he gave to us (Genesis

1:26-27 with Genesis 3) one may conclude that God had the right to start all over again and obliterate us in favor of a new creation. *But he did not!* The reason is as the Psalmist tells us, Ps 136ff:

> [1] O give thanks to the LORD, for he is good,
>   *for his steadfast love endures for ever.*
> [2] *O give thanks to the God of gods,*
>   *for his steadfast love endures for ever.*
> [3] *O give thanks to the Lord of lords,*
>   *for his steadfast love endures for ever;*
> [4] *to him who alone does great wonders,*
>   *for his steadfast love endures for ever;*
> [5] *to him who by understanding made the heavens,*
>   *for his steadfast love endures for ever;*
> [6] *to him who spread out the earth upon the waters,*
>   *for his steadfast love endures for ever;*
> [7] *to him who made the great lights,*
>   *for his steadfast love endures for ever;*

Because of his steadfast love for his creation God did not obliterate us, which we deserved, but *chose instead to save us. It is this very thought that makes Paul's message "good news"*! In place of getting what we deserved we got God's gift of love, forgiveness and justification.

Rom 1:18-32 describes both the depth of depravity to which man had fallen and sets the scene for an appreciation of the depth of God's love for his creation. In view of the extent of this human tragedy God set out on a path of divine love and forgiveness through a covenant he made with Abraham, which reached fulfillment in Jesus. To appreciate the great gift of salvation God provided for us, we need to see clearly how far we have fallen!

The following discussion relating to our text, Rom 1:18-32, clearly outlines the depth of this tragedy. Human depravity results in the absence of a loving God and a personal knowledge of, and relationship with God.

In some ways, a perfunctory read of the text could imply that God had given up on humanity and possibly even his plan for redeeming his creation.

Consider for a moment the consequences of God's banishment of Adam and Eve from Eden, the outcomes of the Noahic Flood, and the consequences of the lascivious sin of Sodom and Gomorrah!

The continuous depravity we read of in so many scenarios in Scripture serves to reinforce how desperate was mankind's need for God's steadfast love, mercy, atoning, and redeeming action.

We learn from the expulsion of Adam, Eve and Cain from God's presence, the destruction of Noah's flood, and Sodom and Gomorrah demonstrate how humanity even in its infancy was bent on destroying itself. In outbursts of God's anger we might even be tempted to suppose that God might have been determined to let them go *completely*, destroyed by their own depravity! After all, the text does on three occasions, Rom 1:24, 26, 28, imply that *God gave them up*! However, a careful read of the text demonstrates that God simply let them have their own way by allowing them to leave him!

If such expressions of his wrath were typical of God's real or ultimate feelings toward the human race, our situation would be hopeless, surrendered to utter despair.

However, Paul's good news was that God is faithful to his creation purpose even in the face of our faithlessness and depravity. God's anger at sinful disobedience highlights the fact, however, that the wrath of God against sin and disobedience should be seen as part of his faithfulness toward us; he wants us to understand how far we have fallen and how deeply we need his divine intervention, salvation, and justification.

But far from implying that in his grace God overlooks human sin, Paul insists that *the anger of God is already being revealed against all unrighteousness,* Rom 1:18, *for the wrath of God is revealed from heaven against all ungodliness and wickedness of men who by their wickedness suppress the truth.*

We need to note that the active verb in this text is a present tense of the verb *apokaluptō* which should be translated as God's wrath *is presently, constantly being revealed from heaven*. God is not willing to wait for the final judgment to express his anger against sin but is already expressing it! Because of this we need to hear and clearly understand God's condemnation of sin, disobedience, and depravity, and hear his gracious call in Jesus and offering of forgiveness.

It is only when we learn the seriousness of our sinful condition that we will turn to God for forgiveness. Karl Barth, famous Swiss theologian of the early twentieth century, once said that every person needs to stand each day at the foot of the cross to hear God's strident NO to sin and his clarion YES offering forgiveness.[3] We need to be broken each day by the reality of our sin, the power of the cross, and put together again by that same power!

This is the story of Paul's Epistle to the Romans, and Rom 1:18-32!

Rom 1:18-32. Paul and the degeneration of all humanity

It's worth noting that Paul begins this section of Romans with God as our sovereign creator, and man's rejection of God and departure from him through disobedience (1:18ff). This is almost the same pattern as seen in Adam's and Eve's disobedience in Eden! They rejected God in favor of a lesser "god," Satan! Paul's stark description of the depraved human situation of moral degradation clarifies in clear terms the depth of mankind's fall away from God and into sin. Anyone denying this depravity is simply blind to the culture in which we live regardless of whether that is in first century Rome, or twenty-first century America, Africa, or Europe! The world in which we live is lost, depraved, and in need of God's loving mercy and atoning love.

---

[3] For a concise discussion of Karl Barth's dialectical theology cf. Herbert Hartwell, *The Theology of Karl Barth*, 1964; Karl Barth, *Evangelical Theology*, 1965; *Der Romerbrief*, 1940; and the PhD Dissertation of Ian A. Fair, *The Theology of Wolfhart Pannenberg as a Reaction to Dialectical Theology*, University of Natal, 1974.

Paul will argue that the corruption and moral degeneration listed in this section begins with man's turning away from the creator God to a creaturely "god" of personal satisfaction and freedom! If we're out of tune with God we're out of tune with creation and our fellow human beings which results in all kinds of sexual immorality and general sinful passion. Paul views our sin not simply as the breaking of some universal laws—our sin is a violation of a personal relationship with God, cf. Rom 3:9-18.

Our stubborn denial of God, our persistent refusal to acknowledge him for who he is and give to him our grateful thanks and honor, blinds us to our sinful condition. Professing to be wise—Gen 3 and the forbidden fruit comes to mind—we became fools, Rom 1:21. Sin disables our minds and rational capacity until we are no longer able to think clearly.

Thinking we are wise, we refuse to listen and be taught by God. Our intellectual gifts are used to serve our own selfish ends. Our sinful nature becomes a vehicle for "explaining" why we should challenge the perspective of God's plan for humanity for another which we substitute in its place.

A reasonable examination of the sinfulness of human depravity listed by Paul in our text, Rom 1:18-32, reveals that our modern twenty-first century culture has followed what Paul was describing regarding his first century culture! Human depravity results in the steady fall into the loss of a real relationship with God!

Thinking to be wise in treating people "equally" and with "dignity" we not only oppose gender-discrimination, but we also completely deny the differences in gender which are part of our being in the image of God (see Gen 1:26-27). We shun marriage commitments in favor of "personal freedom." We deny the God-given decree that in marriage we "both become one flesh," Matt 19:5; Gen 2:24, in favor of a contemporary secular human view that our bodies belong to us and to no one else!

64

We substitute personal gender preferences and alternative lifestyles for God's decree that it is in the marriage bed, Heb 13:4, that sexual gratification should take place.

Thinking it to be wise and in keeping with the "maturation" of human sexuality we do everything to explain away simple decrees and terms such as homosexual sin by inserting "human freedom" and "personal preference." Note Rom 1:26-27; Lev 18:22; 20:13; 1 Cor 6:9 on human sexual freedoms and corruption. Some dislike the term "sexual perverts" as though such a quality does not exist in our culture. If everyone is fine exercising their own private preferences as some claim, then how do we come up with the term pervert!

Some challenge the definition of the Greek word *arsenokoitēs* which refers to *male prostitutes* or *male sexual partners* at 1 Tim 1:10, or the term "sodomites" in favor of the right to practice personal sexual preferences in the privacy of individual rights and freedoms! However, when God is real in our lives there is no such thing as personal human freedom!

Recently, in 2003, during the national discussion of the Episcopalian ordination of a gay priest, an Episcopalian priest explained that the Episcopalian church has grown and matured in their understanding of human sexuality to where Scriptures that are out of date with twenty-first century understanding of sexuality must be reinterpreted to maintain the dignity of human preferences in sexuality!

Not only do we promote the practice of free sexual passion, but we make excuses for those who do, Rom 1:28-32.

As the history of mankind developed and human excuse of evil grew, Paul explains that *God gave man up to perversity and moral derangement*, Rom 1:24, 25, 28. We have already discussed this expression in the context of Rom 1:18-32. It simply means that God let man decide for himself whether he wanted to live with God, so God let men go their own chosen way! God gave them up to their own chosen way!

However, in spite of this depressing narrative, *the good news, euangelion,* explains that God already had a plan prepared in eternity, Jesus Christ! Read Eph 1:3-12 again!

Paul's good news was that God did not desert his creation fallen under sin so that he might be rid of us! He placed all men under the condemnation of sin *so that* we *might see clearly our corrupt and depraved condition.* Paul explains this in order that *"God might have mercy on us all,"* Rom 11:32-36:

32 For God has consigned all men to disobedience, that he may have mercy upon all.

33 O the depth of the riches and wisdom and knowledge of God! How unsearchable are his judgments and how inscrutable his ways!

34 "For who has known the mind of the Lord, or who has been his counselor?"

35 "Or who has given a gift to him that he might be repaid?"

36 For from him and through him and to him are all things. To him be glory forever. Amen.

Perhaps we should see God's giving us up to our wickedness as an act of mercy! Sometimes we are tempted to think that a worsening world is proof that God has abandoned us, but Paul sees it as the merciful wrath of God driving us to a desperate need for the mercy which God is eager to provide.

Our "wisdom" in our arrogance, and our arrogance by God's grace, leads us into an awareness of our abysmal condition out of which we cry for help! God is in Jesus Christ there to provide that help. That is the story of Romans which Paul introduces as good news, euangelion, with this dismal picture of mankind and human depravity!

Rom 2:1-11. Paul and the Jewish predicament

It is natural for *believers in God* and *Christians* to agree with Paul in his vivid description of human depravity and degradation, and to agree with his condemnation of this. Too easily, we are inclined to encourage Paul's narrative of God's condemnation, and say "yes, this depravity deserves God's condemnation!"

This is exactly what the Jews did! They were inclined, as we Christians today might be, to see God's condemnation of the Gentiles as deserved, and a righteous judgment! We can almost hear the Jews saying "*Amen!*" to Paul. Or their cry, "*Go get them, Paul!*"

But the apostle will have nothing of this! He now takes up the Jewish story of sin and disobedience.

The Jew felt superior to the Gentile world Paul had just sketched, but their own Scriptures made it clear that although they *possessed* the *Torah* (God's Law and instruction on covenantal behavior) they had not internalized it! In fact, they had broken it as often as the Gentiles had supposedly done so even though the Gentiles were not under that law!

The Jews had the *Torah* but had not taken God's *Torah* into their hearts. They had all the "*marks*" of God's special favor (like circumcision, the covenants and the *Torah*), but they didn't have the "*heart*" or *lifestyle* that these called for, or to which they were to bear witness.

So, while they called themselves Jews and took pride in the name *Israel,* they weren't *true* to the terms Jew or *Israel* which signified a people *called* by God and *belonging* to God. Paul argued that a true Jew bore, in addition to the physical descent of Abraham, also the *faith* of Abraham. A true Jew had a *circumcised heart* as well as *circumcised body*! The true Jew not only possessed the *Torah*, but he also *lived it*, Rom 2:28-29; 9:6-8:

> *28For he is not a real Jew who is one outwardly, nor is true circumcision something external and physical. 29 He is a Jew who is one inwardly, and real circumcision is a matter of the heart, spiritual and not literal. His praise is not from men but from God.*
> *6 But it is not as though the word of God had failed. For not all who are descended from Israel*

belong to Israel, [7] and not all are children of Abraham because they are his descendants; but "Through Isaac shall your descendants be named." [8] This means that it is not the children of the flesh who are the children of God, but the children of the promise are reckoned as descendants.

Making excuses for sin on the grounds of their "favored" position with God (sounds almost like us Christians) the Jew took advantage of their relationship with God, expecting that being a Jew gave them grace and special privileges. They "supposed" or thought that because they were Jews by nationality they would escape the judgment of God, Rom 2:3-5:

> *[3] Do you suppose, O man, that when you judge those who do such things and yet do them yourself, you will escape the judgment of God? [4] Or do you presume upon the riches of his kindness and forbearance and patience? Do you not know that God's kindness is meant to lead you to repentance? [5] But by your hard and impenitent heart you are storing up wrath for yourself on the day of wrath when God's righteous judgment will be revealed.*

But to their surprise, Paul adds that God shows no partiality, and will judge both Jew and Gentile under the same principles of sin (Rom 2:11).

Rom 2:12-3:8. Paul's most important observations regarding the Jews *and* Gentiles: *Both stand guilty of sin before God.*

Paul included all humanity into his good news and stated that Gentiles *who had in their hearts* what the *Torah* called for would receive eternal life *based on faith* just as surely as the Jew who had lived in honor and faithfulness before God would, Rom 2:6-16:

> *[6] For he will render <u>to every man according to his works</u>: [7] to those who by patience in well-doing seek for glory and honor and immortality, he will give eternal life; [8] but for those who are factious and do not obey the truth, but obey wickedness, there will be*

wrath and fury. [9] There will be tribulation and distress for every human being who does evil, the Jew first and also the Greek, [10] but glory and honor and peace for every one who does good, the Jew first and also the Greek. [11] For God shows no partiality.

[12] All who have sinned without the law will also perish without the law, and all who have sinned under the law will be judged by the law. [13] For it is not the hearers of the law who are righteous before God, but the doers of the law who will be justified. [14] When Gentiles who have not the law do by nature what the law requires, they are a law to themselves, even though they do not have the law. [15] They show that what the law requires is written on their hearts, while their conscience also bears witness and their conflicting thoughts accuse or perhaps excuse them [16] on that day when, according to my gospel, God judges the secrets of men by Christ Jesus.

Does this mean that the Gentile who did not have the Law would be excused of their sin? *No! Certainly not! The Gentile would be judged by God on the basis of their faith in God, not by the Law* (*Torah*) even though they might keep the *Torah*!

Gentiles are under the same principle of faith as the Jew, but not under the same principle of *Torah* as the Jew, even though they might have honored the *Torah* and kept the instruction of God.

Did this mean the Jews had never been peculiarly blessed by God? *No!* Abraham was not a Jew under the Law, but a Gentile from Ur of the Chaldeans! *Yet, he was blessed by God on the grounds of his faith.* Cf. Gen 12, 15, 17 and God's covenant with Abraham and the Gentiles. Of course, for they had been blessed by God if like Abraham *they lived by faith*! Rom 1:18ff clearly states that they had known God at one time but had chosen to give up faith in God and followed their own lusts. *But so had the Jews!* Consider for a moment the sin of Israel and Judah that caused God to judge them and send them into captivity and exile on foreign lands. They turned away from faith in God to serve idols!

Certainly, there was a great blessing in being a Jew if they lived by faith, Rom 3:1; 9:4-5! But when they departed from faith in God all the advantages of being a Jew were lost!

Paul insists that although the Jews had enjoyed special privileges as God's chosen people, they had been just as faithless as the Gentiles had been, and *so in real life Jews were no better off than any other nation!*

Rom 3:9-20. The entire world is guilty before God and under the power of sin.

A collection of texts from the Jewish scriptures, notably the Psalms, which Paul calls the law, which the Jews also saw as *Torah*, showed that the Jews, like the Gentiles, had not given to God what was his due. They had turned away from God, Rom 3:9-20:

⁹ What then? Are we Jews any better off? No, not at all; for I have already charged that all men, both Jews and Greeks, are under the power of sin, ¹⁰ as it is written:

"None is righteous, no, not one;
¹¹ no one understands, no one seeks for God. ¹² <u>All have turned aside, together they have gone wrong;</u>
<u>no one does good, not even one.</u>"
¹³ "Their throat is an open grave,
they use their tongues to deceive."
"The venom of asps is under their lips."
¹⁴ "<u>Their mouth is full of curses and bitterness</u>."
¹⁵ "Their feet are swift to shed blood,
¹⁶ in their paths are ruin and misery,
¹⁷ and the way of peace they do not know."
¹⁸ "<u>There is no fear of God before their eyes</u>."
¹⁹ Now we know that whatever the law says it speaks to those who are under the law, so that every mouth may be stopped, and the whole world may be held accountable to God. ²⁰ <u>For no human being will be</u>

justified in his sight by works of the law, since through the law comes knowledge of sin.

The above citations from the Psalms are not proclamations of hereditary sin, but merely careful observations by the Psalmists of the sinful nature of mankind! The people *turned away,* they *went wrong, their mouth is full of curses and bitterness. They were not born that way, they turned away from God!*

We should remember that the Psalms fall under the genre of Wisdom Literature which impart wisdom for living. The Psalms are astute psychological and sociological observations passed on by inspired writers and chroniclers.

Paul concludes this section of observations from the Psalms by saying what any reasonable person would say observing the way mankind had departed from God; because of universal sin, the *entire world is held under the power of sin and the judgment before God.*

By their behavior, the Gentiles bore the marks of rebellion against God and the sign of his wrath on them, cf. Rom 1:18ff. Likewise, the Jews had the witness of the *Torah* against them that they had not been faithful to God and deserved his judgment.

Notice the striking statement by Paul, Rom 3:9, *"the whole world is under the power of sin."* The RSV correctly translates this as *power* of sin, indicating that sin is not merely a mistake (a Greek concept) but that *sin is a living power that dominates and takes over our lives.*

It's possible for some with "compassionate" hearts, who focus on the suffering of poverty and injustice today to think that God's reaction to sin is something of an *overkill.* Some claim that such condemnation is an *overreaction* to the failures of humanity. A failure to understand the magnitude of sin and a tendency to overlook the reason for the suffering atoning death of Jesus on the cross causes some to overlook the overall nature of human depravity! It was to drive this point home that Paul included the dramatic scene of Rom 1:18-32.

71

The expression *"power of sin"* in Greek is merely the Greek word for sin (*hamartia*). The operative clause, however, develops the concept of *constant living* under the power of sin! In the Greek πάντας ὑφ' ἁμαρτίαν εἶναι the controlling verb is εἶναι, a *present active infinitive* which implies *a constant steady act of being*.

However, we should not interpret sin as *a mistake* as in the Greek world view but should interpret sin as a Jew would understand sin, and how sin is defined in Scripture. Hence, the RSV is correct in translating the expression as *under the power of sin* for sin has a constant living power far more insidious than *making a mistake*.

In the ancient Greek concept, and unfortunately often in our modern view, Christians believe that if we stop a sinful behavior or practice then we've done enough for forgiveness by just simply stopping the sinful behavior.

In the Biblical understanding *sin takes over one's life* and *the only way it can be removed is by the death of Jesus (his blood) and God's grace* and forgiveness which can only be accessed through faith in Jesus Christ, John 14:6, Acts 4:12.

1 John 1:5-2:6 builds on the thought of *not living comfortably with sin* yet realizing that we do *occasionally fall in sin through weakness*, which we all do. John was encouraging Christians to walk faithfully with God and Jesus who can forgive all our sin. This text is worth our attention:

> *⁵ This is the message we have heard from him and proclaim to you, that God is light and in him is no darkness at all. ⁶ If we say we have fellowship with him while we walk in darkness, we lie and do not live according to the truth; ⁷ but if we walk in the light, as he is in the light, we have fellowship with one another* (he most likely means with God and Jesus, but also could mean with our fellow Christians), *and the blood of Jesus his Son **cleanses us** * (present tense verb implies constantly cleanses us) *from all sin. ⁸ If we say we **have no sin** * (do not constantly live with sin), *we deceive*

ourselves, and the truth is not in us. ⁹ If we **confess**
(again. a present tense verb, constantly confess) *our
sins, he is faithful and just, and will forgive our sins
and cleanse us from all unrighteousness. ¹⁰ If we say
we have not sinned* (a perfect past tense verb with
continued present sense), *we make him a liar, and his
word is not in us.*

　*¹ My little children, I am writing this to you so that
you may not sin* (continue to live in sin);[4] *but if anyone
does sin* (sin in error or weakness), *we have an
advocate with the Father, Jesus Christ the righteous;
² and he is the expiation for our sins, and not for ours
only but also for the sins of the whole world. ³ And by
this we may be sure that we know him, if we keep his
commandments. ⁴ He who says "I know him" but
disobeys his commandments is a liar, and the truth is
not in him; ⁵ but whoever keeps his word, in him truly
love for God is perfected. By this we may be sure that
we are in him: ⁶ he who says he abides in him ought to
walk in the same way in which he walked.*

It is only when we understand the power of sin, its
control of our lives, and the consequences of sin, that we
can understand and appreciate fully the grace of God!

It is for this reason, understanding the grace of God,
that Paul has laboured in such detail in the first three
chapters of Romans to describe the power of sin.

Without our understanding of sin being informed by
the will and purpose of God for mankind, and the real
nature of sin, we are not able to understand the nature and
extent of God's loving grace!

Grace without judgment is not grace at all! Evaluating
judgment without understanding the real depravity of man
misses the depth of God's love and grace, and the real
predicament of man!

---

[4] My comments at Rom 1:8, 10, and 2:1 above are based on the tenses
of the Greek verbs, the present active, aorist subjunctive, and perfect
tense verbs.

The cross identifies our sinful nature and clearly defines our real situation! Jew and Gentile together are rebels against God. We see this in the incarnation of God in Jesus and his consequent crucifixion at Calvary. When God came into our human dimension in Jesus the Messiah we rejected him and murdered him on a cross! Explain or debate this as we often do, protest as fiercely as we might, both Jews and Romans, all humanity, showed that *as a race humans became opponents of God when they laid hands on a pure sinless person, Jesus, and murdered him*!

This question has been challenged and debated since the early centuries of Christianity. For example, when Anselm of Acosta, a Benedictine monk, philosopher and theologian, later known as St Anthony, Bishop of Canterbury, 1094-1098, penned his seminal work *Cur Deus Homo, Why God Became a Man*, he debated or dialogued with an interlocutor, Boso, a monk in Normandy *discussing the nature and reason for Christ's incarnation*. In this philosophical work the question regarding the doctrine of *substitutionary atonement* was addressed at length, explaining the reason for God becoming man in the person of Jesus. In summary, Anselm explains that Jesus' divine incarnation in human form *was to do what man could not do for himself, that is, save himself*.

And the situation remains today! Our world lives as though God and his atoning will for man in Jesus do not exist! The seemingly apparent point is *whether the incarnation was really necessary*!

Perhaps the most precise condemnation of humanity is that by ignoring God and his will the result is *there is no fear of God in their eyes*, Rom 3:18.

Paul concludes this dense and intense discussion on the *desperate human situation* by arguing that *no human being* can be justified in God's sight by law keeping, neither Jew nor Gentile! *Their only hope is trusting in the loving grace and atoning work of God through Jesus' faithful substitutionary death and resurrection.*

The reason we cannot be saved by the Law or *Torah*[5] is that the Law or *Torah* was *never given to save or forgive anyone*. Paul explains that the Law was given to Israel, and to the world, to *clarify the nature of sin, to indict mankind for sin, and to instruct them in right living before God*!

Paul argues throughout this great epistle that God never intended the Torah to save mankind, or to *bring them into a righteous relationship with God*, that is, *righteousness*.

Rom 3:20: *For no human being will be justified in his sight by works of the law, <u>since through the law comes knowledge of sin</u>.*

Gal 3:19-22*: Why then the law? It was added because of transgressions, ... [21] Is the law then against the promises of God? Certainly not; for if a law had been given which could make alive, then righteousness would indeed be by the law. [22] <u>But the scripture consigned all things to sin</u>, that what was promised to faith in Jesus Christ might be given to those who believe.*

Rom 7:7: *What then shall we say? That the law is sin? By no means! Yet, <u>if it had not been for the law, I should not have known sin</u>. I should not have known what it is to covet if the law had not said, "You shall not covet."*

2 Cor 3:4-6: *[4] Such is the confidence that we have through Christ toward God. [5] Not that we are competent of ourselves to claim anything as coming from us; our competence is from God, [6] who has made us competent to be ministers of a new covenant, <u>not in a written code but in</u>*

---

[5] Most Christians today refer to the Law of Moses as *the Law*, however, it is more commonly referred to by Jews as the *Torah* which is the Hebrew word for *instruction intended to guide, to teach*. Originally it referred to the first five books of what Christians refer to as the Pentateuch of the Old Testament. However, in time it became common to refer to all of the canonical Scriptures as the *Torah*, or *instruction of God*. I will use the term *Torah* in this study to refer primarily to what we commonly call the Law of Moses which was seen by Paul as *God's instruction through Moses and the Prophets for instruction for right living* or *righteousness*, and not as a vehicle for atonement or *entry* into a right relationship with God.

the Spirit; for the written code kills, but the Spirit gives
life.

Chapter 4 - God's Righteousness: Rom 3:21-31

Context and Message

Christians often have discussions with neighborhood friends on the relationship of faith and baptism where a number of interesting and fundamental questions are introduced!

Central to these discussions is often the relationship between faith, repentance, and baptism.

First, is baptism a work that one experiences because one is already saved by faith, or is it an act of faith that leads to salvation and justification?

Second, is baptism simply an act of a saved Christian's obedience, or is it an obedient aspect of faith **for** salvation?

These and other related questions need some attention!

We will turn to the teachings of the New Testament to answer these questions.

The New Testament teaches that baptism is **for** the remission of sins (Acts 2:38).

Paul teaches at Rom 6:1-6 that baptism is where and how one is united with Christ and in that act, they share in his death and resurrection <u>by faith</u>.

At Gal 3:26, 27 Paul explained that baptism is how one <u>becomes a child of God by faith</u>.

Paul stresses at Rom 6:1-6 and Gal 3:26, 27 that baptism is how one gets into Christ.

Furthermore, at Col 2:12 Paul clearly teaches that baptism is <u>faith in the working of God</u>.

We can safely say that faith and baptism are two ends of a salvation continuum.

Faith is at the beginning and baptism at the end of the continuum.

Remove faith from the faith-baptism continuum and you destroy baptism, for baptism is based in faith.

Remove baptism from the faith-baptism continuum and you get a disobedient faith!

Faith, repentance, confession of one's faith in Jesus, confession of sin, and baptism are all part of the faith principle.

The fall of mankind

The previous lesson closed with the text of Rom 3:19-20 in which Paul charged that *all men are under the power of sin* and in need of forgiveness and justification.

However, he stated clearly that *no human being can be justified in the sight of God* by *Torah,* or Law keeping, Rom 3:19, 20, for the purpose of the *Torah* Law was not to justify, but *to instruct and clarify the true nature and consequences of sin.*

We should remember that in the Jew's mind the *Torah* took on a *divine* character and gave instruction on how to live a righteous life before God.

The righteousness of God

We learned in the first three lessons that the term *righteousness of God* can be interpreted to mean *God's personal righteousness*, and/or the *righteousness that he gives to others*.

Both find their place in Romans!

God is a righteous God because he treats all men equally by making them righteous *by the same method, faith in Jesus Christ*!

There is obviously a double meaning in the expression *the righteousness of God*, with the one concept leading into the other, and Paul often uses the term to imply both meanings!

Context will determine how we should understand the expression.

Righteousness and Justification

First, a brief discussion on the terms *righteousness* and *justification will help*! The terms have a rich Greek background often associated with *the law court* and *justice*.

Both words or concepts are built off the same Greek root stem and are similar in meaning.

The verb form is δικαιόω, *dikaióō*. Zodhiates observes, *in the case of dikaióō, it means to <u>bring out the fact that a person is righteous</u>.*[1]

The two noun forms are δικαιοσύνη, *dikaiosúnē, and* δίκαιος, *díkaios. The root stem of both is* δίκη, *díkē,* which can mean *to be just, right,* or *righteous, declared not guilty.* Zodhiates observes regarding δικαιοσύνη, *dikaiosúnē, righteousness,* that it is used *when a person is in conformity to the claims of higher authority.*[2]

Justification is the *process* by which one is *declared righteous.*

Righteousness is the *result of justification* and *refers to one's standing with the higher authority, in the Jewish and Christian sense, this is God.*

Righteous does not mean sinless, but carries the meaning of judged, *forgiven, and declared not guilty*!

Second. In Jewish and Pauline understanding, *righteousness* meant *to be in a right relationship with God* (that is *forgiven, declared not guilty*).

In Pauline and Christian theology one is not declared righteous by one's ability to keep the law (*Torah*), either *perfectly*, which because of our human nature we have learned is impossible, or *partially*!

God never intended the purpose of the law (Torah) *to forgive or make one righteous.* The purpose of the law was *to clarify sin, show its consequences, and indict one for sin,* Rom 3:19, 20; Rom 7:7.

We will learn from Romans that righteousness with God is on the basis of the faithful righteousness of God and one's *faith in Jesus Christ.* This excludes one's ability to keep the Law (*Torah*) or work for one's salvation.

That is why both Jew and Gentile can be declared righteous even though the Gentile did not have the Law

---

[1] Zodhiates, δικαιόω, *dikaióō, The Complete Word Study Dictionary: New Testament.*
[2] Zodhiates.

(*Torah*), since righteousness is not based on Law keeping, but on faith!

The Jew is not righteous by Law keeping, since they have not, and do not keep the Law perfectly.

For both Jew and Gentile, righteousness is based on faith, but not any kind of faith!

Thus Paul explains, *righteousness*, which is *being declared righteous by God*, is gained only *by faith in Jesus Christ*, which will be the main point of this lesson, Rom 3:21-22.

When the Jews rejected Jesus as the Christ, the Messiah, they did not believe and trust God, although they claimed to do so, since God had proclaimed Jesus to be the Messiah, the miracles of Jesus and his resurrection established this. Remember, Rom 1:4, Jesus was *"designated Son of God in power according to the spirit of holiness by his resurrection from the dead..."*

It was not that the Jew had no faith, they did, but they refused to let that faith mature by hearing God's words, the prophets and their sacred writings.

Paul will later at Rom 10:1-3; 16-19 explain that the faith and zeal of the Jew was *not enlightened, appropriately educated in the Torah,* or focused on Jesus as God's Messiah.

In Paul's understanding of Jewish and Christian theology, *righteousness is always based on faith,* and in the Christian age*, based on faith in the working of God in Jesus Christ, on the cross, and in the resurrection.* These concepts were stumbling blocks to the Jews, Rom 10:17-21, and 1 Cor 1:18ff. Cf also Peter on this,1 Pet 2:6:

> *6 For it stands in scripture: "Behold, I am laying in Zion a stone, a cornerstone chosen and precious, and he who believes in him will not be put to shame."*
> *7 To you therefore who believe, he is precious, but for those who do not believe, "The very stone which the builders rejected has become the head of the corner," 8 and "A stone that will make men stumble, a rock that will make them fall"; for they stumble*

because they disobey the word, as they were destined to do.

Now, in Rom 2:11 Paul has argued that *God is a righteous God* because he treats both Jew and Gentile the same, showing no partiality or favoritism.

Since all, both Jew and Gentile, have fallen short of the glory of God and sinned, both Jew and Gentile will be justified by the same principle, *by God's grace through faith in Jesus*, Rom 3:21-26:

> *But now the righteousness of God has been manifested apart from law, although the law and the prophets bear witness to it, [22] the righteousness of God through faith in Jesus Christ for all who believe. For there is no distinction; [23] since all have sinned and fall short of the glory of God, [24] they are justified by his grace as a gift, through the redemption which is in Christ Jesus, [25] whom God put forward as an expiation by his blood, to be received by faith. This was to show God's righteousness, because in his divine forbearance he had passed over former sins; [26] it was to prove at the present time that he himself is righteous and that he justifies him who has faith in Jesus.*

Rom 3:21-26. Paul's theology of justification

In this text we have the heart of Paul's doctrine of atonement and justification. Here Paul mentions many of the great words that speak of God's forgiveness: justification, redemption, expiation, the blood of Jesus, faith, and righteousness.

For the sake of simplicity, in the following texts we will detail the key features of Paul's theology of justification.

Rom 3:19-21. Justification is not by *Torah* Law of Moses works. *"[19]Now we know that whatever the law says it speaks to those who are under the law, so that every mouth may be stopped, and the whole world may be held accountable to God. [20] For no human being will be*

81

justified in his sight by works of the law, since through the law comes knowledge of sin.

[21] But now the righteousness of God has been manifested apart from law, although the law and the prophets bear witness to it."

Rom 3:9, 19, 22, 23. Both Jew and Gentile, in other words, the entire world, are guilty of sin, *for all have sinned and fallen short of the glory of God and are therefore all guilty before God*!

Rom 3:9, 19. In fact, the *entire world is under the power of sin* and is held accountable to God. We learned at Rom 3:9ff that in the biblical sense sin is seen as *a living power* that controls our lives and is not as in Greek philosophy simply a *passive mistake*!

Rom 3:21-26. *[21] But now the righteousness of God has been manifested apart from law, although the law and the prophets bear witness to it, [22] the righteousness of God through faith in Jesus Christ for all who believe. For there is no distinction; [23] since all have sinned and fall short of the glory of God, [24] they are justified by his grace as a gift, through the redemption which is in Christ Jesus, [25] whom God put forward as an expiation by his blood, to be received by faith. This was to show God's righteousness, because in his divine forbearance he had passed over former sins; [26] it was to prove at the present time that he himself is righteous and that he justifies him who has faith in Jesus.*

But *now* in the Christian age, or the age of the Messiah, *God's righteousness is revealed*—that is, both *God's own righteousness*, and *the righteousness which he gives to those who have faith in Jesus.*

Both views of righteousness are made manifest *in and through Jesus Christ, apart from the Torah Law of Moses.*

The Jews should know this because the prophets had witnessed and testified to this in Scripture, Rom 1: 2; 3:21.

Rom 3:22. The *primary principle of righteousness* is that God by his *grace* and *forgiveness* declares the sinner forgiven, *not guilty, righteous*, in a *right relationship with*

Him. This is *through faith, trusting, in Jesus Christ* for both the Jew and the Gentile.

Notice the emphasis on *faith in Jesus Christ* meaning *trusting in what God has done in Jesus, and what Jesus did on the cross!*

"There is no distinction" in this *principle of righteousness,* for this principle is *the same for all, both Jew and Gentile, on the same grounds.*

Rom 3:23, 24. *[23] since all have sinned and fall short of the glory of God, [24] they (all) are justified by his grace as a gift, through the redemption which is in Christ Jesus.* Since *all* (both Jew and Gentile) have sinned and are accountable to God for their sin, Rom 3:19, *all* (both Jew and Gentile) will be justified by God's grace as a gift, no *exception* is made, no *distinction* by reason of ethnic background, Rom 2:11, 22.

Justification (salvation Eph 2:8) *is a free gift* of God's *grace,* χάρις, *cháris or* graciousness, and implies an *unearned gift* of God's grace, Rom 3:24. *Grace* derives from the Greek *charis* which primarily means *pleasure,* or *undeserved favor.*[3]

Rom 3:24, 5:2. Both Jew and Gentile have access to this grace *through faith in Jesus Christ.*

By God's grace, through faith in Jesus Christ, *all* are *saved* and *justified* through *redemption,* ἀπολύτρωσις, *apolútrōsis,* which carries a clear sign of manumission,[4] *to redeem,* to *purchase back, to deliver* from the death

---

[3] Zodhiates has a helpful discussion of *grace,* χάρις. "Grace derives from the noun *chaírō* ... to rejoice ... particularly that which causes joy, pleasure, gratification, favor, acceptance, for a kindness granted or desired, a benefit, thanks, gratitude. *A favor done without expectation of return*; the absolutely free expression of the loving kindness of God to men finding its only motive in the bounty and benevolence of the Giver; *unearned and unmerited favor. Cháris* stands in direct antithesis to *érga* ... works, the two being mutually exclusive. God's grace affects man's sinfulness and not only forgives the repentant sinner but brings joy and thankfulness to him. It changes the individual to a new creature without destroying his individuality (2 Cor. 5:17; Eph. 2:8, 9).
[4] Manumission, the purchase of freedom for slaves.

sentence of sin. This redemption provided by God *is in Jesus Christ*!

Rom 3:25, 26. God has presented Jesus as an *expiation* for sin. The Greek *hilastērion*, carries the sense of *mercy seat, place of forgiveness*, or *atonement*. The word is used in the OT for *the mercy seat of God* where *sacrificial atonement* took place. Jesus has now become our *hilastērion*, the *means of our sacrificial atonement and forgiveness*. This *expiation* or *atonement* is to be received through *faith, trusting* in Jesus Christ, rather than the *Torah* Law of Moses. Through Jesus we trust in God who is faithful, who will justify <u>*all*</u> by the same principle, *through faith or trusting in what God has done in Jesus Christ*.

Rom 3:27, 28. <u>*"Then what becomes of our boasting? It is excluded. On what principle? On the principle of works? No, but on the principle of faith.*</u> *²⁸ For we hold that a man is justified by faith apart from works of law."* This principle of justification *by God's grace* to which all have access through faith in Jesus Christ, *removes the possibility of all personal boasting in personal ability to keep the Law* or *do enough meritorious work* to warrant justification.

Rom 3:29, 30. *"<u>Or is God the God of Jews only</u>? Is he not the God of Gentiles also?* **Yes**, <u>*of Gentiles also,*</u> *³⁰ since God is one; and he will justify the circumcised on the ground of their faith and the uncircumcised through their faith."* God justified the circumcised Jew <u>*on the basis of their faith not simply on the act of circumcision*</u>. *It was the faith* of their parents *which caused them to be circumcised,* and not the simple fact that they had been circumcised as a Jew. At age 13 the circumcised boy was involved in the religious ceremony of personally accepting the instructions to the *Torah*.[5] God justifies the Gentile likewise *through*

---

[5] The Jewish celebration of *bar mitzvah* is where the circumcised child/son takes on the faith committed by the parents at circumcision. The bar mitzvah is the religious initiation ceremony of a boy who has

their faith in Jesus which caused them to turn to God, Rom 3:30.

However, Paul has already explained that this faith is not any kind of faith, but a *faith focused on Jesus Christ and his death and resurrection*, and in *accepting Jesus as the Messiah*. This principle holds true for both Jew and Gentile.

Rom 3:31. *"Do we then overthrow the law by this faith?* **By no means***! On the contrary, we uphold the law."* This rhetorical question Paul responds to, vehemently, with the powerful rhetorical answer, *me genoito,*[6] *no, no, no, never*! *The faith principle does not destroy the Law, no, no, no, never*; it merely demonstrates the weakness of the Law and sets it in its appropriate role in God's scheme of redemption.

Rom 3:27-31. Paul's *summary* of justification

"Then <u>*what becomes of our boasting? It is excluded. On what principle? On the principle of works? No, but on the principle of faith.*</u> [28] *<u>For we hold that a man is justified by faith apart from works of law.</u>* [29] *Or is God the God of Jews only? Is he not the God of Gentiles also? Yes, of Gentiles also,* [30] *since God is one; and he will justify the circumcised on the ground of their faith and the uncircumcised through their faith.* [31] *Do we then overthrow the law by this faith? By no means! On the contrary, we uphold the law."*

Paul argues that when the Jew's righteousness and justification are centered in any form of personal *Torah* Law keeping *they might be tempted to boast*, but *they had better not do so before God*! All they had achieved through Law keeping was that they had not done so and

---

reached the age of 13 and is regarded to be faithful and ready to observe the *Torah* religious precepts and be eligible to take part in public worship.

[6] Μὴ γένοιτο, *me genoitō*, is a powerful rhetorical expression found in classical debates implying a strong negative response: *no, no, never, never, never.*

were thus sinners needing redemption! In order to boast the Jew would have to keep the Law perfectly, which Paul has already demonstrated in Rom 2 is not what they have done.

Since justification is *not by Law keeping, but by faith in what God has done in Jesus, all human boasting is excluded*, Rom 3:27.

Boasting is excluded because justification is based on the principle of faith and forgiveness, not the *principle* of Law keeping. Interestingly, the Greek word νόμος, *nómos* which is used in this text is normally translated *law*, but can also be translated *principle*,[7] as it is in this text in the RSV at Rom 3:27.

If justification were based on *Torah* Law keeping then *one would have to have two laws and two Gods*, one for the Jew based on *Torah*, and one for the Gentile based on a different principle, in which case then two principles would be necessary, one for the Jew and one for the Gentile. If this were the case, then God would not be a righteous or fair God having two different systems. However, since God treats all in the same manner, he is a righteous God, and there is no need for a second system with another god!

Seven big issues for Paul's doctrine of justification by faith only

Paul's doctrine of justification by faith only set the scene for a series of issues for Jews and Jewish Christians—those with a deep commitment to the *Torah*!

They saw Paul's argument of righteousness based on faith and not the Law *as something new*!

Rom 3:31. *"Do we then overthrow the law by this faith? **By no means**! On the contrary, we uphold the law."*

For the serious Jew, this doctrine would raise several significant questions, some of which Paul later addresses in Romans in a series of related questions and answers.

---

[7] Cf. Zodhiates and Kittel on νόμος, *nómos*.

First, does this "new" Pauline doctrine mean that *God has turned away from, and rejected the Law (Torah)? For a Jew, this is a serious question!*

This would be unthinkable for the Jew, *almost heresy*, for something to take the place of the *Torah* which was considered holy, coming directly from God!

Paul's strident rhetorical response to this question was μὴ γένοιτο, *me genoito, by no means*! *Me genoito* is a technical rhetorical expression Paul uses often in Romans, meaning, *"No, never, never, never; this is unthinkable!"*

Second, to the contrary, Paul argues, justification by faith actually upholds the Law!

Paul returns to this type of question in Rom 5 and 7 where he will argue that the Law is holy, righteous, spiritual, and good when used for the appropriate reason in the right manner.

Rom 4:1. A related question *"Is this doctrine something new?"* To this Paul answers, *"No! It is as old as Abraham!"* We will address this further at Rom 4:1ff:

> *¹ What then shall we say about Abraham, our forefather according to the flesh? ² For if Abraham was justified by works, he has something to boast about, but not before God. ³ For <u>what does the scripture say? "Abraham believed God, and it was reckoned to him as righteousness."</u> ⁴ Now to one who works, his wages are not reckoned as a gift but as his due. ⁵ And to one who does not work but trusts him who justifies the ungodly, his faith is reckoned as righteousness.*

Gal 3:6ff. Paul had previously addressed this point to the Galatian Christians:

> *⁶ Thus Abraham "believed God, and it was reckoned to him as righteousness." ⁷ So you see that it is men of faith who are the sons of Abraham. ⁸ And the scripture, foreseeing that God would justify the Gentiles by faith, preached the gospel beforehand to Abraham, saying, "In you shall all the nations be blessed." ⁹ So then, those who are*

men of faith are blessed with Abraham who had faith....[16] *Now the promises were made to Abraham and to his offspring. It does not say, "And to offsprings," referring to many; but, referring to one, "And to your offspring," which is Christ.* [17] *This is what I mean: the law, which came four hundred and thirty years afterward, does not annul a covenant previously ratified by God, so as to make the promise void.* [18] *For if the inheritance is by the law, it is no longer by promise; but God gave it to Abraham by a promise.*

Rom 9-11. An additional question which would be even more troublesome to the traditional Jew would be, *"Has God then rejected the Jew, his chosen race, in favor of the Gentile?"*

This question was so troublesome to Paul that he later devoted three whole chapters to answering this, Rom 9-11! We will discuss that material in Lesson 9.

Note his closing remarks at Rom 10:17-11:1ff:

[17] *So faith comes from what is heard, and what is heard comes by the preaching of Christ.*

[18] *But I ask, have they not heard? Indeed they have; for*

"Their voice has gone out to all the earth,
and their words to the ends of the world."
[19] *Again I ask, did Israel not understand? First Moses says,*

"I will make you jealous of those who are not a nation;
with a foolish nation I will make you angry."
[20] *Then Isaiah is so bold as to say,*
"I have been found by those who did not seek me;
I have shown myself to those who did not ask for me."
[21] *But of Israel he says, "All day long I have held out my hands to a disobedient and contrary people."*

¹ I ask, then, has God rejected his people? By no means! I myself am an Israelite, a descendant of Abraham, a member of the tribe of Benjamin. ² God has not rejected his people whom he foreknew. Do you not know what the scripture says of Elijah, how he pleads with God against Israel? ³ "Lord, they have killed thy prophets, they have demolished thy altars, and I alone am left, and they seek my life." ⁴ But what is God's reply to him? "I have kept for myself seven thousand men who have not bowed the knee to Baal." ⁵ So too at the present time there is a remnant, chosen by grace. ⁶ But if it is by grace, it is no longer on the basis of works; otherwise grace would no longer be grace. ⁷ What then? Israel failed to obtain what it sought.

Third, we need to address the *faith only* and baptism issue in the larger theological argument of the text.

This question is a perennial issue in discussions with some evangelical believers.

The heart of the discussion and disagreement hinges most often around not interpreting texts and expressions such as *faith only within the larger theological discussion taking place,* as in major Pauline theological arguments in Romans regarding Jewish views of justification by Law keeping.

Consequently, the question of *"faith only"* in most discussions with evangelical Christians,[8] and others of similar persuasion, raises a major concern and initiates serious debate, often a contentious debate!

A classic example of reading personal theology *into the text*, is Julius Mantey in H. E. Dana and Julius R. Mantey, *A Manual Grammar of the Greek New Testament.*

---

[8] Notably Southern Baptist members. The following books on baptism and faith are worth careful study, Beasley-Murray, G. R. *Baptism in the New Testament*, 1973; Cottrell, Jack, *Romans*, College Press, 2 vols., 1996; Cottrell, Jack, *Baptism a Biblical Study*, 1990; Fergusson, Everett, *Baptism in the Early Church: History, Theology, and Liturgy in the First Five Centuries, 2009.*

On the Greek preposition εἰς Mantey argues that his evangelic theology *of faith only requires* that baptism must be *a result of salvation* and not a requirement *for* salvation!

I have discussed this more fully in a manuscript, *A Biblical Theology of Baptism*, HCU Media, 2022 where I demonstrate that in order to preserve his personal evangelic *faith only* theology, Mantey interprets εἰς in the context of *his personal theology* rather than in the *syntactical context of εἰς followed by an accusative noun.* Mantey is patently in opposition to the majority of major New Testament Greek grammarians on *εἰς.* [9] Mantey implies that baptism is *the result of salvation* and not *for salvation* as in most of the major English translations of Acts 2:38.

Thus, Mantey preserves his view of evangelical theology in contrast to what the syntax and grammar of *εἰς* with an accusative noun should read!

The question we must pursue, then, is how to we explain baptism in the context of "faith only?" The problem lies in how we interpret *faith only* and in what context this is relevant.

We should note that Paul's arguments are in his debate with Jews and Judaizing Christian thinkers, as in his

---

[9] All the major Greek English Grammars clearly state that εἰς followed by an accusative noun, is pointing the action *toward* the accusative noun and *not away from* the accusative noun. H. P. V. Nunn, *A Syntax of New Testament Greek;* W. H. Davis, *Beginner's Grammar of the Greek New Testament;* James Hope Moulton and Henry G. Meecham, *An Introduction to the Study of New Testament Greek;* Blass, Debrunner, Funk, *A Grammar of New Testament and Other Early Christian Literature.* Dana and Mantey, *A Manual Grammar of the Greek New Testament,* pp. 91ff. "The *accusative* case relates primarily to *action, and indicates direction, extent, or end.* "*The accusative signifies that the object referred to is considered as the point toward which something is proceeding: that it is the end of the action or motion described...The accusative embraces three ideas: the end, or direction, or extent of motion or action...The root meaning of the accusative is limitation.*" Here, Mantey disagrees with his own Greek Grammar!

Epistle to the Galatians, who claimed that salvation may involve faith in Jesus and baptism, but Christians must also lay the Law of Moses over this salvation principle and keep the Law of Moses for justification! As we have observed above in his *me genoito, no, no, never,* responses Paul will have nothing of this. His point is that salvation is *solely* by the *faith principle,* and *not* by a *works principle.* Cf. Rom 3:25ff:

> *This was to show God's righteousness, because in his divine forbearance he had passed over former sins;* [26] *it was to prove at the present time that he himself is righteous and that he justifies him who has faith in Jesus.*
>
> [27] *Then what becomes of our boasting? It is excluded.* <u>*On what principle? On the principle of works? No, but on the principle of faith.*</u> [28] <u>*For we hold that a man is justified by faith apart from works of law.*</u>

The Greek of the last clause of Rom 3:28 is expressive, πίστει ἄνθρωπον χωρὶς ἔργων νόμου, which translates as <u>*faithfulness*</u> *of man* <u>*separate from*</u> *works of law*! Now, that sounds like *faith only,* but note that it is in the argument of *not by the principle of works of law, but by the principle of faithfulness apart from works of man.* To insert an evangelical interpretation of *faith only* into the context of Paul's theology of justification is to do it a *major and tragic injustice*!

I recently listened to a sermon by a popular and nationally recognized Methodist minister encouraging Christians to understand that the Christian life and faith does not exist simply by believing in God and Jesus, but, citing James 1 and 2:17 he argued that such a *faith without obedient works is a dead faith. A good point!*

However, his Methodist evangelical mindset obviously fell into the *faith only* trap, for as he progressed in his sermon, he simply did not understand the difference between the *doctrinal theology,* which Paul covered in

91

Rom 1-11, and the *practical paranesis,*[10] which Paul developed at Rom 12:1-13:14 and which James discussed in James 1 and 2.

His interpretation of James 1 and 2 was adequate. His rhetorical understanding of the *paranetic*[11] nature of James was fine!

However, he next moved over into a broader context citing Acts 2:38 to define *repentance* and *confession.* He continued to argue that *faith of any kind without an obedient repentance and confession are not biblical faith, for faith must include obedience, repentance, and confession for faith in Jesus to be legitimate.*

Here he jumped track from James' *paranetic* epistle to equating James 2 *paranetic* message with Peter's great *theological* point in his Pentecost sermon of Acts 2. He spoke of an *obedient faith resulting in repentance and confession of faith*! *Here he became confused*! He was quoting Peter's *theological* argument of Acts 2 as an example of James' 1, 2 *paranetic* arguments! I waited keenly to hear him continue Peter's point of Acts 2:38 and speak of *baptism, like repentance and confession being obedient faith for salvation*! *I waited in vain!* He never once mentioned *baptism,* but *baptism* is as much of Acts 2:38 as are *repentance* and *confession*! The components of Acts 2 he was citing to make his argument for an obedient

---

[10] *Paranesis* is an anglicized word based on the Greek word *parainēsis* which originally meant any kind of advice, instruction, or counsel. In New Testament studies it has been used in different ways ... many scholars have sought to understand paraenesis in terms of its ancient meaning as an umbrella term for *any kind of instruction, religious, moral, or otherwise.* "Paranesis," James Star, *Oxford Bibliographies,* referencing David
Aune and Benjamin Fiore.

[11]In this discussion I will speak of *theological* and *paranetic* material. Understanding the difference yet relationship of these terms is critical to the exegetical discussion of certain texts. They speak of *types of contexts* under discussion. *Theology/doctrine* define the *divine reason* or *basis* for our behavior; *paranesis* explains the human or ethical and practical result of our faith and theology.

faith and salvation *also speak of baptism*! *But he never got there*! *For to include baptism in his sermon he would have to agree that baptism is also an obedient faith for salvation*!

OOPS for his salvation by *faith only* evangelical theology!

Peter in his answer to the Jews on Pentecost implied that *faith without repentance and confession is dead because repentance and confession are an obedient faith for salvation*! *But Peter included baptism*! Why did the Methodist preacher not speak of Baptism? It ran contrary to his evangelical view of faith only. *Repentance* and *confession* can be *obedient faith* for salvation, but not baptism. In his view, baptism can be an obedient faith in a paranetic context like James' doing honorable deeds, but not in a theological context as in Acts 2!

I waited patiently throughout his sermon, with anticipation, for him to mention baptism in his discussion of Acts 2, but it did not come! He was correct in his comment that an *obedient saving faith* must be accompanied by repentance and confession *or it is a dead faith*. But he did not mention baptism as Peter did at Acts 2:38! The Methodist preacher did not see that salvation by *faith only without obedient baptism is not saving faith, but a dead faith!*

His problem was the fundamental error of the *faith only* community—a *failure to interpret texts within the major theological point being made by the writer of the text. Conflating* texts like James 1 and 2 with Acts 2:38 without appropriate consideration of their theological context and message results in a confused doctrine, to say the least!

James and Paul are *not in disagreement* on *an obedient faith*, both agree that biblical faith must be associated with obedience. Paul was arguing that salvation and justification *must be based on faith in Jesus Christ and not in works to the Law of Moses*. James was saying that faith in a right relationship *resulting without works* is dead.

93

Paul in Rom 1:1-8 was *theological*, James in James 1, 2 was *paranetic* and there is a major difference theologically between theology and paranesis!

Paul, however, will explain later in Rom 12:1ff that *righteousness* based on an *understanding of the grace and mercy of God, and rooted only in faith* in God and Jesus, and *not simply in works of Law,* should *result in a life of service to others*. That is exactly the point James was making. A righteous relationship with God, based on *faith* (Pauline *faith only*) and not in Law keeping, should result in a life of dedicated worship to God and service to others.

Without service to others as in a life of faith and a righteous relationship with God, *faith is dead*. James' closing thoughts at James 1:26, 27 are a powerful definition of *paranetic* theology growing out of a *theological* stance. *Religion, θρησκεία – worshipping religion,*[12] as James uses it implies *worshipping God. Practical paranetic true worship of God,* flowing out of a *right relationship with God*, must respond *in service to others*:

> [26] *If anyone thinks he is <u>religious</u>, and does not bridle his tongue but deceives his heart, this man's religion is vain.* [27] *<u>Religion</u> that is pure and undefiled before God and the Father is this: <u>to visit orphans and widows in their affliction, and to keep oneself unstained from the world.</u>*

A failure to understand the relationship of *theology*[13]to *paranesis*[14] results in a failure to understand the difference yet similarity of Paul and James and leads to confusion in some evangelical *faith only* positions.

---

[12] Zodhiates, θρησκεία, *thrēskeía*; to worship God, which is from *thrēskos* ... religious, pious. It also refers to the true worship of God (Acts 26:5; James 1:26, 27).

[13] *Theology* – That which motivates us such as justification by faith only and not by works of Law.

[14] *Paranesis* – The result of our theological commitment, the practical ethical life which *results* out of righteousness by faith only.

94

Fourth, as we reflect on the witness of the New Testament Scriptures to the *process* of *salvation,* we learn that it is presented in a *consistent development* in the form of a *salvation continuum.*

We understand a *continuum* to be *a coherent connected collection of parts in a sequence of progression of values that change gradually toward some goal.*[15]

We hold that *salvation* is presented in a *continuum* which originates in the mind and plan of the eternal God, Eph 1:3ff, is revealed in Scripture, 2 Tim 3:14-16, activated in the life and death of Jesus Christ, 1 Cor 1:18-25, and is realized in human experience by man's obedient faith in God and Jesus Christ, Rom 3:21ff.

An excellent example of this is seen in Luke's account of the ministry of the apostolic church in Acts 2. Luke records that the disciples were gathered in one place in Jerusalem, Acts 2:1ff. Suddenly they were surrounded by loud sounds from heaven accompanied by the appearance of tongues of fire resting on the disciples, indicating the presence and activity of the Holy Spirit. Jesus had instructed the disciples to wait in Jerusalem until they were baptized with power and the Holy Spirit, Luke 24:48, Acts 1:4. On this remarkable Day of Pentecost event God and Jesus were inaugurating the plan of salvation God had been working on for centuries. How better to introduce this event than to cite Luke's account, Acts 2:5-16:

> [5] *Now there were dwelling in Jerusalem Jews, devout men from every nation under heaven.* [6] <u>*And at this sound the multitude came together, and they were bewildered, because each one heard them speaking in his own language.*</u> [7] *And they were amazed and wondered, saying, "Are not all these who are speaking Galileans?* [8] *And how is it that we hear, each of us in his own native language?* [9] *Parthians and Medes and Elamites and residents*

---

[15] Based on a range of thoughts in leading dictionaries related to literature or process of ideas. Cf. *Oxford Shorter English Dictionary, Cambridge English Dictionary, Dictionary.com, et al.*

of Mesopotamia, Judea and Cappadocia, Pontus and Asia, [10] Phrygia and Pamphylia, Egypt and the parts of Libya belonging to Cyrene, and visitors from Rome, both Jews and proselytes, [11] Cretans and Arabians, we hear them telling in our own tongues the mighty works of God." [12] And all were amazed and perplexed, saying to one another, "What does this mean?" [13] But others mocking said, "They are filled with new wine."

[14] But Peter, standing with the eleven, lifted up his voice and addressed them, "Men of Judea and all who dwell in Jerusalem, let this be known to you, and give ear to my words. [15] For these men are not drunk, as you suppose, since it is only the third hour of the day; [16] but this is what was spoken by the prophet Joel:

[17] 'And in the last days it shall be, God declares,

that I will pour out my Spirit upon all flesh...'

Beginning with this prophetic promise of God, Peter launched into his remarkable Pentecost sermon:

[22] "Men of Israel, hear these words: Jesus of Nazareth, a man attested to you by God with mighty works and wonders and signs which God did through him in your midst, as you yourselves know— [23] this Jesus, delivered up according to the definite plan and foreknowledge of God, you crucified and killed by the hands of lawless men. [24] But God raised him up, having loosed the pangs of death, because it was not possible for him to be held by it.

Many of the Jews upon hearing Peter recognized the power of his message and *believed* in the message and that they had crucified the Messiah. They were so moved by this that in remorse they cried out to Peter and the apostles, *"Brethren, what shall we do?"* Let Luke tell us this remarkable sequence of events, a key point in the continuum of faith that unfolds in this narrative. Peter preached:

> *36 Let all the house of Israel therefore know assuredly that <u>God has made him both Lord and Christ, this Jesus whom you crucified</u>."*
>
> *37 Now when they heard this <u>they were cut to the heart</u>, and said to Peter and the rest of the apostles, "Brethren, <u>what shall we do</u>?" 38 And Peter said to them, "<u>Repent, and be baptized every one of you in the name of Jesus Christ for the forgiveness of your sins; and you shall receive the gift of the Holy Spirit</u>. 39 For the promise is to you and to your children and to all that are far off, every one whom the Lord our God calls to him." 40 And he testified with many other words and exhorted them, saying, "<u>Save yourselves from this crooked generation</u>." 41 <u>So those who received his word were baptized, and there were added that day about three thousand souls</u>. 42 And they devoted themselves to the apostles' teaching and fellowship, to the breaking of bread and the prayers.*

Note how Luke and Peter fix this remarkable narrative of the first preaching of the Gospel of salvation in Jesus Christ on the Day of Pentecost in the *activity of God and the Holy Spirit*. Peter tied his sermon to the prophetic word of salvation proclaimed by Joel, Acts 2:16ff. Peter then tied his narrative of *Jesus' resurrection* to David stating that David had spoken of the resurrection of Jesus Christ. The flow of thought so aptly captured by Luke really struck a chord with many of the Jews present. When Peter stated that in this resurrection God had made Jesus both Lord and Christ, this shook the confidence of his audience and we have the startling question, *"What shall we do?"*

The line of thought presented by Peter was a natural consequence of their developing faith and *salvation continuum* of Acts. The Jews *believed* they had crucified their Messiah, *they had faith*, at this point they had *emerging faith that needed to be obedient*, and that faith motivated them to hear Peter's call to *repentance* and *baptism*. Luke and Peter demonstrate that a real faith should reveal itself in some obedient action. They had faith but needed to know what to do to *develop* and *fulfill* that faith.

Peter's answer in Acts 2:37, 38 virtually fixes for all time the salvation *continuum* that began in the eternal plan and activity of God. It involved the Holy Spirit and the message of the prophets, it was inaugurated in the death and resurrection of Jesus, and again it involved the remarkable Pentecost activity of the Holy Spirit, the preached word by Peter; *faith, repentance, confession, baptism* for forgiveness; and the indwelling of the Holy Spirit.

> *And Peter said to them, "*<u>*Repent*</u>*, and* <u>*be baptized*</u> *every one of you in the name of Jesus Christ* <u>*for the forgiveness of your sins; and*</u> <u>*you shall receive the gift of the Holy Spirit.*</u> ³⁹ *For the promise is to you and to your children and to all that are far off, every one whom the Lord our God calls to him." *⁴⁰* And he testified with many other words and exhorted them, saying, "*<u>*Save yourselves from this crooked generation.*</u>*" *⁴¹* So those who received his word were* <u>*baptized, and there were added that day about three thousand souls.*</u> ⁴² *And they devoted themselves to the apostles' teaching and fellowship, to the breaking of bread and the prayers.*

A failure to see the developing *salvation continuum* in this remarkable narrative is to refuse the biblical narrative recorded by Luke. It begins with the divine activity of God and his Holy Spirit, flows through prophetic Scripture and the preaching of the gospel regarding the death and resurrection of Jesus, belief in the preached message of Peter, faith, repentance, baptism *for* forgiveness, and the indwelling gift of the Holy Spirit and Peter's call to the Jews to *save themselves* in faith and obedience from the crooked world of sin which Paul explains has captured all men.

Remove any of the ingredients from the *salvation narrative continuum* outlined by Luke *and you destroy the salvation continuum and plan of God*! Remove God's activity and what you have is a false religion. Remove the Holy Spirit from this narrative and Jesus has already condemned you, Mat 12:32! Remove the death and resurrection of Jesus from this continuum and the heart of the Gospel is destroyed, Rom 1:16, 17, 1 Cor 1:18f. Remove faith from this narrative, and it is impossible to please God, Luke 13:3, Heb 11:6. Remove baptism for the forgiveness of sins, and you have a real problem! You do not believe Jesus, Luke, Peter, or Scripture, Luke 24:46f!

Fifth, evangelicals are confused regarding the *role of baptism* in the salvation continuum.

We must ask, is baptism a *result* of faith, that is, faith in God and Jesus *which leads us to baptism for salvation,* as in Acts 2:38, or is baptism in the context of salvation *the result of salvation, that is, consequential to or the result of salvation* as Mantey and some evangelicals imply?

That sounds like the proverbial chicken and egg conundrum! The answer may be neither for they are both essential to one another!

Similarly, which comes first, *baptism* or *salvation*? Likewise, they are both essential to one another, but Scripture does give us an answer we can trust, if we trust Scripture over our personal theology and interpretation of Scripture!

Most *faith only* evangelical arguments are that baptism is the *result* of *salvation*, that is, *consequential* to *salvation*, and not the *result of faith and the cause of salvation*.

The question in simpler words is whether *baptism* is the *result* of *salvation by faith only* as held by evangelicals, or is *baptism for salvation* the result of *faith*!

One Southern Baptist minister years ago in South Africa, a recent arrival from Waco, Texas, tried to convince me that baptism was not *for* salvation, but the name of Jesus Christ was *for* salvation. In some regards he

99

was correct, but his interpretation of Acts 2:38 was miles off course! His interpretation of Acts 2:38 was: *"Repent, and be baptized every one of you in the name of Jesus* anointed *for the forgiveness of your sins; and you shall receive the gift of the Holy Spirit."*

His point was that Peter did not say it was *baptism for* the forgiveness of sins, but that Jesus *anointed for* (the Greek christos meaning the anointed one) the forgiveness of sins. Sounds impressive and smooth, but radically wrong. He simply did not know the difference between *a verb, be baptized* (βαπτισθήτω, a middle passive verb) and *the noun* (Χριστοῦ a genitive descriptive noun) *the anointed one*! Peter did not say Jesus was anointed but that Jesus was the Christ, the anointed Christ.

The arguments of such *faith only* evangelicals are pathetic!

We simply must examine what Peter *actually said to the Jews* in his great sermon on the day of Pentecost as in Acts 2.

Evangelicals see faith, salvation, baptism, righteousness, in the following continuum:

Faith-Salvation-Baptism-Righteousness

Peter at Acts 2:37, 38, (faith) *"what shall we do ... repent and be baptized every one of you in the name of Jesus* (faith) *for the forgiveness of your sins, and you will receive the gift of the* (indwelling) *Holy Spirit'* (a right relationship with God).

We should also consider Peter's comment at 1 Peter 3:21ff: [21] *"Baptism, which corresponds to this, now saves you, not as a removal of dirt from the body but as an appeal to God for a clear conscience* (faith, repentance, confession, obedience), *through the resurrection of Jesus Christ,* [22] *who has gone into heaven and is at the right hand of God, with angels, authorities, and powers subject to him."*

This presents the following continuum: *Faith-Confession-Repentance-Baptism-Obedience-Salvation-Righteousness.*

Paul explains faith, baptism, salvation, righteousness in the following continuum. Cf. Rom 1:16,17; 3:21ff; 5:1ff; 6:1ff; Rom 12:1ff; and Col 2:12,13: *Faith-Baptism-Salvation-Righteousness-Christian living.*

The question we must ask at this point is whether we see baptism as a *sacrament/Christian doctrine* of obedience <u>once we are saved</u> as do the *faith only* evangelicals, or do we see baptism as a *result of faith and repentance* εἰς ἄφεσιν τῶν ἁμαρτιῶν, *for* the *forgiveness of sin.* In this case baptism *results in salvation* as is taught in Acts 2:38.

So, the question is, is baptism a *merit work* principle or a *faith* principle?

Evangelicals are confused on the business of faith! Is faith something we must do or does it happen by accident. *Or is it a work that God does*? Man cannot believe on his own so God intervenes and by selection decides who to bring to faith! Some Calvinistic evangelicals hold such a position! God creates faith in the person through his Holy Spirit! Man is so depraved that he cannot believe on his own so God through his Holy Spirit creates faith in the person. This lies at the root of a Calvinistic doctrine of irresistible grace offered to man by God's predestined view of *who can or should be saved*! *Our answer to that is that simply is not taught in Scripture*!

We might ask a similar question, is *faith* a *work principle*, since it is something *we must do* to be saved in Jesus? It obviously is not something that happens by accident, *we must decide to believe. Is faith then a work that we must do*? If so, *what kind of work is faith*?

Paul has already answered that question! Baptism for Paul is *not a work principle*, but *a faith principle*! It is something *we submit to in faith*, cf. Rom 3:27ff.

Furthermore, baptism as required in the New Testament is *a verb in the passive voice, you must <u>be baptized</u>*! Cf Acts 2:38, μετανοήσατε, φησίν καὶ βαπτισθήτω (*repent and <u>be baptized</u>*, βαπτισθήτω is in the passive voice)! Cf also Acts 22:16, rise and <u>be baptized</u>!

101

We are never taught in the New Testament to baptize ourselves! We are taught to *submit* to baptism *in faith*, that is, *believing* or *trusting* in God's working in baptism.

This implies that *we submit in faith to being baptized.* It is a faith principle, not a work principle!

Sixth, our submitting to God in baptism is where *God does his work* in saving us and *raising us with Christ to a new life in Christ.*

Rom 6:1ff. In baptism we die to our past life of sin and are raised to a new life in Christ.

> *[1] What shall we say then? Are we to continue in sin that grace may abound? [2] By no means! How can we who died to sin still live in it? [3] Do you not know that all of us who have been baptized into Christ Jesus were baptized into his death? [4] We were buried therefore with him by baptism into death, so that as Christ was raised from the dead by the glory of the Father, we too might walk in newness of life.*

Col 2:11,12. Paul explains that baptism is not a work we do, but it is trusting (faith) in *the working of God.*

> *[11] In him also you were circumcised with a circumcision made without hands,* (not what we do) *by putting off the body of flesh in the circumcision of Christ; [12] and you were buried with him in baptism, in which you were also raised with him **through faith in the working of God**, who raised him from the dead.*

We *submit to baptism,* but *it is God who does the work in baptism,* raising us from the dead! We are not doing this work, we merely submit in baptism to God's working, *trusting in God, a faith principle,* and He does the work!

Seventh, is the issue of justification in the faith salvation righteousness continuum.

The process of salvation and justification can be demonstrated as a continuum of *faith-repentance-baptism forgiveness-justification- righteousness.*

We should remember that righteousness in the Jewish and early Christian mindset meant *being in a right relationship with God*. For the *Torah*-minded Jew this meant keeping the Law of Moses which Paul adamantly rejected. Paul's argument in Romans and Galatians was that getting into a right relationship with God was through faith in Jesus Christ and not by works of merit or Law keeping.

Several key and related issues are significant obedient steps or tangent points in the process of the sinner's response to the atoning grace and mercy of God. For the apostolic witness in Scripture, they are all related and essential points in an atoning continuum. One cannot separate faith, repentance, and baptism in this continuum. Peter clarified this in his teaching to persuade Jews at Acts 2:38. Faith, repentance, confession, and baptism form the beginning and end of the atoning continuum revealed in Scripture. Remove the one end or component from the continuum and you destroy the continuum!

Three times in Romans Paul spoke of a *faith* that is *obedient*:

Rom 1:5, where Paul speaks about his apostleship. He defines it as "*to bring about the <u>obedience</u> of faith.*"

Rom 6:17, where he speaks about the Romans who have been "*obedient from the heart*" to the standard of teaching they had heard.

Rom 16:26, 27, where he again speaks about the "*obedience of faith*"
and stresses that faith and obedience are two profound steps in any process of the atoning continuum.

You cannot have faith without obedience! If you do try this, it is no longer faith (trusting in God or Jesus) but honoring your own opinion!

You cannot have obedience without faith. If you do, you have no root in God for that obedience, and can then obey anything that sounds good, even the Law. Without faith and obedience you cannot expect justification! Faith and obedience for Paul are always focused on Jesus, the source of our obedience.

We ask, can a person claim to have faith (trust) in Jesus and refuse to obey him or his apostolic message, especially when they speak of baptism?

Again, we ask, can a person be obedient to Jesus while refusing to believe in him?

In the case of the faith-baptism continuum, if you remove faith from the continuum, you destroy both faith and baptism.

Remove baptism from faith in God's working and what do you have? A person still locked in sin!

Remove faith from baptism and what do you get? A wet unbelieving person!

When one is baptized in faithful obedience to Jesus and Scripture one is *not working for or earning salvation* or *justification*, but merely *submitting to the working of God through faith in Jesus Christ.*

Paul clearly did not consider the faith/baptism continuum a works principle. He clearly saw the relationship between faith and baptism as one process: baptism tied inexplicably to the faith principle.

Gal 3:23-29. Paul clearly contrasted faith and keeping the Law as a work. It was not by Law keeping that one became an heir of Abraham, but by faith and being *baptized into Christ* that one becomes an heir of Abraham.

> [23] *Now before faith came, we were confined under the law, kept under restraint until faith should be revealed.* [24] *So that the law was our custodian until Christ came, that we might be justified by faith.* [25] *But now that faith has come, we are no longer under a custodian;* [26] *for in Christ Jesus you are all sons of God, through faith.* [27] *For as many of you as were baptized into Christ have put on Christ.* [28] *There is neither Jew nor Greek, there is neither slave nor free, there is neither male nor female; for you are all one in Christ Jesus.* [29] *And if you are*

Christ's, then you are Abraham's offspring, heirs according to promise.

Rom 6:1-6. In his closing thoughts of Rom 5 Paul argued that the law had not been introduced to remove sin or trespasses, but *only to clarify the nature of sin, that is, death.* However, what the Law could not do, faith in Christ did, Rom 5:18-20, *"Law came in, to increase the trespass; but where sin increased, grace abounded all the more, [21] so that, as sin reigned in death, grace also might reign through righteousness to eternal life through Jesus Christ our Lord.* Following this at Rom 6:1 Paul stressed the *faith in Christ/baptism principle*:

> *[1] What shall we say then? Are we to continue in sin that grace may abound? [2] By no means! How can we who died to sin still live in it? [3] Do you not know that all of us who have been baptized into Christ Jesus were baptized into his death? [4] We were buried therefore with him by baptism into death, so that as Christ was raised from the dead by the glory of the Father, we too might walk in newness of life.*

Col 2:11-14. Along similar lines to Rom 6:1ff Paul argued in Col 2:11ff

> *[11] In him also you were circumcised with a circumcision made without hands, by putting off the body of flesh in the circumcision of Christ; [12] and you were buried with him in baptism, in which you were also raised with him through faith in the working of God, who raised him from the dead. [13] And you, who were dead in trespasses and the uncircumcision of your flesh, God made alive together with him, having forgiven us all our trespasses, [14] having canceled the bond which stood against us with its legal demands; this he set aside, nailing it to the cross.*

Faith in Jesus, that is, *trusting* in *what God has done* in Jesus, or believing, is something we do but it is not a work of mentor! It is a decision we make to trust in God and his plan of salvation. Faith does not simply happen in us! We must believe.

Faith, repentance, confessing faith, and *baptism* are all *faith principles* set in the *faith-baptism-atonement-salvation continuum.* They work together and depend on one another. *Remove one and you collapse the faith-atonement continuum!*

Chapter 5 - God's Faithfulness and Righteousness are Seen in Abraham and Christ: Rom 4:1-25

Context and Message

Several tricky questions surface in this text!

*Was God's promise to Abraham based on the fact that Abraham was a good person who honored and kept the Torah? Paul answers his question with a strident mē genoito, **No, no, no**!*

*Did God "owe" Abraham any recognition because of what Abraham had done by leaving Ur and travelling to Canaan? **No, no, no!** God owed Abraham nothing other than his love for his creation, his eternal purpose to save his creation, love of Abraham, his grace and his mercy!*

It was God himself who encouraged and called Abraham out of Ur in Chaldea. It was God who, looking into the future, urged the aged and impotent Abraham to trust in His promise of a real biological son and a multitude of descendants, Rom 4:17-21.

*The promises arose out of God's love and concern for Abraham and his descendants, and out of God's eternal purpose and grace. God did **not owe** Abraham anything, least of all a son!*

Certainly, God had called Abraham for a purpose, but both Genesis and Paul explain that the fulfilment of God's promise was grounded not in a debt God owed Abraham, but in promises made to Abraham and Abraham's faith alone. The fulfillment of the promises did not lie in Abraham's circumcision and keeping of the Torah Law which had not yet been given when God made his promises to Abraham and declared him righteous.

Paul wanted to show clearly that the Jew's election by God in Abraham occurred 430 years before the Torah was given[1] and even before Abraham was circumcised. He wanted to emphasize that the Jew's election lay in God's grace and Abraham's faith in God's faithfulness to his promises.

What we see in Rom 4 is God working out his faithfulness to Abraham, the Jews, and to all the nations, and doing this through an uncircumcised, Torah-less Gentile: faithful Abraham!

So what did Abraham have going for him?

He was without physical power, without a fine religious pedigree like the Torah, without moral perfection, without circumcision and without the Laws of Moses!

He lacked just about everything the average traditional Jew said you had to have if you wanted to claim God as your father, and Torah righteousness!

According to the Jew's mindset in Paul's day, Abraham would have been rejected by his own Jewish descendants (which should have told the Jews something) but he was chosen by God without Torah and Jewish legal circumcision!

All he had going for him when God made a covenant with him and declared him righteous was his faithfulness to God, no Law of Moses, no Torah, and no circumcision!

Abraham trusted a righteous and faithful God who would not go back on his commitment to his creation, or to the promises he had made with Abraham, a Gentile. God was offering a new covenant righteousness to Abraham's descendants, the same kind of righteousness and covenant relationship that he had made with their forefather, Abraham. This was a righteousness based on faith and not the Torah!

But God didn't choose Abraham simply to bless him and the Jews! God chose him so that through Abraham's faithfulness God might bless all nations. Abraham's

---

[1] Gal 3:15ff.

glorious place in history was purely a gift and God's grace, based on faith rather than Torah. Abraham's and Israel's blessing and promises were independent of circumcision and the keeping of Torah! Abraham's whole experience with God shows us God being faithful to the entire human race (note Genesis 12:3; 18:18; 22:18).

Israel, then, was not an end to itself! Israel was to be blessed in Abraham along with the Gentiles who through faith in God's promises would all become Abraham's descendants. These promises were not based on Torah Law keeping.

Obviously, Rom 4 discusses Abraham, Sarah, and Isaac and how God blesses them, but the incisive thrust is not about three individuals or the Jews; it is about God and his righteousness! God is a righteous faithful God who treats all people by the same principle: faith in Jesus Christ.

The righteousness of God permeates the whole epistle of Romans as Paul also proclaims a righteousness from God which all people enjoy through our faith in Jesus Christ and God's loving forgiveness.

In addition, it isn't about God's faithfulness only to Israel; it's about God's faithfulness to the entire human race, Rom 4:9-12.

The promise to Abraham was not simply that he would become the father of the Jewish nation, but that he would also become the father of the uncircumcised (Gentiles) who would believe in Him with the faith of Abraham, Rom 4:11-13. In this case neither circumcision nor uncircumcision mean anything, see Gal 5:6; 6:14!

It was because no one, Jew or Gentile, had any moral right to expect God to keep his creation commitments that **God's faithfulness shines all the brighter***!*

Abraham was faithful because he simply trusted God **and was righteous because he was faithful***!*

*So the faithful and righteous God made inheriting the promises made to Abraham **a matter of faith** (trusting rather than earning) **and grace**, rather than Torah Law keeping which would have excluded the Gentiles who did not have Torah.*

*The reason God made righteousness and covenant relationship a principle of grace and not a Torah covenant relationship was so that **all Abraham's children would be able to receive the inheritance**, not only those who possessed the Torah.*

The serious question Paul lays before the Jews, and us, is "Who really are Abraham's seed?"

The answer is "those who have Abraham's faith whether or not they have his fleshly biological descent." Paul will return to this thought again at Rom 9:6-12.

*Abraham looked at his own aged body and Sarah's barren womb and believed that **God could give life to the dead**!*

God, Abraham, faithfulness, righteousness

Rom 1:16, 17; 3:21-31. Paul introduced his theology of righteousness.

In his opening statement at Rom 1:16, 17 Paul indicated that *God is a Righteous God.* At Rom 3:25f he added that God's atonement in Jesus *was to show God's righteousness, because in his divine forbearance he had passed over former sins;* [26] *it was to prove **at the present time** that he himself is righteous and that he justifies him who has faith in Jesus.*

Rom 4:1-25. Paul develops his argument by emphasizing that *Abraham's righteousness* was based on *faith in God's promises*, not in *Torah* Law keeping.

This reasoning should not surprise us for we learn from the Old Testament, and especially the Psalms, cf. Ps 136, that *God's steadfast love never ceases and that he always keeps his covenant promises, as in the case of Abraham!*

God is a God who is *faithful to his creation*, and especially to the human race he created. When sin looked like overtaking and destroying God's creation completely, Gen 6:9ff and Gen 7, God brought the flood to bring about a fresh start in Noah and his family.

So, Paul resorted to Abraham! The point Paul was making *in his Abraham narrative* could be found at Gen 12, 15, 17. The Jew would surely know the Abraham narrative well!

At Gen 12, when God saw the evil of Babylon and elsewhere, he called Abram and his family from Ur of Chaldea and sent them to Canaan to begin the creation of a new nation and people eventually to be called Israel.

Eventually when a famine struck Canaan the sons of Jacob were led into Egyptian captivity from where God delivered them through Moses.

He led Israel in the wilderness and settled them in the land of Canaan which he and earlier promised Abraham.

Throughout these early centuries God was instructing and teaching his people to trust him and keep the various covenants he made with them.

Now, a major problem surfaced for the Jews. Although the Jews still believed in God, they bedded their relationship with God in their ability to keep the *Torah* Laws of Moses.

Paul had learned through his own experience with Jesus on the road to Damascus and subsequent events that Torah Law keeping, although commendable and to be desired, was not a right approach to a relationship with God. Such a relationship with God must be based on faith in Jesus Christ and not in the *Torah*!

This news was the gospel *euangelion*, good news, Paul was teaching. He emphasized that a real covenant relationship with God, that is, *righteousness*, is not based on *Torah* Law keeping, but *solely on faith and specifically **now** in the new age of Christ solely on faith in Jesus.*

The Jew typically had maintained that if the Gentile was to share in this covenant relationship with God it had to be through their keeping the *Torah* Law and circumcision. Paul appropriately rejected and condemned this false covenant relationship view!

Paul had stressed, Rom 3:21ff, that a covenant relationship with God is based *only in faith in Jesus Christ*, and not in Law keeping of any kind. His point was that *a faith only principle is open to all humans*, both Jew and Gentile, without favoritism and ethnic distinction, Rom 1:16, 17; 3:21-31.

That this *covenant relationship* which in Romans Paul calls *righteousness*. It is grounded in *God's grace and faith in Jesus Christ*, and not in *Torah* Law keeping, Rom 3:21-31.

Paul's gospel message deeply disturbed the Jews in a major way, for it seemed to them to undermine all that God had done for them through Abraham and Moses and the *Torah* Law.

Their concern was not simply that God would grant a proselyte covenant relationship to the Gentile that distressed the Jews,[2] it was that this was not through *Torah* Law keeping but now solely through faith in Jesus.

To his Jewish readers, Paul's gospel of grace apart from the Law which included the Gentiles undermined their *Torah* understanding and view of covenant relationship with God.

---

[2] The Jews clearly understood the process of proselytism which granted certain privileges to the Gentile to convert to Judaism as long as they honored the *Torah*. Paul F. Stuehrenberg in *The Anchor Bible Dictionary* observes regarding the Greek word, προσελυτος, proselytes, "In antiquity the term "proselyte" was used only in the context of Judaism. In the LXX it translates Heb *gēr*, a word designating a resident alien or sojourner in the land. *Later it became a technical term for a convert to Judaism*, thus representing one aspect of the more general phenomenon of conversion in antiquity ... The term is used in Matt 23:15 and Acts 2:11."

This also challenged the Jew's perspective of their promised place and role as God's chosen and elected nation and calling through Abraham.

For the Jew, any covenant relationship with God had to be through the *Torah*! Now Paul was challenging this by claiming that a new covenant relationship with God came through faith in Jesus Christ and not through *Torah Law keeping*!

It became necessary for Paul, therefore, to insist that his gospel was *not new* and that it did not nullify or eliminate the *Torah*, or God's election of Israel.

At Rom 3:31f Paul had stated, *But <u>now</u> the righteousness of God has been manifested apart from law, although <u>the law and the prophets bear witness to it</u>, ²² the righteousness of God through faith in Jesus Christ for all who believe. For there is no distinction.*

Paul's one word, **now**, *nuní*, is a loaded expression! It stresses the *now* of the new Messianic age in contrast to the *past then* of the Mosaic system or covenant! Zodhiates notes, νυví, *nuní*; adverb, identical to *nún* ... *now*, strengthened by the demonstrative *i* (iota) for emphasis.[3]

The Jew might have felt that Paul's gospel was something *new* or *not heard of before*, or *innovative*, but at Rom 1:2 Paul had claimed that *his gospel was not something new, for it had been promised in the Old Testament Scriptures*. The Jew ignored this fact.

The Jew probably thought they were morally superior to the Gentiles, and that being a covenant people they had an advantage over the Gentile because of the *Torah*. They knew they were not sinless, their intricate annual sacrificial atoning system reminded them of this, but nevertheless, because they had the *Torah*, and because they believed that it was through the *Torah* that they had a special covenant relationship with God, they felt superior to the Gentile.

This is precisely the point Paul was addressing in Rom 2:17-24 where he argued that the Jews thought they were

---

[3] Zodhiates, νυví, *nuní*.

above the Gentile and were better off than the Gentile *because they had the Torah.*

Paul's argument thus far had been more by way of teaching rather than explanation or providing irrefutable proof of the validity of his message other than Jesus' resurrection, which the Jews rejected. He had stated that the *Torah* and the prophets bore testimony to his message but had thus far given no specific proof to this claim!

So, Paul resorted to a proof that for the Jew should have been indisputable. *Abraham's righteousness*!

Rom 4:1-25. Abraham, the ancestral hero of faith for Israel

Rom 4:1. The interpretation of Rom 4:1ff introduces some interesting possibilities!

The Greek text reads, Τί οὖν ἐροῦμεν εὑρηκέναι Ἀβραὰμ τὸν προπάτορα ἡμῶν κατὰ σάρκα …

There are several textual variants in this text that do not appear on the surface but relate to how to translate the perfect infinitive verb εὑρηκέναι, *heurēkenai, to have found* according to the *flesh*!

The RSV reads "What shall we say about Abraham our forefather according to the flesh?"

The NIV reads "What then shall we say that Abraham, our forefather, discovered in this matter?"

The KJV reads "What shall we say then that Abraham our father, as pertaining to the flesh, hath found?"

The ASV reads "What then shall we say that Abraham, our forefather according to the flesh, has found?

The ESV reads "What then shall we say was gained by Abraham, our forefather according to the flesh?"

The most likely reading of the Greek text literally reads *"What shall we say is to be found about Abraham our forefather according to the flesh?"*

Flesh in Paul's use often represents our *human, carnal, sinful nature.*[4] He normally uses another Greek word for *body*, σῶμα, *sṓma, the parts of the human body* but this is not the word Paul writes here.[5]

This opens up a pivotal argument Paul uses to demonstrate his doctrine of *righteousness by faith only and not by Law or Torah keeping,* and that *God is a righteous God!*

The stubborn Jews needed a stronger argument than Paul had given up to this point, *so he turned to an argument that even the strictest Jew could not reject: Abraham, the father of their race had been declared righteous by faith before the Law had been given!* The *Torah* Law came 430 years *after* Abraham had been declared righteous by God!

Abraham, the source of their promises and covenant relationship with God, was declared righteous by God without any understanding of the *Torah* Law of Moses!

That for the Jew should be irrefutable proof regarding *righteousness by faith without Torah Law keeping!*

The Jew's own Scriptures, Gen 15:1-6, recorded that Abraham in Canaan had been declared righteous by God while still *uncircumcised* and *without the Law,* namely, <u>*when he was still a Gentile*</u>!

Note Paul's comment to the Galatians, Gal 3:15ff:

> *To give a human example, brethren: no one annuls even a man's will, or adds to it, once it has been ratified.* [16] *Now the promises were made to Abraham and to his offspring. It does not say, "And to offsprings," referring to many; but, referring to one, "And to your offspring," which is Christ.* [17] <u>*This is what I mean: the law, which came four*</u>

---

[4] Zodhiates, **σάρξ** *sárx, as implying sinfulness, proneness to sin, the carnal nature, the seat of carnal appetites and desires, of sinful passions and affections whether physical or moral.*

[5] Zodhiates, σῶμα *sṓma,* metonymically referring to the body as the external man, to which is ascribed that which strictly belongs to the person, man, individual.

hundred and thirty years afterward, does not annul a covenant previously ratified by God, so as to make the promise void. [18] For if the inheritance is by the law, it is no longer by promise; but God gave it to Abraham by a promise.

Every Jew, even in Rome, would recognize that Israel's covenant relationship with God, and their election as his people, came from, or moved through Abraham. And this took place *long before the Law had been given*! Abraham's righteousness was simply yet *firmly based on faith in God and his promises* and not on his ability to maintain a law which would only be given to Moses 430 years in the future!

Gen 15:1 reads:

"After these things the word of the LORD came to Abram in a vision, "Fear not, Abram, I am your shield; your reward shall be very great." [2] But Abram said, "O Lord GOD, what wilt thou give me, for I continue childless, and the heir of my house is Eliezer of Damascus?" [3] And Abram said, "Behold, thou hast given me no offspring; and a slave born in my house will be my heir." [4] And behold, the word of the LORD came to him, "This man shall not be your heir; your own son shall be your heir." [5] And he brought him outside and said, "Look toward heaven, and number the stars, if you are able to number them." Then he said to him, "So shall your descendants be." [6] And he believed the LORD; and he reckoned it to him as righteousness."

No Jew would argue that Abraham was not in a covenant relationship with God. Neither would they reject or deny that Abraham and his seed/descendants were chosen by God as a result of Abraham's *faithful obedience to God*!

So, Paul proceeds with his proof that God's promises and covenant relationships are not grounded in *Torah* Law keeping, *but in faith*, and that God's original promise to

Abraham included the Gentiles. Gen 17:4 should seal that argument:

> *¹ When Abram was ninety-nine years old the LORD appeared to Abram, and said to him, "I am God Almighty; walk before me, and be blameless. ² And I will make my covenant between me and you, and will multiply you exceedingly." ³ Then Abram fell on his face; and God said to him, ⁴ "Behold, my covenant is with you, and you shall be the father of a multitude of nations.⁶*

Paul settles his argument in God's promise to Abraham which was based on a faith principle, not the Law or *Torah*, Rom 4:1ff.

Rom 4:1-5. *¹ What then shall we say about Abraham, our forefather according to the flesh? ² For if Abraham was justified by works, he has something to boast about, but not before God. ³ For what does the scripture say? "Abraham believed God, and it was reckoned to him as righteousness." ⁴ Now to one who works, his wages are not reckoned as a gift but as his due. ⁵ And to one who does not work but trusts him who justifies the ungodly, his faith is reckoned as righteousness.*

Paul addresses the Jew's concerns, demonstrating that God's faithfulness to Abraham in the birth promise of Isaac is proof that the basis of the fulfilment of His promise to Abraham was Abraham's faith, and that it included all nations.

The statement *"Abraham believed God, and it was reckoned to him as righteousness"* is drawn from Gen 15:6 which was in the context of God's promise to Abraham that he would have a son and that Abraham's generations would be as many as the stars of heaven.

Rom 4:6. David, citing Psalm 32:1, 2 agreed with Paul on righteousness without works, implying works of *Torah*, long before Paul presented his thoughts. *⁶ So also David pronounces a blessing upon the man to whom God*

---

⁶ Gen 12:1ff; 15:1ff; and 17:4.

reckons righteousness <u>apart from works</u> ⁷ "Blessed are those whose iniquities are forgiven, and whose sins are covered; ⁸ blessed is the man against whom the Lord will not reckon his sin."

Rom 4:9-15. Turning to an argument on circumcision, an article of the Mosaic covenant, Paul argues that Abraham was declared righteous before he was circumcised, demonstrating that Abraham's righteousness was not based on his circumcision but on his faith:

⁹ <u>*Is this blessing pronounced only upon the circumcised, or also upon the uncircumcised?*</u> *We say that faith was reckoned to Abraham as righteousness.* ¹⁰ *How then was it reckoned to him? <u>Was it before or after he had been circumcised? It was not after, but before he was circumcised.</u>* ¹¹ *He received circumcision as a sign or seal of the righteousness which he had by faith while he was still uncircumcised. The purpose was to make him the father of all who believe without being circumcised and who thus have righteousness reckoned to them,* ¹² *and likewise the father of the circumcised who are not merely circumcised but also follow the example of the faith which our father Abraham had before he was circumcised.*

¹³ <u>*The promise to Abraham and his descendants, that they should inherit the world, did not come through the law but through the righteousness of faith.*</u> ¹⁴ <u>*If it is the adherents of the law who are to be the heirs, faith is null and the promise is void.*</u> ¹⁵ *For <u>the law brings wrath,</u> <u>but where there is no law there is no transgression.</u>*

Paul's statement, *where there is no law there is no transgression,* harks back to the fact that Paul has previously made, Rom 3:20, that the law defines sin, and later at Rom 7:5-8 that *"apart from the law sin lies dead"*! The NEB translation of Rom 4:15 is a good explanation of this text, *"where there is no law there can be no breach (transgression) of law."*

Rom 4:13-17. Paul developed this argument further by showing that in these promises, *God had promised that Abraham would be the father of many who were not* *descendants according to the law but were descendants according to promise.*

Rom 4:16. The promise to Abraham was not simply that he would become the father of the Jewish nation, but that he would also become the father of the uncircumcised Gentiles who would believe in Him with the faith of Abraham. In this case neither circumcision nor uncircumcision mean anything, see Gal 5:6; 6:14!

> **Gal 5:6**, *"For in Christ Jesus neither circumcision nor uncircumcision is of any avail, but faith working through love."*
>
> ***Gal 6:14**, But far be it from me to glory except in the cross of our Lord Jesus Christ, by which the world has been crucified to me, and I to the world. ¹⁵ For neither circumcision counts for anything, nor uncircumcision, but a new creation.*

It was because no one, Jew or Gentile, *had any moral right* to expect God to keep his creation commitments that *God's faithfulness shines all the brighter*!

Abraham was faithful because he simply trusted God, and he was righteous because he was faithful!

Rom 4:16-25. Paul developed his argument on Abraham by introducing Sarah and the birth of Isaac.

> *¹⁶ That is why it depends on faith, in order that the promise may rest on grace and be guaranteed to all his descendants—not only to the adherents of the law but also to those who share the faith of Abraham, for <u>he is the father of us all</u>, ¹⁷ as it is written, "<u>I have made you the father of many nations</u>"—in the presence of the God in whom he believed, who gives life to the dead and calls into existence the things that do not exist. ¹⁸ <u>In hope he believed against hope, that he should become the father of many nations</u>; as he had been told, "So shall your descendants be." ¹⁹ He <u>did not weaken in faith when he considered his own body, which was as good as dead</u> because he was about a hundred years old, or when he considered <u>the barrenness of</u>*

*Sarah's womb. [20] No distrust made him waver
concerning the promise of God, but he grew strong
in his faith as he gave glory to God, [21] fully
convinced that God was able to do what he had
promised. [22] That is why his faith was "reckoned to
him as righteousness." [23] But the words, "it was
reckoned to him," were written not for his sake
alone, [24] but for ours also. It will be reckoned to us
who believe in him that raised from the dead Jesus
our Lord, [25] who was put to death for our
trespasses and raised for our justification.*

Paul's irrefutable arguments regarding Abraham's righteousness

Paul uses the timeless and favored story of Abraham
and Sarah to make his point that Abraham's righteousness
was not based on Abraham's works of merit, his
circumcision, or his obedience to a Law and *Torah* that lay
only still in Israel's distant 430-year future.

Paul's reasoning regarding Abraham's righteousness
lay in the promises of a faithful and righteous God to a
faithful Gentile traveler from Ur who *trusted* in God and
His promises.

The *Torah* and keeping the Law had nothing to do
with Abraham's righteousness which lay only in his
faithfulness to God!

Chapter 6 - The Results of Justification by Faith in Christ: Rom 5:1-21

Context and Message

In Rom 5 Paul introduces an interesting yet complicated series of arguments to contend that *in Christ, through faith in Christ* Christians are much *better off than Torah seekers*! This is set in contrast to seeking righteousness through the *Torah* Law, for this only leads to conviction, and not redemption. Twice in this pericope Paul uses the statement *more than*, Rom 5:3,10!

At Rom 5:1-11 we learn of the benefits of justification by faith in Christ. We have peace with God and are strengthened by that faith to where we rejoice in sufferings for in Christ we know that suffering will produce endurance, character, and hope!

Faith, hope, and love feature prominently in Paul's theology. Hope in New Testament theology is fixed firmly in the faith Christians have in the resurrection of Jesus and their own future resurrection when Jesus returns. Cf. 1 Thess 4:13-18 which stresses this. The Thessalonian text is not talking about some supposed "rapture" but is encouraging the Christians to have their future hope fixed on Jesus' return.

Paul was aware that life for both Christians and Jews in Rome was not easy. Several Roman historians, among them Suetonius and Tacitus, ca 100 BCE, recorded that Nero was a brutal leader. Tacitus claimed that Nero, the Emperor of Rome at the time Paul was writing, blamed the Christians for the great fire of Rome. Whether Tacitus is correct or not, Nero was not kind to either the Jews or Christians, or to anyone who he saw as a threat to his Caesar-ship. Although trouble with Nero or Rome was not the reason for Paul's epistle, he was nevertheless aware of their struggles under Roman suzerainship and wanted to encourage them and build up their faith in Christ's kingdom and reign.

In a rich apocalyptic pericope at Rom 8:18ff Paul later will touch on the sufferings all people endure in a cruel world: *I consider that the sufferings of this present time are not worth comparing with the glory that is to be revealed to us.* [19] *For the creation waits with eager longing for the revealing of the sons of God;* [20] *for the creation was subjected to futility, not of its own will but by the will of him who subjected it in hope;* [21] *because the creation itself will be set free from its bondage to decay and obtain the glorious liberty of the children of God.*

In our present pericope Paul adds that we are also encouraged by the knowledge that the Holy Spirit has been given to us to strengthen us.

At Rom 5:6f Paul stresses that God always does things at the right time since he is working on a rich plan of redemption through Abraham and in Christ. At Gal 4:4, 5, Paul had noted "but when the time had fully come, God sent forth his Son, born of woman, born under the law, [5] *to redeem those who were under the law, so that we might receive adoption as sons."*

At Rom 5:13-21 Paul introduces a "two-man" metaphor, Adam/Christ, which contrasts the principles of Adam-Law and sin and Christ-faith and justification.

Paul then complicates the issue by introducing a parenthetic anacoluthon at Rom 5:13 that does not end until Rom 5:17. Scholars are divided over where the anacoluthon ends, but we feel that the best ending of the anacoluthon comes at Rom 5:17.

When studying this pericope, read Rom 5:12 and Rom 5:18-21 without Rom 5:13-17 to get Paul's flow of thought.

Then read Rom 5:13-17 to get the point Paul is making.

One man, Adam introduced Law, sin and death, another man, Christ introduced grace, faith, and life. Which man do you want to follow?

The Story of Romans So Far!

Paul begins his discussion by stressing the most important aspect of his theology: *God is a righteous and faithful God* who always does things at the right time!

Paul had presented the narrative of the fall of man and warned the Jews not to condemn the Gentiles while they were themselves breaking their Law and sinning, Rom 1:18-3:20.

He then showed the preeminence of the gospel of Christ and what people need to know before they can understand God's grace. Of utmost importance is a realization that *the whole world is under the power of sin, and the law of Moses is unable to save them.* The purpose of the Law *Torah* was to instruct people regarding the nature of sin, and hold them accountable for sin, Rom 3:9-20, but not to save them.

Having presented the fallen state of all men, Paul argued that since all men have sinned, justification for all men can be found only in the grace of God and faith in Jesus Christ, Rom 3:21-31.

Since the *Torah* Law can save no one, then all men, Jew and Gentile alike, can only be saved and justified *by God's Grace through faith in Jesus Christ.*

God makes no distinction in regard to justification; all men are treated the same!

In answer to perceived questions the Jews might have regarding Paul possibly *dispensing with the (Torah) Law* and negating God's special *calling* and *election* of Israel, Paul argues that in fact he is not destroying the law but upholding it by emphasizing its proper role in God's eternal purpose.

Neither was he refuting the election of Israel by stressing that no one can be justified by *Torah* Law keeping, not even Abraham was saved by faith and not *Torah* Law. God had originally called Abraham and through him and his faithfulness Israel and the nations were to be blessed by God.

In this lesson Paul will demonstrate the superiority of justification by God's grace through faith in Jesus Christ over attempts to be righteous by Torah Law keeping.

Through faith in Christ, we have peace with God.

Rom 5:1-11:

[1] Therefore, since we are justified by faith, we have peace with God through our Lord Jesus Christ. [2] Through him we have obtained access to this grace in which we stand, and we rejoice in our hope of sharing the glory of God. [3] More than that, we rejoice in our sufferings, knowing that suffering produces endurance, [4] and endurance produces character, and character produces hope, [5] and hope does not disappoint us, because God's love has been poured into our hearts through the Holy Spirit which has been given to us.

[6] While we were still weak, at the right time Christ died for the ungodly. [7] Why, one will hardly die for a righteous man—though perhaps for a good man one will dare even to die. [8] But God shows his love for us in that while we were yet sinners Christ died for us. [9] Since, therefore, we are now justified by his blood, much more shall we be saved by him from the wrath of God. [10] For if while we were enemies we were reconciled to God by the death of his Son, much more, now that we are reconciled, shall we be saved by his life. [11] Not only so, but we also rejoice in God through our Lord Jesus Christ, through whom we have now received our reconciliation.

This text is a powerful statement regarding righteousness; *it is by God's grace and faith in Jesus Christ that we can be declared righteous, not by our own effort*!

Notice the word "*therefore*" in the opening sentence of this pericope which ties the point Paul is making back to *the power of our justification, namely, the death, burial, and resurrection of Jesus Christ,* Rom 4:24, 25.

As we have already learned, the *Torah* Law of Moses was not intended to save anyone! The *Torah* Law can only *clarify the nature of sin* and its consequences. *Torah* keeping cannot save anyone who has sinned, and that includes both the Jew and the Gentile!

It took *the loving grace of God and the faithfulness of Jesus in his sacrificial atoning death to save all sinners.* But Jesus' atoning sacrifice was not only for good people, who the Jew thought themselves to be since they followed the *Torah*! But Paul has already demonstrated the Jew had not kept the *Torah* Law, for they had transgressed the *Torah* Law in many ways!

Paul will state at Rom 5:6ff that it was while we all were lost and sinners, both Jew and Gentile that Jesus died to save us. Salvation was not received by works of *Torah*, or any good works, but only by faith in the sacrificial death of Jesus Christ!

The only power to save and justify sinners, which defines all of humanity, is *God's grace and His powerful work in the death and resurrection of Jesus*, and *our faith in Jesus and God's working.*

Rom 5:2. "*Through him* (Jesus) <u>we have obtained access to this grace in which we stand</u>, *and we rejoice in our hope of sharing the glory of God.*"

So, because we understand the power of our justification by faith in Jesus, <u>we have peace with God</u>! All attempts to be justified and have peace with God by our works and our efforts will *only lead to guilt and frustration*, for we will never be able to live perfectly and above sin. It is only by God's gracious loving forgiveness that we can have any peace! *We have access to God's grace only through faith in Jesus Christ*. It is only in God's grace that we can stand firm and have any hope of redemption and share his glory and presence in heaven.

This *peace with God* comes through <u>the access</u> we *have by Jesus Christ into God's grace in which we stand firm*. There is an interesting Greek textual variant in Rom 5:2 that deserves our attention. This variant is well attested in the relevant Greek manuscripts. Both of the major Greek texts we use most often, the Nestle-Aland *Novum Testamentum Graece,* and the Aland/Martini/Metzger *Greek New Testament,* include the variant in some form of "parenthesis." We have an interesting comment by Metzger who summarizes the discussion in his *Textual Commentary of the Greek New Testament.* Metzger observes that the evidence for and against the variant, τῇ πίστει, *by faith,* is equally divided in the best manuscripts, and that the inclusion or deletion of the variant changes little of Paul's point of view since he has already on several occasions claimed that *justification comes only through faith in Jesus Christ.*

Our normal English translation reads *"we have obtained access to this grace."* The variant if included is well in keeping with the theology Paul has been developing in Romans. *It is only through or **by faith in Jesus** that **we have access** into God's grace!*

Rom 5:3-5. Because we understand these principles, we are in *a most advantageous position in Christ.* Notice the expression *"more than that,"* and *"much more,"* Rom 5:9, 10.

We understand that since our hope is in God's love, grace, and mercy *we can have confidence* in God and look on suffering differently. We have *peace with God* and are *strengthened by that faith* to where we *rejoice in sufferings* for Christ because we learn that *faithful suffering produces endurance, and endurance produces character, and character produces hope*!

Christian hope is not some simple pie in the sky hope! It is based in the confidence Christians have in the resurrection of Jesus and his return, and the promise of a future resurrection to be with God and Jesus. On several occasions Paul stressed the role that hope had in his faith and sense of security in Christ. Hope features prominently in the Christian literature, often built on *faith in the future resurrection.* 1 Pet 1:13, 21 and 1 Thess 4:13-18 build on this connection:

1 Pet 1:13. *Therefore gird up your minds, be sober, <u>set your hope fully upon the grace that is coming to you at the revelation of Jesus Christ</u>. [14]As obedient children do not be conformed to the passions of your former ignorance, [15] but as he who called you is holy, be holy yourselves in all your conduct; [16] since it is written, "You shall be holy, for I am holy." [17] And if you invoke as Father him who judges each one impartially according to his deeds, conduct yourselves with fear throughout the time of your exile. [18] You know that you were ransomed from the futile ways inherited from your fathers, not with perishable things such as silver or gold, [19] but with the precious blood of Christ, like that of a lamb without blemish or spot. [20] He was destined before the foundation of the world but was made manifest at the end of the times for your sake. [21] <u>Through him you have confidence in God, who raised him from the dead and gave him glory, so that your faith and hope are in God</u>.*

1 Thess 4:13. *But we would not have you ignorant, brethren, concerning those who are asleep, <u>that you may not grieve as others do who have no hope</u>. [14] For <u>since we believe that Jesus died and rose again</u>, even so, through Jesus, God will bring with him those who have fallen asleep. [15] For this we declare to you by the word of the Lord, that we who are alive, who are left until the coming of the Lord, shall not precede those who have fallen asleep. [16] For the Lord himself will descend from heaven with a cry of command, with the archangel's call, and with the sound of the trumpet of God. <u>And the dead in Christ will rise first</u>; [17] <u>then we who are alive, who are left, shall be caught up together with them in the clouds to meet the Lord in the air; and so we shall always be with the Lord</u>. [18] Therefore comfort one another with these words.*

In our present pericope Paul adds that we are also *encouraged by the knowledge that the Holy Spirit has been given to us to strengthen us.* Note Eph 3:14ff:

For this reason I bow my knees before the Father, [15] from whom every family in heaven and on earth is named, [16] that according to the riches of his glory he may grant you to be strengthened with might through his Spirit in the inner man, [17] and that Christ may dwell in your hearts through faith; that you, being rooted and grounded in love, [18] may have power to comprehend with all the saints what is the breadth and length and height and depth, [19] and to know the love of Christ which surpasses knowledge, that you may be filled with all the fulness of God.

[20] Now to him who by the power at work within us is able to do far more abundantly than all that we ask or think, [21] to him be glory in the church and in Christ Jesus to all generations, for ever and ever. Amen.

Paul will also discuss the role of the Holy Spirit in the Christian's life at Rom 8:26ff:

Likewise the Spirit helps us in our weakness; for we do not know how to pray as we ought, but the Spirit himself intercedes for us with sighs too deep for words. [27] And he who searches the hearts of men knows what is the mind of the Spirit, because the Spirit intercedes for the saints according to the will of God.

Rom 5:6. *At the right time Christ died for the ungodly.* Since before the foundation of the world God has had a plan of redemption and justification in mind, and has been working on this, cf. Eph 1:3-14. God's call and promises to Abraham were an incisive part of God's eternal plan!

Paul builds on this by stressing that God always does things *at the right time* since he has been working on a rich plan of redemption through Abraham, Moses, and now in Christ. Note Paul's statement at Gal 4:4, 5, *"But when the time had fully come, God sent forth his Son, born of woman, born under the law, [5] to redeem those who were under the law, so that we might receive adoption as sons."*

128

Rom 5:6-10. Since when we were sinners Christ was willing to die for us, and God was willing to forgive us, *how much more* that we are now in a covenant relationship with God as his children, through our faith in Jesus, will God be willing to forgive us and justify us?

> *⁶ While we were still weak, at the right time Christ died for the ungodly. ⁷ Why, one will hardly die for a righteous man—though perhaps for a good man one will dare even to die. ⁸ But God shows his love for us in that <u>while we were yet sinners Christ died for us</u>. ⁹ Since, therefore, we are now justified by his blood, much more shall we be saved by him from the wrath of God. ¹⁰ For if while we were enemies we were reconciled to God by the death of his Son, much more, now that we are reconciled, shall we be saved by his life.*

Rom 5:11. *"Not only so, but we also rejoice in God through our Lord Jesus Christ, through whom we have now received our reconciliation."*

In Torah Law keeping, which defines sin and indicts us for sinning, there can be no joy, only guilt, sadness, and frustration!

So, in contrast to *Torah* keepers made aware of their sin, Christians rejoice because of their reconciliation with God, having experienced his forgiveness!

Rom 5:12-25. *Death* through Adam; *Life* through Christ

> *¹² Therefore as sin came into the world <u>through one man</u> <u>and death through sin</u>, and so death spread to all men because all men sinned— ¹³ sin indeed was in the world before the law was given, <u>but sin is not counted where there is no law</u>. ¹⁴ Yet death reigned from Adam to Moses, even over those whose sins were not like the transgression of Adam, who was a type of the one who was to come.*
>
> *¹⁵ But the free gift is not like the trespass. For if many died through one man's trespass, much more*

*have the grace of God and the free gift in the grace of that **one man** Jesus Christ abounded for many.* [16] *And the free gift is not like the effect of that **one man's sin**. For the judgment following one trespass brought condemnation, but the free gift following many trespasses brings justification.* [17] *If, because of **one man's trespass**, death reigned through that one man, much more will those who receive the abundance of grace and the free gift of righteousness reign in life through the **one man** Jesus Christ.*

[18] *Then as **one man's** trespass led to condemnation for all men, so **one man's** act of righteousness leads to acquittal and life for all men.* [19] *For as by **one man's disobedience** many were made sinners, so by **one man's obedience** many will be made righteous.* [20] *Law came in, to increase the trespass; but <u>where sin increased, grace abounded all the more,</u>* [21] *so that, <u>as sin reigned in death, grace also might reign through righteousness to eternal life through Jesus Christ our Lord</u>.*

Because we are not always sensitive to early Christian and later Jewish thinking and tradition, this passage has been difficult for us to understand! With a little help, thinking like a Christian in Paul's day, we can make some sense out of it!

The ***contrast*** between ***what Adam did*** *and what resulted from this*, and ***what Jesus did*** *and what resulted from this*, is a **key to understanding the passage**; see also a similar contrast of the Adam/Christ metaphor at 1 Cor 15:20-22, *"But in fact Christ has been raised from the dead, the first fruits of those who have fallen asleep.* [21] *For as by a man came death, by a man has come also the resurrection of the dead.* [22] *For as in Adam all die, so also in Christ shall all be made alive."*

We need to understand that the Jew did not differentiate between spiritual death and physical death as though they were two different deaths! For the Jew, death meant *both physical and spiritual ruin and loss*, which resulted in *the cessation of life* or *total ruin* of everything they stand for, *especially their standing and relationship with God.*

The discussion of the Hebrew understanding of death is difficult since the literature of the Old Testament covers a long range of history and Ancient and Near East influences.

K. H. Richards, in *The Anchor Bible Dictionary,* observes:

> On the other hand, the threefold senses domesticate the Hebrew Bible perceptions of death. *A focus on biological cessation undercuts the dynamic intersection of death with life.* Israel, maybe because of its history, is more at home in understanding death through all its faces as *a radical challenge to life. The tripartite understanding unnecessarily isolates Israel's developing monotheistic perspective from its ANE neighbors' polytheistic understandings, which influenced Israel's ideas more than is frequently suggested.* Death can be understood and accepted as a natural part of God's order, *but the people of the Hebrew Bible experienced individual and communal death, <u>which was far more pervasive than biological cessation</u>.*[1]

Elwell, in the *Baker Encyclopedia of the Bible,* observes:

> Death, although a natural ending to life, was never viewed as pleasant. Death cut one off from human community *as well as from the presence and service of God.* God may offer comfort in the face of death (Ps 73:23–28), *but he is rarely portrayed as present with the dead,* and that only in later biblical literature (Ps 139:8). For that reason,

---

[1] Richards, K. H., "Death: Old Testament," *The Anchor Yale Bible Dictionary*, vol. 2, p. 110.

suicide is rare in the OT (1 Sam 31:4, 5; 2 Sam 17:23). *Death was never viewed as the threshold to a better life.*[2]

In the New Testament period death is often portrayed in the context of a certain punishment for sin, and in the light of the resurrection proclaimed by Jesus and the apostolic teachers as a *life after death in eternal punishment in the absence of God.*

For the Christians in Paul's day *death* stood for the *total eternal absence of God* and *everything good.*

Life stood for the defeat of death and victory in the presence of God in a transformed existence with God.

Paul reflected on this at 1 Cor 15:51-57:

Lo! I tell you a mystery. We shall not all sleep, but we shall all be changed, [52] in a moment, in the twinkling of an eye, at the last trumpet. For the trumpet will sound, and the dead will be raised imperishable, and we shall be changed. [53] For this perishable nature must put on the imperishable, and this mortal nature must put on immortality. [54] When the perishable puts on the imperishable, and the mortal puts on immortality, then shall come to pass the saying that is written:

"Death is swallowed up in victory."

"O death, where is thy victory? O death, where is thy sting?" [56] The sting of death is sin, and the power of sin is the law. [57] But thanks be to God, who gives us the victory through our Lord Jesus Christ.

I also like John's statement at Rev 21:1-4:

Then I saw a new heaven and a new earth; for the first heaven and the first earth had passed away, and the sea (in Revelation, the source of evil) *was no more. [2] And I saw the holy city, new Jerusalem, coming down out of heaven from God, prepared as a bride adorned for her husband; [3] and I heard a loud voice from the throne saying, "Behold, the dwelling of God is with*

---

[2] Elwell, W. A., & Beitzel, B. J., "Death," *Baker Encyclopedia of the Bible*, vol. 1, p. 603.

men. He will dwell with them, and they shall be his
people, and God himself will be with them; [4] *he will*
wipe away every tear from their eyes, and death shall
be no more, neither shall there be mourning nor crying
nor pain any more, for the former things have passed
away."

The image of resurrection proclaimed by Jesus and the apostolic teachers promised a future life with God and Christ and all of the saints of the past—not as death, but as life with God; eternal life being the kind of life lived by God. Death was seen as total ruin in the absence of God. Life was seen as being in the presence of God and enjoying his life.

In our present text, Rom 5:12ff, Paul describes death via a metaphor of a choice of Adam/Christ, death/life.

Rom 5:12ff. Paul develops his thought in his *two-man metaphor* contrasting *Adam and Jesus!*

One man represents for all that we are humanly speaking, all that we are according to the flesh — *Adam. Adam, the "old man."*

One man stands for all that we are by God's grace and faithfulness, all that we are according to the Spirit — *Jesus. Jesus, the "new man."*

Death and Life; Adam and Christ!

Paul begins with the simple remark, well known by the Jew, that *sin came into the world through one man, Adam.*

Rom 5:12. Because of the sinful nature we all have, death passed to all men, simply *because, eph ho,* all men sinned!

One way of translating the Greek *eph ho* here could be, *"in view of the fact that,"* or *"in as much as,"* or *"since all men sinned."*

The expression *"and so,* ἵνα ὥσπερ, death spread" can be translated as *"in this manner,"* or *"even so."*

The big question we are considering here is how we understand death. We examined death in some detail

133

above, but here we need to have another glimpse at this topic.

Does death refer to physical death or spiritual death?

The answer is **yes, to both**, or even more. In the Judeo/Christian tradition ca Paul's era, death refers to *total ruin*, both physical and spiritual, in the absence of any relationship with God!

What Paul is in effect saying here is, "*Sin came into the world through one man, Adam, and death,* (the total ruin of man) *came about through sin. In this manner all men experience total ruin through sin. Total ruin became a part of human experience because all men sin*"!

The point Paul is making is simple. "*Follow the example of Adam, choose sin, and the result will be the total ruin of everything in your life.*"

Rom 5:13 introduces an interesting new argument! A challenging comment by Paul here is tricky; "*sin indeed was in the world before the law was given, <u>sin is not counted where there is no law.</u>*"

Notice that in all of our major translations verse 13 introduces a parenthetical, *anacoluthon,*[3] statement:

The KJV puts it in an open bracketed *parentheses - "(For until the law sin was in the world:...)."* The KJV ends the parenthetical statement at the end of verse 17. This view is particularly good and we will come back to this later!

The NIV, the ASV, the NASV, and the RSV begin verse 13 with an "m dash" — indicating that a new parenthetical idea, or *anacoluthon*, is being introduced. The problem is that several of our major translations do not indicate where the parenthetical statement ends!

---

[3] *Anacoluthon,* is derived from the Greek word *akólouthos,* which means "lacking sequence." It is a stylistic device defined as a syntactic deviation, and interruption within a sentence from one structure to another. In this interruption, the expected sequence of grammar is absent. The grammatical flow of sentences is interrupted in order to begin more sentences.

The ASV, like the KJV, carries the paragraph through to the end of verse 17. I agree with this structuring of the *anacoluthon* ending at Rom 5:17. Rom 5:18 begins a new paragraph on the topic

Carefully examine the translation you use, taking it for granted that you use one of the major English translations, and observe where the parenthetical anacoluthon section begins and ends!

A comment or two from some scholars casts some light on this difficult *anacoluthon*. In this citation by Dunn, I have edited Dunn who citing Raisanen, *Paul*, 146 n. 91, observes:

> "The statement ἁμαρτία οὐκ ἐλλογεῖται (imputation) is a mere verbal expedient without any real significance. In this statement the issue is not between man and sin, but between sin and the law. Paul tries to show that, as regards sin and the law, the coming of the law makes a difference to the imputation of sin. But sin was there before the Law and men were held accountable for sin even before the Law was given" (Räisänen, *Paul*, 146 n. 91).[4]

Dunn continues:

> The objection centers not on sin, because it was through sin that death entered (v 12). It centers rather on the nexus between sin and the law: *that sin is not counted except as a breach of the law; and therefore in the absence of the law no acts worthy of death could have happened.* Paul could have met this objection by arguing as he did in chaps. 1 and 2 that those outside the law have a knowledge of God and of his will in terms of which they will be judged (see on 2:14), or by arguing that the law itself was already known in whole or in part already in the garden (see on 7:7). That he chooses not to do so, when he was prepared to take up such ideas elsewhere in the same letter, must be

---

[4] Dunn, *Romans 1–8*, vol. 38A, p. 274.

significant ... The awkwardness of 5:13 is to be explained in large part therefore by the fact that it is like 3:1–8: it foreshadows lines of argument and emphases which Paul is not yet ready to develop.[5]

In literature a parenthetical statement can be lifted out of the body of the pericope without doing harm to the narrative and can then be considered as a separate statement commenting on the main statement!

If this is correct, then the major thought Paul is developing runs like this:

Rom 5:12 *"Sin came into the world by one man, Adam, and death was introduced by sin. In this manner all men died because all men sinned --- vs. 18 Then as one man's trespass led to condemnation for all men..."*

The thought is that *one man, Adam introduced sin and death*, and one man, Adam who sinned, brought in condemnation for all men *since all men follow Adam and sin*!

Paul then makes his contrast between Adam and Jesus.

Sin and death came in through Adam. You will die if you follow Adam and sin! It is in this part of the narrative that the *Torah* which Paul will claim kills one operates.

Life and righteousness came in by one man, Jesus. You can have life and righteousness if you follow (believe or have faith) in Jesus. Similarly, it is in this part of the narrative that faith in Jesus operates.

Rom 5:13-17. The parenthetical anacoluthon argument of Adam/sin and Jesus/life

Now we can go back to the parenthetical passage! Remember that parenthetical or anacoluthon material or arguments are *intended to explain the meaning of a statement made earlier*!

In this parenthetical argument, Paul explains relationship of Adam and sin, and death consequently passing on to all men *because all men follow Adam and sin*!

---

[5] Dunn, *Romans 1–8*, vol. 38A, p. 275.

136

Sin was naturally in the world before the law was given (take for example Noah and the flood). We know God held man accountable for sin before the law was given (take Cain for example, and also Sodom and Gomorrah).

The point is that sin can be, and was counted, even where there was no Torah or Mosaic law!

But Paul now adds this confusing point that where there is no law, sin is not counted!

Is this a contradiction? Surely not!

It might not be contradictory, but it is confusing if one does not follow that Paul is arguing about *the benefits of being in Christ! In Christ sin and the law have no power or imputation.*

Now for the Christian after *faith in Christ*, cf. Gal 3:16-39, there *is* no power of imputation by Law in the sense that the power of the Law to kill through sin has been taken away in Christ!

Regarding Paul's argument, which he is only beginning to develop, and which will be more fully developed in the chapters that follow, we might ask, *"Paul, just where is there no legal imputation by Law, or accountability to Law for sin?"*

Paul's answer would be, *"There is no power of the Law and its consequences of imputation for those in Christ, for in Christ Christians are dead to the Law, released from slavery to the Law!"*

A major point that Paul will make in Rom 8 is that through Christ's death we are freed from the demands of the Law so that in Christ the just requirements of the Law might be fulfilled in us." Paul will argue in Rom 8:1-4 that *what the law could not do*—that is free the sinner from the principle of sin and death and bring them into a covenant relationship with God—*Christ has done for us!*

Humanity between Adam and Moses followed Adam's choice to sin—their own choice—and his condemnation became their condemnation.

The addition of the covenant Law at Sinai was no cure for the human problem with sin and death! The Law was to control sin, not forgive sin!

Rom 5:20. In fact Paul adds, *"The law* (Torah) *came in to increase trespass!"* That is, the *Torah* clarifies the nature of sin and trespass! Cf. the discussion below at Rom 5:20.

At this point Paul is interested only in *summarizing* the human situation of being in Adam and under the Law *without the blessings of being in Christ.*

In Adam humanity is under condemnation and has earned death, but while sin was working so was God's grace which will now be seen in Christ, Rom 6-8!

Rom 5:13-17. Paul contrasts the gifts and legacy of Adam and Christ!

Paul states that *the free gift of God's grace* is not like the "gift" *earned* by following Adam and sin!

*The gift of God's grace in Christ is **life and justification**.*

The *"gift"* of Adam, and of the *Torah* is *sin and death*!

Adam was the *prototype of sinful man*. Adam by his loss of trust in God and disobedience introduced sin and death. Similar action even under the *Torah* Law brings the same result! *Follow Adam and you will die!*

Christ is the *prototype of a new man—a man of faith and obedience! Follow Christ in faith and you have life and righteousness*!

With the introduction of the *Torah*, Adam's sin and the human situation was seen to be even worse than at the first realized, but God's grace responded to the deteriorating human situation by introducing grace in Christ, cf. Rom 5:20-21 below.

Choose who you want to follow; follow Adam and sin, and the *Torah will bring death*!

Or *follow Christ and God's grace*, where the *Torah* Law since Christ has no power, where faith in Christ reigns *which brings righteousness and life*!

Gal 3:16-19:

⁷This is what I mean: the law, which came four hundred and thirty years afterward, does not annul a covenant previously ratified by God, so as to make the promise void. ¹⁸ For if the inheritance is by the law, it is no longer by promise; but God gave it to Abraham by a promise.

¹⁹ Why then the law? It was added because of transgressions, till the offspring should come to whom the promise had been made; and it was ordained by angels through an intermediary. ²⁰ Now an intermediary implies more than one; but God is one.

Rom 5:18-21. Paul returns to a two-man Adam/Christ contrast at Rom 5:12.

Remember, Rom 5:13-17 is an independent discussion introduced by Paul into the two-man Adam/Christ contrast. Now we pick up Paul's primary argument!

¹⁸ Then as <u>one man's trespass led to condemnation for all men</u>, so <u>one man's act of righteousness leads to acquittal and life for all men</u>. ¹⁹ For as by <u>one man's disobedience</u> many were made sinners, so by <u>one man's obedience many will be made righteous</u>. ²⁰ Law came in, <u>to increase the trespass</u>; but <u>where sin increased, grace abounded all the more</u>, ²¹ so that, as sin reigned in death, <u>grace also might reign through righteousness to eternal life through Jesus Christ our Lord</u>.

The key to resolving Paul's argument of Rom 5, however, is this *contrast of Adam/Christ. Christians must choose whom they will follow;* follow Adam by disobeying God in sin where the *Torah* reigns or follow Christ by obeying God and Christ through faith where Christ reigns!

Rom 5:20, 21. "*Law came in, <u>to increase the trespass</u>* …" introduces another interesting misunderstanding or conundrum.

If the *Torah* Law was given *simply to make sin worse,* as Rom 5:20 seems to indicate in a superficial reading, as our English translation may seem to say, "*Law came in, <u>to increase</u> the trespass,*" we do have a problem of sorts! Was

139

it simply the purpose of the *Torah* Law to show the result of sin or the purpose of sin? Was there possibly concealed in this comment a statement of purpose? Obviously, the *Torah* had a deeper purpose than simply to kill or produce death. *We will see that Paul intends to say that the purpose or the end result of the Torah was to define real life by clarifying the nature of sin.*

In the Greek, as in this verse, we have a *hina* clause with an aorist subjunctive verb, ἵνα πλεονάσῃ τὸ παράπτωμα, stressing *in order to* increase sin *Torah stresses the purpose* of the Law rather than *simply the result of the* Law.[6] The subjunctive verb is more clearly stated as *that which is supposed to really take place.* Here the *hina* clause informs us that the *Torah* Law had *the purpose of clarifying or amplifying* the trespass or nature of sin **in order that grace may abound**!

For a comparative *hina* clause see Rom 11:32, ἵνα τοὺς πάντας ἐλεήσῃ ˝*For God has consigned all men to disobedience, (hina, in order) that he may have mercy upon all.˝ The knowledge of sin demonstrates the mercy and purpose of God!*

Although on the surface Paul has sounded negative about the *Torah* Law, in reality he has been positive since his purpose was not against the *Torah* Law but against a false or incorrect use of the *Torah* Law! Paul's purpose was to clarify the real role of *Torah* as instructing Jews how to live *in a righteous relationship with God,* and *not*

---

[6] Zodhiates states regarding a *hina* clause; "ἵνα *hína*; a conjunction. *That, so that, for the purpose of, construed usually with a subjunctive,* seldom with the optative, often with the indicative. *marking the end, purpose.* Also used to indicate the cause for, or on account of which anything is done. It can be translated, "*to the end that,*" "*in order that something might (or may) be.*" It may also be used simply to indicate a happening, event or result of anything, or *that in which the action terminates. Hína* can be translated "so that it was, is, or will be." (I) *Indicating purpose,* end ... in which case we call it a telic conjunction. *It marks the final end, purpose, or cause* and can be translated "*to the end that,*" "*in order that,*" ..."

how to get into a right relationship with God. Ever since Abraham, a relationship of righteousness with God had been based on a *faithful obedience* to God.

Chapter 7 – United with God in Christ
The Fulfillment of *Torah*: Rom 6:1-7:25

Context and Message

Paul discusses the appropriate use of the Torah Law, arguing that failure to understand the proper meaning and use of the Torah Law leads to sin and death since the Torah Law was not intended to save the sinner from transgression of the Law, but to clarify the real nature of sin and sin's consequences for those who transgress the Law.

Rom 6:1-14. Christians are united with Christ in baptism.

This is a great text for understanding what goes on in the Christian experience in baptism.

<u>First</u>, in addition to understanding baptism as the point of obedient faith for salvation, Acts 2:37, 38, Paul explains that baptism is the action by which one is united with Christ through faith in God and his saving activity in Jesus Christ. Paul enlarges on this by stressing that baptism is where one is united with the death and resurrection of Jesus Christ. In baptism one dies with Christ and is symbolically raised with him to begin a new life, a new life in Christ and not the Torah Law.

<u>Second</u>, being united with Christ as their new Lord Christians no longer allow sin to reign in our lives. Sin must have no dominion over the Christian's life. The Christian's life is dedicated to a new Torah Law, Jesus Christ. Since Christians are no longer under the Torah Law, but in Christ they live under God's grace and loving forgiveness as his children.

Rom 6:15-23. Christians in Christ are slaves to righteousness, not to the Torah Law. The wage of sin is death, but the free gift of God is eternal life in Christ Jesus our Lord.

Paul contrasts the life where sin reigns. It reigns in the life governed by the Torah Law which he will enlarge upon in Rom 7. It is a life destined for death. The life in Christ under the grace of God offers salvation, sanctification (ἁγιασμός, *hagiasmós [1]), and eternal life[2] which is life with God. Eternal life is a life emphasizing God's kind of life, a quality of life not intending so much duration of time but divine quality.*

Having been delivered from sinning due to their human propensity to sin, which the Torah should have taught and explained resulted in death, the baptized Christian—now united with and dedicated to Christ—is no longer a slave to sin but is now a slave to God and Christ. In Christ, being set free from the life-crippling power of sin, the baptized Christian is a slave to righteousness, which is a life in a right relationship with God through faith in what God is doing in Christ, and not through faith in the Toran Law.

This does not mean that the Christian will be perfect, only that they have been freed from the controlling power of sin which would kill them, or which would bring their lives to total ruin. Rather than fixing their life to the Torah Law, which they constantly break, Rom 2:17ff, and which condemns them, they fix their life in faith in Christ and what God is doing for them in Christ, that is, forgiving them, saving them, declaring them not guilty, and therefore righteous, in a right relationship with God.

Rom 7:1-6 Paul's marriage analogy.

We need to note that this pericope on marriage law follows immediately on Paul's point that the baptized Christian had died to the Torah and has been freed to a bond with the Torah! To be tied to the Torah and be baptized and tied to Christ was equal to living in adultery!

Scholars are divided as to whether the marriage law Paul discusses is civil marriage law or marriage under the Jewish Torah Law. It would work with both options, but it seems best in the context of what Paul is discussing in Romans that he had in mind the Torah laws on marriage

---

[1] Zodhiates, ἁγιασμός, *hagiasmós* … to sanctify, sanctification, translated "holiness" … separation *for* God, consecrated or dedicated *to* God.

[2] Zodhiates, αἰώνιος *aiŏnios* … Eternal, perpetual, belonging to the *aiŏn* … to time in its duration, constant, abiding. When referring to eternal life, it means the life which is God's and hence it is not affected by the limitations of time. *Aiŏnios* is specially predicated on the saving blessings of divine revelation, denoting those things which are not transitory.

144

which both the Jewish Christians and Jews would understand, and which a Roman Christian would be able to follow. To set this in a New Testament context, Matthew records that Jesus was challenged by the Jewish Pharisees, Mat 19:3ff, regarding Jewish marriage laws indicating that a Jew would be familiar with the Torah laws on marriage.

Paul's point was that when a death occurred in a marriage the bond of marriage was broken, and the freed person could marry again. However, Paul gives the analogy an interesting twist! In Paul's argument the baptized Christian had died with Christ and therefore was no longer tied to the marriage law and free to marry again! An interesting switch! For a Christian to claim to be tied to the Torah, which was what some Jewish Christians were calling for, meant that being married to Christ and the Torah at the same time was adultery!

It is interesting to note that twice for emphasis Paul speaks of living in adultery if one seeks to be tied to the Torah Law and married to Christ in baptism!

Rom 7:7-12. The Law is good, spiritual, and holy, but if used incorrectly is lethal—it will kill you!

Paul explains that it is sin working with the Torah Law that kills one, not the Torah Law on its own. Using the Torah Law as a means of justification will not unite one with God but will only separate one from God. The Torah Law identifies sin, indicts one of sin, and condemns one for sin, resulting in death or total ruin.

In the Jewish tradition, death used metaphorically was not simply physical death or spiritual death, but both or more; it meant total ruin and total separation from God.

Since the Torah came from God it was good, spiritual, and holy with a spiritual dimension. However, like many health medications when abused it can have an opposite negative result. In the case of the Torah, which is essentially good, it will kill you when used inappropriately, because working with sin will separate you from God!

Rom 7:13-25. Paul reflects on a personal and human dimension.

Representing the human condition, Paul personifies his argument. The rhetorical *I* which Paul repeatedly uses here in this pericope, "*I am carnal, sold under sin*" demonstrates a

*universal principle. All honest Jewish people with a sensitivity
to doing right would recognize their own weakness and
failure. They struggle with Torah laws and know they
repeatedly fail to reach the standard of Torah righteousness.*

*Paul's expression, "Wretched man that I am! Who will
deliver me from this body of death?* [25] *Thanks be to God
through Jesus Christ our Lord" opens the door for another
amazing Pauline theological pericope, Rom 8:1-39! Paul's
answer, "It is God in and through Jesus Christ who delivers
us from the consequences of sin!"*

The message of Rom 6

If Paul had put the name Adam at the head of one
ledger, and the name Christ at the head of another, and
listed under them what they both stood for, *sin and death*
would be in the *Adam* list; *life and righteousness* would be
on the other list under *Christ*.

That should puzzle no one, not even a Jew!

*However, it's when Paul puts the Torah Law in the
Adam list that questions fly, and blood pressure rises!*

This is precisely the kind of thing that Jews found
unbearable. It seemed to the Jew that Paul was confused
regarding the *Torah* Law's *role* and *purpose*.

The Jew insisted that the *Torah* Law had brought life
to Israel and kept Israel from sin, and now here we have
Paul claiming that *Torah* Law *only clarified sin and
brought death*, cf. Rom 7:7-12.

Rom 5:20. Paul had claimed that the *Torah* Law was
given to *increase the trespass* or *the knowledge and nature*
of sin, which to the Jew seemed to speak ill of the *Torah* in
that it put the *Torah* on the side of clarifying sin rather than
removing sin! To the pious Jew it seemed that Paul was
arguing that the *Torah* Law only meant death, not life!

In the Jew's mind, if sin reigned through death and the
Torah Law was only given to *increase* or *clarify* the
trespass, then the *Torah* Law must be *anti-life and pro-
death*!

146

But Paul had said at Rom 5:17; 5:20-21 that where *trespass* occurred sin was compounded and clarified by the *Torah* Law. Paul claimed however that *God's faithful grace* was *more than a match* for this, Rom 5:17; 20-21.

For the Jewish mind, this seemed to introduce conflicting and confusing conclusions! *Paul and his doctrine are simply confused*!

If increased sin resulted in increased grace and therefore demonstrated more glory for God, *the logical and right thing to do would be to sin more so that God would get more glory*! Μὴ γένοιτο, *mē genoito*, *"no, no, no, do not think like this"*!

After all, the Jew might argue, that's what people are to live for—*to bring glory to God*!

To the Jew it began to look like Paul despised the *Torah* Law by making it a *"Torah of sin and death Law"*!

To the *obtuse and stubborn* Jew, Paul appeared to be *making sinning a service to God by which God gets more glory*.

Paul's views were becoming a serious and confusing situation!

However, Paul was about to deny and correct this thinking in Rom 6!

Paul's views were a serious challenge to the troubled Jewish mind! So Paul opens Rom 6 with this question, *"What shall we say then? Are we to continue sin that grace may abound?"*

Rom 6 - The baptized believer's response to grace

The following material in this lesson, Rom 6:1-7:25, does not deal directly with the *dynamic* of righteousness, or *the power to overcome sin*, although Paul will mention that.

Paul was more concerned with the resultant *obligation* of the *new man* now *declared righteous* by faith in Christ and consequently freed from *Torah* demands.

Should the man now declared righteous by God by faith live in sin and despise the righteous requirement of the *Torah* so that grace may abound, Rom 6:1? Surely not!

Paul responded to this radical thought with a resounding, μὴ γένοιτο, *"by no means"* or *"no not, never, never, never"*! Paul had already addressed this thinking, Rom 3:8, *"their condemnation is just,"* and Rom 3:31, *"Do we overthrow the law by this faith? Μὴ γένοιτο **By no means**! On the contrary we uphold the law."*

Later in Rom 8:3-4 Paul will pursue this thought by arguing that *Christ had died to condemn sin and sinful flesh*. Here, however, he lays out his fundamental views of defeating sin in baptism into Christ and being united with Christ in his victory over sin!

Rom 6:1-14. Baptism symbolically transfers one into Christ

Paul opens this pericope with the statement, *do you not know*? In a reminder for the Roman Christians Paul discussed what *had happened* to those *who through faith in Jesus had been baptized*. Baptism connects one to Christ, not the *Torah*, or *transfers one into Christ*. Paul's opening statement indicates that *they should already have known this*, but in case they had *not fully realized what had happened to them in baptism*, Paul now introduces one of the strongest and most meaningful discussions of baptism we have in the New Testament, Rom 6:1-14. Notice in the terms Paul uses and how *firm* and *positive* he is in this text; *since, certainty, we believe, must consider*:

> *What shall we say then? Are we to continue in sin that grace may abound? ² <u>By no means</u>! How can we who died to sin still live in it? ³ <u>Do you not know</u> that all of us who <u>have been baptized into Christ Jesus were baptized into his death</u>? ⁴ <u>We were buried therefore with him by baptism into death, so that as Christ was raised from the dead by the glory of the Father, we too might walk in newness of life</u>.*

*⁵ For if or **since**,* (εἰ with the perfect indicative verb γεγόναμεν³) *we have been united with him in a death like his, we shall **certainly** be united with him in a resurrection like his. ⁶ We **know** that our old self was crucified with him so that the sinful body might be destroyed, and we might no longer be enslaved to sin. ⁷ For he who has died is freed from sin. ⁸ But if (**since**) we have died with Christ, we **believe** that we shall also live with him. ⁹ For we **know** that Christ being raised from the dead will never die again; death no longer has dominion over him. ¹⁰ The death he died he died to sin, once for all, but the life he lives he lives to God. ¹¹ So you also **must consider** yourselves dead to sin and alive to God in Christ Jesus.*

¹² Let not sin therefore (Μὴ … βασιλευέτω, indicates a strong qualified negation with the present *imperative, hortatory* verb βασιλευέτω) *reign in your mortal bodies, to make you obey their passions. ¹³ Do not yield* (μηδὲ, disjunctive negative conjunction) *your members to sin as instruments of wickedness, but yield* (again a present *hortatory imperative*) *yourselves to God as men who have been brought from death to life, and your members to God as instruments of righteousness. ¹⁴ For sin will have no dominion* (future indicative verb) *over you, since* (*since* is implied by the strong negative Greek that follows οὐ γάρ ἐστε) *you are not under law but under grace.*

WOW! What a powerful pericope! Strong *hortative imperative* verbs making a powerful statement about baptism!

It is interesting to note that whenever Paul addresses baptism, as here in Romans, he speaks positively in a *hortative imperative manner* to those *who have been baptized* explaining to them what baptism should mean to

---

³ Greek syntax rule, εἰ with an indicative mood verb introduces a strong clause of certainty, not probability.

them! This is clearly the case when Paul addresses Christians regarding baptism, cf. 1 Cor 12:12, 13; Col 2:12, 3:1-17; Gal 3:26, 27.

Here in Romans, Paul obviously has both Jewish and Gentile Christians in mind—*they should know this* about baptism!

For more detailed study on baptism in the New Testament we recommend the following studies on the topic of baptism; Everett Fergusson, *Baptism in the Early Church: History, Theology, and Liturgy in the First Five Centuries, 2009*; George W. Beasley Murray, *Baptism in the New Testament*, 1973; Jack Cottrell, *Baptism a Biblical Study*, 1990.

In Rom 6:3-7 Paul makes the following important comments on baptism:

You are *baptized into Christ*, see also Gal 3:26, 27.

You were also *baptized into Christ's death* which is where atonement for sin took place.

In baptism we are *buried with Christ into death*, we die with Christ to our old life.

In baptism we *are raised with Christ* because of the power of his resurrection to a new life in Christ.

After baptism *we walk (live) in newness of life*, not just a new life, but in a condition of newness.

Since we are united with Christ in a death like his we shall also be united with him in a resurrection like his.

A major point is that in baptism we are united with Christ; we experience in Christ his death, we experience in Christ his resurrection.

Our old man of sin is crucified with Christ so that our sinful nature is dead and destroyed so we are no longer enslaved to sin, Rom 3:9, under the power of sin.

The net result of this we find in Rom 6:8-11, "*So you also must consider yourselves dead to sin and alive to God in Christ Jesus.*"

The point Paul was making is that because Christians have been *united with Christ through baptism, Christians must no longer live under the control of sin*, and *no longer make excuses for sin based on the grace of God they enjoy in Christ!*

Rom 6:15-23. Christians under grace are no longer slaves to sin!

> [15] *What then? Are we to sin because we are not under law but under grace? By no means! [16] Do you not know that if you yield yourselves to any one as obedient slaves, you are slaves of the one whom you obey, either of sin, which leads to death, or of obedience, which leads to righteousness? [17] But thanks be to God, that you who were once slaves of sin have become obedient from the heart to the standard of teaching to which you were committed, [18] and, having been set free from sin, have become slaves of righteousness. [19] I am speaking in human terms, because of your natural limitations. For just as you once yielded your members to impurity and to greater and greater iniquity, so now yield your members to righteousness* (a right relationship with God through Jesus Christ) for *sanctification* (ἁγιασμόν, *dedication, commitment to holiness*).
>
> [20] *When you were slaves of sin, you were free in regard to righteousness. [21] But then what return did you get from the things of which you are now ashamed? The end of those things is death. [22] But now that you have been set free from sin and have become slaves of God, the return you get is sanctification and its end, eternal life. [23] For the wages of sin is death, but the free gift of God is eternal life in Christ Jesus our Lord.*

Since the Roman Christians had been obedient from the heart to that form of doctrine to which they had been committed, namely baptism, they should no longer be slaves to sin regardless of the *Torah* Law! *Christ becomes the definition of righteousness, not Torah law!*

In the context of Rom 6 *the obedience from the heart to the form of doctrine they had received* was a direct reference to *baptism*, which certainly based on faith, was

151

obedience from the heart, or *an obedient faith*, Rom 1:5; 16:26. Cf 1 Pet 3:18ff:

> [18] *For Christ also died for sins once for all, the righteous for the unrighteous, that he might bring us to God, being put to death in the flesh but made alive in the spirit;* [19] *in which he went and preached to the spirits in prison,* [20] *who formerly did not obey, when God's patience waited in the days of Noah, during the building of the ark, in which a few, that is, eight persons, were saved through water.* [21] <u>*Baptism, which corresponds to this, now saves you, not as a removal of dirt from the body but as an appeal to God for a clear conscience, through the resurrection of Jesus Christ,*</u> [22] *who has gone into heaven and is at the right hand of God, with angels, authorities, and powers subject to him.*

Obviously, Jewish concerns for the *Torah* would again surface, so Paul again resorted to a *diatribe* style of discussion in which he introduces an *interlocutor* who would pose a question on behalf of others, and then he answers the question. *"What then? Are we to sin because we are not under law but under grace? By no means!"*

The strident μὴ γένοιτο *"by no means"* at Rom 6:15, which we have previously encountered on several occasions, again demonstrates the *firmness* of Paul's response to the *supposed concern and questions* that arose in the minds of some.

A natural question rephrased in terms of Rom 6:1 would be, *"Since we are no longer under the law and now under grace, can we sin so grace may abound?"* Paul responds with the usual indignant answer at Rom 6:15, *"By no means!"*

Christians should no longer be slaves to sin since they have in Christ become slaves to righteousness, that is, a right relationship with God. *Giving in to sin so that grace may abound is incomprehensible and unacceptable to Paul!*

Slavery to sin results only in death, for *"the wages of sin is death,"* Rom 6:23, and *"the free gift of God is eternal life in Christ Jesus our Lord."*

Notice that in Christ sin <u>*must*</u> no longer have dominion over the baptized, for Jesus is now Lord of their lives!

Rom 6 explains in detail and graphic terms that for the baptized the *Torah*, regardless of how important it might be, and Paul will explain this in Rom 7, *does not control the life of the Christian, but their relationship with Christ does*, for He is now the *torah* instruction of their lives.

Consequently, Christians, although freed from the restrictions of the *Torah, now have a greater torah restriction on sin*, the fact that they are dead to sin and live with Christ!

In one sense, Christ has become the Christian's "torah" or instruction from God on how to live righteous lives.

We encourage the serious student of Romans to carefully read the chapter *A Biblical Theology of Baptism* at the conclusion of this study!

Rom 7:1-25. A continuation of Paul's discussion on the Christian's relationship with the *Torah* Law and Sin

Paul develops his thought on the Christian's relationship to sin and the Law with three arguments:

First, the marriage law analogy, Rom 7:1-6.

Second, the real value of the *Torah* Law, Rom 7:7-20.

Third, Paul's personal struggle with sin, Rom 7:21-25.

Rom 7:1-6. The marriage relationship analogy

[1] Do you not know, brethren—for I am speaking to those who know the law—that <u>the law is binding on a person only during his life</u>? [2] Thus <u>a married woman is bound by law to her husband as long as he lives; but if her husband dies she is discharged from the law concerning the husband</u>. [3] Accordingly, she will be called an adulteress if she lives with another man while her husband is alive. But <u>if her husband</u>

*dies she is free from that law, and if she marries
another man she is not an adulteress.*

*⁴ Likewise, my brethren, you have died to the law
through the body of Christ, so that you may belong
to another, to him who has been raised from the dead
in order that we may bear fruit for God. ⁵ While we
were living in the flesh, our sinful passions, aroused
by the law, were at work in our members to bear fruit
for death. ⁶ But now we are discharged from the law,
dead to that which held us captive, so that we serve
not under the old written code but in the new life of
the Spirit.*

Rom 7:1, 2. William Barclay, noted English New
Testament scholar, observed that "seldom has Paul
written so difficult a passage as this!"[4] Leon Morris[5]
charges that C. H. Dodd took the easy path in saying,
"Paul was confused from the start"!

The key to the discussion is Paul's simple statement
that *the law is binding on a person only during their life!*
There should be no problem with that conclusion!
*However, which law does Paul have in mind? Roman law,
Jewish law, or any law?* But Paul gives it an interesting
twist which raises further questions!

Who is it who has died?

The analogy Paul makes with this marriage law is
creative since in his example it is the person *now married
to Christ who has died.* Thus, the alive person now dead
has broken the previous marriage bond! The Christian now
alive in Christ has died under the *Torah* Law! Thus the
dead person now alive in Christ is no longer bound by that
Torah Law!

It is easy to see why Dodd felt that Paul was confused!

Again, Paul has introduced the discussion with the
expression *"Do you not know…"* indicating that he is using
a diatribe form of argument emphasizing that they *knew*
and *understood these legal arguments*!

---

[4] Leon Morris, *The Epistle to the Romans*, p. 270.
[5] Morris, p. 270.

However, Paul introduces this statement with the "small" or "minor" Greek, *disjunctive*, interrogative, or comparative particle, ἤ, *é,* which introduces or raises a question as to whether they had understood the question, *"don't you know, or, you surely should know!"*

Since Paul was precise in referring to *the law* it seems most likely that he had Jewish Christians in mind, and that the law he is referring to is the *Torah* Law. Some fine scholars (Leon Morris, Sandy and Headlam, Ernst Käsemann, *et al.*) feel that Paul had civil or Roman law in mind, which might have been the case! However, it seems most likely that in the context of Paul's discussion in Romans that he had the Law of Moses in mind (Fitzmyer,[6] Schreiner,[7] Barrett, Cranfield,[8] *et al.*). Certainly, the Jewish law would fit the same argument, and since the discussion is in the context of *Torah* Law, this will work.

In his Gospel Matthew records that Jesus was challenged by the Jewish Pharisees, Mat 19:3ff, regarding marriage and divorce laws indicating that a Jew would be familiar with the *Torah* laws on marriage.

According to most laws, including the *Torah* Law, a marriage lasted only if both partners were alive; simply put, *death broke the marriage bond.*

The surviving partner after a death in the marriage would be free to remarry since that person would then be free from the marriage law that bound their marriage.

Remember, to be baptized into Christ, Rom 6:1-5, meant that the baptized Christian had died to their previous "spouse," the Law!

To both the Jew and the Roman that would be a natural conclusion! One would assume that a Christian Jew would agree!

But Paul gives the marriage-death argument analogy a surprise application! The person who has died is the

---

[6] Fitzmyer, *Romans*, p. 455.
[7] Thomas R. Schreiner, *Romans*, p. 346.
[8] Fitzmyer, *Romans*, p. 455.

Christian who is now freed from the Law and is now free to be remarried to Christ!

No wonder that Dodd felt that Paul had messed up! But Paul was cunning, not messed up!

Rom 7:3. However, here is another commonly known principle, *if one of the partners married while their spouse was alive, this would be adultery*. The Christian must know that they have died and are now no longer bound by law to their previous spouse, the *Torah* Law! To be a Christian and tied to the *Torah* Law was adultery!

The point Paul is making following Rom 6:1-5 and his maturing teaching on the meaning of baptism was that the baptized *Christians had died to their previous life relationships with the Torah Law. In baptism they had now been united in a marriage to a new "spouse," Christ.*

Rom 7:5, 6. Notice, *"while we were living in the flesh, our sinful passions, aroused by the law, were at work in our members to bear fruit for death. ⁶ But now we are discharged from the law, dead to that which held us captive, so that we serve not under the old written code but in the new life of the Spirit."*

Christians do not serve under the old written code, the *Torah* Law which working with their sins only killed them, Rom 7:11. But now they serve in *the new life of the Spirit*, Rom 7:6.

Paul introduces a new point here, the *life-giving power of the Holy Spirit* which he will develop more fully at Rom 8.

Note 2 Cor 3:4-11 where Paul again speaks of the *written code (Torah) which kills* and *the Holy Spirit who is the spirit of life*:

> *⁴ Such is the confidence that we have through Christ toward God. ⁵ Not that we are competent of ourselves to claim anything as coming from us; our competence is from God, ⁶ who has made us competent to be ministers of a new covenant, not in a written code but in the Spirit;* **for the written code kills, but the Spirit gives life.**

⁷ Now if the dispensation of death, carved in letters on stone, (the Torah Law) came with such splendor that the Israelites could not look at Moses' face because of its brightness, fading as this was, ⁸ will not the dispensation of the Spirit be attended with greater splendor? ⁹ For if there was splendor in the dispensation of condemnation, the dispensation of righteousness must far exceed it in splendor. ¹⁰ Indeed, in this case, what once had splendor has come to have no splendor at all, because of the splendor that surpasses it. ¹¹ For if what faded away came with splendor, what is permanent must have much more splendor.

Rom 7:7-12. How Christians relate to the *Torah*

⁷ What then shall we say? That the law is sin? By no means! Yet, if it had not been for the law, I should not have known sin. I should not have known what it is to covet if the law had not said, "You shall not covet." ⁸ But sin, finding opportunity in the commandment, wrought in me all kinds of covetousness. Apart from the law sin lies dead. ⁹ I was once alive apart from the law, but when the commandment came, sin revived and I died; ¹⁰ the very commandment which promised life proved to be death to me. ¹¹ For sin, finding opportunity in the commandment, deceived me and by it killed me. ¹² So the law is holy, and the commandment is holy and just and good.

The setting to this interesting example has also provided scholars a considerable field for discussion!

Just who does Paul have in mind when he uses the pronoun "*I*" (in Greek *ego*) in Rom 7:9?

Several possibilities have been suggested.[9] Among them are the following:

1. He is referring *to himself before conversion* and his personal struggles with sin.

---

[9] Fitzmyer identifies 5 possibilities, but we find three meets the point!

157

2. He is referring *to a Jew in general who struggled with doing right* personalizing this with the "*I*" to include the Jew.
3. *He is referring to unregenerate humanity* personalizing *them* with the "*I*."

Fitzmyer discusses all the options in some detail finding positive thoughts in each one. However, he concludes:

> But in attempting to understand what Paul meant, it is important to keep his perspective in mind, which is unregenerate humanity faced the Mosaic law—but as seen by a Christian.[10]

We will in this discussion adopt #3, *unregenerate humanity* since this seems to be a universal struggle. However, one can make a good argument for all three!

Rom 7:7. Paul returns to another diatribe argument in which a Jewish interlocutor might accuse Paul of a sinful attitude toward the Law. The charge would be "*Paul claims that the law is sin!*"

To both the Jew and Paul this would be blasphemy, so it is obviously not what Paul meant!

Notice again Paul's use of the sharp negative, the μὴ γένοιτο, "*by no means!*" "*No, never, never, ever!*"

In this pericope Paul then makes several important comments about the *Torah* Law:

1. The *Torah* was *good* for it clarified the real nature of sin, Rom 7:7.
2. The *Torah* is *holy* for it is God's *Torah*, and God is Holy, Rom 7:12.
3. The commandments of the *Torah* are *holy and just and good*, Rom 7:12.
4. The *Torah* is *spiritual,* Rom 7:14.

Then what was the problem?

At 1 Tim 1:8 Paul answers this in another context. "*Now we know that the law is good, if anyone uses it lawfully.*"

---

[10] Fitzmyer, p. 465.

The problem was that the Jew was not using the *Torah* Law as God had intended!

God had intended the *Torah*:
1. To be *instruction about Himself*; the word *Torah* means *instruction*.
2. To be *instruction* on *how to live righteously*.
3. To *define His people*.
4. To *define sin* and *indict the sinner*.

The problem was that the Jew had come to use the *Torah* in diverse ways:
1. They used it to *separate themselves from others*, and as the sign of an *exclusive covenant relationship* with God.
2. They used it to *claim preferential treatment*.
3. The used it to *create, introduce* them to, or *bring them into* a *condition of righteousness with God*!

Rom 7:12. *So the law is holy, and the commandment is holy and just and good*.

Rom 7:13-25. The struggle to do the right thing

[13] Did that which is good, (the Law) *then, bring death to me? By no means! It was sin, working death in me through what is good, in order that sin might be shown to be sin, and through the commandment might become sinful beyond measure. [14] We know that the law is spiritual; but I am carnal, sold under sin. [15] I do not understand my own actions. For I do not do what I want, but I do the very thing I hate. [16] Now if I do what I do not want, I agree that the law is good. [17] So then it is no longer I that do it, but sin which dwells within me. [18] For I know that nothing good dwells within me, that is, in my flesh. I can will what is right, but I cannot do it. [19] For I do not do the good I want, but the evil I do not want is what I do. [20] Now if I do what I do not want, it is no longer I that do it, but sin which dwells within me.*

[21] So I find it to be a law (νόμος, *nómos*, a principle) *that when I want to do right, evil lies close at hand. [22] For I delight in the law of God, in my inmost*

159

self, [23] *but I see in my members another law* (νόμος, *nómos,* principle) *at war with the law of my mind and making me captive to the law of sin which dwells in my members.* [24] *Wretched man that I am! Who will deliver me from this body of death?* [25] *Thanks be to God through Jesus Christ our Lord! So then, I of myself serve the law of God with my mind, but with my flesh I serve the law of sin.*

We need to be reminded here that when Paul speaks of "I" he is doing so, not simply regarding his own self, which would be true, but *is referring to the whole human race.*

What he describes in this pericope is *felt by all humans who are sensitive to what is right and wrong,* and *what is expected of them!*

Paul certainly would find himself in this group!

Christians under grace naturally feel the tension of being free from sin and yet struggling with sin! In our times of weakness, it is easy to lose sight of the grace of being *in a right relationship with God and forgiven in Christ.*

Remember 1 John 1:5-10 where John reassures Christians who are aware of their sin that the blood of Jesus constantly cleanses them of *all sin* when they are *walking in the light,* that is, *living faithfully to Jesus.* Paul will pick up on that theme in Rom 8:1ff after expressing in Rom 7:24 human frustration when struggling with personal sin. *Wretched man that I am? Who can deliver me?*

Since the *Torah* Law, although good, spiritual, and holy, led to the awareness of sin and death, how then do Christians live in the presence of a deeply spiritual *Torah*? Jewish Christians would have problems working that one out.

Paul reminds the Romans that the problem lay not in the *Torah,* but in our carnal, fleshly, sinful nature.

Christians know what they should do, or how they should live, they understand "*Torah*" instruction, but

160

because of human weakness they end up failing to do what they intended and are frustrated by their human weakness!

Because Christians recognize their human weakness and know the ideals of righteousness and *"Torah,"* guilt *often sets in*!

Paul expresses this well, *"Wretched man that I am! Who will deliver me from this body of death?* [25] <u>*Thanks be to God*</u> [this is possible] <u>*through Jesus Christ our Lord!"*</u> In this incomplete sentence Paul assumes that the reader will also read, *this is possible* which I have inserted in the appropriate place.

The answer to this cry, almost a cry of desperation, should be anticipated from what Paul has already discussed.

It is "God through Jesus Christ our Lord" who can deliver us!

The answer to Paul's question is that it is **through God and his forgiveness that we find relief from guilt**. Paul devotes the remainder of Rom 8 to respond to this in considerable detail!

Rom 8, which follows, is perhaps the culminating climax of Paul's doctrine which he planned to teach in Rome and Spain, and it certainly is the climax of justification by grace through faith in Jesus, and the confidence Christians gain from this!

Understanding guilt and redeeming freedom

Although the *Torah* Law is *good*, *holy*, and *spiritual*, however, *when used incorrectly* it *brings death, total ruin*, and guilt.

For Christians, and in fact all humanity, knowing and following the instruction of *"Torah"* highlights our own *human weakness; guilt and frustration and their inevitable result; spiritual death.*

The answer to those who cry out in frustration is that *God through Jesus has provided relief* from human weakness, sin, and guilt, and *this relief is found in*

161

covenant relationship with God through faith in Jesus Christ.

Chapter 8 - The Glory and Peace of Being in Christ:
Rom 8:1-39

Context and Message

We must remember that Paul's theological arguments in Romans have focused on *righteousness*, or *our special covenant relationship with God.*

Rom 8 begins in answer to the cry, *"Wretched man that I am, who can deliver me from this body of death?"* Rom 7:24.

Awareness of personal sin in the context of *Torah* requirements inevitably leads to guilt, and when release from guilt is grounded in *Torah* Paul argues the result will be *frustration and personal misery. Paul even likens this to death and total ruin of everything we hold dear.*

However, when the response to personal weakness is grounded in faith in God's *grace* and *forgiveness* and his working in Jesus, the result is the realization that *"there is therefore **now** no condemnation in Christ,"* and *that we are more than conquerors in Christ!"*

When we realize that faith in God, the death of Jesus Christ, and the work of the Holy Spirit have resulted in what the *Torah* could not produce – *justification* and *glorification – then we have confidence and strength in Christ* to face life's difficulties, even to endure persecution and suffering in the knowledge that *our covenant relationship with God is secure!*

In the context of Rome in CE 58, and obvious Neronic Imperial opposition, repeated banishments from Rome, and personal insecurity, *there was one thing of which the Christians could be assured and that is God's faithfulness and covenant relationship with them.*

Physical death may appear to be a hindrance, but Paul assures the Christians that it is only temporary, for in Christ the believer has security in suffering and persecution since the Holy Spirit, Christ, and God are working for the believer to see that even if they die their

163

reward is secure, and not even Roman power and persecution can destroy their covenant relationship with God. The Christian's resurrection with Christ is secured in faith and baptism into Christ.

There is no power that is able to snatch the Christian's covenant relationship with God away from them, or from what God has done for them in Christ!

The Christian's special covenant relationship with God, which the Jew and Paul describe as righteousness, cannot be produced or secured by *Torah* keeping, and cannot be snatched away by suffering, persecution, and Roman power!

We are in Christ more than conquerors through him who loved us!

The glory and peace of no condemnation

Romans 7 closed with the heart wrenching cry from Paul, "*Wretched man that I am,! Who will deliver me from this body of death*?" Rom 7:24, followed by the Christian Paul's response, "*Thanks be to God, this can be through Jesus Christ out Lord.*" Rom 7:25.

Paul, as a representative of humanity, could find no relief by living under the *Torah*, so Paul turns to what God has done in Jesus Christ that the *Torah* could not do, bring peace with God!

Romans 8 takes up this thought and develops it into one of the most encouraging texts in all of Scripture! In this chapter Paul introduces the comforting, yet life giving involvement of the full godhead, including comforting intercession of the Holy Spirit.

Rom 8:1-11. No condemnation in Christ

*¹ There is therefore **now** no condemnation for those who are in Christ Jesus. ² For the law of the Spirit of life in Christ Jesus has set me free from the law of sin and death. ³ For God has done what the law, weakened by the flesh, could not do: sending*

his own Son in the likeness of sinful flesh and for
sin, he condemned sin in the flesh, [4] in order that
the just requirement of the law might be fulfilled in
us, who walk not according to the flesh but
according to the Spirit. [5] For those who live
according to the flesh set their minds on the things
of the flesh, but those who live according to the
Spirit set their minds on the things of the Spirit. [6] To
set the mind on the flesh is death, but to set the
mind on the Spirit is life and peace. [7] For the mind
that is set on the flesh is hostile to God; it does not
submit to God's law, indeed it cannot; [8] and those
who are in the flesh cannot please God.
  [9] But you are not in the flesh, you are in the
Spirit, if in fact the Spirit of God dwells in you.
Anyone who does not have the Spirit of Christ does
not belong to him. [10] But if Christ is in you,
although your bodies are dead because of sin, your
spirits are alive because of righteousness. [11] If the
Spirit of him who raised Jesus from the dead dwells
in you, he who raised Christ Jesus from the dead
will give life to your mortal bodies also through his
Spirit which dwells in you.

In great style Paul begins this section with the assuring statement that *"there is therefore **now** no condemnation for those who are in Christ Jesus."*

Rom 8:1. *There is therefore **now** no condemnation for those who are in Christ Jesus.* The little word ***now**, nún,* functions as an epexegetical eschatological *nún which gives an additional eschatological[1] emphasis.* The Greek *vῦv nún ... now*, emphasizes the *definite present time.[2]* What this means is that *in this eschatological time, the time of the Messiah (the Christian age) there* is ***now** no condemnation for those in Christ Jesus.* What the *Torah* could not do God has ***now** done in Christ!

---

[1] *Eschatological* from the Greek *éschatos, the last, the end, the final age.* Cf. *Anchor Bible Dictionary*, "eschatology," vol 2, p. 566.
[2] Zodhiates, vῦv, *nún,* Fitzmyer, *Romans,* p. 481.

Dunn notes that the two particles ἄρα νῦν, *but now*, are combined for emphasis:

The normal ἄρα phrase used by Paul is ἄρα οὖν (5:18; 7:3, 25; 8:12; 9:16, 18; 14:12, 19). The two particles together *strengthen each other and indicate a conclusion or corollary drawn with immediate force from what has just been said …* The νῦν *is, as usual, eschatological* (as in 3:26; 5:9, 11; 6:19, 21; 8:18, 22; 11:5, 30–31; 13:11; 16:26; as also νυνί in 3:21; 6:22; 7:6, 17). That is to say, *he states the contrast between the two epochs, and between the before-and-after of conversion-initiation,* in simple and sharply antithetical terms, before going on to qualify and soften the antitheses in accordance with the continuing tensions of his (own) experience as a believer. The transition between 7:25 and 8:1 is simply the point at which the more complex analysis of the role of the law in the overlap between the ages has been worked through, at which point Paul pauses and recalls once again the sharply defined terms of his starting point … chap. 7 ended with its note of calm and sober realism. *8:1 therefore signals the beginning of a fresh exposition of the reality of the salvation process in the present,* this time in terms of the Spirit. *Important as it is for Paul to refrain from glossing over the reality of the eschatological tension,* it is equally and more important to be able also to *resort once again to the grand simplicities of faith* (8:1).[3]

Rom 8:1 emphasizes the *present activity of God* in Christ Jesus *in the present eschatological Messianic age!* Under the age of *Torah, there was certain condemnation for sin* since sin working with the *Torah* brought death, Rom 5:12. *However, now,* in the eschatological age, Rom 8:1, that is, the *latest age,* the *last age,* the *age of the Messiah,* the *new age,* or *the Christian age, there is **now** no condemnation for those in Christ*!

---

[3] Dunn, p. 416.

166

*For the serious person struggling under the weakness of carnality and sin under the Torah, there can be no greater news, there is therefore **now** no condemnation for those who are in Christ Jesus!*

The question is, "How does one get into Christ Jesus, and what does this mean?"

Rom 6:3, 4. Paul stated that believers are *baptized into* Christ Jesus:

Do you not know that all of us who have been baptized into Christ Jesus were baptized into his death? [4] We were buried therefore with him by baptism into death, so that as Christ was raised from the dead by the glory of the Father, we too might walk in newness of life.

See also **Gal 3:26, 27**, *"for in Christ Jesus you are all sons of God, through faith. [27] For as many of you as were baptized into Christ have put on Christ."*

Those who *come to God in an obedient faith* and *are baptized into Jesus*, are *united with Christ in his death and resurrection and triumphant victory over death.* They share in *Christ with his victory over sin which the Torah could not do!*

*For those baptized into Christ Jesus, therefore, there is therefore **now no** condemnation! They have been forgiven by God and declared not guilty, and therefore righteous!*

Later in Rom 8:31-39 Paul will develop this thought more fully, but for now, we should ask what it means to be baptized into Christ Jesus? Simply, it means this is where *one is united with Christ and his resurrection and victory over death!*

Now *in Christ* one has died to the fatal destructive power of sin where the *Torah* Law has no power over us *to work with sin and kill us*, Rom 7:7-11!

What then shall we say? That the law is sin? By no means! Yet, if it had not been for the law, I should not have known sin. I should not have known what it is to covet if the law had not said, "You shall not covet."

⁸ But sin, finding opportunity in the commandment, wrought in me all kinds of covetousness. <u>Apart from the law sin lies dead.</u> ⁹ I was once alive apart from the law, but when the commandment came, sin revived and I died; ¹⁰ the very commandment which promised life proved to be death to me. ¹¹ For sin, finding opportunity in the commandment, deceived me and by it killed me.

In Christ we **now** live in the new realm and powerful effective influence of Jesus' atoning death and resurrection!

Rom 8:2. *For <u>the law of the Spirit of life in Christ Jesus has set me free from the law of sin and death</u>.* Paul stresses that in Christ the *law* or *principle of the Spirit of life works and sets us free from the law or principle of sin and death.*

Two *principles* are at work in the arena of human struggle, the *principle* of sin and death, and the *principle* of the Spirit of life.

Here we can legitimately translate the Greek word νόμος, *nómos*, which often in the New Testament is translated as *law*, as *principle,*⁴ such as the *principle* of sin and death, and the *principle* of the Spirit of life.

The *principle* of *sin* is that sin and death work with the *Torah* (law, *nomos*) *to condemn us.*

The *principle of the Spirit of life* is that the Spirit works with faith for those in Christ *resulting in life and no condemnation.*

We encounter here an important doctrine that Paul enunciates elsewhere, 2 Cor 3:6, where *he contrasts the Mosaic Law*, the written code or *Torah, with the Holy*

---

⁴ Νόμος, *nómos.* "The use of νόμος in Paul is not wholly uniform, for he can sometimes employ the term when he does not have the OT Law in view. Nevertheless, he does not start with a general sense which is then predominantly used for the Mosaic Law. His starting point is the traditional use of νόμος for the specific OT Law. Hence it is self-evident what νόμος means, and usually no more precise definition is given." Kittel. *TNDT*, vol 4, pp. 1069f. Fitzmyer, *Romans*, p. 483. Cf. also Zodhiates, νόμος, *nómos.*

Spirit. He writes of being ministers *of a new covenant, not of "a written code but in the Spirit; for the written code kills, but <u>the Spirit gives life</u>."*

In spite of some teachings on the Holy Spirit which emphasize miraculous powers transmitted by the Holy Spirit to some disciples, *the primary ministry of the Holy Spirit is to function as the life giving power of God's atoning and life giving work.*

Unless the Holy Spirit is present in conversion, giving life in the new birth, John 3:3-5, and Titus 3:3-7, *there is no new birth and no real spiritual life! Cf, Tit 3:3-7:*

For <u>we ourselves were once foolish, disobedient, led astray</u>, slaves to various passions and pleasures, passing our days in malice and envy, hated by men and hating one another; [4] *but when the goodness and loving kindness of God our Savior appeared,* [5] <u>*he saved us, not because of deeds done by us in righteousness, but in virtue of his own mercy, by the washing of regeneration and renewal in the Holy Spirit,*</u> [6] *which he poured out upon us richly through Jesus Christ our Savior,* [7] <u>*so that we might be justified by his grace and become heirs in hope of eternal life.*</u>

In the ministry of the Holy Spirit and Christ, God has done what the *Torah* could not do, that is, *give life.* The *Torah* working with the sinful passions of man brought only death, God in Christ and through the working of the Holy Spirit has given us *eternal life,* that is, the *real quality life, God's life.*

It is *the Spirit,* not the *Torah,* working with *faith in Christ's death* on the cross that *the believer in Christ* has life.

Rom 8: 3, 4. *"For <u>God has done what the law, weakened by the flesh, could not do: sending his own Son</u> **in the likeness** <u>of sinful flesh and for sin, he condemned sin</u> in the **flesh,** [4] <u>in order that the just requirement of the law might be fulfilled in us, who walk not according to the</u> **flesh** but according to the Spirit."*

169

Paul adds that the *Torah* Law weakened by the impotence of the *flesh*, that is, *our carnal sinful inclination*,[5] cannot save since that was not its intention. The purpose of the *Torah* Law was to *inform, instruct* the Jew *how to live for God in a covenant relationship*. Hence, the *just requirement of the law, that is, justification, righteousness, a right relationship with God* cannot be restored by the *Torah* Law, because that was not its purpose. The just requirement of the *Torah* Law, *righteousness*, can only be fulfilled by *the principle of faith in Jesus Christ* and *the work of the Holy Spirit*.

Rom 8:5-8. "*For those who live according to the flesh set their minds on the things of the flesh, but those who live according to the Spirit set their minds on the things of the Spirit.* [6] *To set the mind on the flesh is death, but to set the mind on the Spirit is **life*** (ζωή, *zōē*[6]) *and peace.* [7] *For the mind that is set on the flesh is* hostile to God; *it does not submit to God's law, indeed it cannot;* [8] *and those who are in the flesh cannot please God.*"

Paul contrasts the life in the *flesh, sárx,* the *carnal sinful nature of man* which by inclination is opposed to God and his intention, and the *spiritual* side of man, which is led by the Spirit of God. Note Gal 5:16-24 Paul's contrast of *living by the flesh (sárx)* and *living by the Spirit*:

> [16] *But I say,* walk by the Spirit, and do not gratify the desires of the flesh. [17] *For the desires of the* flesh *are against the Spirit, and the desires of the Spirit are against the* flesh; *for these are opposed to each other, to prevent you from doing what you would.* [18] *But if you are led by the Spirit you are not under the law.* [19] Now the works of the flesh are plain:

---

[5] Σάρξ *sárx, Flesh, sinful nature,* Zodhiates, "As implying sinfulness, proneness to sin, the carnal nature, the seat of carnal appetites and desires, of sinful passions and affections whether physical or moral."
[6] Zodhiates and TNDT, ζωή, *zōē,* a manner of life or living, of conduct, *in a moral respect*, Rom. 6:4; Eph. 4:18, "the life of God" *meaning that which God requires, a godly life*; 2 Pet. 1:3.

fornication, impurity, licentiousness, [20] idolatry, sorcery, enmity, strife, jealousy, anger, selfishness, dissension, party spirit, [21] envy, drunkenness, carousing, and the like. I warn you, as I warned you before, that those who do such things shall not inherit the kingdom of God. [22] *But the fruit of the Spirit is love, joy, peace, patience, kindness, goodness, faithfulness,* [23] *gentleness, self-control; against such there is no law.* [24] *And those who belong to Christ Jesus have crucified the flesh with its passions and desires.*

[25] *If (since) we live by the Spirit, let us also walk by the Spirit.* [26] *Let us have no self-conceit, no provoking of one another, no envy of one another.*

The *carnal sinful* nature of man *leads to death*, because of the *Torah* Law indicts him for sin. The *spiritual* side of man, because it is led by the Spirit, *leads to life* (ζωή, *zōḗ, eternal life, a quality of life, God's kind of life) and peace.*[7]

Rom 8:9-11. Paul stresses that Christians must not be controlled by their sinful nature since the Spirit of God dwells in them.

[9] *But you are not in the flesh, you are in the Spirit, **if** in fact the Spirit of God dwells in you. Anyone who does not have the Spirit of Christ does not belong to him.* [10] *But if Christ is in you, although your bodies are dead because of sin, your spirits are alive because of righteousness.* [11] ***If** (since) the Spirit of him who raised Jesus from the dead dwells in you, he who raised Christ Jesus from the dead will give life to your mortal bodies also through his Spirit which dwells in you.*

Rom 8:9, 10. The conditional particles *if* in the Greek construction introduce *first class conditional clauses* and

---

[7] Zodhiates, εἰρήνη *eirḗnē*; peace, particularly in a single sense, the opposite of war and dissension … Metaphorically *peace of mind, tranquility, arising from reconciliation with God and a sense of a divine favor.*

should be understood as **since in fact**[8] *the Spirit of God dwells in you*. There is no doubt in Paul's mind here! *Since the Spirit of God dwells in those who have been baptized into Christ*[9] *there is a new power for good in their lives*— God working through his Holy Spirit, cf. Eph 3:14-21.

The Spirit of God and the life giving power of Jesus' resurrection, will also be the power of the Christian's present and future resurrection and life in and with Christ.

At **Rom 8:10** Paul emphasizes *"But **if** Christ is in you, although your bodies are dead because of sin, your spirits are alive because of righteousness."* The particle *if* here again introduces a 1st class conditional statement which introduces a strong claim, *since* Christ is in you, you are alive *because of righteousness*!

Righteousness is not something we do or earn. It is *the relationship we have with God*!

Since Christ is in us, and since the Spirit dwells in us, we are in *the correct relationship, righteousness*, with God, and therefore have life because of this!

Remember that for the Jew and Paul, righteousness is <u>not</u> *getting it all right*, but being *in the right relationship with God*. Paul recognizes that we will not keep God's *Torah will* perfectly, we will sin, but because we are in Christ and in a right relationship with God through faith, we are *righteous, in a right relationship with God, forgiven, declared not guilty,* and have life with Christ, not death with Adam.

1 John 1:5-10 confirms this:

> *This is the message we have heard from him and proclaim to you, that God is light and in him is no darkness at all.* [6] ***If*** *we say we have fellowship*

---

[8] Dana and Mantey, *A Manual Grammar of the Greek New Testament*, p. 289. Εἴπερ and εἰ, translated *if*, both adverbial conditional conjunctions with verbs in the indicative mood are first class conditional statements which imply certainty, not probability.

[9] See Acts 2:38; 5:32 where Luke informs us that God gives his Spirit to those who obey him, obviously in context, those who have been baptized.

with him while we walk in darkness, we lie and do not live according to the truth; ^{7} *but if we walk in the light, as he is in the light, we have fellowship with one another, and the blood of Jesus his Son* (constantly) *cleanses* ^{10} *us from all sin.* ^{8} *If we say we have no sin, we deceive ourselves, and the truth is not in us.* ^{9} *If we confess our sins, he is faithful and just, and will forgive our sins and cleanse us from all unrighteousness.* ^{10} *If we say we have not sinned, we make him a liar, and his word is not in us.*

This text implies that *if we walk in the light where God is*, we have fellowship with God; in Pauline terms we are in *a right relationship* with God, and the blood of his son, Jesus, constantly cleanses us from all sin. In each case the subordinating conjunction ἐὰν used by John with the present active verb in the subjunctive mood implies *high future probability!* [11]

Rom 8:12-17. Debtors to the Spirit not to the flesh

^{12} *So then, brethren, we are debtors, not to the flesh, to live according to the flesh—* ^{13} *for if you live according to the flesh you will die, but if by the Spirit you put to death the deeds of the body you will live.* ^{14} *For all who are led by the Spirit of God are sons of God.* ^{15} *For you did not receive the spirit of slavery to fall back into fear, but you have received the spirit of sonship. When we cry, "Abba! Father!"* ^{16} *it is the Spirit himself bearing witness with our spirit that we are children of God,* ^{17} *and if children, then heirs, heirs of God and fellow heirs with Christ, provided we suffer with him in order that we may also be glorified with him.*

---

[10] The present tense of the Greek word περιπατῶμεν implies constant action.

[11] Dana and Mantey, *A Manual Grammar of the New Testament*, p. 290.

Note how Paul personalizes his statement. He sees himself writing to fellow Christians, and addresses them by the deep relational term of *brothers*! Several scholars see these two verses as the conclusion of the previous discussion of being dead through sin but alive because of the work of the Holy Spirit. That may be so, but *it is a swing text that introduces the new emphasis of being in the special family of God with a new attitude toward God, Abba Father*, Rom 8:15.

Christians no longer live according to the flesh, or *Torah*! But **now** as *adopted children of God* they live according to the Spirit!

Hidden in this discussion is the contrasting principles; of living according to the *Torah* which only brought death because of our carnal being, or being alive in Christ through the Holy Spirit!

This great texts informs us that *because* of our faith in Jesus Christ and the work of the Holy Spirit *we have been adopted in a spirit of sonship by God into his special family for a life of righteousness.*

This passage builds on the new life in the Spirit Paul has previously just introduced and argues that by the work of the Holy Spirit Christians have put to death the deeds of the body, the sinful nature of man, and have *put on a new life of the Spirit with God.* Those led by the Spirit are children of God; they have been *adopted into his family*, υἱοθεσία, *huiothesia* in Greek carries the sense of *adoption*. In this *spirit of adoption* or *sonship* we now cry in response to God, *Abba Father*! We will discuss the double meaning of *Abba Father* below, but first need to briefly discuss an interesting but possible translation or interpretation of the Greek text.

I particularly like Fitzmyer's comment at this point. "For Paul *huiothesia* denotes *a special status*: because of faith baptized Christians have been taken into the family of God, and have come under the *patria potestas*, "paternal authority," of God himself and have *a legitimate status in that family.*"[12] Possibly also hidden within Fitzmyer's statement is the thought that *seeking legal status* in the *patria potestas* by the *Torah* will not make it! In common contemporary terms seeking status with God by *Torah* results in *illegal immigration status*!

Rom 8:15-17. The Spirit of sonship

> [15] *For you did not receive the spirit of slavery to fall back into fear,* <u>*but you have received the spirit of sonship.*</u> *When we cry,* <u>*"Abba! Father!"*</u> [16] <u>*it is the Spirit himself*</u> *bearing witness with our spirit that we are children of God,* [17] *and if children, then heirs, heirs of God and* <u>*fellow heirs with Christ,*</u> *provided we suffer with him in order that we may also be glorified with him.*

We encounter in Rom 8:15 and 16 a fascinating interpretive problem in the RSV and NIV translations. The translators have not followed the punctuation suggested in the best Greek manuscripts, and have translated the text in agreement with text at Gal 4:4-6:

> *But when the time had fully come, God sent forth his Son, born of woman, born under the law,* [5] *to redeem those who were under the law, so that we might receive adoption as sons.* [6] *And because you are sons, God has sent the Spirit of his Son into our hearts, crying,* <u>*"Abba! Father!"*</u> [7] *So through God you are no longer a slave but a son, and if a son then an heir.*

The issue is one of *punctuation* in Greek at Rom 8:15, 16 which is always a matter of scholarly interpretation since originally there were no punctuation marks in the "original" or our early Greek manuscripts. The Greek manuscripts adopted today by most translators and commentators have the punctuation as follows, "...*the spirit of adoption,* (comma) *in which we cry 'Abba, Father!' The Spirit himself bears witness with us that we are children of God.*"[13]

---

[12] Fitzmyer, *Romans*, p. 500.

[13] Cf. Fitzmyer, *Romans*, p. 497.

The RSV translators rendered these verses as follows, note the difference in punctuation from that which we have just given. "...*you have received the spirit of sonship. (period) When we cry, "Abba! Father!" [16] it is the Spirit himself bearing witness with our spirit that we are children of God...*"

The NIV translates and punctuates these verses in similar fashion to the RSV, but with a slight variation. NIV "...*you received the Spirit of sonship. And by him we cry, "Abba, Father." [16] The Spirit himself testifies with our spirit that we are God's children...*"

However, Fitzmyer, the KJV and the ASV are correct and stay closer to the Greek text than the RSV and NIV!

Hence, the KJV "...*ye have received the Spirit of adoption, whereby we cry, Abba, Father. (period) [16]The Spirit itself beareth witness with our spirit, that we are the children of God...*"

Likewise, the ASV "...*ye received the spirit of adoption, whereby we cry, Abba, Father. (period) [16]The Spirit himself beareth witness with our spirit, that we are children of God...*"

It is better that we interpret these verses as punctuated in the Greek text, and followed by the KJV and ASV, "...*you have received the spirit of adoption in which we cry "Abba, Father"! The Spirit himself bears witness that we are the children of God.*"

Because we have received adoption into God's family, *we cry out to him in excitement, "Abba Father"! The Holy Spirit witnesses to God that we are his children because the Holy Spirit was instrumental in our new birth into God's family*!

In this text we also have also an interesting doubling up of the word father in "*Abba, Father*"! The Greek reads αββα ὁ πατήρ, *abba ho patēr, abba the father.*

The word *Abba* is originally the Aramaic word for *father*. Aramaic was the common "Hebrew" dialect spoken by Jews in the first century. *Abba* in our text has been *transliterated* into the Greek also as *Abba*!

The word *father* in the Greek text is *patēr* which simply means *father*. It is sometimes used as an honorary praise term "Father!"

Interestingly, we have in our Greek text the fascinating doubling of the expression "*Abba*, Father"!

Why?

Simply because the Roman Christians were a mixed group, made up of both Jew and Gentile Greek speaking converts.

Abba would have special meaning to the Jew, "*God has become our Father*!"

To the Gentile Christian the term *Abba* might not be that well known, so Paul adds "*ho pater*," Father.

The doubling means no more than that both Jewish and Gentile Christian now *cry out in joy that God is their Father*!

To translate *Abba* as "daddy" as some are prone to do is a gross error, for no Jew, Christian or otherwise, would ever address God with familiarity as "Daddy"! That is a well-meaning American or western concept, not a Biblical one!

Rom 8:18-25. Spiritual frustration (suffering) and the future hope of glory

[18] I consider that the sufferings of this present time are not worth comparing with the glory that is to be revealed to us. [19] For the creation waits with eager longing for the revealing of the sons of God; [20] for the creation was subjected to futility, not of its own will but by the will of him who subjected it in hope;
[21] because the creation itself will be set free from its bondage to decay and obtain the glorious liberty of the children of God. [22] We know that the whole creation has been groaning in travail together until now; [23] and not only the creation, but we ourselves, who have the first fruits of the Spirit, groan inwardly as we wait for adoption as sons, the redemption of our bodies. [24] For in this hope we were saved. Now hope that is seen is not hope. For who hopes for what he

177

sees? [25] But if we hope for what we do not see, we wait for it with patience.

Paul now shifts gear on us by introducing an interesting, informative, and important piece of literature with a unique literary genre and expression, namely the *apocalyptic genre* which would have been keenly understood by most Jewish readers!

It has to do with the concept of *suffering*, but not simple physical suffering although this is not excluded!

We might ask why Paul introduces suffering into his discussion of the issues of guilt, frustration, *Torah*, righteousness, and the Spirit!

It would be easy and natural to move in the direction of physical suffering and illness, and if we did, the message would still be applicable and valuable.

However, this would be unfortunate and would diminish the real power of the little piece of expressive apocalyptic literature that follows.

From the literary style within the text scholars identify the unique references of the physical world reacting as though it were human suffering with *the focus on the physical world itself suffering because of sin and expressing hope for the future,* a literary style that is well known as *apocalyptic*.

Just as there are keys that inform us of the fact that someone might be telling a fairy tale, such as "*once upon a time,*" so there are literary indicators that *identify certain literary forms as apocalyptic*!

But what is apocalyptic literature or an apocalyptic genre?

An apocalyptic element in Greek and Jewish literature can be identified as early as the seventh century BCE, proliferating in Jewish literature surrounding the Babylonian captivity, Ezekiel, Daniel, Isaiah, and Jeremiah, as well as the literature at the close of the Old Testament prophetic restoration period such as Zechariah and Joel. It was a common Jewish form of expressing *hope for the future when under severe political and religious persecution and suffering.* It is therefore often categorized as *the literature of suffering and persecution.*

Apocalyptic expression flourished in the first 200 years of the life of the Church as Rome sought to forcefully crush the developing challenge of Christianity into the religious paganism of Emperor worship. It is not surprising that John authored the book of Revelation at the close of the first century CE in the apocalyptic genre when the church suffered severe persecution under Emperor Domitian.

When the Seleucid rulers took over the Middle East after the fall of the Alexandrian Empire ca. 323 BCE, and then when Rome captured the whole Mediterranean world, ca. 49 BCE, the Jews entered a period of *harsh religious persecution* which flowed over into the first 300 years of Christianity.

It was during these 400 years of Roman and pagan religious persecution, ca. 49 BCE to 300 CE, that the Jews and then the Christians expressed their *faith, hope for a future with calls for faithfulness* in the literary form of apocalyptic.

Apocalyptic in Christian literature became a common expression of hope under the Roman religious persecution and temptation to compromise as early as Nero's reign ca. 54-68 CE.

Several major commentators of Romans 8:18-25 point to the apocalyptic style of this paragraph.[14] One recent commentator, Ernst Käsemann, in another context appropriately observed that "Apocalyptic is the mother of New Testament theology," indicating that in order to understand the New Testament one must recognize that it was written during a period when Christians were entering

---

[14] Fitzmyer, *Romans*, pp. 506ff; Schreiner, *Romans*, p. 432ff.

a major period of persecution from both the Jews and the Romans.[15]

Why then would Paul introduce this apocalyptic message to the church in Rome?

First, Paul knew that by preaching the good news, the *euangelion gospel* of Jesus Christ as King *Messiah*, which spoke out against righteousness by *Torah* keeping, the Jews would react violently involving some persecution of Christians and suffering.

Second, he knew that this would also cause the Romans to react against the Christians who challenged faith in Caesar as the king, boldly claiming that Jesus was king, not Caesar.

One must remember that it was only a few years, possibly only three years since Nero had banished all Jews, including Jewish Christians, from Rome!

Rom 8:18. In this context Paul speaks of "*the suffering of this present time are not worth comparing with the glory that is to be revealed to us*!"

In typical apocalyptic symbolism Paul personifies the physical creation and demonstrates that even the physical creation has been suffering in some form under man's sinful nature.

The physical creation itself is also looking forward in hope to the coming salvation of mankind at the final end of the world.

Apocalyptic, although sensitive to the salvation experienced by individuals in the present, *looks forward to the future salvation, not only of the individual, but of the whole creation at the end of time.*

Paul's intention in adopting the apocalyptic genre is to *get the Christians to lift their horizons from their present suffering and to see the hope that lies ahead, over the horizon.*

---

[15] Ian A. Fair, "Apocalyptic," *Conquering With Christ*, pp. 34ff; Ernst Käsemann, "The Beginnings of Christian Theology," *Journal for Theology and the Church*, 6, 1969.

The suffering alluded to here by Paul is defined by the very literary genre he uses, namely, apocalyptic. *The suffering is not simply physical suffering, but essentially the spiritual suffering of persecution.* He is well aware of Nero's disposition and the shifting sands of the Christians' lives in Rome.

The whole context of Romans 8 builds on what has transpired in Rom 5-7, namely *Paul's understanding that the Christians under a new covenant relationship with God*, namely, righteousness by faith, *would face both Jewish and pagan Roman opposition.*

Paul is aware of the glorious privilege and covenant relationship Christians have in Christ as opposed to a doomed relationship with *Torah* keeping, and the frustration and guilt resulting from such.

Rom 7 ended with the cry of desperation, *"Wretched man that I am, who will deliver me from this body of death?"*

Paul knew that the suffering of spiritual uncertainty associated with *Torah* keeping and Roman opposition *could only be resolved and alleviated by the indwelling Holy Spirit working in the life of those who by faith in Jesus commit themselves to God's grace*, cf Eph 3:14-21.

Rom 8:26-30. Divine intervention and assurance

26 Likewise the Spirit helps us in our weakness; for we do not know how to pray as we ought, but the Spirit himself intercedes for us with sighs too deep for words. 27 And he who searches the hearts of men knows what is the mind of the Spirit, because the Spirit intercedes for the saints according to the will of God.

28 We know that in everything God works for good with those who love him, who are called according to his purpose. 29 For those whom he foreknew he also predestined to be conformed to the image of his Son, in order that he might be the first-born among many brethren. 30 And those whom he predestined he also called; and those whom he called he also justified; and those whom he justified he also glorified.

181

Rom 8:26. Continuing with the twin focus of Rom 8, the frustration of the wretched man under the *Torah* and the life-giving Holy Spirit, Paul states clearly and strongly that the Holy Spirit is deeply involved in the spiritual man's suffering and weaknesses.

We need to stress again, that although God is concerned with our physical problems, and Christians are enjoined to pray to God on behalf of these, *God's deepest concerns are for our spiritual sufferings and anxieties.*

Too often the pressures of life place great stress on one's spiritual life and one's covenant relationship with God comes under great tension.

We want to cry out to God for help, but often find ourselves crying out to God asking what God is doing with our situation!

Spiritually, our faith batteries tend to run low!

We want to pray *as we ought* but *do not know what to say*!

All we can manage is "*sighs too deep for words*!"

Some commentators want the unspoken of "*ineffable*" sighs *too deep for words* to be the sighs of the Spirit. Others refer the ineffable sighs to the supposed *ecstatic utterance of tongues*, while others prefer to have the inexpressible utterances *belong to humans in their struggles with suffering and frustration.*

The syntax (grammatical form) of the phrase "*sighs too deep*" is in a locative, instrumental, or dative noun case form and could be translated *in* sighs, *with* sighs, or *with reference to* sighs!

Whether it be *the overwhelming sighs of the Christian* or the *indefinable sighs of the Spirit* does not make much difference, for whatever this means *the Holy Spirit intercedes* for the Christian in times *when it is difficult to know what or how to pray*!

Most of us have those moments when we wish we could do better with our prayers. We can take comfort that God through his Spirit knows what to do!

God—who knows the heart of the Spirit and knows that what the Spirit is doing is according to his divine will—will hear those *ineffable* prayers!

So, in our challenging times of spiritual suffering or weakness, the Holy Spirit is on our side and is working for us according to God's will!

Rom 8:28. *We know that in everything God works for good with those who love him, who are called according to his purpose. [29] For those whom he foreknew he also predestined to be conformed to the image of his Son, in order that he might be the first-born among many brethren. [30] And those whom he predestined he also called; and those whom he called he also justified; and those whom he justified he also glorified.*

How do we understand the statement that *God works in everything for good with those who love him*? Obviously, we cannot deny that God can work whatever he desires to work, whenever he desires to do so, within his eternal purpose! However, some take this statement further than Paul intended!

First, there is the temptation to *remove the statement from its context* of discussing *the spiritual needs we have* when attempting to *maintain* our righteousness relationship with God. It is easy for Christians today to stretch this promise further than Paul or the context intended. This can amount to suggesting that God will do what we want him to do for our supposed good!

Second, our problem with interpreting this text lies in the very uncertainty the text itself provides! *The text does not supply the identity of who or what it is that works for us.* Some English translations insert God as the one who works for us, and this may be correct, but that is a translator's insertion! The number of textual variants in our Greek texts indicate that this slight problem of *who is acting* has teased scholars ever since the beginning of the church! The Greek text reads Οἴδαμεν δὲ ὅτι τοῖς ἀγαπῶσιν τὸν θεὸν πάντα συνεργεῖ εἰς ἀγαθόν which translates *"we know for those who love God all things work*

183

together for good." The interpreter has to supply God as the one working, which is reasonable, but the text does not say this!

Third, on top of that, our translations are all over the place in translating this text! The RSV inserts *"in everything God works...,"* the NIV reads *"in all things God works...,"* the NRSV, KJV, ASV, translate it *"all things work together...,"* the NASV reads *"God causes all things to work together..."*

The Greek literally reads *"now we know that to or for the ones loving God all things work together for good...."* However, literal translations are themselves a problem for they often ignore idiom and context.

The verb συνεργεῖ, *works together,* can be translated as either **_he_** works together, **_it_** works together, or **_she_** works together. One would assume that "she works together" does not fit the context!

Fourth, early Greek manuscripts supplied the noun *God* as the one who works together, but the better manuscript evidence is in support of *"everything (it) works together."*

Fifth, further complicating the problem is the adjective *panta* which is variously translated in our translations as *everything* or *all things* since *panta* is either *accusative masculine singular or plural,* or *accusative neuter plural*!

Sixth, then we come to the word *good*! *What kind of good* does Paul have in mind? Is it *physical good, personal good,* personal *health,* personal *wealth, spiritual good,* or *whatever*?

The context of Romans seems to indicate that what Paul does not have in mind is simply physical good. He is concerned in Romans with *spiritual good,* namely *righteousness* or *a special covenant relationship with God.*

Perhaps the best solution to this text is in the first place not to be too emphatic other than to understand that for those who love God good things will take place and that somehow God and his Spirit are involved!

We should remember that the context of this verse is *spiritual suffering* caused by persecution, guilt, or our struggles to overcome our human weaknesses and yet be righteous. The fact is that both God and the Holy Spirit are already involved in our struggles, Rom 8:26.

Our best understanding of this text and its promise is that in our struggles to be righteous in the presence of our human frailty, God and the Holy Spirit participate in every aspect of our spiritual struggle to give us hope and spiritual security!

Rom 8:29. The reason for God's intercession and help

*"**For** those whom he foreknew he also predestined to be conformed to the image of his Son, in order that he might be the first-born among many brethren."*

It is important that we note the connection between Rom 8:28 and Rom 8:29! Paul begins Rom 8:29 with ὅτι *hóti, for,* a demonstrative conjunction[16] which is often used as a causal particle simply translated *because of* or *for.*

The ὅτι, *hóti*[17] of Rom 8:29 explains <u>why</u> or <u>how</u> God works in everything for the *good* of <u>those who love him.</u> *This is so **because** God loves his family,* his *children,* his *adopted children,* and *works for them in their lives as they love him and maintain faith in Jesus.*
Rom 8:29-30. Paul discusses God's *eternal plan* for our Salvation; *it began in eternity before creation,* Eph 1:3-10.

As we have noted above, Paul begins Rom 8:29 with the demonstrative conjunction ὅτι *hóti* which demonstrates *why* God is working for us. He does so **because** he *chose us in Christ before creation,* and has a *plan* to preserve his *creation and family. He began this plan before creation* and is continuing it in the Roman Christian lives!

---

[16] Zodhiates, ὅτι, *hóti*; demonstrative conjunction, *because* (causal) which, introduces the object, contents, or argument *to which the preceding words refer.* As a *causal,* it is particularly equivalent to *diá … for … for this reason,* because, assigning the cause, motive, ground of something.

Careful attention to Rom 8:29, following his discussion of Rom 7:24 *"wretched man that I am…,"* indicates that *it is in the arena of justification or covenant relationship* that he has been working for us, *not in any and every casual, <u>daily</u> or mundane area of our lives. God through his Holy Spirit works to forgive and save* us in Christ.

His real concern is our justification and glorification, and our being conformed to the image of His Son, and *to this end he has been working since before creation, and continues to work today in the eschatological last days, the Messianic or church age!*

The *unique literary construction* of Rom 8:29 and 30 are interesting and most informative!

Rom 8:29, 39. *For those whom he <u>foreknew</u> he also <u>predestined</u> to be conformed to the image of his Son, in order that he might be the <u>first-born</u> among many brethren. ³⁰ And those whom he <u>predestined</u> he also <u>called</u>; and those whom he called he also justified; and those whom he justified he also <u>glorified</u>.*

In Rom 8:29 Paul strings a list of *aorist verbs* together that make *<u>a strong statement of fact</u>*. It is as though he was piling one verb up on another for emphasis! Paul was *reassuring the Christians of an important fact*! At Rom 8:28 he had stated that Christians had been *<u>foreknown</u>* by God in eternity as part of his eternal plan of redemption; God had predestined them to be *conformed to the image of His son*; they were to be like the *firstborn*[18] among God's creation; *<u>predestined</u>*, *<u>called</u>*, and *<u>justified</u>*, in order to be *<u>glorified with</u>* God!

In times of stress, God's plan was something the Roman Christians constantly needed to remember. *They*

---

[18] Zodhiates, Πρωτότοκος, *prōtótokos, the first-born, preeminent one, the one bearing the blessings of the first born in a family.* Remember, Gen 27, Esau and Jacob in the Old Testament story. Jacob "stole" by trickery the first-born privilege of Isaac from his brother Esau. Jacob, the *supplanter*, became the first-born by trickery!

were *chosen, privileged people, adopted by God* according to his eternal purpose.

Scholars have identified a "poetic" lilt or rhythm to the verses that suggest that Paul may have been drawing on a well-known *confession* of faith or early Christian *hymn*. Some even suggest that Paul was drawing on an early Christian baptismal *confession* or hymn!

Within the flow of thought we find good reasons for these suggestions!

The ὅτι, *hóti,* or *for,* with which Paul begins Rom 8:29 answers the *"for what reason"* has God had done this. He has been working in Christ ever since Adam and Eve for the future of his creation! He had known of them before creation and had called them to be saved through Christ, in spite of their sinful nature, *in order that they might be glorified eternally with him*!

Remember Rom 8:15-17, *"When we cry, "Abba! Father!"* [16] *it is the Spirit himself bearing witness with our spirit that we are children of God,* [17] *and if children, then heirs, heirs of God and fellow heirs with Christ, provided we suffer with him in order that we may also be glorified with him."*

It is *for our righteousness and glorification* that he has been working since before creation for his children to be saved in Christ!

Note how Paul concluded this pericope by emphasizing this, *"those whom he foreknew he predestined, he called, he justified, and he glorified"*!

God has had a plan for the believer which began before the creation. He *predestined, decided before time,* that we should be conformed in the image of his Son, Eph 1:3-11:

> [3] *Blessed be the God and Father of our Lord Jesus Christ, who has blessed us in Christ with every spiritual blessing in the heavenly places,* [4] *even as he chose us in him before the foundation of the world, that we should be holy and blameless before him.* [5] *He destined* (προορίσας, προορίζω,

187

proorízō ... to determine or decree beforehand[19])
us in love to be his sons through Jesus Christ,
according to the purpose of his will, ⁶ to the praise
of his glorious grace which he freely bestowed on
us in the Beloved. ⁷ In him we have redemption
through his blood, the forgiveness of our
trespasses, according to the riches of his grace
⁸ which he lavished upon us. ⁹ For he has made
known to us in all wisdom and insight the mystery
of his will, according to his purpose which he set
forth in Christ ¹⁰ as a plan for the fulness of time, to
unite all things in him, things in heaven and things
on earth.

> *¹¹ In him, according to the purpose of him who*
> *accomplishes all things according to the counsel of*
> *his will, ¹² we who first hoped in Christ have been*
> *<u>destined</u> and <u>appointed</u> to live for the praise of his*
> *glory.*

God has *called* people through his Gospel. He *has justified* us *through our faith <u>in Jesus Christ</u>,* and *in this he has <u>glorified us</u>*!

Knowing what God has done for us, and what he is presently doing for us, we should not let *spiritual depression* keep us down.

Rom 8:28-30. All things work together for God for those who love God.

> *²⁸ <u>We know that in everything God works for good with those who love him, who are called according to his purpose.</u> ²⁹ For those whom he <u>foreknew</u> he also predestined to be conformed to the image of his Son, in order that he might be the first-born among many brethren. ³⁰ And those whom he <u>predestined</u> he also called; and those whom he called he also <u>justified</u>; and those whom he justified he also <u>glorified</u>.*

---

[19] Zodhiates, προορίσας, προορίζω.

The first verse presents some textual challenges to our Bible translators since the syntax, or connections, of several words is difficult to determine. Fitzmyer observes:

Verse 28 is problematic in that one cannot be sure whether the discussion about the Spirit comes to an end with it. It is certainly a transitional verse to what follows in vv. 29-30, the problem is mainly one of textual criticism ... the addition or omission of *ho theós*, "God," as the subject of the verb in various manuscripts has resulted in four interpretations ...[20]

Rom 3:28 reads *"We know that in everything God works for good with those who love him, who are called according to his purpose."*

As Fitzmyer and others have indicated, this is a tricky text and according to the translation one might be using, sometimes misleading! The one we are reading here is from the RSV.

However, the Greek manuscript does not stress that **God** *works all things for good*. The RSV translates this as *"we know that <u>in everything God</u> works for good with those who love him, who are called according to his purpose"*! This translation presents an overstatement read into the text from popular thinking!

The Greek reads: Οἴδαμεν δὲ ὅτι τοῖς ἀγαπῶσιν τὸν θεὸν πάντα συνεργεῖ εἰς ἀγαθόν, τοῖς κατὰ πρόθεσιν κλητοῖς οὖσιν. This is best translated as, *"but we know **that for those that love God** <u>all things work for good</u>, according to the things set forth according to his calling,* that is, *according to His eternal purpose"*!

Note how this interesting text has been translated in some Bibles!

NIV. *And we know that <u>in all things God works for the good</u> of those who love him, who have been called according to his purpose.*

---

[20] Fitzmyer, *Romans*, pp. 521ff. We will shortly discuss the different interpretations.

KJV. *And we know that all things work together for good to them that love God, to them who are the called according to his purpose.*

ESV. *And we know that for those who love God all things work together for good, for those who are called according to his purpose.*

NASB. *And we know that God causes all things to work together for good to those who love God, to those who are called according to His purpose.*

RSV. *We know that in everything God works for good with those who love him, who are called according to his purpose*

There is considerable difference in these translations. All of them make some sense, but they can and have been misleading.

Fitzmyer observes that in the Jewish tradition *"all things"* refers to *spiritual* things like *salvation* and *justification*.[21] This is a critical point in the context of the Jewish issues of *Torah* Law Paul has been addressing, and his use of the *eschatological apocalyptic* tradition. Fitzmyer emphasizes that it is necessary to maintain this text in the overall context of *foreknowledge, predestination, calling, justification* that follows in Rom 8:29, 30. Read ahead to Rom 8:37, *all these things*!

Needless, what we have in the above translations makes much the same argument. However, the KJV, the NIV, ESV, are closer to the Greek text!

The following reading is more what Paul had in mind! *"**For those who love God** and who live according to his eternal purpose **in Christ**, all things regarding **salvation** and **justification** will eventually work **for good** according to his eternal plan in Christ!"*

Rom 8:31-39. We are more than conquerors in Christ!

This magnificent statement in this pericope leads into the resounding climax of Rom 8 which had already begun

---

[21] Fitzmyer, *Romans*, pp. 522ff. Schreiner, *Romans*, 449ff.

on a high note, *"There is therefore now no condemnation for those who are in Christ Jesus."*

31 What then shall we say to this? If (**since,** εἰ with a present indicative verb implied) *God is for us, who is against us? 32 He who did not spare his own Son but gave him up for us all, will he not also give us all things with him? 33 Who shall bring any charge against God's elect? It is God who justifies; 34 who is to condemn? Is it Christ Jesus, who died, yes, who was raised from the dead, who is at the right hand of God, who indeed intercedes for us? 35 Who shall separate us from the love of Christ? Shall tribulation, or distress, or persecution, or famine, or nakedness, or peril, or sword? 36 As it is written,*

> *"For thy sake we are being killed all the day long;*
> *we are regarded as sheep to be slaughtered."*

*37 **No, in all these things we are more than conquerors through him who loved us.** 38 For I am sure that neither death, nor life, nor angels, nor principalities, nor things present, nor things to come, nor powers, 39 nor height, nor depth, nor anything else in all creation, will be able to separate us from the love of God in Christ Jesus our Lord.?*

This is one of the most "exciting" and uplifting passages in all of the New Testament. *It proclaims the victory those who love God enjoy.*

It sings the song of the *Revelation* of John, *victory in Christ*!

"We are more than conquerors through Christ who loved us and no one can separate us from the love of God in Christ Jesus"!

We must note the irony of Paul's question, **who can ...?** *The answer is obviously* **No one can!**

Also note the expression *all these things*! Drop back to Rom 8:28. *All these things work together for good, for our eternal salvation*!

Rom 8:31-37. Fitzmyer and most scholars astutely see in this pericope a *hymnic* structure set in *diatribe form,* *sung to the love of God in Christ.*[22] The answers to the questions raised in this pericope are obvious! *God is the judge, God has saved us through Jesus Christ who died for us, who can question God's decisions and power? No one!*

Rom 8:32. In the divine lawcourt where God is the judge, who can question God's decisions in all this business of suffering? *If God is for us*, and he must be since he has been working for us since before the creation, and since he gave his unique son to die for us, *who can be against us*?

The answer to this and the several related rhetorical question in Rom 32-35 comes below at verse 37.

Rom 8:33. *Who is going to bring a charge* against God's elect or chosen ones whom he has forgiven and justified? *No one!*

Rom 8:34. *Who is going to condemn the believer?* Certainly not Christ who died for the believer, and who also intercedes for the believer! For God himself has proclaimed the sinner *not guilty*!

Rom 8:35. Who is able to separate the believer from Christ? *No one!* Only the believer himself!

Paul then lists a number of stressful experiences that were well known to Jews and Jewish Christians of the day, all of which are set in common apocalyptic terms, *tribulation, distress, persecution, famine, nakedness, peril,* and the *sword.*

Rom 8:36. Paul quotes Ps 44 which was a well-known Jewish *community hymn of lament* which was in the sense of a prayer to God for deliverance, and which would be well known to Jewish Christians as a Psalm of those under persecution or oppression.

Rom 8:37-39. *Finally*, as the capstone to the section that began in Rom 8:18 and introduced *suffering*, and then moved through the *Holy Spirit interceding* on behalf of hurting believers, to stressing that *God is working in the trials of believers*, underscoring that *they are secure in*

---

[22] Fitzmyer, *Romans*, pp. 528f. See also Cranfield, Käsemann, Dodd, *et al.*

Christ for *God had been working for them since before creation,* and that God would permit no one to stand or come between them and his love, we come to this resounding note of triumph! **"We are more than conquerors through him who loved us!"**

The Greek behind the statement *"but,* or *on the other hand[23] we are more than conquerors in all these things"* is ἀλλ᾽ ἐν τούτοις ὑπερνικῶμεν διὰ τοῦ ἀγαπήσαντος ἡμᾶς. The present active verb ὑπερνικῶμεν implies *we are winning a more than conquering effort*!

There are no trials imaginable that can separate the believer from the love of God in Christ Jesus!

We note that the beginning of the long section, Rom 8:18-39, and the close of this great passage *focus on the sufferings of believers and the triumph they ultimately enjoy in Christ*!

The language and theology stress that this is a *hymn of triumph over persecution and suffering,* for *the Holy Spirit, God, and Jesus Christ are all involved with the suffering saints throughout their ordeals.*

A former student of mine in a Revelation course once pointed out that the book of Revelation can be summed up in two words: ***We win***!

---

[23] Zodhiates, ἀλλά *allá*; an adversative particle originally the neuter plural of *állos* ... A particle implying in speech some diversity or superaddition *to what preceded.* It serves, therefore, *to mark opposition, antithesis.*

Chapter 9 - Has God Been Faithless with Israel?
Rom 9-11

Context and Message

The primary purpose of these three chapters is to show that *God had not rejected Israel,* as some Jews thought Paul was teaching, *but Israel had rejected God. Israel could still be saved if it returned to God in true contrite heart, believed in the crucified and resurrected Jesus as the Messiah, and restored its faith in God through Jesus Christ* and not through the *Torah,* as great as the *Torah* was when used correctly.

Rom 9. Paul pours out his heart in sorrow in the thought that he wished Israel could be saved by his being accursed and cut off from Christ, but Paul recognized that this was not God's plan for the redemption of Israel.

God's choice of who would be saved is based on his *foreknowledge* and *calling, not on a fleshly human lineage from Abraham* as many Jews wished.

God's calling of Abraham, Isaac, and Jacob were God's *election* prerogative. Not any human privilege or birthright!

Rom 9:19ff. In this chapter we have the fascinating argument of the *potter* and the *clay.* God is obviously the potter, and Israel and the Gentiles are the clay!

Rom 9:30f. *What shall we say, then? That Gentiles who did not pursue righteousness have attained it, that is, righteousness through faith;* [31] *but that Israel who pursued the righteousness which is based on law did not succeed in fulfilling that law.* [32] *Why? Because they did not pursue it through faith, but as if it were based on works. They have stumbled over the stumbling stone,* [33] *as it is written,*

> "*Behold, I am laying in Zion a stone that will make men stumble,*

> *a rock that will make them fall;*
> *and he who believes in him will not be put to*
> *shame."*

The Jews tripped over the stumbling block of faith in Jesus as the Messiah.

So, whom has God chosen in Christ, corporately, according to his foreknowledge, those who have faith, including Abraham, Isaac, the Jews who believed the preaching of Peter in Acts 2, Paul in Acts 9, and the Gentiles like Cornelius in Acts 10, 11 who believed.

Rom 10 begins with Paul emphasizing his love and concern for Israel that they would be saved.

Paul emphasizes that Israel had a zeal for God but this was not enlightened by God's *Torah* word.

Contrary to some Jewish arguments against Paul's message of justification by faith in Jesus and not by works of *Torah* Law keeping, *God has not rejected Israel, Israel has rejected God through unbelief*!

Rom 10:8-10 emphasizes that the Jew could be saved, if they confessed with their mouth and believed in their heart that Jesus is Lord.

Paul assured them that he was not a renegade Jew who disliked Moses and the *Torah*, and insisted that Israel indeed were promised blessings in their fathers Abraham, Isaac, and Jacob, but these promises were not based on *Torah* Law keeping. They were based on faith in God's spoken word of instruction.

Paul claims that mere fleshly descent was not enough to guarantee the Abrahamic blessing.

Paul insisted that the *election* of Israel was not based on the moral goodness of Jacob. Jacob's choice by God was God's election, and *God has a perfect right to choose his own instruments of blessing* since all men have sinned and have no claim on God other than in his *calling* and *blessings*.

The prophets like Israel made it clear that Israel had forfeited their right to blessing and their name as God's people in light of their persistent apostasy, but that God had maintained his faithfulness despite that.

He claims the reason Israel (as a national entity) had missed Messianic blessing is because not only were they *apostate*, had lost their faith in God, and had all along *misread the nature* of the *Torah*.

Israel had become a contrary and disobedient nation not listening to the prophets like Isaiah.

Rom 10:16ff. Paul closes this section of his discussion with the interesting thought: *saving faith* comes from the *oral proclamation of the gospel message of Christ*, not by the preaching of the *Torah* Law!

Rom 11. Israel saw themselves and the *Torah* as a *télos end, final terminal point* to God's purpose, and sought only to establish their own national righteousness in the *Torah* contrary to the Abrahamic faith covenant.

The result *Torah* adherence for righteousness was that the Jews would have excluded the Gentile world.

In truth, the goal, the *télos*, or purpose of the *Torah* was in fact the gospel of God's redemption of both Jew and Gentile. The *télos* points to the eschatological completion or end of God's eternal plan of redemption that was to be found in Jesus the Messiah for all believers. The *Torah* pointed to the past age which had been terminated in Christ's coming. The function of the *Torah* was fulfilled in bringing Israel to faith.

This *télos* reading of God's purpose for the *Torah* was missed by Israel because Israel had repeatedly turned from God in apostasy and had hardened their hearts in unbelief and sin.

In fact, God hardened Israel so that her disobedience would result in the obedience of Gentiles which in turn was meant to result in the renewed faith and obedience of the Jews.

Rom 11:32. God concluded *all* under sin that he might have mercy on *all*.

197

> If Israel seeks salvation it will not be through *Torah* keeping, but *through faith in Jesus on the same grounds as the salvation of the Gentiles*, for God is no respecter of persons, for all have sinned and all need salvation in Jesus, the only means of salvation!
>
> No wonder Paul closes with the doxology of Rom 11:33-36:
>
> *"O the depth of the riches and wisdom and knowledge of God! How unsearchable are his judgments and how inscrutable his ways!* [34] *"For who has known the mind of the Lord, or who has been his counselor?"* [35] *"Or who has given a gift to him that he might be repaid?"* [36] *For from him and through him and to him are all things. To him be glory forever. Amen."*

Background context and message

Romans 1-8 is primarily a major theological discussion regarding the righteousness of God and his plan to save or justify all men, Jew and Gentile, through faith in Jesus Christ.

The discussion of Romans 9-11

Rom 9-11 addresses some concerns the Jews had concerning the righteousness of God who seemed to have turned away from his covenant people.

Paul knew that his message of justification by grace through faith in Jesus would be of considerable concern to Jewish and Gentile Christians who would struggle over his rejection of the *Torah* Law as *a vehicle for justification*. He had spent six chapters explaining that *justification is by faith in Jesus and not by the Torah Law*. This would lead some to believe that Paul had no regard for the *Torah*. He had already answered this concern in the early chapters of Romans. Some would assume from this that God had rejected his chosen people, Israel, since he now in the Messianic age treated Jew and Gentile on the same grounds. Obviously, many Jews would assume that there was no advantage to being a Jew since God seemingly had now turned away from Israel.

Paul then spent three chapters to respond to this false view!

Key thought for understanding Romans 9-11

At Rom 11:26, 27 Paul makes this remarkable statement which unfortunately many have pressed beyond what Paul had intended. He summed up his three-chapter argument by stating that *by faith in Jesus all Israel could be saved.*

Obviously, this would involve the Jew seeing both Jesus and the *Torah* in a different light!

Rom 11:26, 27. *"And so all Israel will be saved; as it is written, "Out of Zion will come the Deliverer; he will banish ungodliness from Jacob." And this is my covenant with them, when I take away their sins."*

However, if we keep this statement within the context Paul has been developing throughout his epistle, there is no real problem. Paul is not preaching **a universal salvation for all Israel** in this statement. We must keep this text within the context of Rom 9-11, *Israel is lost <u>not because</u> God rejected Israel! Israel is lost <u>because</u> Israel has rejected God through unfaithfulness to his Torah covenant*!

Paul had laid out his doctrine regarding Israel being saved at Rom 10:8-11. All Israel had to do to be saved is *believe in Jesus as the Messiah* and *confess their faith in Jesus' death and resurrection*!

[8] But what does it (Scripture) *say?*
  "<u>The word is near you</u>,
    on your lips and in your heart"
*(that is, the word of faith that we proclaim); [9] because <u>**if**</u> <u>you confess with your lips that Jesus is Lord and believe in your heart that God raised him from the dead, you will be saved</u>. [10] <u>For one believes with the heart and so is justified, and one confesses with the mouth and so is saved</u>. [11] The scripture says, "<u>No one who believes in him will be put to shame</u>." [12] For there is no distinction*

between Jew and Greek; the same Lord is Lord of all and is generous to all who call on him. ^{13} *For, "Everyone who calls on the name of the Lord shall be saved."*

To call on the name of the Lord means to believe in him for salvation.

Paul's point is that all Israel can be saved *if they will believe in their hearts and confess that Jesus was raised from the dead*!

So, in this manner, all Israel can be saved! *What manner*? Through *faith in Jesus as the Messiah*!

The same principle is true for all Gentiles, if they believe in Jesus and confess their faith in his resurrection they too will be saved.

Paul's statement *does not eliminate baptism* or discuss this here for baptism was not the issue with Israel or the Gentile being lost; *faith in Jesus and his resurrection were the issue*!

In Romans 9 - 11 Paul answers these concerns

These three chapters are a defense of the righteousness and faithfulness of God in light of what seemed his rejection of the Jewish nation.

These chapters are also a polemic against Gentile arrogance which was being fed by the notion that God had permanently cast off the Jewish people in favor of the Gentiles.

Rom 9:1-5. Paul's Agony Over Israel

I am speaking the truth in Christ, I am not lying; my conscience bears me witness in the Holy Spirit, ^{2} that I have great sorrow and unceasing anguish in my heart. ^{3} For I could wish that I myself were accursed and cut off from Christ for the sake of my brethren, my kinsmen by race. ^{4} They are Israelites, and to them belong the sonship, the glory, the covenants, the giving of the law, the worship, and the promises; ^{5} to them belong the patriarchs, and of their race, according to the flesh,

*is the Christ. God who is over all be blessed
forever. Amen.*

There were those who thought Paul should be
ashamed of what he preached because it seemed to confirm
he was *a renegade Jew who hated his own people.*

Rom 9:1-3. Paul refutes this as *entirely untrue* and
that he would be glad to forfeit his share in the Messiah in
the service of his people.

Rom 9:5. Paul acknowledged the unique opportunities
afforded his nation, *my kinsmen by race*, and *affirms their
privileged position.*

**Rom 9:6-25. Paul emphasizes that any rejection of
Israel lay in the historical apostasy and unbelief of
Israel, not in the unfaithfulness of God.**

Rom 9:11. *But it is not as though the word of God had
failed.*

Paul begins by stressing that *the fault lay not in the
message*, that is, *the word of God.* For example, *the
message of the prophets of Israel* had been proclaimed!

It was the rejection of Israel to the prophets' call for
faith that had led to Israel's historical struggles.

A major problem the Jews encountered was that they
assumed that because they were a descendent of Abraham
and Jacob this constituted their being God's people!

Paul picks up on this by arguing that *not every Jew
was in fact a real "Jew" or every Israelite a real
"Israelite"*!

Paul, by citing Jacob and Esau at Rom 9:12
demonstrated that it was not always the genealogical order
of lineage that counted, for *those who treasured God's
promise and election were favored.*

It is often difficult for those of us who are not Jews to
understand Paul's very Jewish reasoning, so for a while we
must think like a Jew to follow his thoughts!

Inheritance within a Jewish, and Near Eastern culture,
was normally according to *the order in which sons were
born*! The one born first was normally *the favored one*, the

firstborn, prōtótokos, meaning the favored one[1]! But this was not necessarily always the case, consider Jacob and Esau! Esau was born first, but through trickery and dishonesty Jacob *supplanted*[2] his right to be the firstborn, prōtótokos!

In the case of Esau and Jacob they were both legitimate and Esau had been the firstborn, yet because of his lack of faith in God's promise he was excluded from God's choice as *the firstborn*.

The promise to Abraham and his seed, Gen 12:2; 17:4, and the election of Israel through God's promises was a fundamental feature of Jewish thinking and faith. Paul played on this Jewish understanding and heritage!

The Jews recognized that God's promise to Abraham and his descendants, Israel, and his election of Israel as a chosen people, had been God's prerogative and business. They played on this and the concept of calling and election to the exclusion of the Gentiles!

Now to the traditional Jew it appeared that Paul was turning this narrative in a different direction!

Paul's critics may have seen in this a very convenient way to circumvent the force of Paul's arguments! Their point would have been something like "Paul's view argues that God has deviated and rejected Israel as his chosen and favored *firstborn* people"!

Paul disagreed, stating that to have Abraham's *fleshly line* of descent was not enough as the case of Ishmael and Isaac showed. Israel could argue that Ishmael was *illegitimate,* but this would miss God's inclusive promise to Abraham to bless all nations!

Rom 9:6-13. Paul's point is clear; God's choice between Isaac and Ishmael, between Jacob and Esau, and between a superficial Jew and a real "Jew," was a matter of God's divine choice and not human prerogative.

---

[1] Zodhiates, *prōtótokos.*
[2] Carl E. DeVries, "Jacob," *Baker Encyclopedia of the Bible*, vol. 2, p. 1084.

Throughout Paul's sustained argument including Abraham, Isaac, Ishmael, Jacob, and Esau, God's election had been *based on faith*, not genealogy!

Although Paul doesn't mention Deuteronomy 18:15-19, Peter does in Acts 3:22-23 *speaking of un-believing Jews being "cut off from among his people."*

This does not reflect on the faithlessness of God who is sovereign and bestows his grace and mercy in a way he sees fit. *It reflects on the loss of faith in Israel in God's promises to Abraham!*

Rom 9:8-10. In the light of how God in his *mercy* fulfils his *gracious* purposes *through faithfulness,* it is not simply human descent that is counted in hereditary lineage, but *faithfulness.* This point is clear in the descendants of Isaac who were actually the children of promise.

This argument was not new, as Paul had already stressed in Rom 4 and Gal 3:26-29. Inheritance of God's blessings is by faith not the *Torah* Law. One becomes a child and heir of the promises *by faith in Jesus.*

Rom 9:11-16. Paul does not let the opportunity to make his point escape. He states:

*"And not only so, but also <u>when Rebecca had conceived children by one man, our forefather Isaac,</u> [11] though they were not yet born and had done nothing either good or bad, in order that God's purpose of election might continue, not because of works but because of his call, [12] <u>she was told</u>, "<u>The elder will serve the younger.</u>" [13] As it is written, "Jacob I loved, but Esau I hated." [14] What shall we say then? Is there injustice on God's part? **By no means!** [15] For he says to Moses, "<u>I will have mercy on whom I have mercy, and I will have compassion on whom I have compassion.</u>" [16] So <u>it depends not upon man's will or exertion, but upon God's mercy</u>"*

But the critic might urge, Esau was a profane man and was rejected for his profanity. Paul reminds them that this cannot be true, *because God's choice was made while they were in the womb where neither of them had done good or evil.* The point is, *selection is not made according to human standards, but solely by God's foreknowledge, will, and purpose*, as the jew who knew his Old Testament *Tanah* should know!

In any case, by now Paul's point was made; God's blessing and election do not rest on simple human earthly lines, it never had in the past!

Rom 9:14-21. Is God then unjust?

[14] *What shall we say then? Is there injustice on God's part? **By no means**! [15] For he says to Moses, "I will have mercy on whom I have mercy, and I will have compassion on whom I have compassion." [16] So it depends not upon man's will or exertion, but upon God's mercy. [17] For **the scripture**[3] says to Pharaoh, "I have raised you up for the very purpose of showing my power in you, so that my name may be proclaimed in all the earth." [18] So then he has mercy upon whomever he wills, and he hardens the heart of whomever he wills.*

Is there injustice on God's part? Paul answers in the strongest terms, **Mei genoitō**, *No, no, no, by no means,* God was not faithless or fickle for God has not rejected Israel. *Israel has rejected God!*

This means God will work his gracious purpose for the world simply through his choice, as with Pharaoh, or as Israel saw fit!

At Mount Sinai, at the golden calf incident, Moses begged to be cut off from Israel's promises so sinful Israel could be saved, but God curtly rebuked him even though he went on to assure Moses that he would not obliterate Israel simply because of the Golden Calf incident, Exodus 32:30-35 and 33:12-23.

Later at Rom 10:18-21 Paul will enlarge on this and demonstrate that it was *the unfaithfulness of Israel that led to their rejection!*

---

[3] For a sincere Jew, an infallible argument, *"what does the scripture say ..."*

Rom 9:17. An arrogant Pharaoh could have been blotted out by God in an instant but *it served God's purpose to raise him up and harden him in his unbelief*.

An interesting point should be made here, *God only hardened Pharaoh's heart because Pharaoh had already hardened his heart against God,* Ex 8:15, 21, 32.

Rom 9:19-24. The Jew could argue: If that's the case, why should God judge them for disobedience?

[19] You will say to me then, "Why does he still find fault? For who can resist his will?" [20] But who are you, a man, to answer back to God? Will what is molded say to its molder, "Why have you made me thus?" [21] Has the potter no right over the clay, to make out of the same lump one vessel for beauty and another for menial use? [22] What if God, desiring to show his wrath and to make known his power, has endured with much patience the vessels of wrath made for destruction, [23] in order to make known the riches of his glory for the vessels of mercy, which he has prepared beforehand for glory, [24] even us whom he has called, not from the Jews only but also from the Gentiles?

In his potter and clay analogy Paul argues that the potter shapes the clay, not the clay the potter. Israel could have been blotted out immediately at Sinai, Exodus 32:7-10, but out of God's mercy and for his purpose, it suited God's purposes to maintain the covenant with them *for his world redemption purposes*.

Refer back to Rom 9:16; God saves all people out of his sovereign grace and mercy, and not simply because Moses in some way had won God's favor.

So, Pharaoh and Israel serve God's *gracious* purposes in both *obedience and disobedience*!

At Rom 11:7-10, 25 we will learn that throughout the discussion we know God is dealing with sinners *who have first hardened their hearts against God*!

The point is, God does not harden the hearts of the faithful!

However, in spite of the discussion on the hardening of faithless hearts, and God's patient bearing with sinners who have no right to complain, *God as the sovereign creator God still is a sovereign God who acts* as the potter who has the right to do with the clay as he wills! Cf. Jeremiah 18:1-12 which Israel knew very well!

God's aim had always been to be true to the faithful descendants of his promises to Abraham, so God has not been faithless when he rejected unfaithful disobedient people. *He has always kept his promise which was always based on the faith of Abraham and his descendants.*

Rom 9:22. In fact, if there's to be a criticism leveled against God it would have to be that *he was too patient!*

Paul's gospel of faith rather than *Torah* keeping would exclude a host of Jews from Messianic blessings, but this wasn't new because the prophets had done precisely the same thing in their preaching to Israel!

Rom 9:25, 26. Paul makes a *midrashic*[4] parallel argument regarding *Hosea who had proclaimed to the Northern Kingdom that they were not God's people because of their apostasy and harlotry yet who would again be accepted by God as his people*, obviously *by repentance and faith*, referring to the restoration of Israel after the exile! *Paul was obviously reflecting on the repentance of the Gentile and coming to faith, seeing in Hosea possibly also a messianic prophecy!*

Rom 9:27-29. *[27] And Isaiah cries out concerning Israel: "Though the number of the sons of Israel be as the sand of the sea, <u>only a remnant of them will be saved</u>; [28] for the Lord will execute his sentence upon the earth with rigor and dispatch." [29] And as Isaiah predicted,*
> *"If the Lord of hosts had not left us children,*
> *we would have fared like Sodom and been made like Gomorrah."*

---

[4] *Midrash* is a Jewish practice of seeing a parallel commentary between two situations or biblical texts.

Paul cites Isaiah who insisted that *God would save only a remnant* and that if it hadn't been for God's grace they all would have been totally obliterated.

All of this shows that Paul's view that a large number of Israel were outside God's blessing in the Messiah was nothing new, Israel's own prophets had prophesied it. Cf. also Rom 11:2-4.

Even the Torah taught that such rejection is not a lack of God's faithfulness, only that of Israel's!

And *what is just as important is that* the rejection of some of Israel, grounded in God's sovereign will and Israel's sin, *was not to be taken as permanent! There was still an opportunity for Israel to repent, come to faith, confess Jesus as Lord, and be saved.* A point he will make in Rom 10!

Hosea said that Israel would again be called God's people after the exile so the "not my people" status was not intended to be a permanent arrangement. Cf. Rom 11:11,17-24 where Paul discusses the grafting in of the natural branches of the olive tree, branches that had previously been cut off, but who were again part of the olive tree. His reference was to Israel who had been cut off from God because of unbelief, but who could be grafted back into God's family by God's grace through repentance and faith. However, we have already mentioned Paul's *midrashic* use of this text to refer to the Gentile believer's inclusion.

Rom 9:30-33 What shall we say about this?

30 What shall we say, then? That Gentiles who did not pursue righteousness have attained it, that is, righteousness through faith; 31 but that Israel who pursued the righteousness which is based on law did not succeed in fulfilling that law. 32 Why? Because they did not pursue it through faith, but as if it were based on works. **They have stumbled over the stumbling stone,** *33 as it is written,*

> *"Behold, I am laying in Zion a stone that will make men stumble,*

a rock that will make them fall;
and he who believes in him will not be put to
shame."

Paul shakes up the Jewish argument by asserting that the Gentiles who had not pursued righteousness by *Torah* keeping *could now attain it because of their faith*!

The point was that Jews who sought righteousness through the *Torah* did not attain it because that was not the purpose of the *Torah, and because they stumbled over faith in Jesus, the Messiah*!

The fault was not God's fault, nor the fault of his message or the *Torah. The fault lay in Israel who rejected God's covenant in the Torah through lack of faith and idolatry.*

Israel's precarious condition

Rom 10:1-4 Israel is not saved!

In a moving statement, Paul laments the lost condition of Israel and prays that their salvation would be possible.

Brothers and sisters, <u>my heart's desire and prayer to God</u> for them is that they may be saved. [2] I can testify that <u>they have a zeal for God</u>, <u>but it is not enlightened</u>. [3] For, <u>being ignorant of</u> the righteousness that comes from God, <u>and seeking to establish their own, they have not submitted to God's righteousness</u>. [4] For <u>Christ is the end of the law</u> so that there may be righteousness for everyone who believes.

Israel's problem was that *they had a zeal for God*, but that zeal was neither *enlightened* nor *fully formed*!

The NIV translates this as *"For I can testify about them that <u>they are zealous for God</u>, but <u>their zeal is not based on knowledge</u>*!

This suggests that although zeal is noble, *it must be fully informed according to sacred knowledge*, presumably knowledge of God's word as in the *Torah*.

Israel had faith in God, but their faith was *on their own terms*! They were stubborn in not listening to the *Torah* which had predicted the coming of the Messiah. Cf.

Jesus' comment at John 5:39, *"You search the scriptures, because you think that in them you have eternal life; and it is they that bear witness to me; [40] yet you refuse to come to me that you may have life."*

Paul declares that the Christ is the end or the *Torah!* Paul uses the Greek τέλος, *télos* which means *the goal or terminal* of the *Torah*, not meaning that Christ was <u>doing away with the *Torah*</u>, but that Christ was *the direction or goal* to which the *Torah* had been pointing, but which the Jews had missed in their rejection of Jesus as the Messiah! Paul had explained this to the Galatian Christians at Gal 3:19-22:

> [19] *Why then the law?* <u>*It was added because of transgressions, till the offspring should come to whom the promise had been made;*</u> *and it was ordained by angels through an intermediary.* [20] *Now an intermediary implies more than one; but God is one.*
>
> [21] *Is the law then against the promises of God? Certainly not; for if a law had been given which could make alive, then righteousness would indeed be by the law.* [22] <u>*But the scripture consigned all things to sin, that what was promised to faith in Jesus Christ might be given to those who believe.*</u>

Paul argued at Rom 10:2 that Israel was in fact *ignorant regarding the righteousness that comes from God.* Zeal not enlightened by God's word will not save or justify anyone!

It appears that they were seeking a righteousness on their own terms! Righteousness comes from *obeying God in faith*, not by personal obedience to *Torah* instruction. Paul simply states the issue—<u>*they have not submitted to God's righteousness!*</u>

Rom 10:5-13. The message of righteousness had been near the Jew, but they had missed it!

> [5] *Moses writes that the man who practices the righteousness which is based on the law <u>shall live by it</u>.* [6] *But the righteousness based on faith says, Do not say in your heart, "Who will ascend into*

209

heaven?" (that is, to bring Christ down) [7] *or "Who will descend into the abyss?" (that is, to bring Christ up from the dead).* [8] *But what does it say? The word is near you, on your lips and in your heart (that is, the word of faith which we preach);* [9] *because, if you confess with your lips that Jesus is Lord and believe in your heart that God raised him from the dead, you will be saved.* [10] *For man believes with his heart and so is justified, and he confesses with his lips and so is saved.* [11] *The scripture says, "No one who believes in him will be put to shame."* [12] *For there is no distinction between Jew and Greek; the same Lord is Lord of all and bestows his riches upon all who call upon him.* [13] *For, "everyone who calls upon the name of the Lord will be saved."*

Wow, a loaded pericope!

Moses had said that those who sought righteousness by the *Torah must* live by the *Torah*, Lev 18:5. The Greek ζήσεται, *from* ζάω, *záō refers to a lifestyle.* It is in the future indicative mood that implies a *constant lifestyle, not a sporadic lifestyle.*

However, Paul had already shown that *the Jews had failed to live by the Torah because of their stubborn sinful nature and loss of faith!*

Rom 10:6, 7. *The righteousness based on faith* was not something that had been *hidden,* difficult to find, *it was there near to them! It had been revealed from the beginning in Abraham,* the *Torah* Law, and *the prophets' messages!* Righteousness was not a *mysterious difficult lifestyle* that needed going up to heaven or down into the abyss *to bring Christ up from the dead,* to discover!

Righteousness had always lain there *open for all in the Torah* simply in *faith in God and his chosen promises and covenants.*

Rom 10:8. The *word* or *message* of righteousness by faith in God was *near you, on your lips and in your heart (that is, the word of faith which we preach).*

First, Paul uses an interesting word ῥῆμά which implies the *spoken or preached word.*

Second, the word or message, ῥῆμά, *"we are preaching"* κηρύσσομεν, *kērussomen,* is a *plural present* indicative active verb implying the message Paul and his companions *were preaching!*

There is some discussion over what the *content* of the message was; was it *the word of faith and or the confession with the mouth?* Most suggest that the message refers to both the message of the *heart* and the *mouth.* The two refer to the *confession* which was the *message of faith in Jesus.*

Rom 10:9. All the Jew needed to do was *confess with his mouth that Jesus was Lord and believe in his heart that God had raised him from the dead, and they would be saved!* Simple! Israel had *no excuse* for ignorance!

This was true for both Jew and Gentile.

Rom 10:10. *"For man believes with his heart* **and so** *is justified, and he confesses with his lips* **and so** *is saved.*

Here we encounter a text that some use to argue that *all that is necessary* **for salvation,** εἰς σωτηρίαν, *is that* **one believe in Jesus!** Therefore, baptism is not necessary **for salvation,** εἰς σωτηρίαν, but is necessary **because one is saved.** See the general discussions of Acts 2:38, εἰς σωτηρίαν, in many Evangelical commentaries.

The discussion hinges around how we translate the Greek preposition εἰς, *eis!* (That elusive pronoun εἰς again!)

At first glance the verse as translated in the RSV certainly sounds as though it would support such a position!

However, we must keep this discussion in the context of Paul's accusation here and the Jew's *refusal to believe that Jesus is the Messiah* and that *he rose from the dead as their king! The Jews simply refused to believe and confess faith in Jesus!*

So, the **RSV** renders this *"for man believes with his heart* **and** *so is justified, and he confesses with his lips* **and**

211

so *is saved*." *This is how one is justified*! One *believes in Jesus not the Torah* ***and so*** *is justified!*

This is a tricky text for which our translations have offered various solutions.

By translating εἰς, *eis* here as "***and so*** *is saved"* the RSV has created a misleading problem. The fundamental translation of εἰς, *eis* here as ***for*** is far more reliable than ***and so***!

The Greek is simple and reads: καρδίᾳ (locative, instrumental, *dative* noun) γὰρ πιστεύεται εἰς δικαιοσύνην, στόματι (locative, instrumental, *dative* noun) δὲ ὁμολογεῖται εἰς σωτηρίαν. A straightforward translation is "*for the heart believes* ***for*** *righteousness, and the mouth confesses* ***for*** *salvation*!"

What is possibly misleading in this verse are the three words "*and* ***so*** *is justified, or* ***so*** *is saved."*

And so leaves the impression of ***result*** rather than an expectant ***forward pointing*** *to salvation* which is what εἰς, *eis*, ***for***, actually means.

The **KJV** is a better reading and translates eis as "*with the heart man believeth unto righteousness; and with the mouth confession is made unto salvation."*

The **ASV** is similar to the **KJV**, translating this as faith and confession "*unto"* righteousness or salvation.

The **NASV** is similar to the **KJV** and **ASV** translating this as faith and confession "*resulting in"* salvation.

The **NIV** translates this "*For it is with your heart that you believe and are justified, and it is with your mouth that you confess and are saved."*

As we have in our text the **RSV** reading is [10] *For man believes with his heart and so is justified, and he confesses with his lips and so is saved.*

The standard reading of the Greek preposition εἰς, *eis* in this text as ***for*** would be much clearer!

The similar use of εἰς, *eis,* is found at Acts 2:38 where it is translated as ***for***, "*repent and be baptized* ***for*** *the forgiveness of your sins*."

To be a little technical, whenever you place εἰς, *eis,* before a noun in the *accusative* (direct object) case, the εἰς, *eis, points forward toward the accusative noun* and the *accusative noun limits the meaning of the verb* that precedes the **εἰς** *eis*. In Acts 2:38 the verb is *be baptized,* the accusative noun is *forgiveness,* and εἰς, *eis,* stands between *baptized* and *forgiveness* and points from *baptism forward to forgiveness.*

In the case of **Rom 10:10** the translation of the RSV and NIV are unfortunate, the **KJV** and **ASV** do an excellent job of maintaining the meaning of εἰς, *eis,* as *unto,* and the **NASV** is near this with *resulting in.*

By definition, the best translation of εἰς, *eis* coming between the verb *believing* and the accusative noun *forgiveness* would be *for*!

In this case we should translate **Rom 10:10** as *"For man believes with his heart for justification, and he confesses with his lips for salvation."*

This maintains an understanding of the forward-looking meaning of εἰς, *eis* that is in keeping with the Gospels which also mention *repentance* as a requirement *for salvation*!

Paul clearly states that *believing with the heart that Jesus is Lord* is *for* salvation, as is *confessing with the mouth that Jesus was raised from the dead* is *for justification.*

An interesting question here is why Paul does not mention *repentance* and *baptism*?

The answer is simple, *Paul is writing for Jews <u>who refused to believe</u> in Jesus and <u>confess him as Lord</u> and Messiah*! *Baptism was not the issue*!

Repentance and baptism would not have been a problem to the Jews who already believed in Jesus, *but not accepting and believing Jesus as the Messiah was the issue*!

Remember, this section is addressing the question *why the Jews were rejected*. They were not saved *because they did not believe in Jesus*. If they wanted to be saved they must believe in Jesus. They would not confess him if they did not believe in him, neither would they repent nor be baptized if they did not believe in him!

It was not simply because of the *Torah*, that they were not saved, for Paul has already said that the *Torah* was *good*, *holy*, and spiritual, Rom 7:7ff, but it could not save anyone!

It was not that the Word of God was *faulty or uncertain*, the prophetic message from God was clear, cf. Rom 9:6ff, 10:16ff.

The reason the Jew was not saved was that *they refused to believe the message from God regarding Jesus being the Messiah, and rejected the death and resurrection of Jesus as atoning. They simply refused to believe in and confess him as Lord and Messiah.*

In order to be *justified* or *saved* they would *have to first believe in Jesus in faith in order to be justified and saved*!

If they will believe in Jesus and confess him as Lord and Messiah, they could be justified and saved!

Rom 10:14-21. Faith and the preaching of Jesus

This is a tragic text! God has historically called to his people but they had declined to listen to him!

14 But how are men to call upon him in whom they have not believed? And how are they to believe in him of whom they have never heard? And how are they to hear without a preacher? 15 And how can men preach unless they are sent? As it is written, "How beautiful are the feet of those who preach good news!" 16 But they have not all obeyed the gospel; for Isaiah says, "Lord, who has believed what he has heard from us?" 17 So faith comes from what is heard, and what is heard comes by the preaching of Christ.

18 But I ask, have they not heard? Indeed they have; for

> *"Their voice has gone out to all the earth,*
> *and their words to the ends of the world."*

[19]Again I ask, did Israel not understand? First Moses says,

> *"I will make you jealous of those who are not a nation;*
> *with a foolish nation I will make you angry."*
> *[20]Then Isaiah is so bold as to say,*
> *"I have been found by those who did not seek me;*
> *I have shown myself to those who did not ask for me."*

*[21]But of Israel he says, "**All day long I have held out my hands to a disobedient and contrary people**."*

Paul suggests a question that a Jew might ask, "*how are men to believe and call on Jesus if they had not heard of him?*"

Paul will answer, "*But you Jews have heard, but you would not listen, believe, and obey the message!*"

Remember Jesus' discussion at **John 5:39**? He charged that the Jews had searched the Scriptures seeking eternal life, but *these Scriptures had pointed to him and **they would not listen**!*

Now Paul turns to Isaiah in a devastating message! Isaiah had spoken to Israel but they had refused to listen. They had a history of refusing to listen to God's prophets! So Paul, building on this tendency, states that *faith comes from hearing the preaching of God's messengers*, which Israel had historically declined.

Faith comes from **hearing the preached message**, and *what was preached was Jesus Christ the Messiah*, and this the Jews rejected.

Paul's sentence structure is interesting and often missed in our translations!

The **KJV** renders this as *[17]So then faith cometh by hearing, and hearing by the **word** of God.* Our tradition has led us to see this as *faith comes from the preaching of Scripture*, which is a fine thought, but not what Paul actually said!

The **RSV** translates this as *"what is heard comes by the preaching of Christ,"* which is better, but still misses the real strength of what Paul wrote!

Paul wrote ἄρα[5] ἡ πίστις ἐξ ἀκοῆς, ἡ δὲ ἀκοὴ διὰ ῥήματος[6] Χριστοῦ[7]. This reads more precisely as *"consequently,[8] faith comes from what is heard, and what is heard through* <u>*the preached message concerning Christ*</u>.*"*

What was the message *concerning Christ* that Paul and the Apostles had preached? 1 Cor 2:2, *"For I decided to know nothing among you except Jesus Christ and him crucified."*

Then Peter expounded on this at Acts 2:23-36 clearly preaching to the Jews that *Jesus had been crucified by the Jews, but God had raised him from the dead and made him Lord and Christ!*

Rom 10:21. *What was their problem?* Citing Isa 65:2, Paul answered that question! *"All day long I have held out my hand to a* **disobedient** *and* **contrary** *people"*.

Israel was rejected and lost simply because they would not listen to the message of Moses and the prophets regarding a coming Messiah, and Jesus was that Messiah with a public life and ministry to confirm this!

But they could be saved if they only believed in Jesus and confessed him by mouth as their Messiah, Rom 10:9,10!

This is the story Paul will cover again in Rom 11.

---

[5] Zodhiates, ἄρα *ára*; inferential particle. *Then* or *therefore*, and indicating an interrogative. In Classical Greek *it stands after other words in a clause* and is always written *ára*, then, therefore. *As an interrogative,* <u>*it stands first*</u> *in a clause …*

[6] ῥήματος, the *preached word or message*.

[7] Χριστοῦ, objective, genitive, *concerning* Christ.

[8] Dunn translates ἄρα giving it the proper force of introducing a *conclusion or summing up,* "so then, *consequently,*" *Romans 9-16*, p. 623.

Is there a faithful remnant in Israel?

Rom 11:1-10. God has a remnant in Israel that will be saved.

> *[1] I ask, then, **has God rejected his people? By no means**! I myself am an Israelite, a descendant of Abraham, a member of the tribe of Benjamin. [2] **God has not rejected his people whom he foreknew.** Do you not know what the scripture says of Elijah, how he pleads with God against Israel? [3] "Lord, they have killed thy prophets, they have demolished thy altars, and I alone am left, and they seek my life." [4] But what is God's reply to him? "I have kept for myself seven thousand men who have not bowed the knee to Baal." [5] **So too** at the present time there is a remnant, **chosen by grace**. [6] But if it is by grace, it is no longer on the basis of works; otherwise grace would no longer be grace. [7] What then? **Israel failed to obtain what it sought. The elect obtained it**, but the rest were hardened,*

Rom 11:1, 2a. *"I ask, then, has God rejected his people? By no means! I myself am an Israelite, a descendant of Abraham, a member of the tribe of Benjamin. [2] God has not rejected his people whom he foreknew.*

Paul repeats his standard rhetorical diatribe type question with the same profound emphatic answer. Λέγω οὖν, μὴ ἀπώσατο ὁ θεὸς τὸν λαὸν αὐτοῦ; μὴ γένοιτο, *"Therefore I ask, has God rejected his people? By no means!"*

The small interrogative particle, οὖν, *therefore*, or perhaps better still, *consequently I ask* ... Perhaps we can also read this as *"after all, has God turned away from all Israel? Surely not, for I am saved..."* This emphasizes the personal aspect of Paul's own conversion. Paul reminds the Jews of something they knew very well! They should remember that he was a true-blue Israelite of the tribe of Benjamin, and he has been saved! God surely has not rejected or turned away from all Israelites!

God has *definitively not* turned away from *all of Israel*! *He has only rejected those who had rejected him* and *would not believe his message.*

So, Paul continues, *there has always been an elect group in Israel who would believe and be saved*!

Who are they? **It is those who have kept their faith in God**, *"who have not bowed the knee to Baal."*

Paul refers back to Ezekiel and his experience after his battle with the prophets of Ball, and confrontation with Jezebel, 1 Kings 19. When Ezekiel was struggling with doubt and questioned whether he alone was faithful, God assured Ezekiel that *he has always had a remnant in Israel who believed him.*

Definitely, God has not turned away from *all of Israel*! He has rejected *only those who had rejected him* and *would not believe his message. He has a remnant who will believe!*

But, Paul continues, *there has always been an elect group in Israel who would believe and be saved*!

Who are they? **It is those who have kept their faith in God**, *"who have not bowed the knee to Baal."*

The message is that God continues to love Israel, his people, his covenant people, even though they have rejected him and his Mosaic covenant with Israel! This covenant had reached its purpose in Jesus Christ, but God's covenant with Israel continues now in Christ.

Nothing has changed on God's part! He still loves Israel and desires them to be saved!

Only now Israel must accept and believe in his Messiah and his new covenant in Jesus!

Rom 11:2b-10. The problem was that the bulk of the Jews, as in the days of Elijah, *had hardened their hearts and refused to believe*, as Paul explains in Rom 11:1-10.

But this was not God's plan for Israel. He still has a remnant of Jews who would not reject God for "Baal." They could be saved by returning to faith in God believing in his new covenant with Jesus Christ!

However, there was a greater plan in God's dealing with Israel and the Gentiles. The glorious end result to this plan, however, was the salvation of the Gentiles! This demonstrated that those who had rejected God, both Jew and Gentile, _could be grafted back_ into the natural olive tree, the original family of God.

Rom 11:11-32. The salvation of Israel

*[11] So I ask, have they (Israel) stumbled so as to fall (completely)? By no means! But through their trespass salvation has come to the Gentiles, so as to make Israel jealous. [12] Now if their trespass means riches for the world, and if their failure means riches for the Gentiles, how much more will **their full inclusion mean**!*

[13] Now I am speaking to you Gentiles. Inasmuch then as I am an apostle to the Gentiles, I magnify my ministry [14] in order to make my fellow Jews jealous, and thus save some of them. [15] For if their rejection means the reconciliation of the world, what will their acceptance mean but life from the dead? [16] If the dough offered as first fruits is holy, so is the whole lump; and if the root is holy, so are the branches.

[17] But if some of the branches were broken off, and you, a wild olive shoot, were grafted in their place to share the richness of the olive tree, [18] do not boast over the branches. If you do boast, remember it is not you that support the root, but the root that supports you. [19] You will say, "Branches were broken off so that I might be grafted in." [20] That is true. They were broken off because of their unbelief, but you stand fast only through faith. So do not become proud, but stand in awe. [21] For if God did not spare the natural branches, neither will he spare you. [22] Note then the kindness and the severity of God: severity toward those who have fallen, but God's kindness to you, provided you continue in his kindness; otherwise you too will be cut off. [23] And even the others, if they do not persist in their unbelief, will be grafted in, for God has the power to

graft them in again. ²⁴ *For if you have been cut from what is by nature a wild olive tree, and grafted, contrary to nature, into a cultivated olive tree,* **how much more will these natural branches be grafted back into their own olive tree.**

²⁵ *Lest you be wise in your own conceits, I want you to understand this mystery, brethren:* **a hardening has come upon part of Israel,** until **the full number** of the Gentiles come in, ²⁶ **and so** all Israel will be saved; *as it is written,*

"*The Deliverer will come from Zion,*
he will banish ungodliness from Jacob;"
²⁷ "*and this will be my covenant with them*
when I take away their sins."

²⁸ *As regards the gospel they are enemies of God, for your sake; but as regards election they are beloved for the sake of their forefathers.* ²⁹ *For the gifts and the call of God are irrevocable.* ³⁰ *Just as you were once disobedient to God but now have received mercy because of their disobedience,* ³¹ **so they have now been disobedient in order that by the mercy shown to you they also may receive mercy.** ³² *For God has consigned all men to disobedience, that he may have mercy upon all.*

Now this pericope is a mouthful which—if one is not careful to *maintain in the context in which Paul has placed it*—becomes difficult to swallow and digest!

Rom 11:11. We begin by noticing the statement: ¹¹ *So I ask, have they* (Israel) *stumbled so as to fall* (completely)? The Greek reads μὴ ἔπταισαν ἵνα πέσωσιν, "*not to fall (aorist active verb followed by a* ἵνα, *hina, aorist subjunctive clause*⁹) *that it might be a complete fall*"!

Paul's point was that Israel like himself who was a traditional Benjaminite Jew, had not been utterly rejected

---

⁹ This is an interesting coupling of an aorist verb with a ἵνα, *hina*, clause in the subjunctive mood. This can be translated, "*to the end that*, or *that in order* that *it might be.*"

with no hope of salvation. The fall was not necessarily *absolute*, but *conditional*, based on their faithless disobedience and rejection of God's covenant plan in Jesus Christ.

Some Premillennial problems!

This section has led to some fanciful Premillennial interpretations of Rom 11:26, such as, "*In the end, when Jesus returns **so all Israel** will be saved.*"

This passage, and Rom 11:26, simply <u>do not teach or support this claim</u> as that is not what Paul said or implied!

We will discuss this mistaken theology further at Rom 11:26, below.

Paul's Gospel message has always been that the only way either the Jew or the Gentile can be saved is by accepting Jesus as the Messiah, and through faith in Jesus' death and resurrection!

So, in the end, if Israel *is going to be saved* it will be on the same grounds of the gospel Paul preached to both Jew and Gentile, *faith in Jesus Christ and his death and resurrection*!

*If there is **another way** to be saved, then God is **not a righteous God**!*

The gospel preached by Paul, based on God's covenant with Abraham, is that *the Jew will be saved on the same grounds as the Gentile, **through faith in Jesus the Messiah**!*

Paul was not changing his argument or offering a special favor. The *same gospel* argument applied to all, *both Jew and Gentile*, for God is a righteous God!

Rom 11:11, 12. *"Now if their trespass means riches for the world, and if their failure means riches for the Gentiles, how much more will their <u>full inclusion</u> mean!"* If Israel's loss *worked for the glory of the Gentiles*, what should we think of the state of the Gentiles' *rich blessing of inclusion mean*?

The word *fullness* or *full number* in this discussion is a technical term in Greek, πλήρωμα, *plérōma*, [10] found often in the Jewish Apocalyptic tradition. It is translated *full inclusion of the Gentiles* in Rom 11:12, and *full number of the Gentiles* in Rom 11:25. The emphasis is **not** on **number** but on **fulness of blessing**. Thus it carries the meaning of *fulness* in the sense of *fulness* of the *rich blessing of their inclusion*.

In fact the word *number* does not appear in either Rom 11:12 or 25! It is provided by the translators of the text, providing commentators much ground to be ploughed!

Πλήρωμα, *plérōma*, is well translated as *full inclusion* in Rom 11:12, but for some *theological* reason at **Rom 11:25** it is translated as *full number*, which can be misleading! Obviously, the meaning of Rom 11:25 must be shaped also by its context which discusses the salvation of Israel.

The interpretation of this challenging text has been widely interpreted, mostly based on some *theological* position. Fitzmyer observes that at **Rom 11:25** it is possible to translate this as *full number* but this is highly *eisegetical*, [11] meaning *reading meaning into the text* not out of the text, hence my comment that it is a *theological* insert!

Morris makes a good point here arguing that the inclusion of the Gentiles, which would be the completion of God's plan, would not mean the diminution of the Jews blessing, but rather of its enrichment[12].

Rom 11:13. Paul makes the point that he is now speaking to the Gentile believers in Rome.

*[13] Now I am speaking to you Gentiles. Inasmuch then as I am an apostle to the Gentiles, I magnify my ministry [14] in order to make my fellow Jews jealous, and thus save **some** of them. [15] For if their rejection means*

---

[10] Zodhiates, πλήρωμα *plérōma*, figuratively meaning fullness, full measure, abundance.

[11] Fitzmyer, *Romans*, p. 622.

[12] Morris, *Romans*, p. 408.

the reconciliation of the world, what will their acceptance mean but life from the dead? [16] *If the dough offered as first fruits is holy, so is the whole lump; and if the root is holy, so are the branches.*

Paul is aware that he will *not save all of the Jews*, but he *will save **some** of them*!

We must note that Paul is speaking in this paragraph to the Gentiles, but he obviously has the Jews in mind. Both the Gentile and the Jew should know that the inclusion of the Gentiles in God's plan would bring glory to all, to the Gentile, the Jew, and to God!

Rom 11:17. *What then? Israel failed to obtain what it sought. The elect obtained it, but the rest were hardened!* The righteous believing remnant had not hardened their heart!

The hardness of the Jews is seen in their unbelief, but their unbelief need not continue. *They could repent and believe! The inclusion of the Gentiles hopefully would get the stubborn Jews to repent and believe!*

Rom 11:17-24. The parable of the Olive Tree

Paul's point was if the Jews would come to faith, they too, like the believing Gentiles, will be blessed in the Messiah.

In this pericope we have the fascinating "parable" of the natural olive tree, Israel, the people of God, and wild olive branches, the Gentiles. Because of their unbelief, Jewish branches from the natural olive tree have been cut out. Wild olive branches, the believing Gentiles, have been grafted into the natural olive tree *because of faith*. If God can graft wild olive branches, Gentile believers, into the natural olive tree because of their faith, *surely he can graft back into the natural olive tree branches that have been cut out, the unbelieving Jews, if they come to faith*!

So, the solution is that *if Israel wants to be grafted into the true family* of Abraham, and the Abrahamic covenant, after they have been rejected for unbelief, ***all they have to do is return to faith and believe in Jesus the***

Messiah and **confess him as Lord and Messiah**! Cf. Rom 10:9, 10!

Rom 11:18-24. However, Paul sounds a warning for the Gentile believers!

> *[17] But if some of the branches were broken off, and you, a wild olive shoot, were grafted in their place to share the richness of the olive tree, [18] <u>do not boast over the branches. If you do boast, remember it is not you that support the root, but the root that supports you.</u> [19] You will say, "Branches were broken off so that I might be grafted in." [20] That is true. <u>They were broken off because of their unbelief, but you stand fast only through faith. So do not become proud, but stand in awe.</u> [21] For if God did not spare the natural branches, neither will he spare you. [22] <u>Note then the kindness and the severity of God: severity toward those who have fallen, but God's kindness to you, provided you continue in his kindness; otherwise you too will be cut off.</u> [23] And even the others, <u>if they do not persist in their unbelief,</u> will be grafted in, for God has the power to graft them in again. [24] For if you have been cut from what is by nature a wild olive tree, and grafted, contrary to nature, into a cultivated olive tree, <u>how much more will these natural branches be grafted back into their own olive tree.</u>*

Jewish arrogance should not be replaced by Gentile arrogance! When God elected the Jews they became arrogant, and now that Gentiles are included in the elect the temptation is for Gentile Christians to become arrogant.

Gentile Christians are in danger of doing precisely what the Jews did: seeing themselves as an end in themselves with the Jews being completely cast off.

But this would be a violation of the Abrahamic covenant, which was for all nations.

At this point we must remember that in Rom 9-11 Paul has been *refuting the fact that God had rejected all Israel*. It was only *disobedient and faithless Israel that had been rejected*, but God still had a remnant of faithful Jews who would be saved, *but his salvation had always been based in an obedient faith in God*, not by a hereditary legacy or *Torah* works system.

It might be strategically good to refresh our understanding of Paul's key theological thought in Romans, Rom 1:16, 17!

> *[16] For I am not ashamed of the gospel: it is the power of God for <u>salvation to everyone who has faith, to the Jew first and also to the Greek</u>. [17] For in it the righteousness of God is revealed <u>through faith for faith</u>; as it is written, "<u>He who through faith is righteous shall live.</u>"*

Rom 11:25-36. So we come to the final statement of this great discussion of Israel's rejection by God.

> *[25] <u>Lest you be wise in your own conceits, I want you to understand this mystery, **brethren**: a hardening has come upon part of Israel, until the full number of the Gentiles come in</u>, [26] and **so all Israel will be saved**; as it is written,*
>
> *"The Deliverer will come from Zion,*
> *he will banish ungodliness from Jacob;"*
> *[27] "and this will be my covenant with them*
> *when I take away their sins."*
>
> *[28] <u>As regards the gospel they are enemies of God, for your sake; but as regards election they are beloved for the sake of their forefathers. [29] For the gifts and the call of God are irrevocable. [30] Just as you were once disobedient to God but now have received mercy because of their disobedience, [31] so they have now been disobedient in order that by the mercy shown to you they also may receive mercy.</u> [32] For God has consigned all men to disobedience, that he may have mercy upon all.*
>
> *[33] O the depth of the riches and wisdom and knowledge of God! How unsearchable are his judgments and how inscrutable his ways!*
> *[34] "For who has known the mind of the Lord,*
> *or who has been his counselor?"*

^{35} *"Or who has given a gift to him*
that he might be repaid?"
^{36} *For from him and through him and to him are all*
things. To him be glory forever. Amen.

Rom 11:25, 26. Notice that Paul now addresses his readers personally as **brethren**! He has moved on from a general Jewish/Gentile terminology to one of **brethren**, to both groups of Christians in Rome.

Paul refers to this business of Jews and Gentiles being rejected and included as *a mystery of God's will* not necessarily understood by human wisdom. The entire process is God's will and business which Jewish and Gentile Christians should not question, but accept.

^{25} <u>*Lest you be wise in your own conceits, I want you*</u> <u>*to understand this mystery,*</u> **<u>brethren</u>**<u>*: a hardening has*</u> <u>*come upon part of Israel, until the full number of the*</u> <u>*Gentiles come in,*</u> ^{26} *and* **so all Israel will be saved***; as it is written,*

"*The Deliverer will come from Zion,*
he will banish ungodliness from Jacob;"
^{27} *"and this will be my covenant with them*
when I take away their sins."

and **so all Israel will be saved***; as it is written,*

Regarding this mystery of God's will and pattern of behavior, note Paul's closing benediction to this section:

O the depth of the riches and wisdom and knowledge of God! How unsearchable are his judgments and how inscrutable his ways!
^{34} *"For who has known the mind of the Lord,*
or who has been his counselor?"
^{35} *"Or who has given a gift to him*
that he might be repaid?"
^{36} *For from him and through him and to him are all things.*
To him be glory forever

Rom 11:26. Some Evangelical proposals regarding a universal salvation of all Israel being saved has created considerable discussion which we have already addressed at Rom 10:10. But here Paul writes this seemingly discordant statement again, *"and so **all Israel** will be saved"!*

Does Paul mean, as some Premillennial thinkers have stated, that at the eschatological end *all Israel, every Jew, will be saved*?

A gentle nudge, ***think again***!

Is this something new, something different from what Paul has been teaching about salvation and justification *only by faith and confession of Jesus for both Jew and Gentile*?

Is this *a new gospel for the Jews* who in the end, regardless of their repeated unfaithfulness, will be saved! *Surely not*!

Rom 11:26 is interesting, and if taken out of the context of salvation by faith in Jesus Christ can be misleading!

In this text Paul wrote, καὶ **οὕτως** πᾶς Ἰσραὴλ σωθήσεται, *καθὼς γέγραπται,* **"and so** all Israel will be saved, ***just as it is written.***"

First, this cannot be a new different, special dispensational concept, for Paul writes that this salvation of which he now speaks is *just as it has been written*, obviously in scripture. What has been the statement about salvation *throughout scripture*, beginning with Abraham, then the Jews on Pentecost at Acts 2:22-38, with Paul in Acts 22:16, and Jesus' teaching at Luke 13:3? *Scripture* clearly states *Jews will be saved only by faith, notably by faith in Jesus Christ.*

Why all his stuff *in scripture* about Jews needing to believe, repent, and be baptized for forgiveness of sins if in the end all of them will be saved anyhow!

If this Evangelical and Premillennial stuff is true, then Paul was clearly really mixed up and confused!

But what has Paul already said about righteousness and salvation in his leading theological argument at Rom 1:16, 17?

Second, much of the discussion hinges around the word *so*, **οὕτως,** *houtōs,* "*So, all Israel will be saved ...*"

The little *adverb so* in Greek, **οὕτως,** *houtōs. Houtōs* simply means, *"in this manner."*[13]

Dunn adds an interesting thought emphasizing that we should maintain the expression in the *immediate* or *preceding* context of the discussion:

> "but the basic sense of οὕτως is *'thus, in this manner,'* referring to Paul's conviction that *conversion of the Gentiles will be the means of provoking Israel to jealousy and converting them.*[14]

This certainly is possible, but I prefer to see the expression in the context of Paul's previous *overall discussion of salvation—faith in Jesus Christ,* as per Rom 1:16, 17, 3:31, 5:1ff, Rom 10:8-10.

So, in what manner will all Israel be saved? Cf. Rom 10:8-10! *By faith and confession of Jesus the Messiah Israel will be saved!*

If Paul is suggesting some form of universal salvation for Israel, as some Evangelicals claim, then he is contradicting his previous statements that *God does not show favoritism or partiality* to anyone, and Paul's oft made statement regarding a final *universal judgment for all who disobey the gospel,* Rom 1:32; and 2 Thess 1:8-10 where Paul writes:

> *This is evidence of the righteous judgment of God, that you may be made worthy of the kingdom of God, for which you are suffering—* [6] *since indeed God deems it just to repay with affliction those who afflict you,* [7] *and to grant rest with us to you who are afflicted, when the Lord Jesus is revealed from heaven with his*

---

[13] James Swanson, *A Dictionary of Biblical Languages, Greek New Testament,* 1996; Johannes P. Louw and Eugene A. Nida, *Lexicon of the New Testament,* 1989; Leon Morris, *The Epistle to the Romans,* pp. 420f; Fitzmyer, *Romans,* p. 622, who states that this expression should not be translated *and then* as is the practice of some. If Paul *does not have a temporal meaning* it but should be understood as summarizing all that has been said before, meaning *in the manner previously stated;* Louw, J. P., & Nida, E. A., *Greek-English Lexicon of the New Testament: Based on Semantic Domains,* vol. 1, p. 610.

[14] Dunn, *Romans 9–16,* vol. 38B, p. 681. Italics emphases, IAF.

*mighty angels in flaming fire, [8] inflicting vengeance
upon those who do not know God and upon those who
do not obey the gospel of our Lord Jesus. [9] They shall
suffer the punishment of eternal destruction and
exclusion from the presence of the Lord and from the
glory of his might, [10] when he comes on that day to be
glorified in his saints, and to be marveled at in all who
have believed, because our testimony to you was
believed.*

The **"and so,"** καὶ οὕτως, must be understood as *"in
this manner with reference to that which precedes; 'and
so, thus, in this manner"*[15] and not in a resultant forward
looking manner.

So, in this manner, *if all Israel is to be saved*, then *all
Israel will have to come to faith in Jesus Christ which both
Paul and God knew was not likely*!

**Rom 11:28-36. Paul stresses that God can have
mercy upon all whom he decides to have mercy.**

*"As regards the gospel they are enemies of God, for
your sake; but as regards election they are beloved for
the sake of their forefathers. [29] For the gifts and the call
of God are irrevocable. [30] Just as you were once
disobedient to God but now have received mercy
because of their disobedience, [31] so they have now been
disobedient in order that by the mercy shown to you
they also may receive mercy. [32] For God has consigned
all men to disobedience, that he may have mercy upon
all.*

*[33] O the depth of the riches and wisdom and
knowledge of God! How unsearchable are his judgments
and how inscrutable his ways!*

*[34] "For who has known the mind of the Lord,
or who has been his counselor?"*
*[35] "Or who has given a gift to him
that he might be repaid?"*

---

[15] Louw, J. P., & Nida, E. A., *Greek-English Lexicon of the New
Testament: Based on Semantic Domains,* vol. 1, p. 610.

^{36} *For from him and through him and to him are all
things.* **To him be glory forever. Amen.** *"*

Paul opens this intriguing concluding statement to his
argument that Israel is not judged because God has rejected
all Israel! His point has been that Israel has been rejected
because Israel has rejected God by citing Isa 59:20, 21.
Salvation and judgment is God's prerogative, but it has
been since before creation predicated in Christ on his love,
mercy, and grace for those who would trust in him.

> *"The Deliverer will come from Zion,*
> *he will banish ungodliness from Jacob;"*
> ^{27} *"and this will be my covenant with them*
> *when I take away their sins."*

Redemption will come in Christ according to God's
covenant with Abraham, Moses, and Jesus their Messiah.

The overall theme of Isa 40-60 is critical to
understanding this short verse Paul uses, and we know
Paul was fully aware of the meaning and implications of
this great text.

*Israel was despondent, thinking that God had rejected
them! Sounds like Rom 9-11!* But Isaiah writes
encouragement; God will redeem his people; *they will be
his servant to bless both Israel and the nations.*

So, the text Paul cites comes from Isaiah's great
servant Israel/Messiah songs in which Isaiah proclaims a
restoration hope to Israel during Cyrus' Medo-Persian,
former Babylonian captivity. There is hope in God's plan
for Israel for there will be a restoration to Israel, Israel's
homeland.

In this magnificent block of material Isaiah assures
Israel that they will be God's *suffering servant* to usher
redemption to *Israel and all nations*. God promises a
coming suffering servant Messiah who would lead his
people in blessing all nations. *Israel as a co-suffering
servant has a role in God's plan to bless the nations.*

I like Isaiah's statement at Isa 49:6:

> *"It is too light a thing that you should be my
> servant*

> *to raise up the tribes of Jacob*
> *and to restore the preserved of Israel;*
> *I will give you as a light to the nations,*
> *that my salvation may reach to the end of the*
> *earth."*

Paul's citing Isa 59:20, 21 comes as a fine conclusion to his discussion of God not rejecting Israel but blessing them as servants in his eternal plan to bless all nations, Jew and Gentile! *So*, God has chosen to save every Jew *who believes in Jesus Christ, his death and resurrection, and who will confess his name before others, presumably also the Gentiles.*

Every faithful Jew would know that God has the *sovereign right* to carry out his plan of redemption *to save by grace and faith* all who believe in Jesus Christ, Jew and Gentile.

Chapter 10 - How Then Shall We Live?
Rom 12:1-13:14

This chapter is a summary of practical living in a covenant relationship with God which grows out of the heavyweight theological lessons on God's righteousness and mercy in saving all those who trust in Jesus, Jews and Gentiles.

In this lesson Paul applies his doctrinal theology to the practical lives of his readers.

Rom 12:1-13:14 *forms a large block of paranetic, practical ethical and moral material that builds on the theme of how Christians should respond in a practical way to God's great mercy.*

As always for Paul, all doctrine should have practical implications and application! So, at Rom 12:1 he begins to outline a practical application of his theological message relating to a righteous God who desires his people to live in a righteous relationship with him.

Rom 12 :1-2. *First, Paul discusses how the great blessings of God's mercy and calling should impact our everyday lives. The Christian's response should be nothing short of offering their lives to God as a living sacrifice, for such spiritual worship is a reasonable priestly service offered to God.*

God's grace and love are a feasible reason for giving our lives every day and every moment as a holy sacrifice of spiritual service!

We submit to having our minds transformed by his Word and the power of the Holy Spirit as we deny temptation of the world and shape our lives to be pleasing to God.

Rom 12:3-8. *Second, Christians recognize that God's grace and work in saving us should result in a transformation of their lives as they use his many spiritual gifts in a responsible manner of ministry and service.*

Christians must be diligent in discovering and using the practical gifts that God empowers through his Spirit in their lives.

The recognition and awareness of God's grace is a major feature of our Christian service.

Paul lists several practical gifts Christians receive from the Holy
Spirit living and working in their lives.

Dietrich Bonhoeffer in his discerning book The Cost of Discipleship warns against "selling grace cheaply in the marketplace," meaning that Christians too often take God's grace too lightly. God's grace comes to us freely, but when we accept it, it should cost us our very lives in Christian service. Bonhoeffer knew from personal experience the meaning of Rom 12:1, 2, for in the end he died in a Nazi concentration camp for his Christian faith.

Rom 12:9-21. Paul encourages the Christians to realize that the result of their awareness of God's mercy is that they must emulate God's love for one another.

Christian love, like God's love for the world, is more than an emotional feeling for others whom they like. It is like God's love, a seeking to help love that goes beyond an emotional feeling of friendship. Christian love seeks the best for others, friend or foe, like God's love in seeking for and calling the lost in Christ into a deep loving relationship, John 3:16,17, "For God so loved the world that he gave his only Son, that whoever believes in him should not perish but have eternal life. [17] For God sent the Son into the world, not to condemn the world, but that the world might be saved through him."

Strained relationships will exist between Christians; the only reaction to this should be a genuine love and concern for one another in which the other person is always put first. Christians must make every effort on their part to maintain peace and harmony.

Christian love should also overflow toward those outside the Christian faith!

Rom 13:1-7. Living in a hostile environment does not excuse Christians from civil responsible obedience! Christians should set an example of respect for government, especially regarding paying their taxes!

Respect for civil government is part of God's plan for maintaining peace.

Rom 13:8-14. The only real debt that Christians should owe is to love others.

By living with love one fulfils all the requirements of the Torah, note the 10 commandment-like instructions of Jesus' teaching in his great sermon on the mountain, Matt 5-7, and Paul's instructions at Gal 5:13,14: For you were called to freedom, brethren; only do not use your freedom as an opportunity for the flesh, but through love be servants of one another. ¹⁴ For the whole law is fulfilled in one word, "You shall love your neighbor as yourself." ¹⁵ But if you bite and devour one another take heed that you are not consumed by one another.

Christians should realize how important every moment is and should live as though the final hour of Jesus' second coming of salvation and judgment has come.

Christians should not live worldly lives of reveling, debauchery, and licentiousness. Debauchery and licentiousness are terms associated with sexual promiscuity.

How should those redeemed in Christ respond to the love and grace of God and Christ?

Paul shifts his approach in Rom 12 after closing what we might term a heavyweight section of theological instruction on the righteousness of God seen in God's providing an opportunity for a righteous relationship with both the Jews and the Gentiles. He explained to the Jews that God's plan of atoning salvation had never been through *Torah* Law keeping, for ever since his call of Abraham it had always been through faith in God's covenant promises.

Rom 9-11 wrapped up this section by assuring the Jews that God had not rejected the Jews by including the Gentiles in his plan of redemption. Israel's problem was that *they had repeatedly rejected God* in their idolatry and immorality. They had stumbled over receiving his Messiah, Jesus, by refusing to believe in Jesus' divine relationship with the Father, and his death and resurrection.

After his heavyweight theological discussion in Rom 1-11 Paul now explained beginning in Rom 12 that Christians must see the Christian life as *a worshipful response to* God's redeeming grace.

Indicating that these chapters are a response to God's wonderful grace, Paul uses key words to introduce the practical ethical side of his doctrinal teaching.

There are several key terms early in Rom 12 that indicate the introduction of *paranetic* material which is *practical ethical teaching* which flows from doctrinal material or theology to practical responsive practical living.

These terms are *"I appeal,"* *"therefore,"* *"for,"* and verbs in an *imperative* form.

We learn a major point from examining Paul's Epistles; he never lays down doctrinal material just for the sake of doctrine! Doctrine is always followed by practical ethical teaching that grows out of the doctrine!

Technically we call this practical teaching *paranesis* or *paranetic[1]* material. *Paranetic* material always flows out of doctrinal material which shapes it and controls it and *gives life to the doctrinal material.*

What follows in Rom 12:1-15:33 is certainly *a call to a Christian response* to God's gracious redemptive activity. But it is more than simple moral uprightness and

---

[1] *Paranesis* and *paranetic* derive from Hellenistic Greek παραινετικός from παραινέτης, an adviser, encourager, and from ancient Greek παραινεῖν to exhort, advise, *Oxford English Dictionary.*

social behavior! It is the *necessary* righteous behavior in response to what God has done in saving one and granting them a deep relationship with himself, and with Jesus, and the Holy Spirit, *which is what righteousness is all about*! For that reason, the instruction is often in a *hortative imperatival verb form.*

Righteousness has a strong theological Christological foundation to it.

But Christ's atoning work is not only theological, but it also calls for Christlike practical, moral and ethical responses.

The aim of Christ's atoning work is *reconciliation between God and man*, and *this relationship is only complete when man offers to God that which honors His holiness.*

Reconciliation begins in God's work in Christ, but it is fulfilled in man's *parenetic* holy response to God.

Rom 12:1-3 Man's Response to God's redeeming mercy and grace

"*I appeal to you therefore, brethren, by the mercies of God, to present your bodies as a living sacrifice, holy and acceptable to God, which is your spiritual worship. [2] Do not be conformed to this world but be transformed by the renewal of your mind, that you may prove what is the will of God, what is good and acceptable and perfect.*"

Paul's language is strong and vibrant!

Paul *appeals earnestly*, παρακαλέω, *parakaléō,*[2] to the Christians in Rome to *seriously consider God's mercy and grace and the enormous impact of God's grace on human spiritual and emotional understanding*, Rom 7:24, "*wretched man that I am.*" He encourages them to respond to God's grace and mercy in an *appropriate holy devoted*

---

[2] The Greek παρακαλέω, *parakaléō,* can be translated *I encourage,* draws on the concept of *calling to one's side for help,* but carries in it *a sense of urgency to exhort, a desire, to beseech.*

manner in *spiritual worship by presenting their own bodies, lives, as a living sacrifice to God*!

Paul's language here is definitive of *the style and quality of worship he proposes, a living sacrifice.* Louw and Nida note that the word *present* derives from παρίστημι, *to make available, to provide, to present to … offer yourselves as a living sacrifice (to God)'* Rom 12:1.[3]

The verb παραστῆσαι is an aorist active infinitive, pointing to the *direction* or *end result* of the *urging or strong encouragement* of the verb Παρακαλῶ, *I appeal to you …*

Paul's use of the word σῶμα *sōma*[4] translated as *body* is interesting. He is not referring to fleshly body, but *the whole living being* of the worshipper.

This sacrifice of the *body* is to be a *living* sacrifice, θυσίαν ζῶσαν, *thusian zosan of the life of the worshipper!*

The *contrast* could be between *what the Christians are to offer*—a living sacrifice of their own life or body, and *a dead sacrifice as in the Temple cult*—is intended.

Regarding this *living sacrifice* Dunn observes that even when the Temple was destroyed the priests still maintained an emphasis on *daily sacrifices*:

The figurative use of sacrificial language is widely attested, both in Jewish and wider Hellenistic literature, often in criticism, implicit or explicit, of reliance on a superficial ritual performance … There is a significant difference, however. In Jewish critique of a false reliance on sacrifice *it was assumed that ritual sacrifice was still necessary*: the importance of the cult is clearly indicated in such passages as 2 Macc 1:19–22; 3:32–39; Jub. 50.11 … Sib. Or. 3.573–79; and by the flow of temple tax from the diaspora to maintain the daily sacrifice in Jerusalem; the Qumran sect had by no means rejected the cult itself (see the Temple

---

[3] Παρίστημι, Louw and Nida, *Greek English Lexicon of the New Testament.*

[4] Zodhiates, σῶμα, *sōma*; among a wide scope of contexts it primarily means *a body, an organized whole made up of parts and members.*

Scroll!), and even after the destruction of the temple the rabbis show by their continuing concern to regulate for qodašin ("hallowed things") that they regarded the current state of affairs (of Temple Temple) as essentially temporary.[5]

Dunn continues:

> The ζῶσαν is probably chosen to contrast the thought of <u>a sacrifice</u> *which consists in the quality of daily living*, "a constant dedication" ... with a sacrifice which consists in killing an animal ... Here we should recall that σῶμα is not used with reference to sacrifice in the LXX, nor does it occur in Paul in the quite proper Greek sense "corpse" ... Both points underline the implied contrast being made by Paul: the thought of sacrifice has been transposed across a double line—from cultic ritual to everyday life, from a previous epoch characterized by daily offering of animals *to one characterized by a whole-person commitment lived out in daily existence.*[6]

The words *spiritual worship* derived from the Greek λογικὴν, λατρείαν, have provided several alternatives, all reasonable! One version is *a reasonable service*. Another is *a holy sacrifice*. Another, *a living sacrifice*. The RSV and ESV interpretation of a *spiritual worship* is preferred! The NIV translation is also precise, "*a spiritual act of worship.*"

The Greek words λογικὴν λατρείαν are impressive when considered together in this context. Λογικὴν, *logikēn* derives from λογικός, *logikós* which primarily means *reasonable, logical*, but in the context of *worship* carries the sense of *spiritual* rather than *physical rational* thinking.

Λατρείαν derives from *latreías* or *latreúō*, meaning to worship, *to offer devoted service for hire or as a slave, or*

---

[5] Dunn, *Romans 9–16*, vol. 38B, p. 710.
[6] Dunn, *Romans 9–16*, vol. 38B, p. 710.

to offer divine service, obviously here in the sense of *religious context* results in *divine service.*[7]

Thus, Paul encourages the Christians to *present their bodies or lives as a living sacrifice* which incorporates all the above suggested renderings, *encouraging the Christian to respond with a <u>reasoned spiritual life devoted worshiping God!</u>*

The *priestly* and *sacrificial* language Paul uses draws heavily on the Jewish cultic character of worship as reflected in the *Torah* which *defines one's life as an acceptable holy worshipping sacrifice to God.*[8]

Most commentators find in Paul's usage a Jewish *cultic*[9] sense of worship defining the religious side of Jewish religion. However, here he sets this *individual act of worship* in a style typical of the adherents of a Christian cultic religious movement, i.e. the Christian fellowship.

In a long discussion Dunn covers this cultic sense well, commenting also on the Hellenistic understanding of cultic worship.

> The continued use of cultic language is clearly deliberate: of the nine occurrences of λατρεία in the LXX, eight refer to Jewish cultic worship ... λογικός does not occur in the LXX, but is a favorite expression of Greek philosophical, particularly Stoic, thought, in the sense of "belonging to reason, rational." As such *it marks out what is appropriate to man, in distinction from beasts, and what relates him to God*; cf. particularly Epictetus 1.16.20–21: "If I were a nightingale, I should be singing as a nightingale; if a swan, as a swan. *But as it is, I am a rational being (λογικός εἰμί), therefore I must be singing hymns of*

---

[7] Zodhiates, λατρεία, *latreía.*

[8] Dunn, *Romans*, p. 710.

[9] *Cultic, Miriam Webster Dictionary*, a system of religious beliefs and ritual. *The Free Dictionary*,
a system or community of religious worship and ritual,
the formal means of expressing religious reverence; religious ceremony and ritual.

praise to God." This sense naturally lends itself to a spiritualizing antithesis between rational and physical ... All these probably indicate Jewish usage prior to Christian appropriation ... The Hermetic writings also take up the same language, including not least the talk of "spiritual sacrifice" ... A broader usage in Hellenistic Judaism has already been indicated ... *More to the point, Paul has in view not simply a worship offered by the mind, but, in contrast to the Hermetic devotion, a worship expressed in the bodily reality of everyday living* ... similarly *mutatis mutandis* in contrast to Philo ... The implied contrast with ritual worship ... should again not be overplayed ... but again *not be disregarded* ... *if Paul is indeed trying to set out alternative identity markers for the new community of Christians* ... the worship here will be distinct from the cultic hallmarks of traditional Judaism ... The distinctively comparable language of 1 Pet 2:2, 5 (τὸ λογικὸν ἄδολον γάλα ... πνευματικὰς θυσίας εὐπροσδέκτους τῷ θεῷ) may well have been influenced by Paul ...[10]

Although the acts of Christian *logical spiritual worship* Paul is about to delineate is *intrinsically individual* it is a characteristic of the Christian "*cult*" who worship God with their lives as a spiritual marker of distinction from other groups. One should be able to identify the Christian by their daily spiritual activity of offering their lives in service to God and others.

Christians *present* their *lives, or themselves,* to God as a *devoted daily living sacrifice*; one that involves every aspect of their lives.

Rom 12:2. "*Do not be <u>conformed</u> to this world but be <u>transformed</u> by the <u>renewal</u> of your mind, that you may prove what is the will of God, <u>what is good and acceptable and perfect</u>.*"

---

[10] Dunn, *Romans 9–16*, pp 711f. Cf. also Fitzmyer, Romans, pp. 637ff; Schreiner, *Romans*, pp. 644ff.

241

I like J. B. Phillip's translation of Rom 12:2, *"Do not let the world press you into its own mold"*![11]

Rather than being shaped by the world, Christians are to be *transformed by the renewal of their minds.*

Conformed is a fascinating word, συσχηματίζεσθε, from συσχηματίζω, *suschēmatízō,* [12] *to fashion alike, conform to the same pattern outwardly, be conformed to a pattern or mold.* [13]

To the negative to not be conformed, Paul adds the positive, *be transformed,* μεταμορφοῦσθε from μεταμορφόω, *metamorphóō ... from metá ... denoting change of place or condition,* and *morphóō ... to form. To transform, transfigure, change one's form.* [14] It is an imperative *passive* expression indicating that *we must submit to the transformation* that *takes place in our mind* <u>*as our minds are focused on God's saving activity*</u> *and as the Holy Spirit works in us and we are led and transformed by the Spirit of life.*

This is not simply something the Holy Spirit does automatically, but something that happens *when we submit in knowledge to the will of God.*

This act of offering one's life to God and being transformed by the renewal of one's mind *is the will of God.* The Jew would understand this correctly as submitting to the *Torah instruction of God in Christ,* which *behavior is good and acceptable to God!*

Paul expresses the role of being shaped by Scripture well in his admonition to Timothy, 2 Tim 3:14-16:

> *But as for you, continue in what you have learned and have firmly believed, knowing from whom you learned it* [15] *and how from childhood <u>you have been acquainted with the sacred writings which are able to instruct you for salvation through faith in Christ</u>*

---

[11] J. B. Phillips, *The New Testament in Modern English,* 1996.

[12] Zodhiates, συσχηματίζω, *suschēmatízō.*

[13] Swanson, James A., *Dictionary of Biblical Languages with Semantic Domains: Greek (New Testament),* 1997.

[14] Zodhiates, μεταμορφόω, *metamorphóō.*

Jesus. ¹⁶ *All scripture is inspired by God and*
profitable for teaching, for reproof, for correction,
and for training in righteousness, ¹⁷ *that the man of*
God may be complete, equipped for every good work.

Peter, likewise, stresses the need to be shaped by
Scripture at 1 Pet 2:1-3:

¹ *So put away all malice and all guile and insincerity*
and envy and all slander. ² *Like newborn babes, long*
for the pure spiritual milk, that by it you may grow up
to salvation; ³ *for you have tasted the kindness of the*
Lord.

In his second epistle at 2 Pet 1:3ff Peter enlarges on
this thought. God has given us all things that we need to
live godly through the knowledge of him who called us to
his own glory.

His divine power has granted to us all things that
pertain to life and godliness, through the knowledge of
him who called us to his own glory and excellence,
⁴ *by which he has granted to us his precious and very*
great promises, that through these you may escape
from the corruption that is in the world because of
passion, and become partakers of the divine nature.
⁵ *For this very reason make every effort to supplement*
your faith with virtue, and virtue with knowledge,
⁶ *and knowledge with self-control, and self-control*
with steadfastness, and steadfastness with godliness,
⁷ *and godliness with brotherly affection, and brotherly*
affection with love. ⁸ *For if these things are yours and*
abound, they keep you from being ineffective or
unfruitful in the knowledge of our Lord Jesus Christ.
⁹ *For whoever lacks these things is blind and*
shortsighted and has forgotten that he was cleansed
from his old sins. ¹⁰ *Therefore, brethren, be the more*
zealous to confirm your call and election, for if you do
this you will never fall; ¹¹ *so there will be richly*
provided for you an entrance into the eternal kingdom
of our Lord and Savior Jesus Christ.

Rom 12:3-8. The use of God's gifts of grace – interpersonal relationships

For __by the grace given to me__ I __bid__ everyone among you __not to think of himself more highly than he ought to think__, but to think with sober judgment, __each according to the measure of faith which God has assigned him__. [4] For as in one body we have many members, and all the members do not have the same function, [5] so we, though many, are one body in Christ, and __individually members one of another__. [6] __Having gifts that differ according to the grace given to us__, let us use them: if __prophecy, in proportion to our faith__; [7] if __service__, in our serving; he who __teaches__, in his teaching; [8] he who __exhorts__, in his exhortation; he who __contributes__, in liberality; he who __gives aid__, with zeal; he who does __acts of mercy__, with cheerfulness.

First, note that these gifts are *gifts flowing out of God's grace*—we do not deserve them! They are *gifts of faith* that we are to develop and use as an act of *spiritual worship of God*.

They are gifts of faith which with the aid of the Holy Spirit we offer in worship of God!

Notice how the gifts are described by Paul; they are gifts of *service, teaching, exhortation, liberal giving, giving aid* with zeal, doing *acts of mercy* with cheerfulness. *These are gifts for serving others, but they become gifts of worship service to God!*

I am reminded of Jesus' teaching at Matt 25:40:

[31] *"When the Son of man comes in his glory, and all the angels with him, then he will sit on his glorious throne. [32] Before him will be gathered all the nations, and he will separate them one from another as a shepherd separates the sheep from the goats, [33] and he will place the sheep at his right hand, but the goats at the left. [34] Then the King will say to those at his right hand, 'Come, O blessed of my Father, inherit the kingdom prepared for you from the foundation of the world; [35] for I was hungry and you gave me food, I*

was thirsty and you gave me drink, I was a stranger and you welcomed me, [36] I was naked and you clothed me, I was sick and you visited me, I was in prison and you came to me.' [37] Then the righteous will answer him, 'Lord, when did we see thee hungry and feed thee, or thirsty and give thee drink? [38] And when did we see thee a stranger and welcome thee, or naked and clothe thee? [39] And when did we see thee sick or in prison and visit thee?' [40] And the King will answer them, 'Truly, I say to you, as you did it to one of the least of these my brethren, you did it to me."

Most of the gifts are easily understood, but one of them is interesting. It is *giving aid with zeal.* The word translated "giving aid" in Greek is ὁ προϊστάμενος, *ho prohistamenos,* from προΐστημι, *proïstēmi,* which Zodhiates explains has several implications; "to be placed before something or someone, or be over someone, to stand, to cause to stand before, to set over. In the New Testament only in the intransitive, meaning to stand before."[15] This certainly would imply *to teach, to lead,* or even shepherd. In the context it is probably best understood as *to lead people with zeal.* Christians are leaders for Christ!

Second, Rom 12:3, notice Paul's interesting use of *faith* in this context. He does not simply use the word *faith* as a synonym of *belief, what we believe* about God or Christ. In this context, introduced by offering one's body as a living sacrifice, Paul uses the concept of faith to refer to *the stage of maturity in the Christian lifestyle of faith* shaped by one's faith in God and Christ and empowered by the Holy Spirit. Paul uses πίστεως, the descriptive genitive form of πίστις, *pistis,* which can carry the sense of *faithfulness* to the Christian lifestyle. It seems best to see faith here in this context as the *measure of one's growth of living faith in Christ.*

---

[15] Zodhiates, προΐστημι, *proïstēmi.*

Third, note that Paul observes that this ministry is a gift of God's grace *to be performed in service to others*! This defines the nature of the purpose of these gifts. They are *a spiritual service to God* through one's service to others!

Fourth, these *gifts of service* are *according to the measure of faith that God has assigned to us. Faith here is understood as the practical living of our lives in service to God.* When we surrender our lives in spiritual worship to God he collaborates with us in developing our faith to *where we use our faith in spiritual service to others.*

Fifth, Paul expresses *the corporate nature of our faith.* It is not only faith in God, but also *faith for others*! Mounce writes, "The Christian faith is essentially a corporate experience."[16]

Sixth, we live and function in a body greater than our own! "*For as in one body we have many members, and all the members do not have the same function, ⁵ so we, though many, are one body in Christ.*"

Seventh, developing the *corporate nature of our body relationship in Christ*, Paul emphasizes that since we are many, "*we are one body in Christ, and individually members one of another*." Paul's point is that Christians are "estranged" *individuals* redeemed by God and adopted into a *corporate* family of God, *the Church*. As *the body of Christ* the Church is made up of individual members who do not live for themselves but now live for God and Christ, and for one another!

Sometimes this *giving of gifts* involved *miraculous gifts* by the Holy Spirit, 1 Cor 12:4-11, but this does not mean that the only way in which God gives gifts is in a *miraculous* gift! By *miraculous* we imply actual *empowerment by the Spirit* to perform *supernatural or unnatural works* by divine intervention through the Spirit.

That God works in our lives by his Holy Spirit does not necessarily imply miraculous gifts. Many of the gifts

---

[16] Mounce, *Romans* p. 234.

Paul mentions in Rom 12:3-8 *do not require a miraculous power*, only our willingness to let God work in our lives through his Holy Spirit *to assist us to grow*.

That God and Christ distribute gifts to the redeemed is a fundamental doctrine of Paul. Cf. 1 Cor 12:1-32; Eph 4:7-11.

Paul develops these gifts further at 1 Cor 12:4-11 where the context was *the abuse of gifts for personal aggrandizement*, 1 Cor 12:4-11:

> [4] *Now there are <u>varieties of gifts</u>, but the same Spirit;* [5] *and there are varieties of service, but the same Lord;* [6] *and there are varieties of working, but it is the same God who inspires them all in everyone.* [7] *To each is given the manifestation of the Spirit **for the common good**.* [8] *To one is given through the Spirit <u>the utterance of wisdom</u>, and to another the <u>utterance of knowledge</u> according to the same Spirit,* [9] *to another <u>faith by the same Spirit</u>, to another <u>gifts of healing</u> by the one Spirit,* [10] *to another <u>the working of miracles</u>, to another prophecy, to another the ability to distinguish between spirits, to another various kinds of tongues, to another the interpretation of tongues.* [11] *All these are inspired by one and the same Spirit, who apportions to each one individually as he wills.*

Notice the emphasis on *gifts of service to others, for the common good*!

A major point worth noting in Paul's terminology is that gifts given by God *involve ministry or service to others*. God's gifts, whether miraculous or otherwise, were never intended to be for self-aggrandizement, but *for service to others*.

Notice that in describing these gifts in 1 Cor 12 Paul lists gifts that God gives his saints *enabling them to perform* them *in service to others*.

Many charismatic individuals and communities miss this point by focusing on the *personal nature of these gifts* and *not on the community corporate service nature and use of the gifts*.

At Eph 3:14-21 Paul discussed the gift of the Holy Spirit in a different context, one of personal growth so that Christians might *live their lives for the glory of God*, a pivotal point in the Ephesian letter.

[14] For this reason I bow my knees before the Father, [15] from whom every family in heaven and on earth is named, [16] that according to the riches of his glory he may grant you to be strengthened with might through his Spirit in the inner man, [17] and that Christ may dwell in your hearts through faith; that you, being rooted and grounded in love, [18] may have power to comprehend with all the saints what is the breadth and length and height and depth, [19] and to know the love of Christ which surpasses knowledge, that you may be filled with all the fulness of God.

[20] Now to him who by the power at work within us is able to do far more abundantly than all that we ask or think, [21] to him be glory in the church and in Christ Jesus to all generations, for ever and ever. Amen.

Rom 12:9-21. The ideal conduct among those in covenant relationship with God and one another

Paul describes the *motivation* for *Christian behavior and mutual relationships* as *love for one another*.

I am reminded of the three great pivotal theological emphases in Paul's paranetic theology: *faith, hope, and love* which can be traced in almost all of his epistles. Cf. 1 Cor 13:13; 1 Thess 1:2f; Col 1:3.

In his ministry, Jesus emphasized the overall missional impact of *loving one another*. John 13:35:

[34] A new commandment I give to you, that you love one another; even as I have loved you, that you also love one another. [35] By this all men will know that you are my disciples, if you have love for one another."

In the broader context of loving others Jesus taught his disciples *to even love their enemies*, Matt 5:43ff.

[43] "You have heard that it was said, 'You shall love your neighbor and hate your enemy.' [44] But I say to you, Love your enemies and pray for those who

persecute you, [45] so that you may be sons of your
Father who is in heaven; for he makes his sun rise on
the evil and on the good, and sends rain on the just
and on the unjust. [46] For if you love those who love
you, what reward have you? Do not even the tax
collectors do the same? [47] And if you salute only your
brethren, what more are you doing than others? Do
not even the Gentiles do the same? [48] You, therefore,
must be perfect, as your heavenly Father is perfect.

In his First Epistle John goes to great lengths to argue
that one cannot love God without loving one's neighbor or
fellow believer, 1 John 4:7-12ff.

Beloved, let us love one another; for love is of
God, and he who loves is born of God and knows God.
[8] He who does not love does not know God; for God is
love. [9] In this the love of God was made manifest
among us, that God sent his only Son into the world, so
that we might live through him. [10] In this is love, not
that we loved God but that he loved us and sent his Son
to be the expiation for our sins. [11] Beloved, if God so
loved us, we also ought to love one another. [12] No man
has ever seen God; if we love one another, God abides
in us and his love is perfected in us.

In this great text, Rom 12:9-21, Paul obviously reflects on, and projects Jesus' teaching on the situation in Rome!

Jewish Christians had been banished from Rome then
allowed to returned on several occasions. While this was
happening, Gentile Christians had possibly remained in
Rome to continue their ministry. Then the Jewish
Christians returned, sometimes with their ethnic
convictions regarding the *Torah* and food restrictions. Paul
will reflect on this later at Rom 14 & 15.

Tensions must have worn thin on occasions as they
unfortunately still do today between Christian
congregations who hold different opinions on certain

matters and who still have to work through their ethnic differences!

Paul, knowing the issues in Rome from fellow Christian travelers, stressed that the bond that should bind Jewish and Gentile Christians in fellowship in Rome needed to be stronger than was at that time apparent! Hence this striking paragraph at **Rom 12:9-21**.

As you read this amazing paragraph it, reads as though Paul started out emphasizing the importance of loving one another and then his mind moving just kept going from one thought to another! Many of the thoughts just make sense in the context of loving one another, but a few are worthy of further examination!

> _Let love be genuine; hate what is evil, hold fast to what is good; [10] love one another with brotherly affection; outdo one another in showing honor._
> [11] _Never flag in zeal, be aglow with the Spirit, serve the Lord. [12] Rejoice in your hope, be patient in tribulation, be constant in prayer. [13] Contribute to the needs of the saints, practice hospitality._
> [14] _Bless those who persecute you; bless and do not curse them. [15] Rejoice with those who rejoice, weep with those who weep. [16] Live in harmony with one another; do not be haughty, but associate with the lowly; never be conceited. [17] Repay no one evil for evil, but take thought for what is noble in the sight of all. [18] If possible, so far as it depends upon you, live peaceably with all. [19] Beloved, never avenge yourselves, but leave it to the wrath of God; for it is written, "Vengeance is mine, I will repay, says the Lord." [20] No, "if your enemy is hungry, feed him; if he is thirsty, give him drink; for by so doing you will heap burning coals upon his head." [21] Do not be overcome by evil, but overcome evil with good._

Love is a common expression in Christian circles today but is often not fully understood! _Love_ is _not simply an affectionate feeling for another. It goes much deeper than that._

The Greek word ἀγάπη, *agápē,* means *to love others with the intention of doing good for them.* That is all others including fellow Christians, Jews and Gentile Christians, and enemies! It involves *affectionate regard, but also stresses goodwill and unconditional benevolence.* It carries within it a deeply rational and cognitive DNA.

It is best understood in the context of *God's love for the world! God's love is willful direction toward all men with the intention of helping and saving them.*

John 3:16, 17. *"For God so loved the world that he gave his only Son, that whoever believes in him should not perish but have eternal life. [17] For God sent the Son into the world, not to condemn the world, but that the world might be saved through him."*

According to John 3:16, this includes *the entire world,* even man in his unregenerate condition. It involves *God doing what He knows is best for man,* and *not necessarily what man desires.*[17]

Certainly, it involves an emotional element, but it lies not simply in the emotional world but significantly deeper in the cognitive rational world.

One could even say that it incorporates a deep cognitive root that is tangentially attached to the emotive concern for the lost. It does not involve a simple emotional response but initiates an active rational decision to act on behalf of the other.

Paul further defines this love with the term ἀνυπόκριτος, *anupokritos,* which literally means *not like a hypocrite* in an *acting manner* or with *pretension!*[18]

In this mindset for others Christians should *outdo one another in showing honor,* they should *live in harmony,* and *not be haughty*—a temptation with which both Jew and Gentile would struggle.

Christians are to seek fellowship in harmony with others as far as it depended on each one of them, and not simply action in response to others. They should live

---

[17] Zodhiates, ἀγάπη, *agápē.*
[18] Zodhiates, ἀνυπόκριτος, *anupokritos.*

peaceably with all, notably with one another, but also with their non-Christian neighbors!

Christians, reconciled to God and one another by the cross of Jesus, must show the world a better way of living.

Living in a pagan society, in their behavior with others they must overcome evil with good. *This is what God did in Jesus for them!*

Paul will pick up this theme again in Rom 14, 15 when discussing the human tendency to judge others.

Rom 13:1-7. The Christian and the State

Following up on his exhortation in Rom 12:20 Paul suggests a remarkable principle, especially to those living under the shadow of the power of Rome!

Let every person be subject to the governing authorities. For there is no authority except from God, and those that exist have been instituted by God. ² Therefore he who resists the authorities resists what God has appointed, and those who resist will incur judgment. ³ For rulers are not a terror to good conduct, but to bad. Would you have no fear of him who is in authority? Then do what is good, and you will receive his approval, ⁴ for he is God's servant for your good. But if you do wrong, be afraid, for he does not bear the sword in vain; he is the servant of God to execute his wrath on the wrongdoer. ⁵ Therefore one must be subject, not only to avoid God's wrath but also for the sake of conscience. ⁶ For the same reason you also pay taxes, for the authorities are ministers of God, attending to this very thing. ⁷ Pay all of them their dues, taxes to whom taxes are due, revenue to whom revenue is due, respect to whom respect is due, honor to whom honor is due.

This pericope, along with 1 Peter 2:123ff has created considerable discussion among scholars, all along similar lines but with considerable disagreement!

It is difficult for people who have lived in the evil shadow of slavery and suppression endorsed by civil and economic power, and such evil as slavery under Roman hegemony, Nazi brutalism, communist oppression, state ethnic cleansing, and even state religious persecution to wrap their arms around this pericope. We live in a world characterized by open and violent revolution to civil and government power. However, as Fitzmyer will stress bellow, we live under the power of Christ and his kingdom which has greater claim on us than any other power.

Fitzmyer[19] observes that the text was addressed among the hortatory, paranetic practical material of Romans in which Paul is addressing how Christians *should live* under all civil authorities including the Roman situation. He was emphasizing that the new freedom experienced under Christ was *not a license to any form of civil anarchy.*

Although the exhortation emphasizes order, authority, civil obedience, payment of taxes or revenue, and honor for civil authorities regarding "God's servants" (13:6) ... His teaching still has to be understood against the background of that of the lordship of the risen Christ, 10:9f ... and especially of what he says in 1 Cor 6: "Though there are many so-called gods in heaven or on earth, and there are many gods and lords, yet for us there is one God ... and one Lord, Jesus Christ through whom are all things and through whom we exist."[20]

Fitzmyer adds that Paul's teaching still "must be understood against the background of that about the Lordship of Christ ... and of the OT itself in which Israel was instructed. Especially in the time of the exile, to respect governing authorities, even to pray for them, Jer 29:7."[21]

Despite apparent Roman civil opposition to Judaism, and in view of Christ, Paul exhorts the Christians to be subject to their Roman overlords!

---

[19] Fitzmyer, *Romans*, pp. 662ff.
[20] Fitzmyer, *Romans*, p. 662.
[21] Fitzmyer, *Romans*, pp. 663-665.

Today, some like the Jehovah Witness church interpret these governing authorities as the Church authorities, meaning that Paul was not charging the Christians in Rome to obey civil government. The context of this text does not support such an interpretation!

What is more, Paul suggests that civil government is a part of God's program for maintaining peace!

The context of Rom 12 suggests civil rulers, however cruel they may be, have the responsibility of maintaining peace in a community.

1 Pet 2:13-17 likewise charges that Christians should respect civil government, and the context of Peter is certainly Rome.

> Be subject for the Lord's sake _to every human institution, whether it be to the emperor as supreme,_ [14] or _to governors as sent by him_ to punish those who do wrong and to praise those who do right. [15] For it is God's will that by doing right you should put to silence the ignorance of foolish men. [16] _Live as free men, yet without using your freedom as a pretext for evil; but live as servants of God._ [17] _Honor all men. Love the brotherhood. Fear God. Honor the emperor._

Rom 13:8-14. Miscellaneous urgent exhortations regarding one's relations with others

> [8] _Owe no one anything, except to love one another; for he who loves his neighbor has fulfilled the law._ [9] _The commandments,_ "You shall not commit adultery, You shall not kill, You shall not steal, You shall not covet," _and any other commandment, are summed up in this sentence,_ "You shall love your neighbor as yourself." [10] Love does no wrong to a neighbor; therefore love is the fulfilling of the law.
>
> [11] _Besides this you know what hour it is, how it is full time now for you to wake from sleep. For salvation is nearer to us now than when we first believed;_ [12] the night is far gone, the day is at hand. Let us then cast off the works of darkness and put on the armor of light; [13] _let us_

254

conduct ourselves becomingly as in the day, not in reveling and drunkenness, not in debauchery and licentiousness, not in quarreling and jealousy. [14] But put on the Lord Jesus Christ, and make no provision for the flesh, to gratify its desires.

Paul closes this section with two general exhortations, the one *to owe nothing other than to love one another*, the other expressed in the next paragraph, is to *understand the urgency of the hour*!

Rom 13:8ff. *First*, to *owe no one anything other than to love one another* is a general wisdom exhortation as debt can become a ruling principle in the Christian's life. Paul is not prohibiting loans. He is emphasizing *the one major debt we owe one another, that is to love*, Rom 12:9ff.

The principles of loans and repayment of debts was well covered in the *Torah*, as well as under the Roman civil laws.

On *debt*, the *Baker Encyclopedia of the Bible* comments:

> Portions of the legislative sections of the Pentateuch (the first five books of the Bible) regulated the practice of lending in a way that protected the poor and secured each person's right to earn a living and support a family. Many popular Hebrew proverbs dealt with that theme. The positive thrust of the biblical laws was to ensure help for the financially needy, without interest. No personal profit was to be made at the expense of the poor (Ex 22:25; Dt 23:19, 20); God was their special advocate. Thus by lending without interest, the Israelites could demonstrate their reverence for God (Lev 25:35–37).[22]
>
> The apostle Paul instructed Christians to "owe nothing to anyone" (Rom 13:8 NASB), which means at the very least that Christians should make good promptly on loans. On the other hand, a Christian's

---

[22] Elwell, and Beitzel, "Debt," *Baker Encyclopedia of the Bible,* vol. 1, p. 606.

economic activity should be characterized by kindness toward those in need, generosity, and willingness to help (Mt 5:42; Lk 6:35).[23]

Even the Ten Commandments are fulfilled in one commandment – love one another!

Approximately 20 years earlier Jesus had taught this remarkable principle! On the night before his crucifixion John records Jesus' moving instruction to his disciples:

> *Jesus said, "Now is the Son of man glorified, and in him God is glorified;* [32] *if God is glorified in him, God will also glorify him in himself, and glorify him at once.* [33] *Little children, yet a little while I am with you. You will seek me; and as I said to the Jews so now I say to you, 'Where I am going you cannot come.'* [34] *<u>A new commandment I give to you, that you love one another; even as I have loved you, that you also love one another.</u>* [35] *By this all men will know that you are my disciples, if you have love for one another."* [24]

About 60 years after Jesus' great discourse on love which John had recorded, John wrote to the churches in Asia. They were dealing with division regarding he divine nature of the earthly Jesus as the Christ. John wrote:

> [4] *I rejoiced greatly to find some of your children following the truth, just as we have been commanded by the Father.* [5] *And now I beg you, lady, not as though I were writing you a new commandment, <u>but the one we have had from the beginning, that we love one another.</u>* [6] *And this is love, that we follow his commandments; this is the commandment, as you have heard from the beginning, that you follow love.* [25]

Historically sandwiched between these two great Johannine texts, and building off Jesus' early instruction, Paul wrote this great text on love fulfilling all the

---

[23] Elwell and Beitzel, "Debt." *Baker Encyclopedia of the Bible,* vol. 1, p. 607.
[24] John 13:31–35.
[25] 2 John 4–6.

commandments of God to Christians facing relational issues of division! His exhortation:

> *Owe no one anything, except to love one another; for he who loves his neighbor has fulfilled the law.* [9] *The commandments, "You shall not commit adultery, You shall not kill, You shall not steal, You shall not covet," and any other commandment, are summed up in this sentence, "You shall love your neighbor as yourself." [10] Love does no wrong to a neighbor; therefore love is the fulfilling of the law.*

Paul draws attention to the fact love fulfils the law in the sense that even under the *Torah* love was intended to maintain good relations among all people, Lev 19:18, 34.

Paul references the *Torah* speaking of interpersonal relationships by citing several of the principles of what we call the Ten Commandments of Ex 20 which stated, *"you shall not steal, you shall not covet."* Paul stressed that even under the *Torah the whole law was filled by loving one another*. Note Paul's strident proclamation at Gal 5:13,14:

> *For you were called to freedom, brethren; only do not use your freedom as an opportunity for the flesh, but through love be servants of one another. [14] For the whole law is fulfilled in one word, "You shall love your neighbor as yourself." [15] But if you bite and devour one another take heed that you are not consumed by one another.*[26]

Rom 13:11ff. In closing this group of paranetic instructions, Paul introduced a profound *eschatological exhortation*! This one reminded the Roman Christians that *they lived in the last days of God's redeeming and atoning activity*. The *days of the Messiah and the Church are the final last days, age or era, of God working out his eternal plan of salvation*.

Note Acts 2:17 and Heb 1:2 where Luke/Peter and the writer of Hebrews proclaim that *the last days were already in effect at their time of writing,* ca. CE 65.

---

[26] Cf. also Col 3:14; James 2:8.

In his great Pentecost sermon Peter proclaimed that the last days had broken into history in the pouring out of the Holy Spirit, Acts 2:14-17:

[14] But Peter, standing with the eleven, lifted up his voice and addressed them, "Men of Judea and all who dwell in Jerusalem, let this be known to you, and give ear to my words. [15] For these men are not drunk, as you suppose, since it is only the third hour of the day; [16] but this is what was spoken by the prophet Joel:

[17] 'And in the last days it shall be, God declares, that I will pour out my Spirit upon all flesh, and your sons and your daughters shall prophesy, and your young men shall see visions, and your old men shall dream dreams;

Later, in a deeply Christological sermon recorded in the book of Hebrews, the "preacher" wrote, Heb 1:1-3:

[1] In many and various ways God spoke of old to our fathers by the prophets; [2] but in these last days he has spoken to us by a Son, whom he appointed the heir of all things, through whom also he created the world. [3] He reflects the glory of God and bears the very stamp of his nature, upholding the universe by his word of power.

The *last days* is a technical *eschatological*[27] term indicating that the Christian age is the *fulfilment, theological end, of God's plan for man on earth.* We speak of an *eschatological age* as the *last or final age of God's plan of salvation.* After this age when Jesus returns in his second coming, or *parousia*, there will be the final act of judgment.

The end of these last days is not pre-announced and cannot be calculated, so Christians must live in *heightened expectancy*, for Christ could return at any time. I like Paul's encouragement to the young Thessalonian church, 1 Thess 1:9, 10:

---

[27] *Eschatological* derives from the Greek words *éschaton, last, end,* and *lógos, word* or *discussion.* It refers to the *final discussion*, or as it is used theologically, the *last final days.*

For they themselves report concerning us what a welcome we had among you, and how you turned to God from idols, to serve a living and true God, [10] and to wait for his Son from heaven, whom he raised from the dead, Jesus who delivers us from the wrath to come.

At Matt 24, 25, in a major "eschatological" discourse, Jesus discussed the *destruction of Jerusalem*. He predicted it would dramatically occur with considerable visible warnings as the Romans descended in destruction on Jerusalem, ca CE 65/66. Jesus had judged the city of Jerusalem! It would shortly be totally destroyed and never return to its previous glory!

However, at Mat 24:36 Jesus discusses *another day that will come without visible signs; it will come suddenly.* He is referring in this pericope to his *second coming, parousia, or final coming at the end of the age.* Jesus warned the disciples that it will not be possible to predict the end of the world, although men have attempted to do so, even so today. In this additional pericope, Matt 24:36-44, *Jesus charged his disciples to be alert and ready for his sudden and unexpected return.*

At 1 Thess 4:9-11 Paul encouraged the Christians not to mourn the death of fellow Christians for when Christians die they are raised to be with God and Jesus. *When Jesus returns, when the last trumpet sounds*, he will bring with him those who have gone on, *that is those who have already died.* They and the living Thessalonians would all be united with Christ. This all occurs when Jesus returns *at the end of the age, the eschaton*, for the final judgment.

But concerning love of the brethren you have no need to have anyone write to you, for you yourselves have been taught by God to love one another; [10] and indeed you do love all the brethren throughout Macedonia. But we exhort you, brethren, to do so more and more, [11] to aspire to live quietly, to mind your own affairs, and to work with your hands, as we charged

259

you; *12 so that you may command the respect of outsiders, and be dependent on nobody.*

13 But we would not have you ignorant, brethren, concerning those who are asleep (κοιμάω, *koimáō* ,[28] figuratively *died*), *that you may not grieve as others do who have no hope.* *14 For since we believe that Jesus died and rose again, even so, through Jesus, God will bring with him those who have fallen asleep.* *15 For this we declare to you by the word of the Lord, that we who are alive, who are left until the coming of the Lord, shall not precede those who have fallen asleep.* *16 For the Lord himself will descend from heaven with a cry of command, with the archangel's call, and with the sound of the trumpet of God. And the dead in Christ will rise first;* *17 then we who are alive, who are left, shall be caught up together with them in the clouds to meet the Lord in the air; and so we shall always be with the Lord.* *18 Therefore comfort one another with these words.*

Now at **Rom 13:11-14** Paul speaks of an *urgent hour*, using a word for *critical hour*, καιρός, *kairós*, that indicates *a significant or urgent hour*, obviously the hour or time of *the second coming and final judgment.*

11 Besides this you know what hour it is, how it is full time now for you to wake from sleep. For salvation is nearer to us now than when we first believed; *12 the night is far gone, the day is at hand. Let us then cast off the works of darkness and put on the armor of light;* *13 let us conduct ourselves becomingly as in the day, not in reveling and drunkenness, not in debauchery and licentiousness,*

---

[28] Zodhiates, κοιμάω, *koimáō*; contracted *koimṓ* ... to lie outstretched, to lie down. To cause to lie down to sleep. In the NT, generally in the mid. *koimáomai* or *koimṓmai*... to fall asleep, to sleep. Matt. 28:13; Luke 22:45; John 11:12; Acts 12:6; Sept.: Ruth 3:8; 1 Sam. 3:15; Is. 5:27. *Spoken of the sleep of death, to die, be dead*, Matt. 27:52; John 11:11; Acts 7:60; 13:36; 1 Cor. 7:39; 11:30; 15:6, 18, 20, 51; 1 Thess. 4:13–15; 2 Pet. 3:4; Sept.: 1 Kgs. 2:10; 11:43; Is. 43:17.

*not in quarreling and jealousy. [14] But put on the Lord
Jesus Christ, and make no provision for the flesh, to
gratify its desires.*

Since Christians *know* that there will be a final end,
you know, but do not know *when the end will be*, this *adds
urgency to the present*! Live carefully in the present for *the
final end of the age is already in process.*

Because of this sense of urgency, Christians should
not engage in worldly *reveling* and *debauchery*. The words
debauchery and *licentiousness* imply *sexual sin* and *sexual
extravagances.*

A prominent theologian, Wolfhart Pannenberg,[29] has
suggested that Christians should *live in the present as
though it was the final future*. His precise words speak of
the present being the arrival of the future. By the future he
has in mind the *final coming of Jesus.*

*Christians should live each day as though it was
already the day of Jesus' return!*

By this we mean that Christians should *make the most
of their time*, living wisely! This is what Paul instructed the
Ephesian Christians in Eph 5:15, 16 and the Colossians in
Col 4:5!

*[5] Conduct yourselves wisely toward outsiders, making
the most of the time. [6] Let your speech always be
gracious, seasoned with salt, so that you may know
how you ought to answer everyone.*

---

[29] Wolfhart Pannenberg, *passim* in Ian Fair dissertation, *The Theology
of Wolfhart Pannenberg as a Reaction to Dialectical Theology*,
University of Natal, 1975.

Chapter 11 - Living in Christian Community:
Rom 14:1-15:13

Context and Message

In view of a Christian tendency to judge one another and to not be patient with those who are weak in the faith, Paul emphasizes that Christians should all remember that it is only by the grace of God that we are saved, either strong or weak, or Jew or Gentile.

No one of us is better than any other, and none of us deserved to be saved. It is only by the grace of God that the strong and the weak are saved.

It matters not whether one is a Jew or a Gentile, male or female, rich or poor, educated or uneducated, strong or weak in our faith; we are all sinners and saved only by the grace of God!

Those who think they are stronger than others must accept the weaker Christians, especially when it comes to matters of opinion.

Matters of opinion might include what we eat or drink, Kosher food or otherwise, drinking wine or not drinking wine.

Gluttony and drunkenness are of course not to be part of the Christian experience.

Matters of opinion also include personal interpretation of Scripture!

We prefer to think we are right and that our opinion is "doctrine," but even in matters of opinion in interpreting Scripture, we should be careful not to permit such opinions to become divisive and cause another Christian to lose confidence in and leave Christ!

Notice I have spoken of personal opinion in regard to Scriptural interpretation! Every church has a shared system of doctrinal values, and we should be willing to fit our opinion and behavior in with these, or else leave! We do not permit personal opinion to cause division! We should have the freedom to restudy doctrine, but not to *cause division over personal opinion. We should patiently or quietly, even privately, maintain our opinion in the presence of others who disagree with us without causing problems and division!*

Christians do not have the right, nor the mandate to judge God's servants, for they too are only servants, not rulers or judges.

It is only God and Jesus who are in the judging business!

We are in the business of proclaiming the Gospel and teaching the Scriptures and Christian faith, while also being in the loving, patient, and nurturing business!

Christians must be careful not to permit their personal opinion and freedom to cause another whose Christian conscience is not yet fully formed to lose faith and sin by going contrary to their conscience and faith.

Throughout this exhortation the emphasis has been on nurturing and helping the weaker Christian grow in faith and conscience, not permitting personal opinion and freedom to cause another Christian to fall into sin by living contrary to their faith and conscience. We are to be careful not to destroy the saving work of God in another. Our purpose is to bring glory to God in Christ.

Just as Christ welcomed us in our sinful condition, and continues to welcome us in our weakness, we are to welcome others who might not agree with us in matters of opinion!

Paul was keenly aware of the close relationships among the varied house churches in Rome.

Romans 14 and 15 pick up where Paul left off in Rom 12 and 13 in which he spoke of *covenant relations driven by humility and love.*

Fundamental to appropriate covenant relations is the principle that Christians should demonstrate interpersonal love for one another *by not habitually judging one another.* Paul was well aware of interpersonal tensions in Gentile regions, especially close-knit communities such as the churches where Jews were a considerable influence in the community. The exhortation was that Christians should *always put the other person first in a humble way, not with conceited haughty* attitudes as expressed at Rom 12:9ff.

Jesus taught a great lesson on humility at Matt 18:1-20. Although Paul had not been present as a believer when Jesus taught this lesson, Jesus' lessons obviously were repeated by the disciples and as we know these oral sayings became part of the *Jesus tradition* recorded in the Gospels. Matthew wrote:

> [1] *At that time the disciples came to Jesus, saying, "Who is the greatest in the kingdom of heaven?"* [2] *And calling to him a child, he put him in the midst of them,* [3] *and said, "Truly, I say to you, unless you turn and become like children, you will never enter the kingdom of heaven.* [4] *Whoever humbles himself like this child, he is the greatest in the kingdom of heaven.*
>
> [5] *"Whoever receives one such child in my name receives me;* [6] *but whoever causes one of these little ones who believe in me to sin, it would be better for him to have a great millstone fastened round his neck and to be drowned in the depth of the sea. ...* [10] *"See that you do not despise one of these little ones; for I tell you that in heaven their angels always behold the face of my Father who is in heaven. ...* [14] *So it is not the will of my Father who is in heaven that one of these little ones should perish.*

Jesus began with a question to the disciples asking, *"who is the greatest in the kingdom of heaven."* He answered for the disciples, *"Whoever humbles himself like this child, he is the greatest in the kingdom of heaven."*

We learn that in Matthew's Gospel the *little ones* represent new or young disciples.[1] God is concerned not

---

[1] Hagner, *Matthew 14-28*, pp. 517ff.

only for the great disciples, but for every disciple, especially the new or young ones.

Paul's repetition of the essence of Jesus' concern for the young or immature in the faith indicates that it had already become a signature indicator of mature Christian fellowship. As evidenced here in Romans 14, *catechism*, from the Greek word κατήχηση, *katéchésé*, became a form of nurture for new converts early in the Christian system.[2]

Be careful about judging one another.

Rom 14:1-15:9. Paul now focuses on a widespread problem that both the Jew and the Gentile had in common: judging one another *especially across cultures*!

Regarding judging, Jesus warned against being in the frame of mind in which *one habitually finds fault with others*. Matt 7:1 reads, "*Judge not, that you be not judged. For with the judgment you pronounce you will be judged, and the measure you give will be the measure you get.*"

The tense of the verb *judge* in Matt 7:1, κρίνετε, *to judge*, is a present *imperative* verb which when coupled with the Greek negative particle μὴ, *mě*, pronounced *may*, implies *not having a constant continued habitual behavior of finding fault*. Jesus warned the disciples not to develop the practice people often have with others: *finding fault!* Jesus' comment is better translated as "*do not habitually keep on finding fault.*"

In the context of Paul's message in Romans, *God showing no partiality and justifying both Jew and Gentile on the same ground of faith* makes this practical exhortation in Rom 14:1-15:9, *not to judge a man who is weak in faith*, most appropriate and central to maintaining true Christian fellowship.

A practical Christian problem is deciding who is the one who is weak in the faith!

The Jewish Christians might find themselves viewing the Gentile Christians as weaker in the faith due to their

---

[2] *Britannica Dictionary, catechism.*

not following all the *Torah's kosher* food laws. Likewise, there might be the tendency for the Gentile Christians, who were more settled in Rome, to constantly be finding fault with the Jews *who kept on leaving and returning*, although not by their fault, nevertheless *creating an unstable situation among the house churches.*

It is amazing how easily well-meaning Christians find themselves in situations in which they consider themselves to be the stronger ones, and in which they tend to find fault with their weaker brethren!

This seems to be an age-old human fault which many Christians have not been able to overcome, but which they should be able to control with help from God and his Holy Spirit.

It seems to be a natural and historically present problem of *loving one another with a genuine love* and yet being inclined to find fault with others. Check the number of divisions within any denomination of the Christian faith to verify this!

But then, this is what these two chapters are all about!

Understanding God's grace and the fact that God and Jesus have welcomed us into their family should motivate us to do the same for one another without constantly judging or finding fault with one another!

Notice that this material is enclosed by two statements which technically we call an *inclusio. Welcome one another* at Rom 14:1 and Rom 15:7. *Inclusios* function like parentheses, binding material together between the first and the second repeated thought of a pericope to emphasize the central thought of the pericope's teaching and emphasis.

This whole pericope of Rom 14 and Rom 15 hinges around the pivotal thought of *welcoming or accepting one another* in Christian fellowship in spite of our different religious maturity, ethnic, or cultural differences.

Rom 14:1-3. *As for the man who is weak in faith, welcome him, but not for disputes over opinions.* ² *One* *believes he may eat anything, while the weak man eats only vegetables.* ³ *Let not him who eats despise him who abstains, and let not him who abstains pass judgment on him who eats; for God has welcomed him.*

Paul begins with the exhortation regarding the weaker Christian, *"welcome him"*! Rom 15:7 begins with the similar statement that Christians should *"welcome* one another, therefore, *just as Christ has welcomed you, for the glory of God"*!

Whatever this passage teaches it teaches that *Christians should welcome one another just as Christ has welcomed them, full of our weaknesses, but welcomed for the glory of God*!

Key to understanding this exhortation is the meaning of the word *welcome*! The word *welcome* in Greek is προσλαμβάνω, *proslambánō,* from *prós, to,* and *lambánō* meaning *to take or receive, to accept,* or *to welcome.* Putting these two words together we come up with *welcome, to receive,* or *to accept.*

In our text Paul is instructing Christians to *receive* or *accept* the *weaker Christians just as God has accepted them*!

So, who is the one who is weaker in the faith?

A fascinating question!

In our human experience it is usually the other person!

If this is the case, then we are to *accept the other person just as God has accepted us*!

However, we can come to some conclusion in Romans as to who the person is who is weaker in the faith!

Remember, *context* is the determining factor in the meaning of words or expressions.

In Rome, or Paul's Roman epistle, it is the person who possibly does not understand the *Torah health or food instructions* as well as some Jews might expect! This person is irregular and not thoughtful in the eating habits! Note Rom 14:2, 5-6.

Rom 14:5-12. Judging God's servants!

Christians must be aware of the danger of judging others in matters of opinion!

Sometimes our opinions may be on an interpretation of Scripture!

We excuse ourselves by claiming that the dispute is over a doctrinal issue, but often it is over our opinion on a doctrinal issue!

Even on doctrinal issues we will not always agree!

Christians must realize that they are not their own, all Christians belong to the Lord Jesus Christ *as his bond servants*, which a Roman would understand.

Therefore, we should not judge others who belong to the Lord!

Christians do not live to themselves and their own opinions, they belong to the Lord and his opinions, and he will judge all according to his opinions not ours!

Rom 14:5.

> *"One man esteems one day as better than another, while another man esteems all days alike. Let everyone be fully convinced in his own mind.* <u>Let everyone be fully convinced in his own mind.</u>
> *[6] He who observes the day, observes* <u>it in honor of the Lord</u>*. He also who eats, eats in honor of the Lord, since he gives thanks to God; while he who abstains, abstains in honor of the Lord and gives thanks to God. [7]* <u>None of us lives to himself, and none of us dies to himself.</u> *[8] If we live, we live to the Lord, and if we die, we die to the Lord; so then,* <u>whether we live or whether we die, we are the Lord's</u>*. [9] For to this end Christ died and lived again, that he might be Lord both of the dead and of the living.*
>
> *[10]* <u>Why do you pass judgment on your brother? Or you, why do you despise your brother? For we shall all stand before the judgment seat of God;</u> *[11] for it is written,*
>
>> *"As I live, says the Lord, every knee shall bow to me,*

and every tongue shall give praise to God."
[12] So each of us shall give account of himself to God.

We do not have the privilege or right to judge God's servants, for only God has that right!"

Primarily, it might be good for Christians to recognize that they are not in the judging business!

Note the following parables, Matt 13:24-30, *the Parable of the Wheat and Tares*, and Matt 13:47-50, *the Parable of the Dragnet*. Jesus taught that only he and his chosen angels will do the judging!

The Christian's work is to teach and preach the gospel, God and Jesus will do the converting, saving, and judging; we do the welcoming!

We have no business deciding who can be our brother or sister in a right relationship with God. God our Father does that, *we do the loving and welcoming*!

Certainly, we have on occasion to decide whether we can fellowship with a person who is caught up in immorality, 1 Cor 5:6-13, but not to decide whether they can be in a right relationship with God and go to heaven or not!

Rom 14:5-9. Dedicating certain days or food to the Lord *is a personal opinion and we have no business judging the decisions of others. We have no business binding our opinion regarding days, food, or personal preferences on others*!

[5] One man esteems one day as better than another, while another man esteems all days alike. Let everyone be fully convinced in his own mind. [6] He who observes the day, observes it in honor of the Lord. He also who eats, eats in honor of the Lord, since he gives thanks to God; while he who abstains, abstains in honor of the Lord and gives thanks to God. [7] None of us lives to himself, and none of us dies to himself. [8] If we live, we live to the Lord, and if we die, we die to the Lord; so then,

whether we live or whether we die, we are the
Lord's. *9 For to this end Christ died and lived*
again, that he might be Lord both of the dead and
of the living.

Again, Paul stresses that our whole lives are dedicated to God in worship and service. Having been purchased from slavery to sin by the death of Jesus we now live for God in the freedom of Christ.

Rom 14:10-12. We who will one day stand before the judgment seat of God should not put ourselves in the judgment seat of God regarding others!

10 Why do you pass judgment on your brother? Or
you, why do you despise your brother? For we shall all
stand before the judgment seat of God; 11 for it is written,
> *"As I live, says the Lord, every knee shall bow to*
> *me,*
> *and every tongue shall give praise to God."*
12 So each of us shall give account of himself to God.

Paul cites Isa 45:23 where God reminded Israel that he was the sovereign judge over all the earth, even Cyrus!

The ultimate judge of everyone is God, so why presume on his sovereignty and judge others?

Rom 14:13-23. Becoming a stumbling block to others

13 Then let us no more pass judgment on one
another, but rather decide never to put a stumbling
block or hindrance in the way of a brother. 14 I know
and am persuaded in the Lord Jesus that nothing is
unclean in itself; but it is unclean for anyone who
thinks it unclean. 15 If your brother is being injured by
what you eat, you are no longer walking in love. Do
not let what you eat **cause the ruin** *of one for whom*
Christ died. 16 So do not let your good be spoken of as
evil. 17 For the kingdom of God is not food and drink
but righteousness and peace and joy in the Holy Spirit;
18 he who thus serves Christ is acceptable to God and
approved by men. 19 Let us then pursue what makes for
peace and for mutual upbuilding. 20 Do not, for the
sake of food, destroy the work of God. Everything is

indeed clean, but it is wrong for anyone to make others fall by what he eats; ²¹ <u>*it is right not to eat meat or drink wine or do anything that makes your brother stumble.*</u> ²² **The faith that you have, keep between yourself and God;** *happy is he who has no reason to judge himself for what he approves.* ²³ **But he who has doubts is condemned, if he eats, because he does not act from faith; for whatever does not proceed from faith is sin.**

Paul begins by speaking of Christians being a *hindrance* and *stumbling block* to others. He includes injuring others and becoming *the ruin* of some. He is obviously speaking of *spiritual matters* of faith and not simply addressing principles of hygiene!

Christians should not let their freedom in Christ cause those who are weaker in their faith to act in a way that is not determined by their faith and understanding of their freedom in Christ!

He sets this whole discussion in the context of *the work of God*, obviously speaking of *God's atoning work in Jesus Christ*!

We should note here that Paul is not simply speaking about *offending* some by exercising their freedom. It is obvious that some Jews would be offended by the Christians' freedom to eat food outside of Jewish *kosher* laws, which laws were instruction to Israel coming out of pagan practices in Egypt and facing all kinds of pagan customs in Canaan, and which laws as part of the Mosaic covenant had been annulled by Christ's death.

Paul had previously addressed these food and special day principles to the Colossians, Col 2:16-23:

¹⁶ *Therefore* <u>*let no one pass judgment on you in questions of food and drink or with regard to a festival or a new moon or a sabbath.*</u> ¹⁷ *These are only a shadow of what is to come; but the substance belongs to Christ.* ¹⁸ *Let no one disqualify you, insisting on self-abasement and worship of angels, taking his stand on visions, puffed up without reason by his sensuous mind,* ¹⁹ *and*

not holding fast to the Head, from whom the whole body, nourished and knit together through its joints and ligaments, grows with a growth that is from God.

[20] If with Christ you died to the elemental spirits of the universe, why do you live as if you still belonged to the world? Why do you submit to regulations, [21] "Do not handle, Do not taste, Do not touch" [22] (referring to things which all perish as they are used), according to human precepts and doctrines? [23] These have indeed an appearance of wisdom in promoting rigor of devotion and self-abasement and severity to the body, but they are of no value in checking the indulgence of the flesh.

We need to examine several terms used by Paul in this interesting pericope: Rom 14:13-23.

Rom 14:13. *First,* Christians should first understand what a *stumbling block* means! Paul uses two words that are somewhat synonymous, "a *stumbling block* or a *hindrance*"

The first word *stumbling block* derives from πρόσκομμα, *proskomma,* meaning *an occasion of stumbling.* Christian freedom should not become an *occasion of stumbling* for others!

The second word σκάνδαλον, *skándalon as used in the New Testament means something that causes someone to stumble in sin and ruin.* The word σκάνδαλον, *skándalon,* in its broader common day sense means *a trap!*[3] However,

---

[3] Zodhiates observes, σκάνδαλον *skándalon*; the trigger of a trap on which the bait is placed, and which, when touched by the animal, springs and causes it to close causing entrapment. The word and its derivatives. belong only to biblical and ecclesiastical Greek. In the Septuagint it answers to the word for *pagís* ... trap. However, *pagís* always refers simply to a trap hidden in an ambush and not to the results; whereas *skándalon* involves a reference also to the conduct of the person who is thus trapped. *Skándalon* always denotes an enticement to conduct which could ruin the person in question. See Sept.: Lev. 19:14.; Josh. 23:13; 1 Sam. 18:21. In the NT *skándalon* is used figuratively in a moral sense. It is concerned mainly with the fact

as used by Paul and other places in the New Testament, it implies an action that *produces certain behavior which can lead to ruin.*

Cf. **Matt 18:7** in the RSV (and NIV similarly) where σκάνδαλον, *skándalon is translated temptation to sin!*:

> *"Woe to the world for temptations to <u>sin</u>! For it is necessary that temptations come, but woe to the man by whom the temptation comes!* [8]*And if your hand or your foot causes you to <u>sin</u>, cut it off and throw it away; it is better for you to enter life maimed or lame than with two hands or two feet to be thrown into the eternal fire.* [9] *And if your eye causes you to <u>sin</u>, pluck it out and throw it away; it is better for you to enter life with one eye than with two eyes to be thrown into the hell of fire."*

At **Matt 18:7f** above I have underlined the word *sin* in our RSV translation. The context of Matthew clearly shows that the word *skándalon, stumbling block,* can be used as a synonym for *a stumbling block for sin and ruin*!

Second, these two words, *stumble* and *hindrance*, do not mean doing *something that <u>someone else might object to</u>*! *The words imply doing something that would <u>cause someone to stumble and sin in ruin</u>!*

Christians must be careful not to act *in a manner in which their freedom from Torah might cause another person to fall and sin.*

Paul urges Christians to refrain from judging, and to decide never to act in a manner that might cause someone who might be <u>*weaker in the faith to stumble and sin*</u>!

Rom 14:15-17. Paul teaches that *there is more to the kingdom than opinions about eating and drinking,* and yet too often we cast a shadow over the kingdom by *squabbles over our opinions* regarding food restrictions, special days, or even doctrinal opinions!

---

that *it produces certain behavior which can lead to ruin* (Rom. 9:33; 11:9; 14:13; 16:7; 1 Cor. 1:23; Gal. 5:11; 1 Pet. 2:8; 1 John 2:10; Rev. 2:14).

The essence of the kingdom is living under the principles of Christ and the *evangelistic missional nature of the kingdom*. The spirit of the kingdom is loving others just as Christ loved us and gave himself for us.

The question is, how much of ourselves will we give up for others and the kingdom?

Rom 14:19 again stresses the need that Christians must then *pursue what makes for peace and for mutual upbuilding*. Squabbling over *opinions* does not make for peace, but creates friction that too easily leads to divisions in the living body of Christ, the church!

A significant point in Rom 14:19 is that Christians should *strive for mutual upbuilding*, which means to *give others time to grow*, and to make every effort to help them to mature in Christ by Christian example and teaching.

The heart of Christian faith is helping others to study and to grow in their faith, and not to dispute over opinions that create division!

Rom 14:20. Paul exhorts the Christians in Rome *not to destroy for the sake of food the work of God in saving both Jew and Gentile!*

The point here is that Christians can so easily destroy God's work of saving someone by squabbles over opinions!

Rom 14:20-22. *Everything is indeed clean, but it is wrong for anyone to make others fall by what he eats;* [21] *it is right not to eat meat or drink wine or do anything that makes your brother stumble.* [22] *The faith that you have, keep between yourself and God; happy is he who has no reason to judge himself for what he approves.* [23] *But he who has doubts is condemned, if he eats, because he does not act from faith; for whatever does not proceed from faith is sin.*

Paul encourages the Christians not to permit their freedom regarding food and wine to cause a weaker Christian to stumble, that is, to *sin against their faith or conscience*, perhaps in ignorance because they follow the example of a supposedly stronger Christian.

Elsewhere in his epistles Paul has spoken of clean/unclean food clarifying that there is nothing inherently unclean in food other than the attitude Christians have in their freedom to eat food. Cf. 1 Tim 4:4, *"For everything created by God is good, and nothing is to be rejected if it is received with thanksgiving; ⁵for then it is consecrated by the word of God and prayer."* Under the Mosaic system certain foods had been decreed unclean and off limits, but Christ had annulled that Law on the cross.

The restrictions of the Mosaic *Torah* Laws must be interpreted under the cultural and pagan corruption of Egypt and Canaan and God's holy plan to display the difference between pagan religious practices and the holiness[4] of God's covenant with Israel.

How Christians use their freedom in observing special days, eating foods, and drinking wine is always difficult yet important to grasp. It sometimes equates to walking a narrow line by giving up personal freedoms.

Note **Gal 5:1, 13f** where Paul speaks of the freedoms we have in matters of opinion but *sets some parameters to this freedom*. Note *the parameter of love and concern for others and their faith*!

¹ For freedom Christ has set us free; stand fast therefore, and do not submit again to a yoke of slavery.

¹³ For you were called to freedom, brethren; only do not use your freedom as an opportunity for the flesh, but through love be servants of one another. ¹⁴ For the whole law is fulfilled in one word, "You shall love your neighbor as yourself." ¹⁵ But if you bite and devour one another take heed that you are not consumed by one another.

Rom 14:22. In this exhortation Paul speaks of not permitting *personal faith* to destroy the faith of another. By *faith* here Paul has in mind *one's conscience*—that which has come to be definitive of one's faith.

---

[4] We should remember that a root meaning of *holiness* is that which is God's—an absolute difference from that which is practiced on earth in human behavior.

Conscience is that inner sense of right and wrong that is informed and shaped by our knowledge of God and Christ. In the case of a Jew, the instruction of the *Torah*, but in the case of a Christian it could be the instruction we have from Christ and his Apostolic witnesses. Ultimately, we are shaped by the example of Christ and living for him and his and God's glory—a tall order and challenge!

Whatever the Christian conscience permits, and it should be shaped by our Christ-life example and instruction, we should *use freedom with care and concern for others* to ensure that we do not cause a weaker Christian to sin against their *faith and conscience*.

A necessary principle here is for all Christians, both weak and strong, to be constantly *nurtured in their faith, instructed from Scripture* and their knowledge of Christ, and given time to mature.

Two important Scriptures are 2 Tim 2:15,16 and 2 Tim 3:14-17.

2 Tim 2:15,16:

> [15] *Do your best to present yourself to God as one approved, a workman who has no need to be ashamed, rightly handling the word of truth.* [16] *Avoid such godless chatter, for it will lead people into more and more ungodliness,*

2 Tim 3:14-17:

> *But as for you, continue in what you have learned and have firmly believed, knowing from whom you learned it* [15] *and how from childhood you have been acquainted with the sacred writings which are able to instruct you for salvation through faith in Christ Jesus.* [16] *All scripture is inspired by God and profitable for teaching, for reproof, for correction, and for training in righteousness,* [17] *that the man of God may be complete, equipped for every good work.*

Third, we are *not speaking* in this discussion of those matters of strong Christian opinion that shape the core of the Christian faith such as the divinity of Jesus, his death and resurrection and second coming, and God's plan of redemption through faith in Jesus, repentance, and baptism into Christ. Some certainly might not like, or might disagree in matters of primary Christian doctrine! Paul was not addressing here the primary theological principles of the Christian faith, but was addressing the paranetic Christian behavior based on the primary Christian principles.

Paul was concerned in this text with the use of Christian freedom in regard to the weaker Christian's life behavior. He was addressing the cultural differences between Jewish, Roman, and Christian faith and the freedom that might cause the *new Christian's faith to weaken and cause them to behave contrary to their faith/conscience mindset.* He was primarily concerned for those whose faith was still young and vulnerable!

For a Christian to disregard conscience, however weak or strong that conscience or faith may be, personal or otherwise, is sin!

In exercising their rightful freedom, Christians can sin by causing others to act contrary to their conscience and faith!

Finally*, there are nevertheless clear principles in this text of Rom 14, 15 that warn against Christians judging one another under all conditions, for it is not the Christian's role to judge, but to teach, encourage, and nurture other Christians in their faith.*

In summary, Paul was encouraging stronger Christians to be careful not to cause weaker Christians, or new Christians, to act in ways not determined by their faith or a commitment to Christ. To cause a weaker Christian to stumble or lose their faith by excessive inconsiderate exercise of freedom is sinful!

In contrast to judging Christians weaker in the faith the stronger Christians should *welcome them into the faith* by patiently encouraging them to live for Christ and to grow in their faith.

Rom 14:1ff: *As for the man who is weak in faith, welcome him, but not for disputes over opinions*

278

Following Christ's example

Rom 15:1-6. Patience with the weakness of others

"We who are strong ought to bear with the failings of the weak, and not to please ourselves; [2] let each of us please his neighbor for his good, to edify him. [3] For Christ did not please himself; but, as it is written, "The reproaches of those who reproached thee fell on me." [4] For whatever was written in former days was written for our instruction, that by steadfastness and by the encouragement of the scriptures we might have hope. [5] May the God of steadfastness and encouragement grant you to live in such harmony with one another, in accord with Christ Jesus, [6] that together you may with one voice glorify the God and Father of our Lord Jesus Christ."

Strong Christians through their example should *patiently bear with the failings of the weak*! They should *not ignore them, and should not constantly be judging them.* They should *encourage* them, *nurture them, teach* them, and *demonstrate the appropriate life in Christ*!

Note Paul's use of *"we who are strong" ought*[5] to *bear*[6] *with the failings of the weak,*[7] *that is, to be patient with those who are weaker in their faith, and to support them,* (βαστάζω, *bastázō*) *as they mature.* The word *ought,* ὀφείλω, *opheílō, carries the sense of we owe it to them*!

Strong Christians do not ignore the failings of the weak, and do not make a fuss about their failings! They do this so the weaker Christian can be taught, encouraged, edified, and strengthened.

Edification comes from the example of others, from prayer and study, and from giving others time to grow!

---

[5] Zodhiates, ὀφείλω, *opheílō; to owe them, to be indebted to them.*
[6] Zodhiates, βαστάζω, *bastázō; ... To raise upon a basis, to support. In the NT, generally it means to take up and hold, to bear.*
[7] Zodhiates, ἀσθένημα, *asthénēma ... to be weak or powerless.* The result of being weak, as indicated by the suffix *-ma.* Rom. 15:1, in the plural, referring to *the scruples which arise by being weak in the faith.*

The Christian example in this is obviously Christ and his giving himself, patiently, for us, and his continuing patient endurance of our weaknesses!

Paul prays that God, who is patient with all Christians, may grant that Christians live in harmony with one another, in accord with Christ, which means *just as*, καθώς, *kathōs*, Christ is patient with them.

Rom 15:7-13. We ought to welcome one another just as Christ has welcomed us.

"Welcome one another, therefore, as Christ has welcomed you, for the glory of God. [8] For I tell you that Christ became a servant to the circumcised to show God's truthfulness, in order to confirm the promises given to the patriarchs, [9] and in order that the Gentiles might glorify God for his mercy. As it is written,

"Therefore I will praise thee among the Gentiles, and sing to thy name";
[10] and again it is said,
"Rejoice, O Gentiles, with his people";
[11] and again,
"Praise the Lord, all Gentiles, and let all the peoples praise him";
[12] and further Isaiah says,
"The root of Jesse shall come, he who rises to rule the Gentiles; in him shall the Gentiles hope."
[13] May the God of hope fill you with all joy and peace in believing, so that by the power of the Holy Spirit you may abound in hope."

Rom 15:1. Remember that the word *welcome*, προσλαμβάνω, *proslambánō*, means *to receive and accept others where they are in their faith!*[8]

This does not mean that we do nothing about their weakness in the faith! Likewise it does not mean that we constantly find fault with them and judge them.

---

[8] Cf. Rom 14:1

But it does mean that we are patient as we work with them and encourage them to grow and mature, just as Christ has been doing with us!

Paul focuses attention on the tendency that Jews (informed by the *Torah*) might have in finding fault with Gentiles (who might not be informed by the *Torah*). The *Torah* is no longer a standard for measuring a true relationship with God. The *Torah* "rules" have been annulled by Christ and his death on the cross! Trusting in Jesus and living in Jesus is the *standard* of the *new covenant.*

Christ became the "*suffering servant Messiah*" of the Jew (the circumcised) and the Gentile (the uncircumcised) so that both Jew and Gentile could be confirmed as beneficiaries of the promises to Abraham.

Paul had addressed the circumcision issue in his Galatians epistle:

[11] See with what large letters I am writing to you with my own hand. [12] It is those who want to make a good showing in the flesh that would compel you to be circumcised, and only in order that they may not be persecuted for the cross of Christ. [13] For even those who receive circumcision do not themselves keep the law, but they desire to have you circumcised that they may glory in your flesh. [14] But far be it from me to glory except in the cross of our Lord Jesus Christ, by which the world has been crucified to me, and I to the world. [15] For neither circumcision counts for anything, nor uncircumcision, but a new creation

Rom 15:7. *Welcome one another, therefore, as Christ has welcomed you, for the glory of God. [8] For I tell you that Christ became a servant to the circumcised to show God's truthfulness, in order to confirm the promises given to the patriarchs.* Jesus is the New *Torah* example and standard of how Christians should welcome the weak in faith. Christians should *welcome* and *accept* one another *just as Christ welcomed them for the glory of God.*

Rom 15: 9. Paul then cited Psalm 18:49 and the *Torah* in support of the rejoicing of the Gentiles having received their redemption.

As Christ has been patient with the Jews, so the Jewish Christians must be patient with the Gentile Christians, for the work of God among the Gentiles, and the glory of God!

Christians do this so they do not destroy the work of God by their lifestyle, Rom 14:20, and so that *they might bring glory to God*, Rom 15:7.

We do not focus on ourselves and our opinions, but on the other person, *on their needs, on Christ and his example, and on God for his glory*!

Believing in God and Christ should bring glory to God through the believers living in peaceful community harmony in Christ, not disharmony and dissension.

Chapter 12 - Concluding Remarks:
Rom 15:14-16:17

Context and Message

Paul's concluding comments spread over Rom 15:14-16:17 may be seen as merely closing comments to a great theological epistle, but that would be missing the fact that the information scattered throughout these verses is profoundly important to understanding the purpose of Paul writing the epistle prior to visiting Rome.

First, it explains in some detail that this epistle is very much a mission related epistle written by an experienced missionary with a divinely commissioned mission to take the gospel to both the Jew and Gentile, but primarily to the Gentile.

Second, that he is keenly aware of the issues Jews might have over the content of his message, justification by faith in Jesus and not torah Law keeping.

Third, he is also keenly mindful of the ethnically diverse nature of the house churches in Rome, each holding both religious and ethnic prejudices.

Fourth, knowing well the dangers of certain false teachers upsetting congregations or house churches he warns against permitting them to take root in their groups.

Fifth, although he knew he had done an excellent job defining acceptable faith as focused on Jesus and not the Torah he felt the need in closing to remind the Romans that faith and obedience are dynamically connected in a saving continuum that ranged from believing through repentance and obedient baptism in the gospel message.

Finally, in keeping with an epistle that repeatedly praises God for his faithfulness and righteousness, he closes with a magnificent doxology to the epistle.

Some scholars suggest that in this concluding section we have at least two conclusions, possibly three! The proposal is that the epistle actually closed at Rom 15:7 with two possible appendices added to the epistle at Rom 15:14 and Rom 15:22.

The suggestion is that someone else, possibly someone close to Paul, later added some material to Paul's epistle.

That there does seem to be some interesting observations regarding the conclusion to the epistle does not mean that Paul was not the author of the whole epistle.

An interesting fact is that no copy of Romans has appeared in any form different from the one we have, raising some questions regarding an earlier epistle to which someone added an appendix!

The conclusion to the epistle includes some informative comments as to why Paul wrote the epistle, plus some commendations and greetings to a variety of Christians in Rome. This suggests to some that since Paul had not yet been to Rome that this section, which seems to demonstrate a knowledge of the churches in Rome, must have been written by someone other than Paul which is not that impressive an argument. Finally, there is a beautiful doxology to the epistle.

Paul's reasons for writing the epistle

Rom 15:14-21. From Jerusalem to Illyricum!

"I myself am satisfied about you, my brethren, that you yourselves are full of goodness, filled with all knowledge, and able to instruct one another. [15] But on some points I have written to you very boldly by way of reminder, because of the grace given me by God [16] to be a minister of Christ Jesus to the Gentiles in the priestly service of the gospel of God, so that the offering of the Gentiles may be acceptable, sanctified by the Holy Spirit. [17] In Christ Jesus, then, I have reason to be proud of my work for God. [18] For I will not venture to speak of anything except what Christ has wrought through me to win obedience from the Gentiles, by word and deed, [19] by

the power of signs and wonders, by the power of the
Holy Spirit, so that from Jerusalem and as far round as
Illyricum I have fully preached the gospel of Christ,
²⁰ thus making it my ambition to preach the gospel, not
where Christ has already been named, lest I build on
another man's foundation, ²¹ but as it is written,
> *"They shall see who have never been told of him,*
> *and they shall understand who have never heard of*
> *him."*

Paul began by expressing his confidence in the churches in Rome.

He observes that he is writing by way of reminder, demonstrating no superior attitude toward the Christians in Rome.

He comments on the fact that God appointed him to be an apostle to the Gentiles, see Acts 9:15; Gal 1:16.

Paul mentions his ministry of taking up a contribution from the Gentile Christians for the Jewish Christians in Jerusalem, Rom 15:16, 26, which was intended to demonstrate the unity of the faith to the Jewish and Gentile Christians in Rome.

Paul is concerned over how the Jewish Christians and Jews in Jerusalem would receive him and asks for the prayers of the Roman Christians in his behalf for when he arrived in Jerusalem. Paul knew that should the Jewish Christians reject the Gentile gift that it would set his ministry back considerably.

We learn from Acts 21:17 that the Christians in Jerusalem received him "gladly." Cf. 1 Cor 16:1-4; 2 Cor 8:1-5; and 9:1-5 on this Gentile/Jewish Christian contribution.

Rom 15:22-33. Paul's future mission plans

"This is the reason why I have so often been
hindered from coming to you. ²³ But now, since I no
longer have any room for work in these regions, and
since I have longed for many years to come to you, ²⁴ I
hope to see you in passing as I go to Spain, and to be
sped on my journey there by you, once I have enjoyed

your company for a little. ²⁵ At present, however, I am going to Jerusalem with aid for the saints. ²⁶ For Macedonia and Achaia have been pleased to make some contribution for the poor among the saints at Jerusalem; ²⁷ they were pleased to do it, and indeed they are in debt to them, for if the Gentiles have come to share in their spiritual blessings, they ought also to be of service to them in material blessings. ²⁸ When therefore I have completed this, and have delivered to them what has been raised, I shall go on by way of you to Spain; ²⁹ and I know that when I come to you I shall come in the fulness of the blessing of Christ.

³⁰ I appeal to you, brethren, by our Lord Jesus Christ and by the love of the Spirit, to strive together with me in your prayers to God on my behalf, ³¹ that I may be delivered from the unbelievers in Judea, and that my service for Jerusalem may be acceptable to the saints, ³² so that by God's will I may come to you with joy and be refreshed in your company. ³³ The God of peace be with you all. Amen."

Paul discussed the reason he had been detained from visiting Rome; *he was busy elsewhere*! He had preached al over Palestine, Asia, and Eastern Europe (from Jerusalem to Illyricum).

Now that he had completed that ministry he wanted to go on via Rome to Spain.

It was Paul's policy not to become a located preacher or to preach where others had laid a foundation for Christianity, like the Starship Enterprise in *Star Trek*, Paul wanted to go where no man had ever gone before!

In Rom 15:24 Paul uses a technical term to indicate that he hoped the Christians in Rome, Jew and Gentile, would pay some of his expenses for the journey to Spain. *"²⁴ I hope to see you in passing as I go to Spain, and to <u>be sped on</u> my journey there by you, once I have enjoyed your company for a little."* The expression "to be sped" on my way draws on a Greek term *propempō* which in essence implies to be sent.[1]

While on the subject Paul took the advantage of explaining why he had had taken so long in reaching out to Rome. He had been busy on God's commission to take the gospel out into the world, notably in Macedonia, Asia, Achaia, and Galatia. At the same time he drew attention to the fact that Christians, both Jew and Gentile, had given freely to the support of the gospel. *"*[25]*I am going to Jerusalem with aid for the saints.* [26] *For Macedonia and Achaia have been pleased to make some contribution for the poor among the saints at Jerusalem;* [27] *they were pleased to do it, and indeed they are in debt to them, for if the Gentiles have come to share in their spiritual blessings, they ought also to be of service to them in material blessings.* [28] *When therefore I have completed this, and have delivered to them what has been raised, I shall go on by way of you to Spain."*

Paul closed this pericope with an appeal for prayer, that the Christians in Rome would pray for his safety and the success of the gospel.

Rom 16:1-23. Personal commendations and greetings

"I commend to you our sister Phoebe, <u>a deaconess of the church at Cenchre-ae</u>, [2] *that you may receive her in the Lord as befits the saints, and help her in whatever she may require from you, for she has been a helper of many and of myself as well.*

[3] *Greet Prisca and Aquila, my fellow workers in Christ Jesus,* [4] *who risked their necks for my life, to whom not only I but also all the churches of the Gentiles give thanks;* [5] *greet also the church in their house. Greet*

---

[1] Zodhiates, προπέμπω, *propémpō* ... from *pró* ... *before*, and *pémpō* ... *to send*. To send on before, send forward or forth. In the New Testament, *to send forward on one's journey*, bring someone on his way, especially to accompany for some distance in token of respect and honor ... Hence, generally to help one forward on his journey (Acts 15:3; Rom. 15:24; 1 Cor. 16:6, 11; 2 Cor. 1:16; Titus 3:13; 3 John 1:6).

my beloved Epaenetus, who was the first convert in Asia for Christ. [6] Greet Mary, who has worked hard among you. [7] Greet Andronicus and Junias, my kinsmen and my fellow prisoners; they are men of note among the apostles, and they were in Christ before me. [8] Greet Ampliatus, my beloved in the Lord. [9] Greet Urbanus, our fellow worker in Christ, and my beloved Stachys. [10] Greet Apelles, who is approved in Christ. Greet those who belong to the family of Aristobulus. [11] Greet my kinsman Herodion. Greet those in the Lord who belong to the family of Narcissus. [12] Greet those workers in the Lord, Tryphaena and Tryphosa. Greet the beloved Persis, who has worked hard in the Lord. [13] Greet Rufus, eminent in the Lord, also his mother and mine. [14] Greet Asyncritus, Phlegon, Hermes, Patrobas, Hermas, and the brethren who are with them. [15] Greet Philologus, Julia, Nereus and his sister, and Olympas, and all the saints who are with them. [16] Greet one another with a holy kiss. All the churches of Christ greet you."

Rom 16:1 has generated considerable discussion regarding Phoebe whom the RSV here describes as *a deaconess:*

> *"I commend to you our sister Phoebe, <u>a deaconess of the church at Cenchre-ae</u>, [2] that you may receive her in the Lord as befits the saints, and help her in whatever she may require from you, for she has been a helper of many and of myself as well."*

The KJV, ESV, ESV, and NIV all translate this as Phoebe, "<u>*a servant* of the church at Cenchreae.</u>"

So what is the issue? Was she *a servant* or *a deaconess* of the church? The answer is *yes, both,* if we correctly understand the meaning of *diákonos,* as a *servant!* Originally, the words *diakonos* and *diakonía* meant *a servant* or a *special kind of servant.*

Zodhiates observes:

διάκονος *diákonos*; a masculine, feminine, noun. *A minister, servant, deacon.* The derivation is uncertain … Also used in the NT as a technical term side by side with *epískopos* ... bishop or overseer (1 Tim. 3:8, 12; Phil. 1:1). The deacons in this sense *were helping or serving the bishops or elders*, and this is why they were probably called deacons. *They did not, though, possess any ruling authority as did the elders.* Tychicus was called a deacon in his relation to Paul (Eph. 6:21; Col. 4:7 [cf. Acts 19:22]). The origin of this relationship is likely found in Acts 6:1–4. *Stephen and Philip were deacons and were first chosen as distributors of alms and other forms of aid, but soon appeared alongside the Apostles and as their helpers and as evangelists* (Acts 6:8–10; 8:5–8). *The care of the churches fell upon the deacons as the helpers of the elders who held distinct offices.*[2]

It is possible that we can get a rich understanding of what it means to be a *deacon* from the verbal form of *diakonos*, διακονέω, *diakoneō, to serve.*

Beyer, in a lengthy but helpful article in Kittel's *Theological Dictionary of the New Testament*, brings us close to a deeper meaning of the concept of being a deacon:

> "In the NT διακονέω is first used in the original sense of "to wait at table": Lk. 17:8: ἑτοίμασον τί δειπνήσω, καὶ περιζωσάμενος διακόνει μοι ἕως φάγω καὶ πίω; Jn. 12:2: ἐποίησαν οὖν αὐτῷ δεῖπνον ἐκεῖ, καὶ ἡ Μάρθα διηκόνει, ὁ δὲ Λάζαρος εἷς ἦν ἐκ τῶν ἀνακειμένων σὺν αὐτῷ. At table there is a palpable distinction between the worthy man reclining on the couch and the girded servant or the attentive woman. It is thus a high honour for the vigilant servants when their returning lord rewards them by girding himself, setting them at table and coming to serve them (Lk. 12:37). The astonishing act of Jesus in the appraisal of

---

[2] Zodhiates, διάκονος *diákonos.*

289

service is to reverse in ethical estimation the relation between serving and being served (Lk. 22:26 f.) ...[3]

Martha's care for her guest is described as διακονεῖν in Lk. 10:40, the narrower sense being included as in Jn. 12:2. Peter's mother-in-law cares for her guests in the same way in Mk. 1:31 and par. The word also seems to be used in this sense of the angels who ministered to Jesus after the temptation (Mk. 1:13; Mt. 4:11); their ministry consisted in bringing Him food after His period of fasting.

The same change in evaluation as we find in respect of waiting at table applies everywhere in the NT to διακονεῖν in the wider sense of "to be serviceable." Sometimes the link with waiting at table may still be discerned, as when it is said of the women who accompany Jesus: αἵτινες διηκόνουν αὐτοῖς (or αὐτῷ) ἐκ τῶν ὑπαρχόντων αὐταῖς (Lk. 8:3). Cf. also Mt. 27:55; Mk. 15:41. In Mt. 25:42–44, however, Jesus comprises under the term διακονεῖν many different activities such as giving food and drink, extending shelter, providing clothes and visiting the sick and prisoners. The term thus comes to have the full sense of active Christian love for the neighbor and as such it is a mark of true discipleship of Jesus. For what the Christian does to even the least of his fellowmen he does to the Lord Himself.[4]

This reversal of all human ideas of greatness and rank was accomplished when the Son of Man Himself came, not to be *ministered* unto (→ 84, in exposition of Lk. 22:26), but to *minister*. The new feature as compared with Lk. 22:26 is that in Mk. 10:45 and Mt. 20:28 *Jesus does not stop at the picture of table service. διακονεῖν is now much more than a comprehensive term for any loving assistance rendered*

---

[3] Beyer, H. W., *διακονέω, διακονία, διάκονος*, in G. Kittel, G. W. Bromiley, & G. Friedrich, *Theological Dictionary of the New Testament (TDNT)*, vol. 2, p. 84 ff.

[4] Beyer, *TDNT*.

to the neighbor. It is understood as full and perfect sacrifice, as the offering of life which is the very essence of service, of being for others, whether in life or in death. Thus the concept of διακονεῖν achieves its final theological depth. And what is true of Christ Himself is made a command for all His disciples in Jn. 12:26." [5]

So what are we to draw from this?

First, diakonos is not simply a *male* or *masculine* term! It is both masculine or feminine according to context!

Second, simply put, a *diakonos* is a *special servant* of the church, either male or female, depending on the context under discussion. As Beyer has pointed out Martha was referred to as one *who served*, diakoneō, others. In a distinct way, Martha was a *deaconess* who *served others*. No special authority is attached to the term other than authority to *be a special servant*. A female teacher of children in church is a special servant, a *diakonos*!

Third, the terms *deacon, diakonia, diakonos*, do not refer to an office, but refer to a *ministry serving function*.

Fourth, Church of Christ tradition has shied away from the concept of *deaconess* since deacons in the Roman Catholic and Episcopal Churches have *special authority* and a special *office*. Hence, to steer away from the Catholic and Episcopal implications, Churches of Christ have favored the term *servant* to avoid misunderstandings. Greek speaking churches would normally have no problem understanding that Phoebe was a *special-special servant* of the church!

Rom 16:3-16. House churches in Rome

Most scholars recognize that this pericope indicates that there were several house churches in Rome. Opinions

---

[5] Beyer, *TDNT*.

differ as to how many house churches Paul greeted, but the consensus is that there were at least five.[6]

Dunn favors several house churches as opposed to some suggestion that the members mentioned in this pericope were all members of the same church:

> The suggestion is attractive that the groupings indicate at least five different house churches in Rome (vv 5, 10, 11, 14, 15; e.g., Minear, *Obedience*, 7), and is more likely than Zahn's suggestion that those mentioned in vv 5–13 were all members of the home church of Prisca and Aquila, which would imply a double greeting on Paul's part (v 5a, vv 5–13). The extensive use of second-person greetings (Mullins, 425) may simply reflect Paul's awareness that the letter would have to be read several times within the different home churches; 1:7 is hardly sufficient evidence that Paul envisaged a single reading to the whole community gathered in one place ...[7]

Paul warning against those who create division in the fellowship of Christians

Rom 16:17-18. In keeping with his encouragement of the Roman Christians to quit judging one another, Paul also sternly warns the Christians not to permit those who cause division (that is the meaning of *dissentions* and *difficulties*) in opposition to doctrine (the teaching of the faith) to remain in close fellowship since they would divide the church. Such persons are to be avoided as dangerous to the fellowship and unity within the church, and this is one of the main purposes for Paul having demonstrated that in God there is no partiality, and that Jews and Gentiles must get along in the church, or in covenant relationship with one another and with God.

"I appeal to you, brethren, to take note of those who create dissensions and difficulties, in opposition to the doctrine which you have been taught; avoid them.

---

[6] Schreiner, *Romans*, p. 797; Dunn; Fitzmyer; Morris.

[7] Dunn, *Romans 9–16*; Fitzmyer, *Romans*, pp. 734ff.

^{18} For such persons do not serve our Lord Christ, but their own appetites, and by fair and flattering words they deceive the hearts of the simple-minded. ^{19} For while your obedience is known to all, so that I rejoice over you, I would have you wise as to what is good and guileless as to what is evil; ^{20} then the God of peace will soon crush Satan under your feet. The grace of our Lord Jesus Christ be with you."

Greetings from Paul's associate missionaries

Rom 16:21-23. *"Timothy, my fellow worker, greets you; so do Lucius and Jason and Sosipater, my kinsmen. ^{22} I Tertius, the writer of this letter, greet you in the Lord. ^{23} Gaius, who is host to me and to the whole church, greets you. Erastus, the city treasurer, and our brother Quartus, greet you."*

Paul closes his epistle with greetings from *Timothy* and several others indicating that they were known by quite a few of the Roman Christians, otherwise why mention them by name. *Timothy* had been a *fellow missionary* of Paul's on several occasions and would have been widely known. Three fellow Jews, *Lucius, Jason, and Sosipater,* whom he calls *my kinsmen*, are mentioned without further explanation at this point. *Gaius, who is host to me and to the whole church, greets you* as do *Erastus, the city treasurer, and our brother Quartus.* These last three were Corinthian Christians who were also known to the Romans, possibly through Aquilla and Priscilla who travelled back and forth between Rome and Corinth. The brief comment *and to the whole church* may indicate that the church, or at least some of the Corinthians, may have assembled in Gais' home which was Paul's base for writing the Roman letter.

I Tertius, the writer of this letter indicates that Tertius was Paul's scribe or amanuensis for the Roman letter.[8] It was common for teachers and philosophers of the day to use an amanuensis for official letters. The fact that Paul would have a Roman Christian *Tertius* write the letter may indicate that Tertius was from Rome and possibly known to the Roman Christians. Tertius was a Latin name.[9]

Paul's Doxology

Rom 16:25-27. *"Now <u>to him who is able to strengthen you according to my gospel and the preaching of Jesus Christ</u>, according to the revelation of the mystery which was kept secret for long ages [26] but is now disclosed and through the prophetic writings is made known to all nations, according to the command of the eternal God, to bring about the obedience of faith— [27] to the only wise God be glory for evermore through Jesus Christ! Amen."*

In rich Jewish tradition Paul *praises God for his gracious work of redemption*. The word *doxology* draws on the Greek word δόξα, *doxa*. The full word is δοξολογία, *doxologia*, implying *glory to God* and λογία, *logia, a saying*. A doxology is usually a short hymn of praises to God. The tradition derives from a similar practice in the Jewish synagogue, where some version of the Kaddish serves to terminate each section of the service.

Paul prays that God will strengthen the Christians in Rome, both Jewish and Gentile, and *suggests three ways in which God does this*; 1) according to the preaching of the Gospel; 2) according to the revelation of the mystery, that is, how in one body God reconciles both Jew and Gentile to himself; 3) according to the command of the eternal God who desires an obedient faith.

In Pauline and biblical theology, one cannot think of, or speak of faith *without implying that faith is obedient*. James, the brother of Jesus, a church leader in Jerusalem, certainly builds on the *parenetic* aspects of *faith without*

---

[8] Morris, *The Epistle to the Romans*, p. 543; Schreiner, *Romans*, pp. 807f.

[9] Fitzmyer, *Romans*, p. 749.

works being dead, James 2:14-26. Paul, however, stresses that faith and obedience cannot be separated for they are theologically symbiotically united. Three times in Romans Paul speaks of, or alludes to, *a faith that must be obedient,* Rom 1:5; 6:17; 16:26.

Rom 1:5. *"Jesus Christ our Lord,* ⁵ *through whom we have received grace and apostleship <u>to bring about the obedience of faith</u> for the sake of his name among all the nations,* ⁶ *including yourselves who are called to belong to Jesus Christ."*

Rom 6:17. *"But thanks be to God, that you who were once slaves of sin <u>have become obedient from the heart to the standard of teaching to which you were committed,</u>* ¹⁸ *and, having been set free from sin, have become slaves of righteousness."*

Rom 16:25, 26. *"the preaching of Jesus Christ, according to the revelation of the mystery which was kept secret for long ages* ²⁶ *but is now disclosed and through the prophetic writings is made known to all nations, according to <u>the command of the eternal God,</u> <u>to bring about the obedience of faith</u>."*

An *obedient faith* obviously was something of great importance to Paul since he includes this in the context of God's eternal command!

Brief Excursus in Biblical Predestination:
Rom 8:29, 30

Context and Message

We live in an environment of religious history in which several different views of predestination are encountered. The discussion has continued through the centuries as theologians have debated the fall of man, the loss and meaning of the Imago Dei, and how God has gone about restoring what was lost through human sin.

Roman Catholic, Reformed theology, and Calvinistic views have adopted the view that man is born inheriting the sin of Adam in some form or definition. They hold that in the fall of man (Adam's sin) man lost his image of God (the Imago Dei) and in consequence lost the cognitive ability to fully understand or identify with God.

It is only through the direct intervention and action of the Holy Spirit that man can fully cognitively understand God and come to faith. An atoning faith is thus not man's working, but the work of the Holy Spirit.

Some Evangelical theologians influenced by Jacob Arminius and Arminianism have adopted the view that the individual is free to respond of his own will individually in faith to God's predetermined corporate salvation in Christ. Believers are saved corporately in Christ by their own faith in Jesus Christ and the Holy Spirit's regenerative power.

These views impact our doctrine of predestination in the sense that Calvinistic predestination builds off the total depravity of man and the loss of his cognitive Imago Dei so that God in his sovereign will has predetermined that certain men should be saved and certain lost.

Evangelistic "Armenian" predestination adopts the view that in his loss of the Imago Dei man lost his rightful <u>relationship</u> with God through sin which relationship with God can be restored through

*individual faith in God's redemptive work in Jesus'
death and resurrection. The Imago Dei refers to man
being in a right <u>relationship</u> with God; it is <u>relational</u>,
not <u>cognitive</u>.*

*What God predestined was a <u>corporate</u> redemption
in Christ through faith in Christ, and not an individual
divine arbitrary redemption.*

Introduction

Predestination is a biblical topic and doctrine, but as
Paul uses it his view is vastly different from Calvinistic
Predestination.

In Rom 8:29, 30 Paul briefly discusses a concept of
predestination.

He writes *"We know that in everything God works for good
with those who love him, who are <u>called according to his
purpose</u>. [29] For those whom he <u>foreknew</u> he also
<u>predestined</u> to be conformed to the image of his Son, in
order that he might be the first-born among many
brethren. [30] And those whom he <u>predestined</u> he also <u>called</u>;
and those whom he called he also <u>justified</u>; and those
whom he justified he also <u>glorified</u>."*

The Greek word translated *predestined* is προορίζω,
proorizō, pronounced *"pro-horidzo."*

The word literally means *"to see before"* but is
understood to mean *"to decide beforehand,"* or *"to
determine or decree beforehand."* [1]

In Eph 1:5 προορίσας from προορίζω, *proorizō* is
translated *"destined"* and from the context we understand
that God *decided beforehand* that we should be his sons in
Christ according to his preordained will.

In Rom 8:29 and 30 the word simply means that *"God
knew something beforehand"* (*foreknew*), and based upon
this he *decided beforehand* (*predestined*) that we should be

---

[1] Zodhiates, προορίζω, *proorizō.*

298

conformed to the image of his son. He therefore *called us* for this purpose and *in order to be justified and glorified.*

God knew certain things and based on his *foreknowledge* he decided to act so we could be his children. He *decided beforehand* to call Abraham and then send Jesus to die for our sins. He then called us to faith through the gospel message proclaiming Jesus' death.

Calvinistic Predestination, see below, holds that God *arbitrarily* decided beforehand that some *persons* (individuals) should be saved, and some *persons* (individuals) *should be lost.*

Pauline and biblical predestination hold that based on God's *foreknowledge* that man would sin God, God had a *preordained* plan and "*decided beforehand*" according to that plan that Jesus would die for our sin. Through Jesus' atoning death, or in Jesus Christ, believers would, or could become God's sons, or as Paul puts it "*be conformed to his image.*"

God *predestined, decided beforehand* according to his *foreknowledge*, that his creation would need his *atoning intervention* so believers in Christ could be saved!

This is a *corporate* predestination, not an *individual* predestination. Paul posits a corporate predestination; Calvinism posits an *individual* predestination. We might argue that God knows before we obey him that we will believe, and that we will become his children, but *the predestination Paul describes is a <u>corporate</u>* predestination that proclaims that *<u>those in Christ</u> would be saved and become God's children.*

Due to the choice in words preferred by some there are degrees of understanding of the topic. Some prefer to speak of *predestination*, others prefer *election*. Both topics, however, focus on God's advance *selection* or *choosing* as reflected in texts such as Eph 1:3f-11 and Rom 8:29, 30.

Ewell and Beitzel observe that the words predestination and election "thus indicate God's prerogative in deciding what shall happen, independently of human choice."[2] They add,

> "The use of the word "*election*" emphasizes that membership of God's people is *due to God's initiative*, prior to all human response, made before time began (Eph 1:4; cf. Jn 15:16, 19). It is God who has called men and women to be his people, and those who respond are therefore the *elect*. God's call does not depend on any virtues or merits of humankind. Indeed, he chooses the foolish things by worldly standards to shame the wise, the weak to confound the strong, and the low and insignificant to bring to nothing those who think that they are something, 1 Cor 1:27, 28. The effect of election is to leave no grounds whatever for human boasting in achievement and position. Whoever the elect is, they owe their calling entirely to God's grace and mercy, and cannot boast or compare themselves with other people."[3]

Karl Barth proposed an alternative solution. Instead of teaching that God has chosen *to save some of mankind and has passed by the others* or *chosen to reject them*, Barth noted how Jesus is spoken of in Scripture as "*the elect One.*" Jesus is the object or sphere both of God's rejection and of his election! *In Christ* you are *elect, outside of Christ* you are *not the elect*! *In him the human race was rejected and endured judgment for its sins, Barth argued, but in him also the race is chosen and appointed to salvation. It is thus in Jesus Christ that we are chosen by God* (Eph 1:4). ... Barth insisted that a person may reject his or her calling and election.[4]

---

[2] Elwell, W. A., & Beitzel, B. J., "Elect, Election," *Baker Encyclopedia of the Bible,* vol. 1, p. 682.

[3] Elwell, W. A., & Beitzel, "Elect, Election."

[4] Elwell, W. A., & Beitzel, B. J., "Elect, Election," *Baker Encyclopedia of the Bible.*

"Calvinistic" Predestination[5]

Briefly speaking, Calvinistic Predestination arises out of the Catholic doctrine of inherited sin and total depravity.

Out of this mindset, Calvin adopted the Roman Catholic mindset and developed his doctrine of predestination.

Calvinistic, Reformed theology, and Lutheran theology hold that in the fall of man (Adam's sin) man lost his *image of God* (*Imago Dei*) and in consequence *lost the ability to fully understand or identify with God.*

It is only through the *direct intervention and action* of the Holy Spirit that man can fully understand God and *come to faith*; *atoning faith is thus not man's working, but the work of the Holy Spirit.*

Luther held that unregenerate man could understand the *outer clarity* of Scripture, but without the Holy Spirit man cannot understand the *inner meaning* of Scripture.

Most scholars recognize that Evangelicals differ widely over the topic of hereditary sin, the rational nature of the *Imago Dei*, and predestination.

Some Evangelicals today are *Calvinistic* in their understanding of the *Imago Dei* and man's rational ability to respond appropriately to God, other evangelicals are more *Arminian* in their thinking.

Arminianism is a branch of Protestantism based on the theological ideas of the Dutch Reformed theologian Jacobus Arminius (1560–1609) and his attempt to challenge the doctrines of Calvinism related to its interpretation of *predestination*.

Classical Arminianism, to which Arminius is the main contributor, and Wesleyan Arminianism, to which John Wesley is rooted, are two main contributors to evangelical

---

[5] For more detailed information on *predestination*, Roman Catholic and Calvinistic *total depravity*, cf. Richardson, Alan, *A Dictionary of Christian Theology*, London: SCM Press, 1969; Guthrie, Donald, *New Testament Theology*, Downers Grove: IVP, 1981, Bloesch, Donald G., *Essentials of Evangelical Theology*, Vol. 2, New York, Harper and Row, 1982.

thought. Many Christian denominations have been influenced by Arminian views *regarding the will of man being freed in* grace *prior to regeneration and salvation.* This was true notably of the British Baptists in 17th century, the Methodists in the 18th century, and the Pentecostals in the 20th century.

Many Evangelicals adopt an Arminian view that the individual is free to respond *of his own will individually in faith* to *God's predetermined corporate salvation in Christ.* Believers are *saved corporately in Christ* by *their own faith in Jesus Christ* and the Holy Spirit's *regenerative* power.

In a Calvinistic view each individual's salvation, or eternal rejection, is *predetermined* by God according to His *predetermined* will and election decision. Fundamental to this doctrine is the view that all men are by nature sinners and do not deserve eternal salvation. This doctrine abuses the context of Paul's statements at Rom 3:9-18.

It is difficult, almost impossible, to narrow the broad evangelical thinking to one conclusion, we must recognize that evangelicals are divided over *how* they understand *predestination* and *election.* For some salvation or rejection is definitively "Calvinistically" predetermined based on man's hereditary sinful lost condition and man's *inability* to come to faith through personal reflection of Scripture. Others are more open to an "Arminian view" of God's *predetermined* plan of *corporate salvation in Christ,* and man's *individual* openness to respond personally in faith.

William S. Sailer in the *Baker Encyclopedia of the Bible* observes:

"Evangelicals in the Arminian tradition ... distinguish *foreknowledge* from *foreordination* (predestination) of events. While the *plan of salvation* of the world and human history is *foreknown corporately* in Christ which is *predetermined* by God, they are *saved in Christ,* and *lost outside of Christ.* God does not predetermine their individual salvation.

While evangelical Christians differ in their description of the relationship between the eternal all-knowing God and the individual's freedom in the events of human history, it should be kept in mind that Scripture teaches both God's *foreknowledge* of all things, *the corporate nature of Christ* in salvation, and the *responsibility of humans* for their choices. Hence God *can foreknow* an event *without directly decreeing that event to take place.*[6]

Some summarize Calvinistic Predestination under the acronym TULIP.

T represents *total depravity* and holds that every person is born inheriting Adam's sin and is therefore totally depraved and unable to understand God.

U represents *unconditional election.* God chose some to be saved and some to be lost as an arbitrary choice by his grace and we have no say in his choice since we all deserve condemnation for our sin.

L represents *limited atonement.* Jesus died only for the elect; God limits his choice and calling.

I represents *irresistible grace* which means when God chooses you he sends his Holy Spirit to bring about your conversion, and you cannot resist the working of the Holy Spirit.

P represents *preservation of the saints.* The Holy Spirit sees to it that you cannot and do not fall away from grace. No matter what happens, you will get to heaven! It is on this point that we have the doctrine held by some that once you are saved, you are always saved.

The Origin of Faith

In classical restoration Church of Christ and Christian Church thinking, the understanding of the origin of an individual's faith was influenced by John Locke (ca. 1700) and Alexander Campbell (ca 1800); both classical

---

[6] Sailer, W. S., "Foreknowledge," *Baker Encyclopedia of the Bible*, vol 1, p. 808.

rationalists, who held that the *Scriptures are rational and can be understood by rational man. Faith,* then results from man's *rational comprehension of Scripture* and his *personal decision* to accept that rational conclusion.

Although Campbell had an appreciation for the working of the Holy Spirit he would not condone the direct operation of the Holy Spirit on man in the *initial development of faith* in the individual. Faith must be a rational conclusion to the evidence of Scripture.

Some of Campbell's followers took Campbell's views to the extreme and held that the only way the Holy Spirit ever works in one's life was through the Word.

This may help us understand why some members of the Church of Christ have until recently had a challenging time accepting the work of the Holy Spirit in that by doing so they may *detract from a rational approach* and comprehension of Scripture.

This is unfortunate and has led to a diminution of appreciation of the working of the Holy Spirit in the *maturation of faith.*

It would have been better had members of the Church of Christ paid closer attention to Barton W. Stone, who although similar in approach to Campbell in a rational understanding of Scripture, also accepted the working of the Holy Spirit in the development of faith! Stone had perhaps a more balanced approach than that adopted by Campbell's extremely rationalist followers!

Several Scriptures support the conclusion that faith results from a rational hearing, learning, and comprehension of Scripture.

2 Tim 3:15, 16: [14] *But as for you, continue in what you have learned and firmly believed, knowing from whom you learned it,* [15] *and how from childhood you have known the sacred writings that are able to instruct you for salvation through faith in Christ Jesus.* [16] *All scripture is inspired by God and is useful for teaching, for reproof, for correction, and for training in righteousness,* [17] *so that* *everyone who belongs to God may be proficient, equipped for every good work.*

Rom 10:16: [16] *But not all have obeyed the good news; for Isaiah says, "Lord, who has believed our message?"* [17] *So faith comes from what is heard, and what is heard comes through the word of Christ.*

[18] *But I ask, have they not heard? Indeed they have; for*
"Their voice has gone out to all the earth,
and their words to the ends of the world."
[19] *Again I ask, did Israel not understand? First Moses says,*
"I will make you jealous of those who are not a nation;
with a foolish nation I will make you angry."
[20] *Then Isaiah is so bold as to say,*
"I have been found by those who did not seek me;
I have shown myself to those who did not ask for me."

John 5:39: [39] *"You search the scriptures because you think that in them you have eternal life; and it is they that testify on my behalf."*

It seems obvious that Scripture and the understanding of Scripture have a large part to play in the development and maturation of faith, but this does not exclude prayer and the working of God, Holy Spirit, and teaching in the development and maturation of faith.

The issue or difference between a restoration Church of Christ view of faith and that of Lutheranism and Calvinism is that Calvinism and Lutheranism hold that without the *initial operation* of the Holy Spirit one cannot come to Christian faith. Lutheranism holds that without the *assistance* of the Holy Spirit *one is not able to understand the inner meaning of Scripture.*

Both Calvin and Luther held to the importance of Scripture but in addition both held that without the direct intervention of the Holy Spirit one would not be able to understand Scripture.

Both the Calvinistic and Lutheran views are committed to some concept of the loss of the *Imago Dei* being related to *one's rational ability.*

305

Conclusion to Calvinistic Predestination

We have not attempted to develop a full Calvinistic doctrine of Predestination, only to comment on the main direction of such theories or doctrines.

Our purpose has been only to give an overview of the doctrine as held by most Roman Catholics, Calvinists, and Lutherans.

In spite of earnest attempts to sustain Calvinistic Predestination from a biblical standpoint, it simply is not supported by Biblical doctrine or theology!

A Biblical Theology of Baptism

Introduction

The topic of baptism has been encountered in most forms of Christian religion since the very origins of the Christian faith. It appears in the beginnings of the Gospel story as recounted by Mark, Matthew, and Luke in their Gospels, and was encountered early in the life of Jesus at his baptism by John.

The interpretation of this doctrine has been shaped by numerous cultural and sociological opinions ever since the first century CE.

For instance, early in the life of the Corinthian Church, ca CE 56, a doctrine of baptizing for the dead, 1 Cor 15:29, surfaced which Paul criticized as being without biblical foundation and centered in the Corinthian Greek culture and concern for those who had died in a philosophy that denied any doctrine of resurrection. The Greek rejection of a resurrection was the cultural determinant in this strange doctrine of a baptism for the dead which had no roots in either the Old Testament or New Testament systems. Notice Paul's condemnation of this rejection of the crucifixion and resurrection at 1 Cor 1:18-25 and 1 Cor 15:1-58.

As the church spread into the Roman world and became a Christianized religion, concern for the sinful nature of man surfaced, cf. the Augustinian Pelagian controversy, ca CE 350. The net result of this has been the Christianized form of pedobaptism, child baptism, since it was believed that the baby was born tainted by original sin and needed to be baptized for salvation and initial entrance into the church.

For several reasons, this pedobaptism shifted from immersion in water to sprinkling with specialized holy water. This form of sprinkling or pedobaptism is practiced by many churches in the Roman Catholic and Reformation traditions. The Greek Orthodox tradition practices a form of baptism similar to Roman Catholic sprinkling but adapts

307

this into a *pouring* of holy water over an infant seated in a baptism laver.

A form of Christian baptism by immersion is found in certain African Christo-pagan churches. Repentant members are immersed numerous times on the same occasion to drive out the evil spirits inhabiting the person. The baptism is repeated until the member manifests an emotional emetic reaction to being purged by the water. In some variations of this repeat baptisms are practiced on all the members to maintain a pure membership.

In the early 1500 CE era a movement arose in the context of debates on the role of baptism among Ulrich Zwingli and some reformers who opposed infant or pedobaptism. Out of this movement the religious group commonly identified as the anabaptists surfaced. The term anabaptism derives from the Greek word for *repeated, ἀνά,* and *baptism.* The term was somewhat derogatory since the anabaptist movement argued against infant baptism in favor of adult baptism. More modern forms of anabaptism are found among the Mennonites, Hutterites, Amish, and Brethren movements. Baptism by immersion upon the confession of faith and repentance among these fellowships is generally associated with salvation and membership in the church.

Thomas R. Schreiner, *Believers Baptism: Sign of the New Covenant in Christ,* opens his recent study on Baptism with this observation:

> Some within the Christian confession claim that baptism should be classified as a minor issue. *Such a sentiment is misdirected, for baptism is regularly connected in scripture with belief and salvation.* Baptism, as this book will demonstrate, is the initiation rite into the Christian church. Those who label it as minor are *imposing their own categories onto the Scriptures instead of listening to the Scriptures.* Timothy George reminds us that those who practiced believer's baptism during the Reformation risked "persecution and martyrdom," and hence did

not view baptism as a minor matter. We are not claiming, of course, that a right understanding of baptism is necessary for salvation. Still, to say that a right understanding of baptism is unnecessary for salvation does not lead logically or biblically to the conclusion that baptism is inconsequential. In saying the above, we do not wish to engage in a polemical debate which ratchets up the temperature to a fever pitch. *Our hope is that this book will defend believer's baptism with a charitable and irenic spirit.* We realize that other evangelical believers disagree with us, but we hope to persuade many that the course we chart fits with the scriptural witness.

Baptism is important precisely because it is tied to the gospel, to the saving work that Christ accomplished in his death and resurrection. We do not think baptizing infants is merely a minor mistake, even though we rejoice in the evangelical credentials of many with whom we disagree.[1]

As indicated above, the discussion on baptism we often encounter is not necessarily a *biblical* theology of the subject, but is one more influenced by ecclesiological history, current philosophical persuasions, and sociological developments.

This study, however, is intended to be an advanced *inductive* study of the *biblical texts* and doctrine of Baptism, and the biblical meaning and occasions of the words βαπτισμός, *baptismós* and βαπτίζω, *baptízō* in the New Testament. We will reflect on some scholarly biblical studies as a context for our study.

We will begin by examining in some detail the words *baptism, baptize, baptized, Baptist, baptizer*. They are found at least 95 times in the New Testament (Revised Standard Version).

---

[1] Thomas R. Schreiner; Shawn Wright. *Believer's Baptism: Sign of the New Covenant in Christ,* 2006. Emphases, IAF.

Of the 95 occurrences in the New Testament, the words are found 50 times in the Gospels. They are found in all fours Gospels, Acts, Paul, and Peter.

Brief Bibliography

The Bible Dictionaries cited in this study are a good beginning point for examining the doctrine of baptism in the New Testament and its subsequent practice in the Christian tradition:

Everett F. Harrison, Geoffrey W. Bromiley, et al., *The Yale Anchor Bible Dictionary*, 1992.
Everett F. Harrison, Geoffrey W. Bromiley, et al., *Baker's Dictionary of Theology*, 1987.
George Arthur Buttrick, Thomas Samuel Kepler, *The Interpreter's Dictionary of the Bible*, 1962.
Gerhard Kittel, *Theological Dictionary of the New Testament*, 1976.
Spiros Zodhiates, *Complete Word Study Dictionary: New Testament*, 1993.
In addition to some excellent commentaries which will be listed below the following studies on baptism will be helpful and informative.

G. R. Beasley-Murray, *Baptism in the New Testament*, 1962.
Everett Ferguson, *Baptism in the Early Church: History, Theology, and Liturgy in the First Five Centuries*, Eerdmans, 2009.
Jack Cottrell, *Baptism: A Biblical Study*, College Publishing Company, 2000.
Thomas R. Schreiner, *Believers Baptism: Sign of the New Covenant in Christ*, B & H Academic, 2007.

This study on Baptism

As indicated above this study will provide a critical inductive scholarly examination of the *biblical* doctrine of baptism. We begin with a brief study of the word family that surrounds the doctrine of baptism. Following this we will notice several theological statements made by leading scholars, Bible dictionaries, and theological works from a variety of religious persuasions. We will then examine the occurrence of this family of words in the New Testament. Finally we will draw together conclusions from the biblical statements on baptism and offer a biblical theology of baptism that has its roots within the biblical framework.

Outline of the Study
1. The Words
2. Remarks in the Yale Anchor Bible Dictionary
3. Some general theological discussions
    a. Alan Richardson, Anglican Dean of York, Professor of Christian Theology
    b. Geoffrey W. Bromiley, Professor of Church History and Historical
       Theology
4. Baptism Texts in the Gospels, Acts, Paul, and Peter
5. Theological Discussion on the Textual and Linguistic Analysis
    a. Pre-Christian Practice of Baptism
    b. The Baptism of John the Baptist
    c. Christian Baptism
6. Biblical theological discussion on the texts: Acts
7. Biblical theological discussion on the texts: Paul, John, and Peter
8. Summary and conclusion of Baptism study

The Words
    These are the Greek words with their literal English meaning from which the English words are transliterated:
βαπτίζω, **baptizō** – verb, to baptize, dip, immerse, dip oneself (middle voice), wash, plunge, sink, drench, overwhelm
βaptismós, baptismós – noun, baptism, dip, wash
βάπτισμα, **báptisma** – noun, baptism
βαπτιστής, **baptistés**, noun baptizer
βάπτω, *báptō*– to dip, dip into, cover with.

311

The Yale Anchor Bible Dictionary

Below, we present an extract from the Yale Anchor Bible Dictionary on Baptism.

The *Anchor Bible Dictionary defines baptism as "A rite of incorporation employing water as a symbol of religious purification."*

In a discussion of the Greek words *The Anchor Bible Dictionary* makes the following observations, v. 1pp. 583ff:

> 1. Greek Terminology. The Gk verb for "baptize," baptizein, is formed from baptein, "dip," and means "dip frequently or intensively, plunge, immerse."
>
> By Plato's time and onwards it is often used in a figurative sense (e.g., in the passive, "soaked" in wine, Plato 176 B).
>
> It appears 4 times in the LXX: 4 Kingdoms 5:14 (Naaman in the Jordan), Jdt 12:7 (purification), Sir 34:30—in English 34:25 (purification after touching a corpse), Isa 21:4 (figuratively of lawlessness).
>
> The noun báptisma is only used in Christian literature, where it refers to the baptism of John or to Christian baptism.
>
> The word baptismós is used in a wider sense for dipping, washing (of dishes Mark 7:4), of ritual washings (Heb 9:10; John's baptism, Joseph. Ant. 18.117; Christian baptism, Col 2:12 (variant).
>
> A synonymous noun is loutron "bath" used of both ordinary and ceremonial baths, but in the NT only with reference to baptism.
>
> The corresponding verb *louein* "wash, bathe" is encountered in its everyday use in, e.g., 2 Pet 2:22 and John 13:10. It refers to ceremonial baths in Lev 15:11 and to Christian baptism (probably) in the compound form *apolouein* in 1 Cor 6:11.
>
> Rites of immersion were common in the world in which early Christianity developed.

One type of symbolism with which they were frequently connected was that of purification: from sin, from destruction, from the profane sphere before entering a holy area, from something under a taboo. See, e.g., Lev 16:4, 24 (the high priest before and after the rites of atonement); Leviticus 15 (on menstruating women); 1 QS 3:5–9 (cleansing from sins); Sib. Or. 4.165 (a baptism of repentance); Joseph. Ant. 18.117 (on John's baptism); Joseph. Life. 11 (on Bannus' ablutions for purity's sake); Apul., Met. 11.23 (purification at the initiation into the Isis mysteries); b. Yebam. 47 ab (on proselyte baptism).

Such cleansings can take place when one stands on the verge of a new state in life or is entering into a new community or upon a new phase of life. (Emphasis, IAF).

Thus they can function as rites of initiation or as rites of passage. Depending on the way in which one regards the situation being left behind and the one being entered, such rites can be connected with ideas of a new birth, of a new life, or of salvation as contrasted to nothingness, chaos, death, or destruction.

As already intimated, many religions in antiquity practiced different washings and baths.

This holds true for the mysteries of Eleusis, of Mithras, and of Isis. The OT prescribed several ablutions to be performed, rules which were observed by Jews also in NT times (John 2:6).

The Qumran community laid a particular stress on them, and Bannus (Joseph. Life. 10) and John the Baptist were not alone in practicing baptisms outside of mainstream Judaism.

Other baptismal movements also appeared in the Transjordanian/Syrian area.

Sometime during the 1st century c.e. proselyte baptism was introduced in Judaism

When baptism received a principal place in Mandeism, the rite as such was certainly no novelty, regardless of whether it should be regarded as pre-Christian or not.

One should beware of assigning the same or even similar meanings to these rites. As rites they are open to several interpretations; in each case it is to be expected that the meaning of the rite is provided by the ritual context or otherwise through instruction or tradition.

General Theological Discussion

The majority of mainline, traditional, churches hold to some form of baptismal tradition. In most cases, baptism is seen as a means of transition from a past life into a new lifestyle and relationship with Christ and the church.

In this sense, baptism has traditionally been seen as one of the two main sacraments of the church, the other being the Eucharist, Communion, or Lord's Supper. The term sacrament is a technical term (sacrament derives from the Latin term *sacramentum* which meant an oath of allegiance to someone) that infers a relationship with, or commitment to, Christ and the church. Baptism is the sacramental initiation into the church and relationship with Christ, and the Eucharist (Lord's Supper) is the continued intimate relationship or communion with both.

Cf. Alan Richardson, ed., *A Dictionary of Christian Theology*, SCM Press, 1969, under the section *Initiation* Richardson makes the following observations on baptism:

"From apostolic times the initiation of new members into the Church has been by baptism (cf. Acts 2:38, 41)... Theologically baptism signifies what God has done for our salvation through Christ...and also what God does for men individually and corporately through the mediating work of Christ. Baptism, like the other dominical sacrament, the Lord's Supper, is a proclamation of Christ's death and resurrection...The going down into the water

314

symbolizes a burial and the coming up from the waters a resurrection... As we are born into a natural family on earth, so at baptism we are reborn ('regenerated') into the family of our heavenly father..."

Cf. Everett F. Harrison, ed., *Baker's Dictionary of Theology*, Baker Book House, 1960, 1983, under "Baptism and Believers."

"Baptism: In essence the action of baptism is an extremely simple one, though pregnant with meaning. It consists in a going in or under the baptismal water in the name of Christ (Acts 19:5) or more commonly the Trinity (Matt 28:19). Immersion was fairly certainly the original practice and continued in widespread use up to the Middle Ages."

"Theologically, the insistence upon believers' baptism in all cases seems better calculated to serve the true significance and benefit of baptism and to avoid the errors which so easily threaten it. Only when there is personal confession before baptism can it be seen that personal repentance and faith are necessary to the salvation through Christ, and that these do not come magically but through hearing the word of God. With believers' baptism the ordinance achieves its significance as the mark of a step from darkness and death to light and life. The recipient is thus confirmed in the decision he has taken, brought into the company of the regenerate, which is the true church..., and encouraged to walk in the new life which he has begun."

Geoffrey Bromiley, Professor of Church History and Historical Theology, Fuller Theological Seminary.

Pre-Christian Practice of Baptism

We have already noticed above that several religious groups outside of the Judeo-Christian tradition held to some form of baptism or immersion as a form of ceremonial cleansing or washing in the case of certain taboos such as touching a corpse, or the cleansing from some "sin" or ceremonial misdeed. In some cases (Isis) baptism by immersion was part of the process or ceremony of initiation into the group.

Baptismal cleansing was also practiced among the Jews as a means of ceremonial cleansing prior to John the Baptist and the Christian movement. Not only were people cleansed from ceremonial uncleanness, but utensils used in the home or religious functions were also cleansed by immersion. *Mikvahs* (spelled variously) were a common part of prayer places and synagogues before the time of John the Baptist and Jesus Christ. (A *mikvah* is a large "pool" or cistern in which a person could be immersed for this ceremonial cleansing. Rules relating to the type of water and ceremony were established in early Judaism. *Mikvahs* have been discovered in many archaeological digs of Jewish communities and synagogues.)

From the Dead Sea Scrolls we have learned that the community at Qumran (and other Dead Sea religious communities) practiced baptism as a form of ceremonial cleansing. In this community baptism was not a once for lifetime experience as in Christian baptism, but one repeated as often as the necessity demanded for ceremonial holiness.

It is not surprising that John the Baptist came preaching a baptism for the forgiveness of sins that was characterized by repentance.

First, we learn from Luke 7:29, 30 (but the Pharisees and the lawyers rejected the purpose of God for themselves, not having been baptized by him) that John's baptism was not his idea, but that of God, for as we notice, Luke tells us that the Pharisees rejected the purpose of God by not being baptized. John (Jn 1:33) records that John the Baptist understood that God sent him to baptize with water.

Second, some scholars suggest, with reasonable grounds, that John may have been raised by one of the Jewish communities in the wilderness (such as the one at Qumran). If so, he must have been familiar with ceremonial baptisms such as those carried out by the Qumran community.

Third, from at least the time of John the Baptist, ceremonial cleansings in *Mikhahs* was already a practice fairly common among the Jews. That the crowds flocked out to hear John and to be baptized by him indicates that they were not surprised by John's insistence that they be baptized demonstrating repentance, and that this baptism was for the forgiveness of sins.

The point we are making here is that baptism was not a new novelty invented by the Christian community.

The Baptism of John the Baptist

When John came preaching the urgent and long anticipated message that the kingdom of God was at hand, and demanded repentance and baptism from the Jews, his message had within it certain eschatological (end time) implications. The Jews had long anticipated the coming of a Messiah who would judge the nations and restore God's kingdom to Israel. John came as the forerunner to the Messiah (Matt 3:1-3; Mk 1:1-4, Lk 3:2-9; Jn 1:19-23). His message of repentance and baptism held within it both the promise of cleansing and renewal, and the imminent arrival of the Messianic kingdom.

Mark explains in the clearest terms the nature of John's baptism.
"John the baptizer appeared in the wilderness, preaching a baptism of repentance for the forgiveness of sins. And there went out to him all the country of Judea, and all the people of Jerusalem; and they were baptized by him in the river Jordan, confessing their sins." (Mk 1:4, 5)
We need to understand the nature of the forgiveness offered under John's baptism. Forgiveness of sins was not something new, for such was available through the Mosaic annual sacrificial offering for sin and day of atonement. Repentance and confession of sins was required under the mosaic system, but the sacrifices had to be repeated every year. The forgiveness of sins offered through John's

317

baptism was part of this Mosaic system with the new ingredient of baptism as a sign of true repentance. The initiative for this repentance was the imminence of the Messianic kingdom to be inaugurated by Jesus.

Such was the power of John's message that many (all Judea) went out to hear him preach and to be baptized. The exception, however, were the Scribes and Pharisees whose traditional piety was superficial (Jesus calls them hypocrites) and who desiring to make a show of their "righteousness" also came out to hear John, only to hear a scathing rebuke regarding the nature of their false repentance.

The core, or dynamic of John's message was repentance in view of the imminence of the Messianic kingdom. Its purpose was to prepare the Nation of Israel for the coming of the Messiah and the inauguration of his kingdom. John the Baptist clearly claims that his purpose in baptizing was to reveal the Messiah to Israel (Jn 1:31). John's baptism, characterized as it was by repentance, was an indication that the recipient was prepared for the breaking in of God's eschatological kingdom. Baptism was the visible expression of one's faith and repentance, and the goal of that baptism was the forgiveness of sins and preparation for the imminent kingdom of God and the Messiah.

The key points we should note are:

1) The baptism of John was accompanied by repentance.

2) It offered forgiveness of sins under the Mosaic system.

3) It was a forerunner to the inauguration of the Messianic kingdom.

4) It operated under the Mosaic system of animal sacrifices which had to be renewed every year.

Years later (Acts 19:3-5) Paul encountered some who had been baptized under John's baptism. He encouraged them to be baptized in the name of Jesus, not the name of John: "*v3. And he said, "Into what then were you baptized?" They said, "Into John's baptism." v4. And Paul said, "John baptized with the baptism of repentance, telling the people to believe in the one who was to come after him, that is, Jesus." v5. On hearing this, they were baptized in the name of the Lord Jesus."*

Once Jesus' kingdom had been established, John's baptism was no longer effective and valid.

Jesus' Personal Baptism falls under the category of John the Baptist's baptism. Three of the Gospels record Jesus' baptism (Matthew 3:13-17; Mark 1:12, 13; and Luke 3:21, 22) and the fourth, John, alludes to it (John 1:29-34).

Matthew (in view of his Jewish audience) gives us the more detailed explanation of Jesus' baptism. It is Matthew that includes the interesting dialogue between Jesus and John regarding the necessity for Jesus being baptized. John wanted to resist Jesus' baptism, claiming that he needed to be baptized by Jesus rather than Jesus being baptized by John. Jesus responds that his baptism was necessary "to fulfil all righteousness." What Jesus meant by this was that in order to keep in a right relationship with God (righteousness in the Jewish context implied a right relationship with God by doing his will) he needed to be baptized. He had no reason to repent and no sins that needed forgiveness, yet he still needed to keep the will of God in order to be righteous and in a right relationship with his Father. This adds to the importance of John's baptism, since Jesus implies that John's baptism related to doing the will of the Father! (See also Lk 2:20, 30.)

When Jesus came up out of the water the Holy Spirit descended on him in the form of a dove, and God acknowledged Jesus as "my beloved son in whom he was well pleased."

In John's baptism of Jesus we see a transition from John's ministry of pointing to Jesus as the Messiah, and Jesus beginning his ministry as the Messiah.

In this significant narrative we find John "passing the torch" to Jesus with the fascinating words:

319

"I baptize you with water for repentance, but he who is coming after me is mightier than I, whose sandals I am not worthy to carry; he will baptize you with the Holy Spirit and with fire. 12 His winnowing fork is in his hand, and he will clear his threshing floor and gather his wheat into the granary, but the chaff he will burn with unquenchable fire." Matt 3:11, 12

Whereas John's baptism was with water for repentance (and forgiveness - Mark 1:4), Jesus' baptism was to be *with the Holy Spirit and fire*. This brief expression, recorded also in Mark and John (albeit not as fully as in Matthew), presents an interesting study.

First we note that the best translation is "with the Holy Spirit and fire," not repeating the "with" as in "with the Holy Spirit and with fire." *The Greek construction ties Holy Spirit and fire together as one thought, not two.*

Second, although the next verses speak of the winnowing fork and fire as judgment, this statement Holy Spirit and fire speaks not only of judgment but *also of sanctification and purification as in the new birth.* Fire in the Jewish tradition could represent *both judgment* (Isa 5:22; Isa 34:8-10; Isa 66:15, 16, 24) *and purification* (Zech 13:9; Mal 3:2). Notice the statement in Zech 13:8, 9:

> *8 In the whole land, says the Lord,*
> <u>*two thirds shall be cut off and perish,*</u>
> *and one third shall be left alive.*
> *9 And I will put this third into the fire,*
> *and <u>refine them as one refines silver,</u>*
> *<u>and test them as gold is tested</u>.*
> *<u>They will call on my name,</u>*
> *<u>and I will answer them.</u>*
> *<u>I will say, 'They are my people';</u>*
> *and they will say, 'The Lord is my God.'*

Coupled with the reference to the Holy Spirit the statement "he will baptize you with the Holy Spirit and fire" *speaks of the purification by the Holy Spirit in the new age or the Messianic kingdom* (see Hagner, in his

320

commentary *Matthew 1-13*,[2] and Isa 44:3; Ezek 36:25-27; 39:29; Joel 2:28, *passim*, and the Dead Sea Scroll text 1QS 4:20-21).

Whereas John's baptism pointed to or announced the imminence of the Messiah and the Messianic kingdom, Jesus' baptism (the baptism instituted by Jesus, namely Christian baptism) *ushers in or inaugurates* the Messianic kingdom and the purification and forgiveness offered in the Messianic kingdom.

The mention here of the Holy Spirit in conjunction with the baptism that Jesus would bring indicates the inauguration and institution of the new birth (Jn 3:3-5) and forgiveness (Acts 2:38) in the Messianic kingdom.

> [3] *Jesus answered him, "Truly, truly, I say to you, <u>unless one is born anew</u>, he cannot see the kingdom of God." [4] Nicodemus said to him, "How can a man be born when he is old? Can he enter a second time into his mother's womb and be born?" [5] Jesus answered, "Truly, truly, I say to you, <u>unless one is born of water and the Spirit, he cannot enter the kingdom of God</u>. [6] That which is born of the flesh is flesh, and that which is born of the Spirit is spirit. [7] Do not marvel that I said to you, 'You must be born anew.' [8] The wind blows where it wills, and you hear the sound of it, but you do not know whence it comes or whither it goes; <u>so it is with everyone who is born of the Spirit</u>."[3]*

> [37] *Now when they heard this they were cut to the heart, and said to Peter and the rest of the apostles, "Brethren, what shall we do?" [38] And Peter said to them, "Repent, and <u>be baptized every one of you in the name of Jesus Christ for the forgiveness of your sins; and you shall receive the gift of the Holy Spirit</u>. [39] For the promise is to you and to your*

---

[2] Donald Hagner, *Matthew 1-13*, World Biblical Commentary, 1993, p. 52.
[3] John 3:2–8.

*children and to all that are far off, every one whom
the Lord our God calls to him."[4]*

When John records that Jesus baptized disciples (John
3:22), this was under *the baptism instituted by God
through John the Baptist*, and like John's baptism
functioned under the Mosaic legal system of sacrifices.
This should not be confused with the baptism Jesus
instituted and commanded (Matt 28:18, 19; Mark 16:15,
16) and the Apostles taught (Acts 2:38, passim).

Thus, the baptism Jesus commanded and instituted,
and the Apostles taught, we refer to as *Christian baptism.*

The great Commission and Christian Baptism

In the following discussion we summarize the Great
Commission of Jesus.

In Matt 28:19, 20 and Mark 16:15, 16, Jesus
commanded his Apostles to *go out into all the world and
make disciples of all nations, baptizing them and teaching
them, and that those who believed and were baptized
would be saved.*

> *And Jesus came and said to them, "All
> authority in heaven and on earth has been given to
> me. [19] Go therefore and make disciples of all
> nations, baptizing them in the name of the Father
> and of the Son and of the Holy Spirit, [20] teaching
> them to observe all that I have commanded you;
> and lo, I am with you always, to the close of the
> age." [5]*

> *[15] And he said to them, "Go into all the world
> and preach the gospel to the whole creation. [16] He
> who believes and is baptized will be saved; but he
> who does not believe will be condemned.[6]*

Thus what Jesus instituted and the Apostolic church
carried out we call Christian Baptism.

---

[4] Acts 2:37–39.
[5] Mat 28:18–20.
[6] Mark 15:15, 16.

We have already noted above that John the Baptist had announced this category of baptism with the statement that Jesus would baptize with the Holy Spirit and fire.

The baptism of Jesus would usher in the Messianic kingdom, the new birth into the kingdom, and the new life in the Spirit.

The Gospels do not explain *the act of baptism* in any detail other than in the discussion by John the Baptist mentioned above, and in Jesus' Great commission.

It is to the Book of Acts and the Epistles of Paul and Peter that we must turn *for details and clarification of the nature, purpose, and act of Christian Baptism.*

We should stress again, however, that *Christian Baptism was instituted and commanded by Jesus* and *carried out* by the Apostolic church.

Brief introductory discussion on the texts of Baptism in Paul, John, and Peter

Baptism in Paul

A unique feature of Paul's use of, and theology of baptism is that in his epistles he is writing to Christians who have already been baptized!

Unlike Acts where Luke is recording the Apostolic preaching to Jewish and Gentile unbelievers, Paul is writing to believers, members of the church, those who have already been baptized!

Baptism in Paul's use and theology is the means of *reminding* Christians *of what happened to them when they were baptized*, baptism introduced a radical change in their lives, they had experienced a death and resurrection, a new birth introducing a new life. Things in the Christian's life are different because the Christian has been baptized and has entered into a new union with Christ, and with one another! Because they have been baptized they are now members of Christ's body, the church, and should behave accordingly!

We will consider baptism in Paul's thought somewhat chronologically, revealed through his primary epistles..

We will begin with Gal 3:24ff:

> [24] ... *the law was our custodian until Christ came,*
> *that we might be justified by faith.* [25] *But now that*
> *faith has come, we are no longer under a*
> *custodian;* [26] for in Christ Jesus <u>you are all sons of</u>
> <u>God, through faith.</u> [27] <u>*For as many of you as were*</u>
> <u>*baptized into Christ have put on Christ.*</u> [28] <u>*There is*</u>
> <u>*neither Jew nor Greek,*</u> *there is neither slave nor*
> *free, there is neither male nor female;* <u>*for you are*</u>
> <u>*all one in Christ Jesus.*</u> [7]

Galatians was possibly one of Paul's earliest epistles
written to both Jews and Gentiles emphasizing that they
are *no longer two people*, Jews and Gentiles, but are now
one family in Christ; *they were united in one baptism into*
one body in Christ, Eph 4:1ff:

> [1] *I therefore, a prisoner for the Lord, beg you*
> *to lead a life worthy of the calling to which you*
> *have been called,* [2] *with all lowliness and meekness,*
> *with patience, forbearing one another in love,*
> [3] *eager to maintain the unity of the Spirit in the*
> *bond of peace.* [4] *There is one body and one Spirit,*
> *just as you were called to the one hope that belongs*
> *to your call,* [5] *one Lord, one faith, one baptism,*
> [6] *one God and Father of us all, who is above all*
> *and through all and in all.* [8]

In Galatians Paul is incensed that some were following
a new gospel, not one which he had preached, and one that
called Christians back to keeping the Law of Moses and
circumcision.

> *I am astonished that you are so quickly*
> *deserting him who called you in the grace of Christ*
> *and turning to a different gospel—* [7] *not that there*
> *is another gospel, but there are some who trouble*
> *you and want to pervert the gospel of Christ.* [9]

---

[7] Gal 3:24-28
[8] Eph 4:1–6.
[9] Gal 1:6–7.

His argument is that the Law had served a purpose of leading the Jew to Christ, but now that Christ had come they were no longer under the Law, they were under Christ and faith in Christ. All Christians, both Jewish and Gentile, are children of God through faith in Jesus, and not through keeping the Law. Notice Gal 3:27 where Paul introduces the subject of baptism. *It was through their baptism that they were united with Christ and put on Christ.* The introductory word *"For"* explains how they became children of God through faith, for, through baptisms they became part of Christ, they were united with Christ, the ultimate son of God! Baptism takes faith beyond the sense of believing or trusting, and translates or transfers one into Christ.

In similar vein, Paul wrote to a congregation divided into several opposing groups of disciples, some following Paul, some Peter, some other leaders. He argued that Christians are one people, not divided into sectarian groups.

Almost as though he were building on his argument in Gal 3 that we are all one in Christ through faith in Christ, Paul discusses a problem plaguing the Corinthian church, namely, that of division. They had been baptized into one group, followers of Jesus, not of Paul or Peter! Note this emphasis at 1 Cor 1:12-17 and 1 Cor 12:13:

> *[12] What I mean is that each one of you says, "I belong to Paul," or "I belong to Apollos," or "I belong to Cephas," or "I belong to Christ." [13] Is Christ divided? Was Paul crucified for you? Or were you baptized in the name of Paul? [14] I am thankful that I baptized none of you except Crispus and Gaius; [15] lest anyone should say that you were baptized in my name. [16] (I did baptize also the household of Stephanas. Beyond that, I do not know whether I baptized anyone else.) [17] For Christ did not send me to baptize but to preach the gospel, and not with eloquent wisdom, lest the cross of Christ be emptied of its power.*

1 Cor 12:13:

13 For by one Spirit <u>we were all baptized into one body</u>—Jews or Greeks, slaves or free—and all were made to drink of one Spirit.

Paul's argument against dividing into subgroups favoring certain church leaders is that the body of Christ is not divided, that *the disciples were not baptized into Cephas, or Apollos, or anyone else. They were all baptized into Christ, and Christ is not divided. Baptism was not the core of Paul's preaching; Christ was.* Paul argues throughout that although baptism is important, the Corinthians, because of their baptism were one body in Christ. They may be different nationally, but because of being baptized into Christ they were one people, one body. Although in this context Paul's emphasis was on preaching only Christ, baptism still features prominently in Paul's theology and argument, for he has just made an argument from baptism; they were not baptized in the name of Paul, but of Christ! In 1 Cor 12:13 he continued this argument by showing that by one Spirit (the Holy Spirit) *they were all baptized into one body, the body of Christ.* As we learn from Acts 2:38 and John 3:3-5, the Holy Spirit is present in baptism bringing about a new birth. We are born into one family, the family of God *through our faith in Jesus Christ and by being baptized into Christ!* We are baptized into one body, the one body of Christ. Division and favoring one human being over others is against the will of Christ and the work of the Holy Spirit.

In the course of developing his argument against being divided over allegiance to church leaders, Paul makes this interesting statement: 1 Cor 1: 14ff:

14 I am thankful that I baptized none of you except Crispus and Gaius; 15 lest anyone should say that you were baptized in my name. 16 (I did baptize also the household of Stephanas. Beyond that, I do not know whether I baptized anyone else.) 17 For Christ did not send me to baptize but to

preach the gospel, and not with eloquent wisdom,
lest the cross of Christ be emptied of its power.

One could take this to mean that baptism was not important in Paul's theology. However, there are two major flaws in this reasoning:

First, this would lift the comment out of the context which Paul is discussing which is the core of his message and theology, namely, the gospel is all about *the cross of Christ, and being in Christ.* 1 Cor 1:18 emphasizes this:

"For the word of the cross is folly to those who are perishing, but to us who are being saved it is the power of God."

Paul's purpose in 1 Cor 1:17ff was to emphasize being in Christ rather than in the one who baptized them is more important than the one who baptized them!

Second, this thinking would lift baptism out of Paul's own practice into the core of his theology, being in Christ! In the same text Paul mentions that he did baptize Crispus, Gaius, and the household of Stephanas! The point Paul is making in the context of this text is that being baptized by Paul was not that important. Being united in Christ by baptism is all important. Notice verse 15: *"lest anyone should say that you were baptized in my name."* In Pauline theology the only manner by which one may be united with Christ, or enter Christ, was *to be baptized into Christ!*

We now turn to one of Paul's most profound comments on baptism,

Rom 6:1-9: *being united with Christ in Baptism.*

¹ What shall we say then? Are we to continue in sin that grace may abound? ² By no means! How can we who died to sin still live in it? ³ Do you not know that all of us who have been baptized into Christ Jesus were baptized into his death? ⁴ We were buried therefore with him by baptism into death, so that as Christ was raised from the dead by the glory of the Father, we too might walk in newness of life.⁵ For if we have been united with him in a death like his, we shall certainly be united

327

*with him in a resurrection like his. [6] We know that
our old self was crucified with him so that the sinful
body might be destroyed, and we might no longer
be enslaved to sin. [7] For he who has died is freed
from sin. [8] But if we have died with Christ, we
believe that we shall also live with him. [9] For we
know that Christ being raised from the dead will
never die again; death no longer has dominion
over him. [9] For we know that Christ being raised
from the dead will never die again; death no longer
has dominion over him. [10] The death he died he
died to sin, once for all, but the life he lives he lives
to God. [11] So you also must consider yourselves
dead to sin and alive to God in Christ Jesus.*

In his epistle to the Romans Paul was explaining the
core of the doctrine he preached everywhere to both Jew
and Gentile, which gospel he planned to preach in Spain.
*His point was that both Jew and Gentile are justified by the
same principle, grace through faith in Jesus Christ.*

Baptism is central to this message in that it brought the
believing and repentant believer into contact with the death
and resurrection of Jesus, the heart and power of that
gospel! Justification is not through personal works, Jewish
heritage, the Law, or human effort. *Justification is solely
on the principle of grace through faith, for the Jew and for
the Gentile.* Paul's point was that in the gospel God shows
no partiality. Both Jew and Gentile are lost through sin.
Both will be saved by the same gospel, and obedient faith
in Jesus! Paul has demonstrated that the entire world is
under the power of sin and because of this will die. Paul's
argument in Romans is that the Law, although holy,
spiritual, and good, served the purpose of indicting man for
sin, not redeeming him from sin. The Law cannot save. It
only indicts, and because of sin, the law, therefore, kills.
Anticipating arguments that since we are now under grace
and no longer under sin, we could sin and grace could
abound! Paul will have nothing of this nonsense! *Μὴ
γένοιτο,* "*No, no, not ever*"! His argument is that all are

once dead in sin, but can now be alive in Christ. *When we were baptized into Christ's death we die to sin and a new person was born.* In baptism we are buried with Christ and raised with Christ. The old man is dead, the new man is alive. *In baptism we are united with Christ, in a death like his, and in a resurrection like his. It is in baptism we that are united with Christ.*

This is a powerful message that lies at the very heart of redemption.

Eph 4:1-6. We will note that in this pericope baptism is *central to maintaining the unity of the Spirit in the bond of peace, the purpose of God in Christ*:

> *"I therefore, a prisoner for the Lord, beg you to lead a life worthy of the calling to which you have been called, ² with all lowliness and meekness, with patience, forbearing one another in love, ³ eager to maintain the unity of the Spirit in the bond of peace. ⁴ There is one body and one Spirit, just as you were called to the one hope that belongs to your call, ⁵ one Lord, one faith, one baptism, ⁶ one God and Father of us all, who is above all and through all and in all."*

Paul's point in Eph 4 stresses the urgency of maintaining the unity into which the Holy Spirit has brought us through being baptized into one body, 1 Cor 12:13, *"For by one Spirit we were all baptized into one body—Jews or Greeks, slaves or free—and all were made to drink of one Spirit."*

Paul's instruction is that Christians should so live that they treat one another equally, maintaining the unity of the body of Christ. A divisive spirit will destroy the unity of the body of Christ which the Holy Spirit has created! So, Christians should live worthily of the Christian calling to maintain the unity of Christ! Disunity in the body of Christ is brought about when Christians no longer forbear one another in love. In the context of developing his argument for maintaining the unity of the Spirit, Paul demonstrates the foundation or reason for this unity. *There is only one*

Holy Spirit who baptizes us into one body, therefore, there must be unity. *There is only one faith, one Lord, and one God the Father, therefore there can be only one body. Since there is only one baptism by which we are baptized into the one body*, there cannot be two bodies, one for Jews another for Gentiles! There must be Christian unity for the one body of Christ to survive. *Here baptism plays a pivotal role in Paul's argument for unity in the body. There is only one baptism! There can be only one body*!

At Col 2:11-13 Paul returns to his theme of being buried with Christ in Baptism.

> [11] *In him also you were circumcised with a circumcision made without hands, by putting off the body of flesh in the circumcision of Christ;* [12] *and <u>you were buried with him in baptism, in which you were also raised with him through faith in the working of God, who raised him from the dead.</u>* [13] *And <u>you, who were dead in trespasses and the uncircumcision of your flesh, God made alive together with him, having forgiven us all our trespasses,</u>* [14] *having canceled the bond which stood against us with its legal demands; this he set aside, nailing it to the cross.* [15] *He disarmed the principalities and powers and made a public example of them, triumphing over them in him.*

In this text, so much like Rom 6:1ff, Paul proclaims the symbiotic connection between baptism and the death of Jesus. However, the context here is Paul's view of the all-sufficiency of Christ. Philosophy may have a sense of wisdom, but in providing security from an evil spiritual world, philosophy fails completely. It is only in Christ, *in whom all the fullness of deity dwells, that we have no fear of the spiritual world.* Circumcision of the flesh cannot help, only in being buried and raised with Christ is there hope. *In baptism we are buried with Christ, but it is God who works in baptism, not us!* Baptism is not a work of merit or of law. *It is submitting in faith to the working of God. In baptism, man is passively submitting to the will and working of God*, and it is God through his power and the Holy Spirit who works with our faithful obedience and raises us to new life in Christ.

We draw attention to an excellent article on *Baptism in Colossians* by Jeffrey Peterson, Professor of New Testament, Austin Graduate School of Theology, "The Circumcision of the Christ": The Significance of Baptism in Colossians and the Churches of the Restoration," *Restoration Quarterly*, Vol 43/2, 2001.

Peterson makes three salient points:

First, as a symbolic climax of the Colossians' conversion, baptism signifies the convert's transfer of allegiance to Jesus Christ as Lord.

Second, baptism signifies entry into the eschatological covenant people (church, IAF) of God.

Third, baptism signifies the moral transformation of the people of God into the image of his Son.

We recommend careful reading of this article.

Summary of New Testament teaching on Baptism

Baptism in Paul

Paul's theology of baptism is primarily paranetic or practical, that is, Paul uses baptism to explain how Christians should live because they have died in baptism to their old life of sin and been raised in baptism to a new life in Christ. Being united with Christ in baptism, Christians should live like Christ, not like the world. It is through baptism that people enter Christ, are united with Christ, and are therefore, in Christ, wherein are all spiritual blessings.

Baptism in John

John does not openly develop a significant theology of baptism, but there are instances in which we see a baptismal theme underlying the message of John.

We find the usual Gospel references to John regarding the Baptists baptism of Jesus, and Jesus and his disciples regarding baptizing, but beyond this little is said directly regarding baptism.

However, in John 3:3-5 Jesus discusses the new birth with Nicodemus.

> *³ Jesus answered him, "Truly, truly, I say to you, unless one is born anew, he cannot see the kingdom of God." ⁴ Nicodemus said to him, "How can a man be born when he is old? Can he enter a second time into his mother's womb and be born?" ⁵ Jesus answered, "Truly, truly, I say to you, unless one is born of water and the Spirit, he cannot enter the kingdom of God. ⁶ That which is born of the flesh is flesh, and that which is born of the Spirit is spirit.*

Key words in this discussion of the new birth are "*unless one is born of water and the Spirit*." The expression "*born of water and the Spirit*" in the Greek read ἐὰν μή τις γεννηθῇ ἐξ ὕδατος καὶ πνεύματος "*unless one is born of water and Spirit*." The small coordinating conjunction καὶ, *and* forms a construction scholars call *hendiadys* in which two nouns in the same case are tied together in one context. Thus, one cannot separate *water* and *Spirit* into *two births* as some would do, having the water refer to physical birth and Spirit referring to spiritual birth. *The birth Jesus has in mind is the new birth, or the birth from above. Being born of water is a reference to baptism in which the Spirit is also active, hence one is born again, born anew, or born from above at baptism by the Holy Spirit.*

Although John does not present any fully developed baptismal theology we do see a form of baptismal development in this passage on the new birth in John 3:3-5:

A parallel passage in Paul would be Tit 3:3-5:

> *³ For we ourselves were once foolish, disobedient, led astray, slaves to various passions and pleasures, passing our days in malice and envy, hated by men and hating one another; ⁴ but when the goodness and loving kindness of God our Savior appeared, ⁵ he saved us, not because of deeds done by us in righteousness, but in virtue of*

*his own mercy, by **the washing of regeneration** and renewal in the Holy Spirit, [6] which he poured out upon us richly through Jesus Christ our Savior, [7] so that we might be justified by his grace and become heirs in hope of eternal life. [8] The saying is sure.*

Paul's use of the Greek words, *regeneration* and *renewal*, λουτροῦ παλιγγενεσίας, the *laver or washing of regeneration*, and ἀνακαινώσεως πνεύματος ἁγίου, the *renewal of the spirit are interesting*! It does not take any effort to see the parallel thought to Jesus' and John's 3:3-5—*the water of new birth and born again by the Spirit*!

Baptism in Peter

The family of baptism words is found only once in Peter, that is, in
1 Pet 3:13-23:

> *Now who is there to harm you if you are zealous for what is right? [14] But even if you do suffer for righteousness' sake, you will be blessed. Have no fear of them, nor be troubled, [15] but in your hearts reverence Christ as Lord. Always be prepared to make a defense to anyone who calls you to account for the hope that is in you, yet do it with gentleness and reverence; [16] and keep your conscience clear, so that, when you are abused, those who revile your good behavior in Christ may be put to shame. [17] For it is better to suffer for doing right, if that should be God's will, than for doing wrong. [18] For Christ also died for sins once for all, the righteous for the unrighteous, that he might bring us to God, being put to death in the flesh but made alive in the spirit; [19] in which he went and preached to the spirits in prison, [20] who formerly did not obey, when God's patience waited in the days of Noah, during the building of the ark, in which a few, that is, eight persons, were saved through water. [21] Baptism, which corresponds to this, now saves you, not as a removal of dirt from the body but as an appeal to God for a clear*

conscience, through the resurrection of Jesus Christ, [22] *who has gone into heaven and is at the right hand of God, with angels, authorities, and powers subject to him.*

This is an interesting passage in which Peter discusses a challenging thought of *Jesus having reached to those who are now in prison.* There is much debate on the *preaching to those in prison,* but the salient point is that Peter compared *the Noah flood experience to baptism which now saves!* Peter encourages his readers to reverence Christ in their hearts, and to be willing to suffer for him. He introduces Noah and his family and their salvation from the flood! Having said that eight souls in Noah's day were *saved by water, Peter adds that baptism corresponds to the salvation of the eight by water. His statement is clear, "baptism...now saves you!"* This salvation is not simply the removal of dirt from the body, but results from a clear conscience in regard to God. *The power of the salvation of baptism here in Peter's mind is the resurrection of Jesus. Somehow baptism connects one with the resurrection of Jesus.* This should not surprise us since Paul has also made this connection between baptism and the resurrection (Rom 6:3ff). Furthermore, baptism is the appeal, some translations *have answer of a good conscience. God through Jesus has commanded baptism, baptism is a response to the command of God and Jesus. Baptism results in a clear conscience before God.*

Baptism and Salvation in Peter: Luke-Acts.

Although the above is the only passage in Peter in which he discusses baptism, we do have two significant passages in Acts in which *Luke has recorded Peter's two key sermons in which baptism features.* The first was the great *Pentecost sermon* and *the first Jewish converts* (Acts 2:38), the other *the sermon to Cornelius and his household, the first Gentile converts* (Acts 10:48). In both these sermons Peter "commands" that the believers be baptized for salvation associated with the death and resurrection of Jesus.

334

Baptism and Salvation in Luke-Acts

Several texts in Luke's book of Acts stand out in any study of Baptism. We need to remember that Luke explains that his book is all about what Jesus began to do and which are furthered in Acts.

Note Acts 1:1-8:

> *In the first book, O The-ophilus, I have dealt with all that Jesus began to do and teach, [2] until the day when he was taken up, after he had given commandment through the Holy Spirit to the apostles whom he had chosen. [3] To them he presented himself alive after his passion by many proofs, appearing to them during forty days, and speaking of the kingdom of God. [4] And while staying with them he charged them not to depart from Jerusalem, but to wait for the promise of the Father, which, he said, "you heard from me, [5] for John baptized with water, but before many days you shall be baptized with the Holy Spirit."*
>
> *[6] So when they had come together, they asked him, "Lord, will you at this time restore the kingdom to Israel?" [7] He said to them, "It is not for you to know times or seasons which the Father has fixed by his own authority. [8] But you shall receive power when the Holy Spirit has come upon you; and you shall be my witnesses in Jerusalem and in all Judea and Samaria and to the end of the earth."*

Luke's responsibility in Acts was to demonstrate that the gospel of salvation in Jesus was meant for all men, not only to the Jews, but also to the Gentiles.

He begins his story of baptism and salvation in Jesus' death and resurrection with his grey sermon on the Day of Pentecost, Acts 2:1ff. We will merely pick up on that section that introduces baptism associated with the death and resurrection. When many Jews heard his sermon on the death and resurrection they were moved and believed that they had crucified their *Messiah*. They asked Peter what they should do! His powerful response:

³⁷ Now when they heard this they were cut to the heart, and said to Peter and the rest of the apostles, "Brethren, what shall we do?" ³⁸ And Peter said to them, "Repent, and be baptized every one of you in the name of Jesus Christ for the forgiveness of your sins; and you shall receive the gift of the Holy Spirit. ³⁹ For the promise is to you and to your children and to all that are far off, every one whom the Lord our God calls to him." ⁴⁰ And he testified with many other words and exhorted them, saying, "Save yourselves from this crooked generation." ⁴¹ So those who received his word were baptized, and there were added that day about three thousand souls.

We have already noted in this study the symbiotic relationship between faith, the death and resurrection of Jesus, baptism, and the working of the Holy Spirit. Peter brings them all together with the message of repentance in this profoundly important text. We will note in another study on Acts 2:38 that some evangelical ministers substitute *because* of the remission of sin for the Greek preposition εἰς, *for*, but this is untenably incorrect, for εἰς followed by an accusative noun as in Acts 2:38 points forward in direction and not backwards. Our English translations of this text are correct in translating this as for! Cf the KJV, ASV, RSV, NIV, and other excellent translations.

The next text in Acts that we will examine is Acts 8:26-38. On this occasion Phillip, an early Christian was sent by the Holy Spirit to preach to an Ethiopian Eunuch, possibly a Jew.

But an angel of the Lord said to Philip, "Rise and go toward the south to the road that goes down from Jerusalem to Gaza." This is a desert road. ²⁷ And he rose and went. And behold, an Ethiopian, a eunuch, a minister of the Candace, queen of the Ethiopians, in charge of all her treasure, had come to Jerusalem to worship ²⁸ and was returning; seated in his *chariot, he was reading the prophet Isaiah. [29] And the Spirit said to Philip, "Go up and join this chariot." [30] So Philip ran to him, and heard him reading Isaiah the prophet, and asked, "Do you understand what you are reading?" [31] And he said, "How can I, unless someone guides me?" And he invited Philip to come up and sit with him. [32] Now the passage of the scripture which he was reading was this:*

> *"As a sheep led to the slaughter*
> *or a lamb before its shearer is dumb,*
> *so he opens not his mouth. [33] In his humiliation*
> *justice was   denied him.*
> *Who can describe his generation?*
> *For his life is taken up from the earth."*

[34] And the eunuch said to Philip, "About whom, pray, does the prophet say this, about himself or about someone else?" [35] Then Philip opened his mouth, and beginning with this scripture he told him the good news of Jesus. [36] And as they went along the road they came to some water, and the eunuch said, "See, here is water! What is to prevent my being baptized?" [38] And he commanded the chariot to stop, and they both went down into the water, Philip and the eunuch, and he baptized him.

Several salient points surface in this text! *First*, this represents the spread of the gospel message beyond the borders of Jerusalem and Judea! The man was from Ethiopia, possibly a devout Jew of proselyte – he had just travelled to Jerusalem for the feast. Second, he was reading the *Torah* and was concerned about whom the prophet was speaking. *Second*, Philip told him it was about Jesus who had been slain as a lamb for in humiliation without justice, obviously regarding Jesus' trial before the Romans and his subsequent death and resurrection. *Third*, the Eunuch believed him and when they arrived at a place where there was water he asked why he would not be baptized. *Fourth*, obviously, Philip had preached belief in Jesus and baptism. *Fifth*, this baptism obviously involved enough water for baptism, not simply for sprinkling for they would most assuredly have had some water with them in the chariot! *Sixth*, they stopped the chariot, the Eunuch and Philip *went down into the water for baptism, immersion*, and came up out of the water. *Seventh*, the Eunuch went on his way rejoicing! Why? He had just been saved by the death and resurrection of Jesus through his baptism!

Paul, as the Jewish Saul living under the *Torah* or old covenant, enters our story in a new and profoundly significant way! He was still making war on the Christians, but was about to enter a new kind of life, one in Christ! We read about this on two separate occasions, first at Acts 9:1-19, where Luke recounts Paul's conversion, and then at Acts 22:1-16 where Paul fills in some of the details!

> *"But Saul, still breathing threats and murder against the disciples of the Lord, went to the high priest [2] and asked him for letters to the synagogues at Damascus, so that if he found any belonging to the Way, men or women, he might bring them bound to Jerusalem. [3] Now as he journeyed he approached Damascus, and suddenly a light from heaven flashed about him. [4] And he fell to the ground and heard a voice saying to him, "Saul, Saul, why do you persecute me?" [5] And he said, "Who are you, Lord?" And he said, "I am Jesus, whom you are persecuting; [6] but rise and enter the city, and you will be told what you are to do." [7] The men who were traveling with him stood speechless, hearing the voice but seeing no one. [8] Saul arose from the ground; and when his eyes were opened, he could see nothing; so they led him by the hand and brought him into Damascus. [9] And for three days he was without sight, and neither ate nor drank.*
>
> *[10] Now there was a disciple at Damascus named Ananias. The Lord said to him in a vision, "Ananias." And he said, "Here I am, Lord." [11] And*

the Lord said to him, "Rise and go to the street called Straight, and inquire in the house of Judas for a man of Tarsus named Saul; for behold, he is praying, [12] and he has seen a man named Ananias come in and lay his hands on him so that he might regain his sight." [13] But Ananias answered, "Lord, I have heard from many about this man, how much evil he has done to thy saints at Jerusalem; [14] and here he has authority from the chief priests to bind all who call upon thy name." [15] But the Lord said to him, "Go, for he is a chosen instrument of mine to carry my name before the Gentiles and kings and the sons of Israel; [16] for I will show him how much he must suffer for the sake of my name." [17] So Ananias departed and entered the house. And laying his hands on him he said, "Brother Saul, the Lord Jesus who appeared to you on the road by which you came, has sent me that you may regain your sight and be filled with the Holy Spirit." [18] And immediately something like scales fell from his eyes and he regained his sight. Then he rose and was baptized, [19] and took food and was strengthened."

I have tried to simplify this story but have come to realize that you cannot tell it better than Luke! Note some high points. Under the *Torah*, Saul thought he could *see the light*, but it was not until he encountered the Holy Spirit and Jesus that he did. He was blind until the power of God and the Holy Spirit transformed him. It is intensely striking that all this took place under the guidance of God, Jesus, and the working of the Holy Spirit, and that this took place when he was baptized!

The importance of Saul's or Paul's experience takes on new light when Paul later explains this in his defense of his ministry at Acts 22:1-16. For convenience I will focus more on a few words as Paul tells the story! It heightens the significance of baptism in the gospel story as well as in Paul's life and gospel message!

339

[12] *"And one Ananias, a devout man according to the law, well-spoken of by all the Jews who lived there, [13] came to me, and standing by me said to me, 'Brother Saul, receive your sight.' And in that very hour I received my sight and saw him. [14] And he said, 'The God of our fathers appointed you to know his will, to see the Just One and to hear a voice from his mouth; [15] for you will be a witness for him to all men of what you have seen and heard. [16] And now why do you wait? Rise and be baptized, and wash away your sins, calling on his name.'"*

The Holy Spirit led Peter into introducing a new major step in the gospel narrative, the inclusion of the Gentiles into the kingdom of Jesus!

At Acts 10 and 11, we read of Peter, who had preached the first sermon on the Day of Pentecost to Jews, instructed by the Holy Spirit to preach to a Gentile, Cornelius! Luke was moving the story from Jerusalem, Judea, and Samaria into *all the world*, for *the Gentile world was another world*, a different world!

Acts 10:1-48: This is a long text but so important to the gospel theology that we must look at it in some detail! Bear with me!

"At Caesarea there was a man named Cornelius, a centurion of what was known as the Italian Cohort, [2] a devout man who feared God with all his household, gave alms liberally to the people, and prayed constantly to God. [3] About the ninth hour of the day he saw clearly in a vision an angel of God coming in and saying to him, "Cornelius." [4] And he stared at him in terror, and said, "What is it, Lord?" And he said to him, "Your prayers and your alms have ascended as a memorial before God. [5] And now send men to Joppa, and bring one Simon who is called Peter; [6] he is lodging with Simon, a tanner, whose house is by the seaside." [7] When the angel who spoke to him had departed, he called two of his

340

servants and a devout soldier from among those that waited on him, ⁸ and having related everything to them, he sent them to Joppa.

⁹ The next day, as they were on their journey and coming near the city, Peter went up on the housetop to pray, about the sixth hour. ¹⁰ And he became hungry and desired something to eat; but while they were preparing it, he fell into a trance ¹¹ and saw the heaven opened, and something descending, like a great sheet, let down by four corners upon the earth. ¹² In it were all kinds of animals and reptiles and birds of the air. ¹³ And there came a voice to him, "Rise, Peter; kill and eat." ¹⁴ But Peter said, "No, Lord; for I have never eaten anything that is common or unclean." ¹⁵ And the voice came to him again a second time, "What God has cleansed, you must not call common." ¹⁶ This happened three times, and the thing was taken up at once to heaven.

¹⁷ Now while Peter was inwardly perplexed as to what the vision which he had seen might mean, behold, the men that were sent by Cornelius, having made inquiry for Simon's house, stood before the gate ¹⁸ and called out to ask whether Simon who was called Peter was lodging there. ¹⁹ And <u>while Peter was pondering the vision, the Spirit said to him, "Behold, three men are looking for you. ²⁰ Rise and go down, and accompany them without hesitation; for I have sent them.</u>" ²¹ And Peter went down to the men and said, "I am the one you are looking for; what is the reason for your coming?" ²² And they said, "Cornelius, a centurion, an upright and God-fearing man, who is well spoken of by the whole Jewish nation, was directed by a holy angel to send for you to come to his house, and to hear what you have to say." ²³ So he called them in to be his guests.

The next day he rose and went off with them, and some of the brethren from Joppa accompanied *him. ²⁴ And on the following day they entered Caesarea. Cornelius was expecting them and had called together his kinsmen and close friends. ²⁵ When Peter entered, Cornelius met him and fell down at his feet and worshiped him. ²⁶ But Peter lifted him up, saying, "Stand up; I too am a man." ²⁷ And as he talked with him, he went in and found many persons gathered; ²⁸ and he said to them, "You yourselves know how unlawful it is for a Jew to associate with or to visit any one of another nation; but God has shown me that I should not call any man common or unclean. ²⁹ So when I was sent for, I came without objection. I ask then why you sent for me."*

³⁰ And Cornelius said, "Four days ago, about this hour, I was keeping the ninth hour of prayer in my house; and behold, a man stood before me in bright apparel, ³¹ saying, 'Cornelius, your prayer has been heard and your alms have been remembered before God. ³² Send therefore to Joppa and ask for Simon who is called Peter; he is lodging in the house of Simon, a tanner, by the seaside.' ³³ So I sent to you at once, and you have been kind enough to come. Now therefore we are all here present in the sight of God, to hear all that you have been commanded by the Lord."

³⁴ And Peter opened his mouth and said: "Truly I perceive that God shows no partiality, ³⁵ but in every nation anyone who fears him and does what is right is acceptable to him. ³⁶ You know the word which he sent to Israel, preaching good news of peace by Jesus Christ (he is Lord of all), ³⁷ the word which was proclaimed throughout all Judea, beginning from Galilee after the baptism which John preached: ³⁸ how God anointed Jesus of Nazareth with the Holy Spirit and with power; how he went about doing good and healing all that were oppressed by the devil, for God was with him. ³⁹ And

we are witnesses to all that he did both in the country of the Jews and in Jerusalem. They put him to death by hanging him on a tree; ⁴⁰ but God raised him on the third day and made him manifest; ⁴¹ not to all the people but to us who were chosen by God as witnesses, who ate and drank with him after he rose from the dead. ⁴² And he commanded us to preach to the people, and to testify that he is the one ordained by God to be judge of the living and the dead. ⁴³ To him all the prophets bear witness that everyone who believes in him receives forgiveness of sins through his name."

⁴⁴ While Peter was still saying this, the Holy Spirit fell on all who heard the word. ⁴⁵ And the believers from among the circumcised who came with Peter were amazed, because the gift of the Holy Spirit had been poured out even on the Gentiles. ⁴⁶ For they heard them speaking in tongues and extolling God. Then Peter declared, ⁴⁷ "Can anyone forbid water for baptizing these people who have received the Holy Spirit just as we have?" ⁴⁸ And he commanded them to be baptized in the name of Jesus Christ. Then they asked him to remain for some days."

Fortunately, to understand the full impact of this Cornelius event, Luke continued his narrative in Acts 11. I am including a few verses to fill out the impact of these events. When the Jewish Christians heard of Cornelius' baptism, they were concerned that Peter had preached to and baptized a Gentile, so Peter explained this "disturbing" and "confusing" event for them, Acts 11:12-18. Speaking of the three men who had come to Peter from Cornelius, Luke records:

"And the Spirit told me to go with them, making no distinction. These six brethren also accompanied me, and we entered the man's house. ¹³ And he told us how he had seen the angel standing in his house and saying, 'Send to Joppa and bring Simon called

Peter; [14] *he will declare to you a message by which you will be saved, you and all your household.'* [15] *As I began to speak, the Holy Spirit fell on them just as on us at the beginning.* [16] *And I remembered the word of the Lord, how he said, 'John baptized with water, but you shall be baptized with the Holy Spirit.'* [17] *If then God gave the same gift to them as he gave to us when we believed in the Lord Jesus Christ, who was I that I could withstand God?"* [18] *When they heard this they were silenced. And they glorified God, saying, "Then to the Gentiles also God has granted repentance unto life."*

Notice the series of theological points that Luke covers in this Cornelius narrative.

First, the story told by Peter includes the activity of the Holy Spirit. The *effective involvement* of the Holy Spirit is evident throughout the events of the narrative.

Second, it relates the story of the *death and resurrection* as the heart of the gospel message.

Third, the preaching or teaching of the death and resurrection of Jesus is primary to the events and activity of the Holy Spirit. The death and resurrection of Jesus is *the power of the gospel message*, as explained by Paul at Rom 1:16, 17.

Fourth, The gospel message has to be *heard, believed*, and *obeyed*, culminating in *the baptism of the believer for* the remission of sin and a new birth in Christ. Cf. Acts 2:37, 38; Acts 8:37, 38; Acts 9:17, 18; Acts 10 and 11; and Acts 22:12-16.

Fifth, the narrative of Acts 10 and 11, falls within the theology of Luke's narrative, which involves both Jews and Gentiles in the conversion story—the gospel is a *universal* gospel message! It was not only for the Jews, but for everyone who would believe and obey it, Jew and Gentile, without partiality, which is the theological story of Paul's Roman message. At Acts 2:38 Peter's instruction, although directed here to the Jewish believers, had the universal element embedded within it; *Peter said to them,*

"Repent, and be baptized every one of you in the name of Jesus Christ for the forgiveness of your sins; and you shall receive the gift of the Holy Spirit."

Summary list of Baptism texts in the New Testament

Baptism in the Gospels

Although the family of baptism words appear only twice in the Gospel of John (both in John 3) the words appear at least 50 times in the Gospels. The words appear basically in four different settings:

1) John the Baptists' practice of baptism
Baptism: Matt 3:6; Matt 21:25; Mk 1:4; Mk 11:30; Lk 3:3;
Lk 7:29; Lk 20:4
Baptize: Matt 3:11; Lk 3:16; Jn 1:26; Jn 1:33
Baptized: Matt 3:6; Matt 3:13, 14, 16; Mk 1:5, 8, 9; Lk 3:7, 12,
21; Lk 7:29, 30; Jn 10:40
Baptizer: Mk 1:4; Mk 6:14, 24
Baptist: Matt 3:1; Matt 11:11, 12; Matt 14:2, 8; Matt 16:14;
Matt 17:13; Mk 6:25; Mk 8:28; Lk 7:20, 33; Lk 9:19
2) Jesus' and his disciples' practice of baptism.
Baptize: Jn 4:2;
Jn 3:22, 23
3) Christian baptism. *Baptize*: Matt 3:11; Mk 1:8; Lk 3:16;
Mk 16:16
4) *Symbolic uses.* Mk 10:38, 39; Lk 12:50; Mk 10:38, 39;
Lk 12:50

Baptism in Acts

The baptism family of words is found at least 26 times in Acts.

1) *John the Baptist's Baptism*, 10 times: Acts 1:5; Acts 1:22; Acts 19:3, 4; Acts 10:37; Acts 11:16;

Acts 13:24; Acts 18:25;
Acts 19:3, 4

2) *Christian Baptism*, 16 times: Acts 1:5; Acts 2:38, 41; Acts 8:12, 13, 16, 36, 38; Acts 9:18; Acts 10:48; Acts 11:16; Acts 16:15, 33; Acts 18:8; Acts 19:5; Acts 22:16

Baptism in Paul

This family of words is found at least 14 times in Paul:

Christian Baptism: Rom 6:3, 4; Eph 4:5; Col 2:12; 1 Cor 1:13, 14,
15, 16, 17; 1 Cor 12:13; 1 Cor 15:29

Symbolic: 1 Cor 10:2

Baptism in Peter

Christian Baptism: 1 Pet 3:21

Acts 2:38: Baptism *for* the Forgiveness of Sins

Rationale for the Topic

This study is written in response to some evangelical attempts to reinterpret Acts 2:38.

> *38 And Peter said to them, "Repent, and be baptized every one of you in the name of Jesus Christ for the forgiveness of your sins; and you shall receive the gift of the Holy Spirit.*
>
> 38 Πέτρος δὲ πρὸς αὐτούς· Μετανοήσατε, (φησίν) καὶ βαπτισθήτω ἕκαστος ὑμῶν ἐπὶ τῷ ὀνόματι Ἰησοῦ Χριστοῦ **εἰς** ἄφεσιν τῶν ἁμαρτιῶν ὑμῶν καὶ λήμψεσθε τὴν δωρεὰν τοῦ ἁγίου πνεύματος.

As we will note below, all major English translations translate Acts 2:38 as *"Repent, and be baptized every one of you in the name of Jesus Christ **for** the forgiveness of your sins; and you shall receive the gift of the Holy Spirit,"* or something close to this!

Some evangelicals, predominantly Southern Baptists, would reinterpret this text to read *"Repent, and be baptized every one of you in the name of Jesus Christ **because of** the forgiveness of your sins; and you shall receive the gift of the Holy Spirit."* In this interpretation they suggest that *because of* means *as a result* of the remission of sins.

We reject this evangelical translation as unsound Greek syntactical[1] translation, and one influenced by denominational theology rather than careful biblical Greek syntactical grammatical context.

Bibliography on Baptism

We recommend the following studies on Baptism:
Beasley-Murray, G. R., *Baptism in the New Testament*, Eerdmans, 1962.

---

[1] I refer to syntactical translation since all Greek words are influenced and shaped in relation to their immediate grammatical context rather than personal or denominational theological views. This will be discussed in detail below.

347

Beasley-Murray is a Baptist scholar who has taught at some of the finest Baptist universities and seminaries. He was professor emeritus at Southern Baptist Theological Seminary in Louisville, Kentucky, and a former principal of Spurgeon's College, London. Beasley-Murray discusses all of the major baptism texts in the New Testament, including Acts 2:38 and the other baptism texts in Acts.

Ferguson, Everett, *Baptism in the Early Church: History, Theology, and Liturgy in the First Five Centuries*, 2009.
Ferguson is a distinguished, internationally acknowledged Professor of Church History and Biblical Studies at Abilene Christian University.
Schreiner, Thomas R. and Shawn D Wright, *Believers Baptism: A Sign of The New Covenant in Christ*, 2006.
Cottrell, Jack, *Baptism: Zwingli or The Bible?*, 2022.
Cottrell, Jack, *Baptism A Biblical Study*, 1999.
Zodhiates, Spiros, *The Complete Word Study Dictionary: New Testament*, 1993.
Kittel, Gerhard, *Theological Dictionary of the New Testament,* 1964.
Arndt, William F. and Gingrich, F. Wilbur, *A Greek-English Lexicon of the New Testament*, 1967.

Our Response to Some Evangelical Reinterpretation of Acts 2:38

This study explores the meaning of Peter's response in Acts 2:38 to the Jews gathered in Jerusalem on the day of Pentecost. After preaching a sermon on the Holy Spirit and Jesus' Death and Resurrection based on Joel 2:28 and Psalm 16, Peter concluded *"Let all the house of Israel therefore know assuredly that God has made him both Lord and Christ, this Jesus whom you crucified."* Luke continues *"Now when they heard this they were cut to the heart, and said to Peter and the rest of the apostles, "Brethren, what shall we do?"* We can safely assume that at this point these Jews believed in Jesus; that he was both Lord and their promised Messiah, that they had crucified

348

him, and that God had raised him from the dead. Peter responded telling them to *"Repent, and be baptized every one of you in the name of Jesus Christ for the forgiveness of your sins; and you shall receive the gift of the Holy Spirit."*

It is clear from Luke's account of this sermon that these Jews really believed in Jesus. When they asked what they should do, Peter did not respond, "You do not have to do anything, you now believe and are therefore saved." His instructions were *"repent and be baptized every one of you."* But why should they be baptized? Quite clearly his answer gave the reason, *"for the forgiveness of sins."* Luke tells us that Peter then encouraged them *"with many other words and exhorted them, saying, "Save yourselves from this crooked generation."* The result was that *"those who received his word were baptized, and there were added that day about three thousand souls."*

This brief account of the baptism of the 3000 on Pentecost is not difficult to understand. They heard Peter's preaching concerning Jesus; they *believed in Jesus*; they asked what they should then do; they were told to *repent,* and *every one* of them to *be baptized in the name of Jesus Christ for the forgiveness of their sins.* They were then encouraged to save themselves from their crooked generation. They responded in faith by being baptized.

Some evangelical Christians have difficulty reconciling this brief narrative with their doctrine of *salvation by faith only.* They consider baptism a *work of obedience* in response to salvation, and not faith responding *for* salvation.

There is no question regarding the fundamental Christian doctrine of justification or salvation by grace through faith in Jesus! This is deeply embedded in New Testament and Christian doctrine. *The question is how baptism fits into this equation.* The evangelical response is that baptism is *a work of obedience* experienced *after salvation.* Baptism in their view is *because of* the salvation already received and in response to that salvation. Baptism

349

in Peter's view in Acts 2:38 is *the result of faith and repentance, and is for or unto salvation*. The error in evangelical views of baptism is that baptism is not simply a work of obedience *because of*, or after salvation, but *is in fact faith expressing itself in response to grace and for salvation*. This is clearly what Peter laid out in Acts 2:38 stressing that baptism is not a work we engage in, but it is faith in the working of God.

At Col 2:12 Paul clearly explains that baptism is *faith in the working of God*. Baptism is not faith in our working as an act of obedience, but *faith in God's working!*

We will argue that baptism and *faith* are *both "acts, activities, or actions"* we must *personally engage* in for salvation. The debate we have with many evangelicals relates to *how one interprets works*, as works of *merit* or works of *faith*!

Jesus, in a discussion with some Jews regarding the works that God desired of us explained that faith is the work God requires of us! John 6:28, 29: "*Then they said to him, "What must we do, to be doing the works of God?"* [29] *Jesus answered them, "This is the work of God, that you believe in him whom he has sent."*

Baptism is as much a work of faith as are believing and repenting! They represent *action in response* to God's saving grace and redemptive activity in the death and resurrection of Jesus Christ!

No one has faith *for us*; *we must believe* or have faith in Jesus for ourselves. Likewise no one is baptized for us; we must personally submit to being baptized as a matter of faith in Jesus! *Faith and baptism are therefore acts we must experience and engage in. However, neither faith nor baptism are acts or works of merit from which we earn salvation.*

Salvation has its roots in God's love and is a free gift of God's grace, for which believing, repenting, and baptism are faith responding to God's grace. We respond to the preaching of God's grace and the Gospel message through faith, trusting and believing the preached gospel message of his atoning death and resurrection. As in Acts 2:36 with the Jews on Pentecost, this gospel message challenges us to repent and submit to God's working in baptism *for* the forgiveness of our sins.

Faith is not something we do that earns us salvation or gains us merit! Faith and baptism are however the *appropriate response to God's grace.*

This is what Peter explained in 1 Pet 3:21 when he discussed Noah and baptism. After stating that Noah was *"saved through water"* Peter added, *"Baptism, which corresponds to this, now saves you, not as a removal of dirt from the body **but as an appeal to God for a clear conscience**, through the resurrection of Jesus Christ..."* Baptism is the *response* of *a good conscience in faith to God's call for faith and obedience*, and as Peter explains in both Acts 2:38 and 1 Pet 3:21, baptism is *for the purpose* of *forgiveness* and *salvation.*

Faith and baptism are *intricately connected* as two *indispensable poles in a continuum pointing to salvation* and not as two separate but important points. The minute you separate faith from baptism you end up in a situation of no real faith! To say you believe in and trust Jesus and separate baptism from that equation you no longer trust in Jesus and his Word! To separate baptism from faith in the equation of Acts 2:38 you likewise end up in a situation of no real faith and no salvation!

Whichever way you approach salvation, it is a matter of God's saving grace and not your effort, either in having faith or in being baptized. Salvation remains a matter of God's saving and powerful grace bound in Acts 2:38 to faith and baptism, and in 1 Peter 3:21 to salvation bound to baptism! To separate baptism from either faith and salvation in either text is to abuse and denigrate the text! The Greek preposition καὶ is a coordinating conjunction[2]

---

[2] Zodhiates, καὶ ... *As simply joining single words and clauses, As a continuative in respect to time, i.e., connecting clauses and sentences in the order of time, As continuative in respect to sense, i.e., before the*

351

joining or coordinating words or clauses in a sentence or statement! In this case, Acts 2:38, Μετανοήσατε ... καὶ βαπτισθήτω ἕκαστος ὑμῶν ἐπὶ τῷ ὀνόματι Ἰησοῦ Χριστοῦ εἰς ἄφεσιν τῶν ἁμαρτιῶν, *repent and be baptized each one of you in the name of Jesus for the forgiveness of sins.* Peter does not speak here of *faith* or *belief* since that would have been redundant as they had already confessed their faith in Jesus in the response to Peter's sermon!

Furthermore, baptism is not a work we do, that is an active verb, but something that is done to us as we submit to baptism! Baptism in Acts 2:38 is expressed in the *passive voice,* βαπτισθήτω, *baptisthētō,* and not the active voice. This is likewise true at Acts 22:16, Rom 6:1ff, and Gal 3:26! We submit *in faith* to *being baptized,* and *it is God who works salvation in our submission to baptism!*

It is interesting to note a smooth move here on the part of Mantey and some evangelicals! All Greek lexicons recognize that one meaning of *eis* can be *causal, because of,* or *for unto!* However, *because of* does not necessarily *look back* and mean *as a result of forgiveness!* That is clarified by the use of an *accusative noun* following *eis,* i.e. ἄφεσιν, *forgiveness,* which indicates that *eis* points forward to the direction of the action of the verb, βαπτισθήτω, *be baptized!*[3] Mantey clearly and intentionally ignores the syntax of *eis* ἄφεσιν in Acts 2:38. A smooth but false move!

The translation **for** *the forgiveness of sins* or **unto** *the remission of sins* is the translation found in all major English translations of Acts 2:38, KJV, ASV, NASV, RSV, NRSV, NIV.

---

apodosis and connecting it as a consequent with the protasis as its antecedent, As an explicative copula meaning, i.e., namely, to wit, even, between words and clauses, between nouns which are strictly in apposition...

[3] Check this in any of the Greek-English lexicons cited in this study. See the discussion of this below!

In similar fashion those adopting this false solution to Acts 2:38 should reinterpret the final statement of the Nicene Creed[4] to fit into their own doctrine of atonement. The Nicene Creed reads *"We acknowledge one baptism for (unto) remission of sins."* In similar fashion Mantey would have us interpretate the Nicene Creed as **because** *of the remission of sins.*

We reject this tendency to change the reading of Acts 2:38 and the Nicene Creed to fit a particular doctrine of salvation by faith only!

In light of these problems, this study of Acts 2:38 is written with the purpose of examining the meaning of the Greek preposition εἰς, *eis* in Acts 2:38. We will also examine the implications of this for New Testament theology in general.

Since many evangelicals follow the proposals of Julius R. Mantey in regard to Acts 2:38, and his preference for *because of* in place of *for* or *unto*, much of the following discussion is focused on Mantey's thought as set out specifically in Dana and Mantey, *A Manual Grammar of the Greek New Testament*, 1957. We will notice that Mantey falls into the same error as some modern evangelical groups in that he interprets *eis according to his personal doctrine of atonement rather than according to normal Greek syntax and use.*

---

[4] The Nicene Creed is the most common creed used in Christianity. The creed was originally formulated in 325 at the council of Nicea. It was later revised at the council of Constantinople in 38. At the time the church was struggling with the Arian heresy, which denied that Christ was truly God, but rather that he was a created being. The creed was formulated to repudiate Arianism and clearly states that Christ is eternal and part of the trinity of Father, Son and Holy Spirit. It clearly reflects the New Testament views on Baptism as *for* or *unto* and not *because of*! In most branches of Christianity, the creed is widely used or referenced today.

The Translation of Acts 2:38 in the Major English Translations

KJV 1611 [38] *Then Peter said unto them, Repent, and be baptized every one of you in the name of Jesus Christ* **for** *the remission of sins, and ye shall receive the gift of the Holy Ghost.*

ASV 1901 [38]*And Peter said unto them, Repent ye, and be baptized every one of you in the name of Jesus Christ* **unto** *the remission of your sins; and ye shall receive the gift of the Holy Spirit.*

RSV 1973/77 [38] *Repent, and be baptized every one of you in the name of Jesus Christ* **for** *the forgiveness of your sins; and you shall receive the gift of the Holy Spirit.*

NASV 1977 [38] *Repent, and let each of you be baptized in the name of Jesus Christ* **for** *the forgiveness of your sins; and you shall receive the gift of the Holy Spirit.*

NIV 1984 [38] *Peter replied, "Repent and be baptized, every one of you, in the name of Jesus Christ* **for** *the forgiveness of your sins. And you will receive the gift of the Holy Spirit.*

NRSV 1989 [38] *Peter said to them, "Repent, and be baptized every one of you in the name of Jesus Christ* **so that** *your sins may be forgiven; and you will receive the gift of the Holy Spirit.*

NASV 1995 [38] *Peter said to them, "Repent, and each of you be baptized in the name of Jesus Christ* **for** *the forgiveness of your sins; and you will receive the gift of the Holy Spirit.*

Not one of the recognized major English translations interprets the Greek *eis* as *because of* as does Julius Mantey and some evangelicals!

The question we are addressing here I touched on above relating to the syntax of eis ἄφεσιν. On what grounds do some translate or interpret the Greek ***eis****, **for**, as "**because of**?"* Certainly not on the Greek syntax of the preposition and noun it modifies, *but solely on a preconceived doctrinal view!*

354

The Meaning of the Greek Preposition *Eis*

Bauer, Arndt, and Gingrich, *A Greek English Lexicon of the New Testament and Other Early Christian Literature*, **1957.** This is a standard and widely recognized Greek English Lexicon (Dictionary).

Arndt and Gingrich, list over 20 different uses of *eis*.

A leading and important consideration regarding this preposition *eis* is that *eis* with the *accusative* noun (simply put, the direct object in a sentence), *indicates motion toward or into something, or into its immediate vicinity.*

Arndt and Gingrich list the following ways in which *eis* can be translated:

a. Of place, *into, to, toward*
b. With verbs of sending, *to, into, among*
c. It can simply mean direction, *toward something*
d. Of time, *to the end*
e. Indicating degree, *fully*
f. Indicating goal, *to, toward*
g. The result of an action, *into, to, so that*
h. To denote purpose, *in order to, to*
i. With the dative noun, *for*
j. They list one reading as <u>controversial</u>, namely as *because*, and indicate that this possibility derives from J. R. Mantey, of whom much will be said below!
k. *Regarding Acts 2:38*, they indicate that ***it denotes purpose***, *in order to, so that.*

Kittel, The Theological Dictionary of the New Testament, TNDT

Kittel lists several categories in which eis must be considered:

a. Spatial, cosmic and psychological
b. Temporal
c. Modal
d. In logical connection *stating reason*

e.   With a noun or <u>pronominal accusative</u>, *a final sense*

f.   With Personal reference, *with reference to*

The critical point emphasized here is that the noun or *pronominal accusative* used with *eis* indicates ***a final sense or result***.

> In Greek, the accusative *indicates the limitation, result, direction, or end of the verbal action.*
> (Simply put, pronominal refers to a pronoun. A pronominal accusative is a pronoun serving as *a direct object*.)

Spiros Zodhiates, A Complete Word study of the New Testament.

Zodhiates explains, εἰς eis; a preposition governing the accusative with the primary idea of motion into any place or thing; also of motion or direction to, toward or upon any place, thing. The antithesis is expressed by ek ... out of.[5]

The Greek Preposition *Eis* and Greek Syntax

Syntax refers to how words work together in any language, especially in Greek.

In Greek, prepositions work in conjunction with and define nouns and other grammatical forms such as the infinitive.

Dana and Mantey, *A Manual Grammar of the Greek New Testament*, 1927/1957, p. 103, states that *eis* occurs more than 1,700 times in the Greek New Testament, and *only with the accusative form of noun*.

Blass, Debrunner, and Funk, *A Grammar of New Testament and Other Early Christian Literature*, 1961, agree with Dana and Mantey.

Dana and Mantey argue that the fundamental compositional meaning of *eis* is *into, in, to go inside*.

They demonstrate that in conjunction with the *accusative* noun the resultant meanings of *eis* are *into, unto, to, for*.

---

[5] Zodhiates, *The Complete Word Study Dictionary: New Testament.*

Several remote meanings are offered such as *upon, against, among, with respect to, in reference to.*

As we have noted above, at this point Mantey demurs and argues for an interpretation that some (Arndt and Gingrich) have termed *a controversial meaning*, implying that it is not generally recognized as such by grammarians! Mantey argues for a translation of *eis* which *might* or *could* read as *because of.*

We will discuss Mantey's controversial and unusual interpretation in detail below demonstrating that it is *forced* to meet Mantey's doctrinal theological stance on baptism, salvation, and *faith only*, and not based on the normal meaning as used in the Greek of the New Testament.

Greek Grammars on *Eis* and the Accusative Case of the Noun.

Most Greek grammars indicate that *the accusative case*, simply stated, *limits* or *describes extension.* By this they mean that *the accusative indicates the limit or direction of the verbal action.* In relation to the preposition *eis*, the *accusative* case *indicates the direction or limitation of the preposition eis.* This can be observed and corroborated in the following standard Greek Grammars.

H. P. V. Nunn, *A Syntax of New Testament Greek.*

W. H. Davis, *Beginner's Grammar of the Greek New Testament.*

James Hope Moulton and Henry G. Meecham, *An Introduction to*
   the Study of New Testament Greek.

Blass, Debrunner, Funk, *A Grammar of New Testament and Other*
   Early Christian Literature.

Dana and Mantey, *A Manual Grammar of the Greek New Testament*, 1927/1957, pp. 91ff. "The *accusative* case relates primarily to *action, and indicates direction, extent, or end.* "*The accusative signifies that the object referred to is*

considered as the point toward which something is
proceeding: that it is the end of the action or
motion described...The accusative embraces three
ideas: the end, or direction, or extent of motion or
action...The root meaning of the accusative is
limitation."

Discussion on Mantey's Arguments for Translating *Eis* as *Because*

As mentioned previously we have considerable
disagreement with how Julius Mantey manages the Greek
preposition in his comments in the Dana and Mantey
Greek Grammar included in our bibliographies. This
comment should not be interested as a criticism of the
Grammar, only of Mantey's observations on *eis*! In this
section we will examine reasons why Mantey
translates *eis* as *because* or because of rather than
as *for, toward, unto.*

 a. As indicated above, none of the major translations
   deviates from the normal translation of *eis*!

 b. Mantey's discussion of the normal translations
   of *eis* in his grammar are excellent and to the point.
   Eis indicates *direction* and with the accusative it
   indicates *limitation*, not source or origin!

 c. The major reason for Mantey seeking a different
   translation from the norm is his difficulty in taking
   Acts 2:38 at face value!
   "Repent, and be baptized every one of you in the
   name of Jesus Christ *for* the forgiveness of your
   sins; and you shall receive the gift of the Holy
   Spirit."

 d. We quote Mantey's argument on Acts 2:38 in
   detail:
   "When one considers in Acts 2:38 repentance as
   self-renunciation and baptism as public expression
   of self –surrender and self-dedication to
   Christ, *which significance it certainly had in the
   first century (Italics IAF)*, the expression εἰς ἄφεσιν

τῶν ἁμαρτιῶν may mean *for the purpose of the remission of sins*. But if one stresses baptism, without its early Christian import, as a ceremonial means of salvation, he does violence to Christianity as a whole, for one of its striking distinctions from Judaism and Paganism is that it is a religion of salvation by faith while all others teach salvation by works..."

Here in this last sentence we find the root of Mantey's problem or faulty theology. He reads modern day evangelical thoughts or doctrine of *salvation as faith only* into both the text and theology of Judaism and Christianity. We will demonstrate below that the definition of faith only cannot and is not supported by the teachings in either the Old or New Testaments! Mantey and other evangelicals confuse Paul's teaching of *faith only* by taking it out of the context of Paul's argument against strict Judaism that would bind works of Law on salvation and justification, which Paul radically challenges by stressing that it is *only by faith in Jesus* and not by works of Law that one is saved or justified.

Here we find the root of Mantey's problem! He sets his Greek interpretation in the context of his evangelical theology of faith only and not in the context of Greek syntax.

One should set *theology* in the context of Peter's proclamation in Acts 2:38, Luke in Acts *passim*, and Paul in his doctrine of justification by faith only in Jesus and not the Law of Moses.

One should set one's grammar in the context of Greek literature as a whole, Greek words, Noun cases, Verb tenses and actions, pronominal pronouns, and the unique syntax of Greek and not evangelical theology!

We pause here to examine Mantey's argument in some detail at this point.

Mantey points out that in the context of the first century Greek syntax *eis afesin may mean for the purpose of the remission of sins*! Yet he demurs from this!

359

Why, if it could be, and most likely was, translated in this manner in the first century should it not be translated in the same manner in the 20th or 21st centuries?

The reason is that it does not fit Mantey's and some evangelical 20th century doctrinal positions!

First, the translation *for the purpose of the remission of sins* does violence, not to the remaining teachings on baptism in the New Testament, but only to Mantey's doctrinal position.

Second, Mantey's description of Paganism teaching salvation by works may be correct, but his understanding of Judaism is faulty when he maintains that Judaism taught salvation by works! Refer to recent studies on Judaism by E. P. Sanders, W. D. Davies, *et al.* who argue correctly that 2nd Temple Judaism at the time of Christ did not see justification as a result of works, but of faith.

Third, furthermore, since the New Testament apparently does teach salvation or the washing away of sin as a result of baptism (see Acts 22:16, 1 Pet 3:21) then we must assume, according to Mantey, that the New Testament teaches salvation by works! However, this does not follow. What is defective is Mantey's understanding of the relationship of works, faith and baptism in the New Testament. Cf G. R. Beasley-Murray, **Baptism in the New Testament** *passim* for an excellent theology of faith and baptism at this point.

Fourth, we return now to the Dana and Mantey grammar's primary argument on εἰς with a comment they make on Mat 12:41: μετενόησαν εἰς τὸ κήρυγμα Ἰωνᾶ, *"they repented at the preaching of Jonah."* Mantey argues from this text for a *causal* point. We have no question on that, but lurking in our mind is the question "what kind of causal understanding does Mantey hold?"

> "The sentence *"metanohsen eis to kerugma Iona"* in Mt. 12:41 and Lk. 12:32 is *forceful evidence for a causal use of this preposition*. What led to their repentance? Of course it was Jonah's preaching."

We should note that there are different senses of *because of*; it could mean *as a result of*, looking back, or *for the reason of* looking forward! Context and syntax with pronouns will define the meaning, which in regard to Acts 2:38 is missed by many evangelicals. *Eis* with the accusative noun points *forward*, not backward.

We should examine Mantey's argument on Mat 12:41 closer which he considers *forceful evidence for a causal use* of *eis*!

> "The RSV translates this as "for they repented *at* the preaching of Jonah."
> The KJV translates this as "because they repented *at* the preaching of Jonas."
> The ASV 1901 likewise translated this as "for they repented *at* the preaching of Jonah."
> The NASV likewise translated this as "they repented *at* the preaching of Jonah."
> We can safely assume that the eis in these translations should be rendered as *at!*

We ask, "how does Mantey render or understand *at*?"

Adopting Mantey's own category of "remote meanings" for *eis* he suggests "*with respect to, with reference to*" as possible meanings for *eis*. In this case we can translate Mat 12:41 "they repented *with reference to the preaching of Jonah*" or "*with respect to*" the preaching of Jonah"!

The question we must ask is what has this to do with Acts 2:38? The context of Mat 12:41 and Acts 2:38 are radically different! As Mantey himself has indicated it would be permissible to translate ὅτι μετενόησαν εἰς τὸ κήρυγμα Ἰωνᾶ as *because they repented at the proclamation of Jonah* to mean *they repented* **with respect to the preaching of Jonah!**

According to Mantey's own correct meaning *with respect to*, then Acts 2:38 could be translated *repent and be baptized with respect to (for) the remission of sins*!

Mantey has done nothing less than argue for being baptized for the remission of sins! He argues

361

grammatically for the major translation of *eis* as *for* or *unto*!

Mantey's *forceful argument* for his *theological* translation of Acts 2:38 as baptism *pointing back* to or *resulting from* their salvation is unsustainable based on Greek Grammar and syntax!

Arndt and Gingrich likewise suggest that when used with a person or thing that *eis* can be translated as "*with respect* or *reference to*" the person or thing. In Mat 12:41, they interpret *eis* as "repented *with respect to* the preaching of Jonah!"

Mantey has in regard to Mat 12:41 agreed with most that *eis* can be translated safely as "*with respect to* the preaching of Jonah," but this is not a forceful argument for translating *eis* as *because of looking back to salvation* as indicated by Mantey with eis *look back to salvation* rather than baptism *eis with respect to* or *for* salvation!

The *supposed evidence* assumed by Mantey above is not *a forceful reason* at all, as he would have us believe! In fact it is no argument at all for a *causal because of, looking back to salvation* in Acts 2:38, as he claims!

Again, we return to Mantey:

> "Mt 3:11 furnishes further evidence: *ego men humas baptizō en hudati eis metanoian.* Did John baptize that they might repent, or because of repentance? If the former we have no further Scriptural confirmation of it. If the latter, his practice was confirmed and followed by the apostles… In connection with this verse we have the testimony of a first century writer to the effect that John the Baptist baptized people only after they had repented. Josephus, Antiquities of the Jews, book 18, chapter 5, section 2…"

Once again, Mantey fails to permit the translation of the text to work within his own category of definitions, that is, *eis* being understood as *in reference to*. In this case the translation would be "I baptize you in water *with reference to* (your) repentance!"

However, contrary to Mantey the NASV translates Mat 3:11 as "*I baptize you with water **for** repentance.*"

Likewise, the KJV translates this as "*I indeed baptize you with water **unto** repentance.*"

The RSV and NIV translate this as "*I baptize you with water **for** repentance.*"

Our conclusion is that Mantey has proven nothing at all! He is merely inserting his definition of *eis* into the equation of Mat 3:11 to prove his point, ignoring the context of what Mat was stating. In agreement with the KLV, RSV, and NIV we conclude from the context of the discussion that it was *for the purpose* of *encouraging* repentance that John was baptizing!

As our major translations indicate, there are categories within the accepted possibilities for *eis* that would be suitable for translating Mat 3:11 without resorting to categories not normally accepted that would fit one's own doctrinal biases as does Mantey!

His forceful evidence falls far short of being either forceful or convincing!

Every argument Mantey has proposed can be better explained from within Dana and Mantey's "*Resultant*" or "*Remote*" meanings, without resorting to what Arndt and Gingrich call a "controversial" translation *because of.* Well within the *resultant meanings* our major translations translate grammatically and syntactically without resorting to doctrinal presuppositions as does Mantey.

There is, however, yet a far greater problem for Mantey's and some evangelical's proposals!

This has to do with how we use or read Scripture, and how we determine theology and doctrine!

Mantey reads Scripture *deductively* through *the lens of preferred doctrine*, rather than determining doctrine through *the lens of Scripture in an indictive approach* which works *from* within a Scriptural reading *toward* a theological meaning!

A major question we must ask theologians: *Do we interpret Scripture from within our doctrine, or do we interpret our doctrine from within Scripture?*

Mantey wants us to interpret Scripture so it agrees with a particular doctrine he holds dear!

However, we do not interpret Scripture according to our doctrine, but we interpret our doctrine according to Scripture.

What Mantey and similar evangelical arguments do is called *deductive theology*, as opposed to *inductive theology*, in which they interpret things, even Scripture, *from within their own doctrine*, or *to agree with their own doctrine.*

In Mantey's deductive system he moves from doctrine to Scripture, rather than from Scripture to doctrine.

Biblical theology works differently from the way Mantey proposes! In Biblical theology you move inductively from Scripture to doctrine and interpret doctrine from within Scripture.

New Testament Scriptures with Similar *Eis* Constructions to that of Acts 2:38

There are a number of New Testament texts related to *baptism* and *forgiveness* which are not translated in our major translations as *because* or *because of.* We will note that they retain the traditional *for, into,* or *unto* translation.

We will examine several of these texts in which *eis* is in a parallel construction with Acts 2:38, and where *eis* was *preceded* by the *verb form baptize* and is followed by a noun in the *accusative* case.

The purpose of this section of the study is to demonstrate that there are many Greek constructions in the New Testament that are parallel to Acts 2:38 where none of the major translations have been compelled to follow Mantey's controversial handling of Acts 2:38!

The only reason Mantey and some evangelicals translate *eis* in Acts 2:38 as *because of* is that they ignore

the rules of Greek Syntax which require a rendering
of *for* or *unto* when used with an accusative noun which
would then *violate their specific doctrine of salvation by
faith only!* Mantey himself describes the form of
translation as seen in the major translations as *"doing
violence to Christianity as a whole"* by not stressing *faith
only* as opposed to *salvation by works* as the ground of
forgiveness that he sees in early Judaism and Christianity.[6]

We stress again, that doctrine should be shaped by
Scripture, and not Scripture by doctrine!

First, we begin by examining Matt 26:28 since it
contains wording and syntax similar to Acts 2:38.

In order to demonstrate the parallel nature of this text
with Acts 2:38 we will quote both Matt 26:28 and Acts
2:38. For those not familiar with the Greek text we will
also demonstrate the parallel nature of the texts
by underlining the parallel words in the Greek text.

> Matt 26:28 - τοῦτο γάρ ἐστιν τὸ αἷμά μου τῆς
> διαθήκης τὸ περὶ πολλῶν ἐκχυννόμενον <u>*εἰς* ἄφεσιν
> ἁμαρτιῶν</u>.
> "this is my blood of the covenant, which is *poured
> out **for** <u>many for the forgiveness of sins</u>*"
> Acts 2:38 - <u>βαπτισθήτω</u> ἕκαστος ὑμῶν ἐπὶ τῷ
> ὀνόματι Ἰησοῦ Χριστοῦ <u>*εἰς* ἄφεσιν τῶν ἁμαρτιῶν</u>
> Acts 2:38 "be <u>baptized</u> every one of you in the
> name of Jesus Christ ***for*** <u>*the forgiveness of your*
> *sins*</u>."

None of the major translators translate Matt 26:28 as
Mantey would have us do with Acts 2:38, *"this is my blood
of the covenant, which is poured out for many <u>because
of the forgiveness of sins</u>."*

In fact, at the time Matthew is describing at Matt
26:28, Jesus' blood had not yet been shed. His blood *was
to be shed in the very near future **for** the forgiveness of
sins*. Jesus is not saying that his blood was

---

[6] Dana and Mantey, *A Manual Grammar of the Greek New Testament*,
p. 104. Reading Mantey is enlightening!

shed *because of* forgiveness, but **_for_** the forgiveness of sins!

The sense of Jesus' statement was that his blood was to be shed *with respect to* or *in regard to* the forgiveness of sins.

There is no need to translate this text other than according to the normal criteria for standard Greek grammar and Syntax (and in accordance with Dana and Mantey's own primary criteria), which is what the major translations have done.

I find the diagram illustrating the direction of prepositions in their Manual for Greek Grammar to be most informative and helpful! It clearly describes direction *forward into* for *eis*, and not *out of* as in *ek*!

Neither is there any grammatical ground for translating Acts 2:38 as Mantey would—*because of*. On both occasions the **eis** should be translated *for the forgiveness of sins*.

Second, let us turn to Rom 6:3 which reads *"Do you not know that all of us who have been baptized **into** Christ Jesus were **baptized** into his death?"* ἢ ἀγνοεῖτε ὅτι, ὅσοι ἐβαπτίσθημεν **εἰς** Χριστὸν Ἰησοῦν, **εἰς** τὸν θάνατον αὐτοῦ ἐβαπτίσθημεν.

Notice in Rom 6:3 that as in Acts 2:38 the **eis** follows a *baptism* verb, *baptized*, and is followed by an *accusative noun, death, θάνατον.*

The natural translation of this text calls for the English preposition into as in the major translations, and not *because of* as Mantey argues at *Acts 2:38!*

The construction of the clause of Rom 6:3 closely parallels Acts 2:38!

Third, at Gal 3:26 Paul writes *"for in Christ Jesus you are all sons of God, through faith.* [27] *For as many of you as were baptized into Christ have put on Christ."* Πάντες γὰρ υἱοὶ θεοῦ ἐστε διὰ τῆς πίστεως ἐν Χριστῷ Ἰησοῦ· [27] ὅσοι γὰρ **εἰς Χριστὸν ἐβαπτίσθητε**, Χριστὸν ἐνεδύσασθε.

Notice again that the preposition eis is preceded by the baptism verb, and followed by a noun in the accusative case, *Christ, Χριστὸν.* In this case the word order in Gal 3:26 is a little different, for the baptism word follows *eis.* We are reminded that Greek does not follow the English conventions of word order, but changes word order for emphasis.

Here the preposition *eis* is correctly translated and interpreted in our English translations as *into,* not *because.*

Notice in Gal 3:26 that Paul considers baptism to be a matter of faith, not works!

We become children of God *through faith, for* as many as have been *baptized into Christ* have <u>put on Christ</u>. The Greek particle or conjunction *gar, for,* indicates the *reason* or *ground* for their becoming children of God through faith. Dana and Mantey observe that the conjunction *gar,* "may express a ground or reason, an explanation, a confirmation or assurance..."[7]

Following the context of Paul's argument in Gal 3, Christian baptism may not be removed from the faith dynamic and considered a work without doing baptism and faith an injustice.

Baptism is a faith principle, not a work principle, just as repentance and confession of faith are faith principles and not work principles.

Fourth, in fact, Paul explains in Col 2:10-12 that *baptism is <u>faith in the working of God</u>*!

> *you have come to fulness of life in him, who is the head of all rule and authority. [11] In him also you were circumcised with a circumcision made without hands, by putting off the body of flesh in the circumcision of Christ; [12] <u>and you were buried with him in baptism, in which you were also raised with him **through faith in the working of God**, who raised him from the dead.</u> [13] And you, who were dead in trespasses and the uncircumcision of your flesh, God made alive together with him, having forgiven us all our trespasses...*

---

[7] Dana and Mantey, *Grammar,* p. 242f.

Fifth, Rom 10:10 is a fascinating case for
an *accusative* noun
following *eis* in *justification* and *salvation*.

The construction is almost parallel to Acts 2:38
here *forgiveness* stands for *salvation*!

RSV: "For man believes with his heart (*eis*) *and so* is
justified, and he confesses with his lips (*eis*) *and so* is
saved."

ASV: "for with the heart a person believes,
(*eis*) *resulting in* righteousness, and with the mouth he
confesses, (*eis*) *resulting* in salvation."

KJV: "For with the heart man
believeth *unto* righteousness; and with the mouth
confession is made *unto* salvation."

The NIV is somewhat different, yet still conveys the
same meaning, "For it is with your heart that you
believe *and are justified*, and it is with your mouth that you
confess *and are saved*."

The Greek reads καρδία γὰρ πιστεύεται εἰς
δικαιοσύνην, στόματι δὲ ὁμολογεῖται εἰς σωτηρίαν... Both
nouns following *eis* are accusative nouns!

Notice that in each case above the *eis* points forward to
the accusative nouns following, that
is, *righteousness* and *salvation*!

Presumably Mantey and those evangelicals who follow
Mantey's views of Christian doctrine stressing *salvation by
faith only* would have no problem with the first part of this
verse! Using the ASV, "*For with the heart man
believes resulting in righteousness.*" There should be no
problem here since salvation is by faith, the faith principle,
but not works principle!

But with the second part, "*with the mouth he confesses,
(eis) resulting in salvation*" they should have problems
*since confessing with the mouth should be a work in their
definition*! In this case they would need to translate the
second clause "*with the mouth he confesses, because
of salvation*"! However, by doing this they would destroy
the syntactical parallelism Paul has used to make his point.

The only way around Mantey's problem is to argue that *confessing faith* is *a faith principle and not a work principle*! But that is what we have been saying all along!

However, if confessing with the mouth that Jesus is Lord is a faith principle, why is confessing one's faith in baptism a work principle?

We stress here that *believing in Jesus Christ is <u>something we do</u>*, as is *repenting of one's sins <u>something we do</u>*, as is <u>*confessing one's faith something we do*</u>!

Yet both actions are considered by evangelicals as *faith principles and not work principles*! Yet *you have to do both!*

Likewise we stress that baptism is something we surrender to <u>as a faith principle</u> and not something we do to merit or earn forgiveness.

Sixth, we now turn to examine Mk 1:4. In a section above we considered Mantey's arguments on Matt 3:11 and found them faulty. In similar fashion we examine Mk 1:4.

> RSV: "John the baptizer appeared in the wilderness, preaching a
> baptism *of* repentance *for* the forgiveness of sins."
> KJV: "John did baptize in the wilderness, and preach the baptism *of* repentance *for* the remission of sins."
> NASV: "John the Baptist appeared in the wilderness preaching a
> baptism *of* repentance *for* the forgiveness of sins."
> NIV: "And so John came, baptizing in the desert region and preaching a
> baptism *of* repentance *for* the forgiveness of sins."

The Greek reads ἐγένετο Ἰωάννης (ὁ) βαπτίζων ἐν τῇ ἐρήμῳ καὶ κηρύσσων <u>βάπτισμα</u> μετανοίας <u>εἰς</u> ἄφεσιν ἁμαρτιῶν·

Notice that John was preaching a *baptism of* repentance, that is, a baptism *characterized by* repentance (the genitive construction of repentance provides the *of* repentance), and that this *baptism* was *for* (εἰς) the *forgiveness* of sins.

Notice also that the Greek construction εἰς ἄφεσιν ἁμαρτιῶν, *for the forgiveness of sins* here in Mk 1:4 is *exactly parallel to that of Acts 2:38*, εἰς ἄφεσιν τῶν ἁμαρτιῶν, *for the forgiveness of sins* other than for the presence of the definite article τῶν, *the* in Acts 2:38 which does not impact or effect the syntax of the sentence at all.

Now if we were to follow Mantey's Acts 2:38 reasoning in Mk 1:4, then the translation would be, "*John the Baptist appeared in the wilderness preaching a baptism of repentance because of the forgiveness of sins*"! We know from our study of the Gospels that John would not baptize anyone unless they demonstrated repentance! Mantey's interpretation would, therefore, have *John baptizing unrepentant sinners because of forgiveness* already received before they had in fact repented!

This demonstrates Mantey's confused theology! We then have people baptized *because* they had been forgiven *before they had repented*!

This does not fit in with Peter's instruction in Acts 2:38 that the believing Jews must *repent and then be baptized*!

What Mark was implying was that John was preaching a baptism *for* the forgiveness of sins, that is, a baptism being *characterized by repentance*!

We should note here a technical but important syntactical point in the clause κηρύσσων βάπτισμα μετανοίας εἰς ἄφεσιν ἁμαρτιῶν, *preaching a baptism of repentance*. The noun preceding *for forgiveness* is βάπτισμα, an accusative noun modifying the verb *preaching*, κηρύσσων. This accusative noun βάπτισμα is in turn modified by a *descriptive genitive noun*, μετανοίας, which defines the accusative noun βάπτισμα and modifies the *nature of the baptism!* Thus the baptism preached is *characterized by a repentance*, as in Acts 2:38!

Let me have another swing at this interesting text. Μετανοήσατε, *repentance*, is a *genitive* noun modifying the *nominative* noun *báptisma*, so it was not John preaching *repentance for forgiveness* but a *baptism, characterized by repentance, for forgiveness*!

Likewise, in Acts 2:38, Peter was preaching *a baptism, characterized by faith and repentance, for the forgiveness of sins*.

Seventh, Luke 3:3, Luke's parallel statement regarding John's preaching, follows the same pattern as does Mark. ³ καὶ ἦλθεν εἰς πᾶσαν (τὴν) περίχωρον τοῦ Ἰορδάνου κηρύσσων βάπτισμα μετανοίας εἰς ἄφεσιν ἁμαρτιῶν, "*and he went into all the region about the Jordan, preaching a baptism of repentance for the forgiveness of sins*."

A Survey of Some important Scriptures on Baptism and Salvation that Teach that Baptism has a Major Role in Salvation.

Mk 16:15, 16: "Go into all the world and preach the gospel to the whole creation. *¹⁶ He who believes and is baptized will be saved*; but he who does not believe will be condemned."

This text has been contested by some on the grounds that the ending of Mark's Gospel is uncertain. Whether or not one accepts the text as original to Mark, one must as the early church did, acknowledge the *apostolicity* of the text and consider the *teaching of the text to be consistent with New Testament doctrine*. It is considered apostolic even by the most ardent challengers who question its being part of Mark's Gospel.

The text clearly connects belief and baptism as conditions of salvation.

Again, some evangelicals argue that since the second clause of the verse does not expressly mention *not baptized*, for example, "*but he who does not believe "*and is not baptized" *will be condemned"* this negates the strong connection of baptism to the first clause believe.

371

Typical of this is a statement in an article by the NT Restoration Foundation: *"Notice, however, those who Jesus said would be condemned: "whoever does not believe." No mention was made of not being baptized. The emphasis is on unbelief, not baptism. Condemnation comes as a result of unbelief, not the lack of any ritual activity."* The article continues, *"Indeed, it is unthinkable that anyone would believe in Jesus and refuse to be baptized"*!

Did the NT Restoration Foundation miss the point? By their own confession *it is unthinkable* that one who does not believe will want to be baptized!

However, the NT Restoration Foundation did miss the point! It would be redundant for Jesus to add *not baptized* after *not believing*, for those not believing would not want to be baptized!

The statement *"and is not baptized"* in the second clause would be redundant and is not necessary and self-explanatory!

Acts 22:16: *"And now why do you wait? Rise and be baptized, and wash away your sins, calling on his name."* Καὶ νῦν τί μέλλεις; ἀναστὰς βάπτισαι καὶ ἀπόλουσαι τὰς ἁμαρτίας σου ἐπικαλεσάμενος τὸ ὄνομα αὐτοῦ. Interestingly, the Greek is stronger than the RSV translation, it reads *rising be baptized and wash away your sins calling on his name!* The verbal command is an active aorist participle, ἀναστὰς, that can, *and should be* interpreted as *"rising up*, be baptized, and wash away your sins calling on the name of Jesus! The καὶ, *and,* is a coordinating conjunction that acts as an epexegetical conjunction emphasizing *why* he should rise and be baptized – *to wash away his sins*. All of this is predicated by *faith in Jesus, calling on his name,* implying believing in Jesus.

In this text Paul is explaining to the Roman Tribune the circumstances of his conversion (see Acts 9 for his conversion). That he believes in Jesus is obvious from the context of his conversion. He explained that Ananias called on Paul telling him to *arise and be baptized*, but for what purpose? Mantey and evangelicals would have his baptism *because of his forgiveness and cleansing*, and see baptism as an act of obedience following salvation.

However, *that is not what the text clearly states!* In keeping with Mark 16:15, 16, and Acts 2:38, *baptism here clearly preceded cleansing and the forgiveness of sin.*

Beasley-Murray makes a strong point that in both Acts 2:38 and Acts 22:16 baptism is associated with the name of Jesus, either *"in the name of Jesus Christ"* or *"calling on his name."* This would imply that the power of salvation lies primarily in the person of Jesus, and not in the believing, repenting, and baptizing! Beasley-Murray argues that there is more in the expression *"in the name of Jesus"* than merely the authority of Jesus. *It is in his death and resurrection that salvation is focused,* and "in the name of Jesus Christ" or "in the person of Jesus Christ" *connects us dynamically with his death and resurrection.*[8]

Rom 6:1-5: *Paul's argument is critical to our understanding of what happens in baptism.* We symbolically die to ourselves and our old manner of life and are united with Jesus in baptism! Likewise, we are symbolically buried and raised with Christ to begin a new birth and walk in life! The baptism is real but in it we are symbolically united with Jesus and his death!

> *What shall we say then? Are we to continue in sin that grace may abound?* [2] *By no means! How can we who died to sin still live in it?* [3] *Do you not know that all of us who have been baptized into Christ Jesus were baptized into his death?* [4] *We were buried therefore with him by baptism into death, so that as Christ was raised from the dead by the glory of the Father, we too might walk in newness of life.* [5] *For if we have been united with him in a death like his, we shall certainly be united with him in a resurrection like his.*

---

[8] G. R. Beasley-Murray, *Baptism in the New Testament*, 1973.

Paul's leading point is that in baptism *we are united with Christ and his death, with the life giving power of the gospel*, Rom 1:16, 17!

If we are saved before baptism, as per Mantey and some evangelicals, then according to this verse *we are saved before dying to our old sinful life and being united with Christ in a new life like his!*

According to Mantey's view, by being baptized we are then *dying **to** a salvation and an experience of a new birth!* We are dead to salvation! This argument patently misses the point Paul is making!

The new birth Paul is describing is not the result of our working. It is the heart of the atoning gospel he has been preaching.

The new birth spoken of by Jesus to Nicodemus and his disciples, and our new life in Christ comes about through our faith in the working of God, our dying to our past life of sin in baptism, and our being raised with Christ to walk in newness of life!

Col 2:12, 13: Paul writes to the Colossians stressing that now in Christ they must live lives radically different from their pagan or Jewish neighbors! He based his argument on the same major point that he later stressed in Rom 6, *"you were buried with him in baptism, in which you were also raised with him through faith in the working of God, who raised him from the dead. [13] And you, who were dead in trespasses and the uncircumcision of your flesh, God made alive together with him, having forgiven us all our trespasses."*

In this text, Paul is making the point that the Colossian Christians were not in a covenant relationship with God through physical circumcision, as had been the case with Israel prior to Christ's atoning death on the cross. Their covenant relationship with God was through a *"circumcision not made with hands."* Which he equates with baptism. He continues to explain that they had entered this new covenant relationship with God by dying to their past lifestyle and being raised in a new birth with Jesus, cf.

374

Rom 6:1-5 above. Their covenant relationship was based on *what God had worked and brought about through Jesus*, and their connection with this new covenant had taken place through *their baptism which expressed their faith in the working of God.* Note the parallel statement of Col 2:12 and Rom 6:1-5:

> *"And you were buried with him in baptism, in which you were also raised with him through faith in the working of God, who raised him from the dead."*

Christians take on a new life by dying to their old life and being born again, anew, with Christ through their faith and baptism into Christ. Paul clearly teaches in Rom 6 and in this Colossian text that this takes place at baptism. It is in baptism that they were united with Christ in a death like his and raised with him to a new life.

At Col 3:1ff Paul built on this theme by stating that *since*[9] they had been raised with Christ—*in baptism*—they should therefore seek the things of Christ, things that are above!

This text emphasizes that in baptism the believer is *trusting (faith) in the working of God*, not in their own working. *In baptism we surrender in faith to the working of God.*

1 Pet 3:21. *"For Christ also died for sins once for all, the righteous for the unrighteous, that he might bring us to God, being put to death in the flesh but made alive in the spirit; ¹⁹ in which he went and preached to the spirits in prison, ²⁰ who formerly did not obey, when God's patience waited in the days of Noah, during the building of the ark, in which a few, that is, eight persons, were saved through water. ²¹ Baptism, which corresponds to this, now saves you, not as a removal of dirt from the body but as an appeal to God for a clear conscience, through the resurrection of Jesus Christ, ²² who has gone into heaven*

---

[9] Εἰ ... συνηγέρθητε, *ei* with the indicative verb, a first class conditional clause, *since they had been raised.*

and is at the right hand of God, with angels, authorities, and powers subject to him."

Peter clearly connects salvation to water and baptism in this verse!

Peter is making an analogy to Noah's experience in the flood, observing that eight souls were saved on that occasion by water. He then connects his analogy to Christian baptism.

We should note that the salvation of Noah and his family experienced in the flood came about as a result of God's grace and Noah's obedient faith in God, not in his own ability to build a boat! His faith resulted in his obedience, but *he was saved by his faith in God!* Notice what the writer of Hebrews says regarding Noah, Heb 11:7:

> "*By faith Noah, being warned by God concerning events as yet unseen, took heed and constructed an ark for the saving of his household; by this he condemned the world and became an heir of the righteousness which comes by faith.*"

Now notice Peter's statement regarding Noah and Christian salvation, "*God's patience waited in the days of Noah, during the building of the ark, in which a few, that is, eight persons, were saved through water. [21] Baptism, which corresponds to this, now saves you, not as a removal of dirt from the body but as an appeal to God for (eis) a clear conscience, through the resurrection of Jesus Christ.*"

Peter clearly states that Christians are saved by water and baptism.

We must note that it was not the water that saved Noah or that saves the Christian in baptism. *It is faith in God expressed in an obedient baptism.*

However, in this action baptism becomes the prayer, request, or appeal to God *for (eis) a clear conscience.*

It would take a stretch of imagination to translate this in a way that would imply that baptism is an appeal to

376

God *because of* a clear conscience, as Mantey would be forced to do to be consistent in his theology! That is what some evangelical theology would imply, but it is clearly not what Peter implied or stated very clearly!

In this case in Peter's argument and reference to Noah, what is baptism an appeal to God for, if not for salvation!?

The task of the translator

This section discusses the task of the translator in making a translation of the Greek text. I have included it in light of Julius Mantey's and some evangelical's wrong-headed process of doing theology!

C. H. Dodd, noted New Testament scholar, once observed that the translator must realize that he undertakes an impossible art!

Dodd would agree that his observation was an overstatement, but would observe that it indicates the difficulty faced by translators who translate from an ancient text into a modern language.

The following are principles that the translator must take seriously when translating from one age, language, culture, and era to a modern era.

The translation should:
a. Be true to the idiom, language, and message of the original text.
b. Speak accurately in the idiom of the readers.
c. Be clear and intelligible.
d. Strive toward a measure of consistency in its choice of words.
e. Manifest a literary style that is suitable to the tenor of the message.
f. Be accurate in its reproduction of the original message.
g. Be true to the Gospel of Jesus Christ, rather than to a particular theological or denominational persuasion.
h. Be made by a committee that is reasonably widespread in theological conviction, and

qualified in the field of textual criticism and translation.

It is patently obvious that Mantey was not faithful to these proven principles!

The task of the interpreter, commentator, teacher, preacher, or theologian[10]

a. The interpreter must be true to the language, syntax, and wording of the original message.

b. The interpreter must faithfully render the meaning of the original text.

c. The interpreter must be careful not to read into the text or his/her interpretation his/her own religious convictions.

d. The interpreter must work from (out of) the text toward doctrine, and not from doctrine back into the text. Technically we refer to this as *exegesis* (out of the text) rather than *eisegesis* (into the text).

e. The exposition of the text must be true to the words, idiom, grammar, and syntax of the original text.

f. The meaning of words and sentences must be determined from the historical, sociological, and theological context of the original writer and not from that of the interpreter.

Problems with Mantey's and some Evangelical interpretations of Acts 2:28

a. Mantey in his grammar recognizes that the syntax of the text calls for *eis* to be translated *for* or *unto*, but forces his interpretation to comply with his preferred Christian doctrine.

b. Mantey shapes his interpretation according to his preferred doctrine, rather than have Scripture shape his doctrine.

c. Mantey is inconsistent in applying his views of *because of* to texts that are parallel, but which do not threaten his doctrine.

---

[10] Bruce Metzger, *The Bible in Translation, passim*, Baker Academic, 2001, F. F., Bruce, *A History of Translations*, 1961.

Ian A. Fair (PhD)
Professor Emeritus of New
Testament and New Testament
Theology
Graduate School of Theology
College of Biblical Studies
Abilene Christian University

TEACHING &
SPECIALIZATION
Revelation
Romans
Prison Epistles
Synoptic Gospels: Matthew
1 & 2 Thessalonians
Leadership

SEMINARS AND
WORKSHOPS
Revelation
Romans
Matthew
Strategic Planning
Leadership
Unity in Diversity

Education
Ph.D. in Systematic Theology, University of Natal, South Africa
Dissertation: *The Theology of Wolfhart Pannenberg as a Reaction to Dialectical Theology*
MA in New Testament Theology, University of Natal, South Africa
Thesis: *The Resurrection of Jesus in Three Contemporary Theologians*
BA Honors in Bible and Theology, University of Natal, South Africa
BA in Bible, Abilene Christian University, Abilene, Texas, USA.

Books by Ian Fair published by HCU Media

Conquering in Christ: Commentary on the Book of Revelation

Ephesians: Studies in the theology of Paul's Letter to the Ephesians

Paul's Epistle to the Galatians

Philippians: A Remedy for the Spiritual Blahs

A Biblical Theology of Worship

A Biblical Kingdom Theology

Paul's Epistles to the Colossians & Philemon

A Biblical Theology of Righteousness

WHO WE ARE
HCU MEDIA LLC

Publishing in support of

Heritage Christian University – Ghana (HCU Ghana)

www.hcuc.edu.gh

HCU media has been established to support the publication of
materials, both paper and electronic, created by faculty and
friends of HCU Ghana. These materials will be offered
initially in the USA & Ghana but may become available globally
via other outlets.

381